D0998995

INTERNATIONALIZATION
OF STUDENT AFFAIRS AND SERVICES

NASPA
Student Affairs Administrators
in Higher Education

Kenneth J. Osfield and Associates

INTERNATIONALIZATION
OF STUDENT AFFAIRS AND SERVICES

An Emerging Global Perspective

NASPA
Student Affairs Administrators
in Higher Education

WASHINGTON, D.C.

NASPA
Student Affairs Administrators
in Higher Education

Internationalization of Student Affairs and Services: An Emerging Global Perspective

Copyright © 2008 by the National Association of Student Personnel Administrators (NASPA), Inc. All rights reserved.

Published by NASPA – Student Affairs Administrators in Higher Education
1875 Connecticut Ave., NW
Suite 418
Washington, D.C. 20009
www.naspa.org

No part of this publication may be reproduced, stored in a retrieval system, or transmitted in any form or by any means, now known or hereafter invented, including electronic, mechanical, photocopying, recording, scanning, information storage and retrieval, or otherwise, except as permitted under Section 107 or 108 of the 1976 United States Copyright Act, without the prior written permission of the Publisher.

Additional copies may be purchased by contacting the NASPA publications department at 301-638-1749 or visiting http://bookstore.naspa.org

NASPA does not discriminate on the basis of race, color, national origin, religion, sex, age, gender identity, gender expression, affectional or sexual orientation, or disability in any of its policies, programs, and services.

Library of Congress Control Number: 2008937184

ISBN 978-0-931654-44-2

Printed and bound in the United States of America
FIRST EDITION

CONTENTS

PART IV
LOOKING AHEAD

TABLES AND FIGURES

A PERSONAL PERSPECTIVE

Eighteen years ago, compiling a book with 36 authors from all around the world would have been a daunting task. But the subsequent revolution in technology has made such a project possible—though still challenging enough. We relied heavily on e-mail, which allowed us to communication regardless of time zone or geographic location.

From the beginning of this project, the goals were: to reach out to as many student affairs and services professionals in as many areas of the world as possible to produce a comprehensive book on the development of student services around the world; to show how student services are actually delivered to students around the world; and to give students an opportunity to learn about worldwide student services delivery models.

It should be noted that the idea for this book came from the Jossey-Bass publication *Beyond Borders: How International Developments are Changing Student Affairs Practice* (Dalton, 1999). The Dalton monograph was a good start, but more information from other countries was needed. Dalton points out that the "literature on internationalization in the student affairs profession is still quite sparse" (p. 1). He made that statement only a few years ago, and though there is more literature available today, it remains quite sparse.

Coordinating a book project with 28 chapters and 36 authors has been an interesting experience. Even though I devoted many hours to this project—more time than I had anticipated—I would do it all over again without hesitation. In fact, this book was never meant to be inclusive of all countries, but rather a starting point. Although this book is complete, the project should not stop here. There are many countries that are not represented in this book, and a second edition currently being developed. Japan, Eastern Europe, Scandinavia, South America, South Africa, México, and more countries in the Middle East are but a few of the countries and regions that are missing from this publication. If your country is not represented in this edition and you would like to be involved in the next edition, please contact me, Kenneth J. Osfield, via e-mail at osfield@ufl.edu.

Kenneth J. Osfield
June 26, 2008
Gainesville, Florida

Reference

Dalton, J. C. (1999, Summer). Beyond borders: How international developments are changing student affairs practice. *New Directions for Student Services, 86*. San Francisco: Jossey-Bass.

ACKNOWLEDGMENTS

This book could not have been completed without the support and encouragement of many people. I extend a sincere thank you to all the chapter authors: Modh Razali Agus, Annie Andrews, R. Ambihabathy, Lisa Bardill, Françoise BIR, Edward T. Bonahue, Tony W. Cawthon, Doris Ching, Jon C. Dalton, Suan Eng, Dala Taji Farouki, Annie Grant, Jennifer Hanson, Pamela A. Havice, Achim Meyer auf der Heyde, Enrique Iglesias Hidalgo, Sandy Hubler, Sharon Karkehabadi, Barry Kehoe, Kwok Hung Lai, Roger B. Ludeman, Daniel Mackeben, Jeanna Mastrodicasa, Julie Adkins Nhem, Leslie A. Owen, Ouyang Ke-Quan, Olga Rybalkina, Rob Shea, Cathy Stevens, Martha Sullivan, Carol Tang, Manuel M. Tejido, Howard S. Wang, Jeanine Ward-Roof, and Heidi Huang Yu.

I wish to single out Howard Wang, who worked tirelessly to secure all the chapters from our friends and colleagues in the Asian Pacific region. Howard deserves recognition for securing the chapters on The Philippines, Mainland China, Hong Kong, Singapore, and Malaysia.

I acknowledge with thanks NASPA Executive Director Gwen Dungy and Associate Executive Director Kevin Kruger for their continued support for the international initiatives of the association, as well as Director of Publications Melissa Dahne for managing the editing and production of this book. Thanks also to the NASPA International Education Knowledge Community members and all NASPA International Symposium supporters.

The use of computers today is taken for granted, but I do not want to take for granted the contribution of Mike Bielby (University of Florida), who provided technical support during the course of this project. A special thank you goes to Dana L. Wallace (Baylor University) for her editing assistance with this project. She took time out of her busy work and graduate program schedule to look over various chapters. Finally, I would be remiss if I did not thank two former NASPA presidents for their roles in bringing NASPA into the area of international student services and student affairs: Dr. James E. Scott (NASPA President 1994–95) and Dr. Jon C. Dalton (1995–96). This book would not have been possible without their efforts and the efforts of so many other NASPA leaders.

PART I

THE GLOBAL GROUNDWORK

ONE

AN EMERGING GLOBAL PERSPECTIVE

Kenneth J. Osfield

The title for this book was up for discussion throughout the entire design and writing phases of the project. The final title reflects a combination of suggested titles from some of the contributing authors. What is "the internationalization of student affairs and services in higher education"? And why is it "an emerging global perspective"?

Internationalization

Everyone who uses the term *internationalization* will probably define it differently (McGill Peterson, 2002). For purposes of this book, internationalization has been defined as "the process by which a university changes the infrastructure or the campus ecology to keep up with the changing demand for more direct links to higher education outside their own country of origin." Peterson (2002) defined it as activities that

> ...relate to a primary goal of creating an educational program that moves significantly beyond the local and national culture in which our institutions are located and providing knowledge and competencies for our students that extend well beyond the singularity of their own cultural experience or understanding.

Each reader will define it within the context of his or her environment.

Within this book many of the authors (Dalton and Sullivan, chapter 2; Hubler and Mackeben, chapter 5; Owen, chapter 7; Ambihabathy and Agus, chapter 11; Heyde, chapter 17; Ludeman, chapter 25; Bonahue, chapter 26) specifically address both internationalization and globalization of student services, and in those chapters the terms are defined further.

Emerging Global Perspective

Internationalization was part of the fabric of politics and the economy long before it became a topic for discussion in higher education (Ping, 1999). The concept of internationalization in higher education has been receiving more press in the past few years, even though pro-

grams such as the Fulbright Scholar Program[1] (founded in 1947 and discussed in chapter 5) and People to People[2] (founded in 1956) have been devoted to the internationalization of our educational system for many years.

What these two programs have in common is the goal of bringing the people of the world together in order to understand one another and learn from one another. The Association of International Educators (NAFSA, n.d. a) addresses the importance of internationalizing education for U.S. citizens. NAFSA (n.d. a) reports that those students who "study abroad, participate in scholarly exchange programs, or study foreign areas and languages are far better prepared for the demands of the 21st century" (p. 2).

Internationalization of the U.S. educational system is an emerging trend and not yet part of the fabric of what we do. In chapter 2 (section on benefits of international contacts and experiences), Dalton and Sullivan address a conversation with a group of senior student affairs officers (SSAOs) about the importance of international activities. The response from one SSAO was, "Why does this matter to me?" If we have not sold it to our senior student affairs staff, we have a long way to go. Dalton and Sullivan introduce the importance of expanding the global hori-

---

[1] U.S. Senator J. William Fulbright proposed the Fulbright Program in 1945. International collaboration and exchange are the basis for the Fulbright Scholar program. Fulbright (as cited in CIES, n.d.) viewed the program as an instrument for promoting "mutual understanding between the people of the United States and the people of other countries of the world." The Fulbright programs, through exchange and collaboration, seek to make the world a more compassionate and understanding place. It is a unique program in that it funds both U.S. citizens and nationals from other countries. The Fulbright Program is funded by the U.S. government and foreign governments through their bi-national commissions and foundations (CIES, n.d.).

[2] Another similar program worth noting is the People to People International (PTPI) program as it too seeks to provide opportunities for people to become immersed in the culture of other countries. The mission of PTPI is "to enhance international understanding and friendship through educational, cultural, and humanitarian activities involving the exchange of ideas and experiences directly among peoples of different countries and diverse cultures. It will cooperate with any and all other organizations which are of similar nature and purpose." (PTPI, n.d.)

zons of student services in higher education, and in chapter 5, Hubler and Mackeben continue the discussion and address the importance of staff and student involvement in international activities.

Peterson (2002) says that institutions of higher education need to take the buzzword *internationalization* and develop a more coherent and strategic approach in order to make the buzzword an operative term. I believe that it is a term often thrown into the mission statements of institutions for accreditation purposes but that schools often lack the significant financial resources and administrative staff needed to entrench it in campus life.

Global Competencies for All

The Association of International Educators (NAFSA, 2003) in its *Report of the Strategic Task Force on Education Abroad* urges the accreditation organizations in the United States to require global competencies of all students who graduate (p. 15). Making global competency a graduation requirement or part of the licensing criteria will go a long way to internationaling higher education. Zhao, Kuh, and Carini (2005) address the need for higher education to produce culturally competent people who have the ability to work with people from all walks of life. How can higher education assist in the development of students and staff who are globally and culturally competent? One way would be to infuse both international exchange opportunities and internationally themed coursework into the curriculum, thus making it part of the fabric of higher education. Another way would be to make it a program requirement, graduation requirement, or licensing requirement. University administrators must find ways to incorporate international experiences and opportunities into the curriculum and work environment, so that internationalization will become part of the overriding philosophy of a university.

I am not so naïve as to think that everyone will have the resources, funding, and opportunity to spend time in another country, but there are other ways that students and staff can become involved internationally. They can become involved in organizations on campus aimed at international students and staff. They can host international students and staff for visits and meals and can set up times to meet regularly with international students and staff to talk about life, experiences, politics, and family. Faculty can internationalize their courses to ensure that students are exposed to life outside their country of origin. Administrators can assist student groups interested in international issues and topics by offering planned opportunities for involvement. Ambihabathy and Agus in chapter 11 (student development section) report that there is "an increasing focus on providing an opportunity for students to spend two weeks in a foreign host university. As a start, the unit is only focusing on South East Asian countries with future plans to include all other

countries around the globe." If the University of Malaya can set such a lofty goal, then why can't the wealthier countries around the globe?

NAFSA (2003) proposed that it is the responsibility of the federal government, the local state government, and the colleges and universities to ensure that study abroad opportunities become integrated within higher education. A partnership must be forged in order for students and staff around the world to experience a true international curriculum and academic experience. I propose that it is also the responsibility of our students, staff, and families to assist in every way possible to make study abroad and international exchange a reality at all levels of education. As citizens, we each bear some of the burden to become globally competent in this fast-changing society.

According to Peterson, in a 14-nation Carnegie Foundation study of the academic profession, only about "45% of faculty agreed that further steps should be taken to develop a more global educational approach" (p. 2). The same survey found that "while 90% of the faculty from 13 countries believed that a scholar must read books and journals from abroad to keep up with scholarly developments, only 62% of the U.S. faculty believed that was necessary" (Peterson, p. 2). Until internationalism is entrenched within the curriculum and campus ecology it will stay as it is now, a misunderstood and overused buzzword. In chapter 26, Bonahue states that for global competency to succeed, the community college must "promote global competencies in their students through internationalization of the curriculum, student services, and workforce partnerships. If the goal of the institution is to internationalize in such a way as to reach all its students, however, these initiatives should be pursued together." It is Bonahue's premise that for internationalization to succeed, it must be intertwined within all the activities of the institution, and by integrating it into the lifeblood of the institution all students will be affected.

To assist students and staff in becoming globally competent two things need to take place. First and foremost, study abroad must become ingrained and integrated within our educational systems. Second, there must be government support to make it a reality (NAFSA, 2003).

International Collaboration and International Exchange

U.S. presidents of both parties have held similar views on international collaboration and exchange. In 1966, President Lyndon B. Johnson (as cited in NAFSA, n.d. b) summed up the importance of international collaboration when he said, "International education cannot be the work of one country. It is the responsibility and promise of all nations. It calls for free exchange and full collaboration … The knowledge of our citizens is one treasure that grows only when it is shared" (para. 7). In 1989, President George Bush (as cited in NAFSA, n.d. b) addressed the significance of international exchanges when he said, "International exchanges are not a great tide to sweep away all differences, but they will slowly wear away at the obstacles to peace as surely as water wears away a hard stone" (para. 2). And Ronald Regan (as cited in NAFSA, n.d. b) summed it up best when he said, "There is a flickering spark in us all which, if struck at just the right age ... can light the rest of our lives, elevating our ideals, deepening our tolerance, and sharpening our appetite for knowledge about the rest of the world. Educational and cultural exchanges ... provide a perfect opportunity for this precious spark to grow, making us more sensitive and wiser international citizens" (para. 3). The type of international educational and cultural exchange referred to here is a well thought out, well constructed, and meaningful experience designed to fully immerse oneself into the culture, language, experiences, and people of the host country. It is not meant as a vacation or an opportunity to get away from campus, for this type of attitude will only lead to the demise of the overall experience of international exchange. One of the goals of this book is to raise a thirst in each reader to find out more about what is going on in this world. There is more to student affairs and services than what is taking place in the United States, and it is another goal of this book to convey how other countries provide services to the students on their campuses. Yu, Ke-Quan, and Wang in chapter 9 (concluding remarks section) address this very point when Wang reported that importing "the U.S. concept of professionalization of student affairs management and its model of graduate student personnel preparatory programs may not be appropriate for Asian countries and their students." This is a point of note and should be considered.

Chapters 8–24 of this book (country-specific student service delivery models) address the methods by which other countries support their campuses with the delivery of student services. Look at the similarities and differences in each country and then compare them to the delivery method on your own campus. As individuals, we have much to learn from one another, especially from our colleagues from different countries, backgrounds, and life experiences. Reach out and share in the experience of international education.

Willi Brandt, former chancellor of the Federal Republic of Germany, in a speech at the Aspen Institute for Humanistic Studies on September 28, 1970 said:

> We shall have to devote time and effort to each other. We must get to know each other; still more, we must learn to live with each other. More young Europeans must have the opportunity of exploring the social landscape of America, of discovering America's outlook on life, of becoming familiar with its history, and the process must be reciprocal. In this we cannot put our faith in the governments alone (V. Ekechukwu, personal communication, July 29, 2005).

Today the same comment can be applied more broadly to the people of the world. The simple truth is, we must reach out to one another and learn about each other. One way to do that is through the international exchange of ideas, experiences, and friendship.

References

Council for the International Exchange of Scholars (CIES). (n.d.). *About Fulbright*. Retrieved July 8, 2005, from http://www.cies.org/about_fulb.htm

McGill Peterson, P. (2002, January). *Addressing the challenge to internationalize our academic institutions: How are we doing?* Speech presented at the meeting of the American Council on International Intercultural Education, Seattle, WA.

NAFSA (Association of International Educators). (2003, November). *Securing America's future: Global education for a global age*. Washington, D.C.: Author.

NAFSA (Association of International Educators). (n.d. a). *International education: Advancing global understanding*. Retrieved November 30, 2004, from http://www.nafsa.org/template.cfm?section=publicpolicy&navmenuid=50

NAFSA (Association of International Educators). (n.d. b). *The U.S. presidents on Fulbright and international exchange programs*. Retrieved October 5, 2005, from http://www.nafsa.org/about.sec/about_international_education/resources/quotes_by_u.s._presidents

Ping, C. J. (1999, Summer). An expanded international role for student affairs. In J. C. Dalton (Ed.). *Beyond borders: How international developments are changing student affairs practice* (pp. 13–21). *New Directions for Student Services* (86). San Francisco: Jossey-Bass.

People to People International (PTPI). (n.d.). *About us*. Retrieved July 7, 2005, from http://www.ptpi.org/about_us

Zhao, C. M., Kuh, G. D., & Carini, R. M. (2005). A comparison of international student and American student engagement in effective educational practices. *The Journal of Higher Education, 76*(2), 209–231.

TWO

EXPANDING GLOBAL HORIZONS

Jon C. Dalton and Martha H. Sullivan

The traditional boundaries of the work of student affairs professionals in higher education are changing rapidly with the new global trends and developments of the 21st century. The growing involvement of student affairs professionals in international travel, professional collaboration and exchange, global communication, and information exchange represents one of the most important developments in the student affairs profession in the past three decades. Charles Ping (1999) describes this development as a "late-twentieth century expansion of the educational role of student affairs" (p. 13). In this chapter the authors examine the various types of international contact and involvements that have been occurring over the past 25 years and discuss the benefits of internationalization and its implications for the future of the student affairs profession.

Student Affairs Involvement in International Activities

Student affairs professionals have been engaged in international travel and involvement for many years but most often in individual and informal contexts. Most have had regular contact with international students and faculty on their own campuses, and many have had responsibility for the administration of their institutions' international student services and programs. Some student affairs staff have traveled extensively and participated in international programs and exchanges. But until quite recently, such international involvements were on the periphery of the profession and outside the mainstream of professional activities and responsibilities. In the last 25 years, however, international travel and exchange has entered the mainstream of attention and concern for student affairs professionals as well as for the professional associations that serve them. Today, more than ever before, student affairs professionals travel abroad, participate in international conferences and exchange programs, study foreign languages, communicate regularly with international colleagues, and follow international developments. This movement has been prompted by

more convenient and inexpensive transportation, global developments in communication, expanding professional development opportunities, and a shift in the priorities and values of the profession that gives more emphasis to cross-cultural and international experiences. Higher education has played a leading role in promoting global development, and student affairs professionals are becoming more active partners in the international efforts of their institutions. In many instances, it has been student affairs leaders who have served as campus catalysts to encourage greater institutional partnerships and educational exchange with higher education institutions and colleagues in other countries.

Another important indicator of the growing influence of internationalism in the profession is the formal attention it receives from professional associations. Some associations related to student affairs in higher education (the Association of College Unions International and the Association of College and University Housing Officers-International) have had international members for many years and have acknowledged international ties through changes in their associations' names. These student service associations were founded early and developed contacts with their counterparts in other countries because the student services they represent were often some of the first to be provided by colleges and universities, both in the United States and in other countries. Despite their early recognition and involvement in international contact, exchange and collaboration with colleagues in other countries have been limited. Throughout much of the latter half of the 20th century, economic retrenchment, state and institutional restrictions on out-of-country travel, and parochial social and political attitudes have often hindered student affairs professionals and others in American higher education from seriously engaging in international exchange.

The two large generalist student affairs professional associations in the United States, NASPA–Student Affairs Administrators in Higher Education and ACPA–College Student Educators International, have also had longstanding interests in international contact and development, but only in the last 25 years have they made substantial efforts to integrate these priorities into their formal programs and services. Over the past 25 years, NASPA has developed extensive opportunities for its members to participate in international professional development and exchange programs and has added an international pre-conference program to its annual conference. NASPA has also developed an International Education Knowledge Community within its organizational structure to promote international activities and awareness. We will review some of the other NASPA international activities a little later.

The ACPA has also emphasized international exchange and professional development and includes international themes and programs in its conferences and member programs. In 2004, the ACPA executive council formally changed its name from Association of College Personnel Administrators to College Student Educators International to reflect the association's commitment to international education (M. Morgan, personal communication, August 23, 2005). It is also actively promoting international conferences and professional exchange opportunities for its members and the profession.

What Are the Factors Driving International Involvement?

There are many influences that have converged to create the internationalization movement in student affairs, but six factors in particular have been formative.

1. Global Connectedness. The global connections fostered by modern communications, travel, economics, and politics have created a much smaller world and much more frequent contact among people across national borders. The communications revolution made possible by the Internet, satellites, and cell phones has helped downsize the planet and create a much smaller and more intimate international community. There are no global boundaries with this new technology, and it is possible to move easily through this seamless universe. The personal contact and communication across national borders made possible by modern communications has been the most important influence in internationalizing the student affairs profession, and indeed, much of society at large.

2. Internationalism and the Leadership Culture in Higher Education. American higher education has played a pivotal role in promoting global connectedness through its leadership in basic and applied research, study abroad programs, international conferences, and international collaboration and partnerships. College presidents, provosts, and academic deans are frequently involved in international academic exchange programs, meetings, travel abroad, and recruiting international faculty and students. Academic leadership today requires a global perspective and sufficient international experience to appreciate the opportunities and challenges presented

by an increasingly global community. This international perspective was described earlier as an important aspect of the current leadership culture in higher education (Dalton, 1999). The leadership culture is the prevailing mindset that reflects the most important values, convictions, and dispositions of higher education leaders today. Leaders in student affairs have recognized the increasing international orientation of leaders in higher education and have begun to develop their expertise in this area as well. It is important for student affairs professionals to develop these skills so that they are not marginalized in the leadership culture by being regarded as primarily campus-oriented officials.

3. The Internationalizing Influence of Foreign Students. According to estimates by the Institute of International Education, more than 550,000 foreign students study in the United States and contribute more than $12 billion a year into the economy (Study Trend, 1997). Colleges and universities recruit international students for both financial and educational considerations. For many colleges and universities, international students represent a very important component of their overall institutional enrollment strategies. The other important incentive for recruiting foreign students is that they bring diversity of experiences and perspectives into the educational setting. Having international students on campus enriches the social and cultural interactions of students and adds a variety of political, religious, and historical perspectives that enhances academic discussion and learning. Because student affairs staff spend more time with students than anyone else in higher education and because they respond most directly to students' personal needs, they also have developed an appreciation and understanding of the needs of international students on campus. As student affairs staff have interacted with international students and sought to create welcoming campus environments for an increasingly diverse student body, they have themselves become more engaged and aware of international perspectives and issues. Given the presence of so many international students on campus and their importance for educational and enrollment strategies, it is critical for student affairs staff to develop a more international outlook and expertise. Student affairs staff have also been influenced by the friendships and personal interactions they have had with students, staff, and faculty from around the world. The authors have known many student affairs leaders who have visited other countries at the invitation of international students with whom they developed personal friendships during their study in the United States. This person-to-person contact is one of the most positive benefits of having international students on campus.

4. The Influence of International Study and Travel. Another important influence in the growth of international awareness and contact among student affairs staff has been the dramatic increase in foreign study and travel by students and faculty. American colleges and universities created hundreds of study abroad programs in response to the growing student interest in spending some time abroad as part of the undergraduate experience. Almost every American college or university now has some arrangement for their students to study abroad, and increasingly these programs are administered or coordinated locally. Study abroad programs add prestige and variety to a college's reputation and curriculum and often generate substantial revenue. Student affairs staff have often been exposed to international travel and interests through their involvement with their institution's study abroad programs. Many of them also have served as leaders or participants in study abroad programs and frequently have responsibility for administering them.

5. *Organized International Programs for Student Affairs Professionals.* One of the most important ways in which student affairs professionals develop interests and expertise in international activities is through organized programs for higher education professionals. The Fulbright Scholar Program in particular has provided many student affairs professionals with opportunities to travel to European and Asian countries. This successful and well-funded federal program provides opportunities for faculty and staff to make short-term visits abroad for professional development, teaching, research, and study. Many student affairs leaders have received Fulbright grants and have benefited richly from opportunities to participate in these excellent international professional development experiences. Student affairs recipients of Fulbright grants have been some of the profession's most influential advocates for the importance of international travel and expertise. In the 1990s, NASPA launched an extensive program of international professional exchange programs and an international pre-conference component to its annual meeting. Beginning with the Centre National des Œuvres Universitaires et Scolaires (CNOUS) in France and followed by the Studentenwerk in Germany, NASPA established regular exchange programs for student affairs professionals in the United States and their counterparts in these countries. This exchange initiative has grown into more than 11 international exchange programs in countries around the world. In 1994, NASPA added its first international member to the board of directors. The vice rector of student affairs at the Instituto Tecnológico in Monterrey, México, was invited to serve as an at-large member. This monograph is another example of NASPA's efforts to create awareness and support the development of international exchange in the student affairs profession.

6. *Student Affairs and Diversity.* One of the central issues and priorities of student affairs work in higher education during the past 20 years has been the concern for enhancing awareness and appreciation of human diver-

sity. As college campuses have become more diverse and pluralistic with racial, religious, ethnic, and international differences represented among their students and staff, student affairs professionals have had increasing contact with and responsibility for diversity issues. Concern about the human problems created by increasing diversity has helped to foster more awareness and expertise about international issues among student affairs staff. Student affairs staff members are often the first ones called upon to respond to the human conflicts and problems of bias and discrimination that often accompany diversity on campus. They routinely encounter campus situations involving international students, and these experiences have broadened international knowledge and awareness. This was especially true following the September 11, 2001, terrorist attacks. Reactions to the terrorism created a volatile situation on many campuses and brought new attention to the importance of understanding the Islamic religion and those who practice it. Student affairs staff were often the leaders on campuses who helped create a climate of dialogue and openness and moderate the strong emotions generated by the circumstances of that time. Understanding interfaith differences may well be the most important arena of diversity education for higher education in the future.

Re-conceptualizing the Meaning of Community

One of the important responsibilities of higher education in today's world is expanding students' understanding of the meaning of community. Nash (2002) suggests there are several levels of what we regard as community. The first level of community is centered on one's closest personal relationships. The second level is formed by one's participation in social groups and organizations. Interactions with peers, faculty, administrators, and others who are a part of campus culture form the core of this community in the higher education setting. A third level of community involves the broader societal realm in which work, citizenship, civic life, schools, and religious organizations define the roles and values of community life.

Today a fourth level of community life is emerging that is global in nature and connects people across the diminishing barriers of national borders. Colleges and universities can play an important role in helping students expand their vision of community to include the global dimension and to enlarge students' conceptions and commitments to the global community. College students have naturally strong attachments at the more intimate levels of community that focus on personal relationships and contacts, but they are often are not engaged when it comes to civic connections at global levels. Exposing students to the world beyond the local levels of community helps to enlarge their understanding of and commitment to a richer and more layered vision of community. To do this effectively, student affairs staff must themselves become more knowledgeable and comfortable in the broader global community.

The idea of community has always been central to the purposes of higher education in the United States. Ernest Boyer (1987) wrote that "... our democratic way of life and perhaps our survival as a people rest on whether we can move beyond self-interest and begin to understand better the realities of our dependence on each other" (p. 8). Moving beyond self-interest, particularly at the level of nationalism, is one of our greatest challenges in a shrinking world. Higher education can be one of the best places to help students better understand an expanded view of community that includes interdependency and shared interests across national boundaries.

The rich diversity of people on campus, including international students and scholars, is one of higher education's greatest resources for introducing students to the global community. Colleges and universities are good at promoting a strong sense of school spirit and community, but far too little effort is made to prepare students for participation in international living and community.

Internationalism in a Time of Terrorism

International travel and cross-cultural contacts by Americans throughout the past 20 years have served to promote a more global consciousness and respect for cultural differences in the United States. Since the events of September 11, 2001, however, the concern about terrorism in the United States has created greater fear of some people from certain areas of the world and tighter restrictions on immigration and travel in the United States and other parts of the world. A shift in social and cultural values also has occurred in the United States to reflect a more conservative orientation. This shift in values tends to focus more on domestic issues and less on international relationships and exchange. Thus, student affairs professionals often find themselves at the nexus of two powerful social and political movements, one that pushes to expand global awareness and interchange, and another that pushes in the opposite direction. One of the challenges for our profession is to find ways to continue international exchange and collaboration that recognize the risks and dangers of living in today's world but that does not succumb to the fear and insularity that such dangers can often promote. This fear and insularity is today reflected in the attitudes and behaviors of some students who create hostile conditions on campus for international students because of their religious or political views. One of the great challenges for student affairs professionals today is helping students resist the impulse to fear differences and learn from those who see life from a very different vantage point.

Building Bridges to New Places and People

While professional exchange programs and international travel have expanded the international horizons of many student affairs professionals, much of their international experience has been limited to Western Europe. Similar trends also are reflected among students. Despite the growing interest in international study and travel, only 1%–2% of U.S. students study abroad, and most are female (65%) and White (84%) (Christie & Ragans, 1999, p. 80). A large number of U.S. travelers go to the United Kingdom, France, Italy, Germany, Spain, and the other countries of Western Europe. Travel in Western Europe is an important gateway to global experience and awareness, but it does not provide Americans with experiences of some of the more diverse social, cultural, and political differences that deepen our understanding of human diversity. Travel to Asia, Africa, and the Middle East is still limited, and the events of September 11, 2001, have made many Americans even more cautious about travel to these regions.

Yet these regions are especially important in today's world because of economic, political, and cultural conflicts and shifts in strategic interests. Travel and international exchange do not necessarily solve these problems, but they can provide a basis for understanding and communication that help to bridge differences and foster a wider sense of community. Student affairs staff can be important catalysts on campus for encouraging greater contact and communication with people and institutions in these non-traditional travel destinations.

It is becoming increasingly difficult to separate the spheres of our lives into separate categories of domestic and foreign, national and international. When the cars we drive are produced and assembled in Asia, our breakfast fruit is imported from Latin America, our shirts are manufactured in Bangladesh, and our dinner wine is produced in the Andean highlands of Chile, it is no longer possible to think of ourselves and our work as defined by national borders and parochial interests. Our students are quickly becoming citizens of a much more integrated and expanding world. Such changes can be intimidating, but they can also be a powerful stimulus for growth and development. A major goal in student affairs for the new millennium should be to expand our vision and our work beyond borders to better educate our young citizens for this new global future.

Benefits of International Contacts and Experiences

After one of the authors talked with a group of senior student affairs administrators from major research institutions and urged them to become more involved in the international activities of NASPA, one participant asked quite earnestly, "Why does this matter to me?" To those of us who have already traveled abroad, the professional and personal benefits of international involvement seem self-evident. But perhaps they are not so obvious to many student affairs professionals.

When we examine more closely how the internationalization of higher education has affected student affairs services within the United States, we may be forced to conclude that its influence has been far too limited. International travel and exchange is an area in which student affairs professionals lag behind their academic colleagues. They lag even farther behind their student affairs colleagues in many other parts of the world, who are working to improve student mobility and to reduce the barriers of international borders. In recent years, the major focus of student services in the European Union has been student mobility. Under the aegis of their organization ECStA (European Council for Student Affairs), student services professionals are making remarkable progress in opening higher education across borders and providing greater ease of access and matriculation. This important global objective is not even on the table in discussions with leaders of student affairs in the United States. Too often, many in the United States think that what is happening in the rest of the world is irrelevant to our responsibilities or strategically unimportant. Hence, it has little impact on our long-term planning. Long at the forefront in providing services to college students, student affairs professionals in the United States seem to be asleep at the wheel when it comes to internationalization, especially compared to the innovative efforts of some of our international colleagues.

While there are certainly many in the profession who are working actively to promote international exchange and collaboration, there is still no concerted and coordinated strategic planning in the profession to work intentionally to address issues of internationalization. Thus, instead of being integral partners in international efforts in higher education, we are often not included in discussion and planning of such efforts.

We must examine our own personal and professional complacencies about cultural differences and recognize that our limited contact with others can foster narrowly perceived notions of how people should act and relate to one another. Few things are more important to our development as professionals in a global society than the recognition of our own deeply ingrained cultural biases. Experiencing the culture, language, social patterns, and systems of other cultures can help us feel what it is like to be in the position of the outsider, i.e., the foreigner, the one who does not quite fit in, the person who may not only look different but is distinctive by dress and habits. When we participate in exchanges in other countries, we often become more cognizant of our own privileges and resources that may be unknown to many of our international colleagues. But we also learn about their accomplishments and innovations.

Also, the experience can cause us to reflect on how to navigate a social and cultural system quite different from our own and how to recognize the written and unwritten rules and customs. We notice, for example, the clarity (or lack thereof) of the instructions in the residence halls and dining facilities. How many of us communicate policies and procedures on our campuses thinking from the inside out rather than from the outside in? Unwittingly, we use jargon that translates either poorly or not at all to those for whom English is a second or third language. Even brief experiences as an outsider can cause us to reflect on how we can make our student services and programs more accessible to people from a wide range of social and cultural backgrounds.

Not only does an international experience add to our professional development, it also provides us an excellent opportunity to work collaboratively with our international colleagues. Why is this important? Through collaboration with our international counterparts, we may be able to develop new international experiences for our staff and students. Being the host of an international delegation or a guest in another country are both tremendous learning experiences. For our students, such experiences can provide a doorway to new possibilities in their personal and professional futures as citizens of a more global society. For our staff, working with international colleagues and learning the challenges others face can give them a broader perspective of and appreciation for what they are doing on their own campuses.

Both students and staff who have had meaningful international experiences return more interested in the activities and lives of our international students on campus, tend to attend more international programs on campus, and are more cognizant of the impact of events around the world. They not only become more interested participants in international issues, they themselves become more interesting people and influential leaders as they broaden their scope of contacts.

Implications of Internationalization for Future Developments in the Student Affairs Profession

What are the implications of internationalization for future developments in the student affairs profession? In the first place, we must begin to understand developments in student affairs in other countries. Rather than simply benchmarking our efforts against peer institutions in the United States, we must also begin to compare our professional efforts with those of colleagues in other countries. As a matter of national priority and foreign policy, an increasing number of countries are working aggressively to promote their institutions of higher education as a means of guaranteeing future stability and national prominence. Many national leaders regard this strategy as a means of ensuring that future world leaders understand and appreciate the history, culture, and values of their country. They are anxious to foster connections between their country and the world community, so higher education can be an important vehicle for this global strategy. For example, most Web pages of student affairs organizations in other countries use their own native language but also make the information available in English since English is increasingly becoming the universal language.

While the organizational structure of student services in higher education differs from country to country, student services professionals in various countries share many things in common and confront many similar issues. What differs is often only context and language. The increasing mobility of students and the ease of global communications serve to increase the common aspects of student services work in many international settings. Rather than simply focusing on local campus issues such as international student enrollment, student visa processing, and cultural programming, we are now exchanging information with our international counterparts on such far-ranging issues as residence hall designs, town–gown relations, student health issues, staff development, student government, business management, disability access, and the ongoing challenge of assuring adequate financial aid for students. Finally, each of us needs to consider what our own personal international and cultural enrichment can mean for the students and staff we serve. How does our participation in international exchanges affect the services we offer to our students, both domestic and international? For many student affairs staff, international travel and exchange has been genuinely transforming for their professional work and leadership.

For many years, U.S. student affairs staff and their institutions have developed exchanges with other institutions around the world, but few have approached study abroad exchange agreements with particular attention to student services. Understandably, most in higher education focus on the academic side of study abroad and student mobility. Increasingly, however, we are finding that we must include student services considerations in developing and administering study abroad and student exchange programs. Housing, food service, financial aid, orientation, career services, international student services, counseling, disability services, and student associations are all student service areas that are integral to operating successful student study and exchange programs. Whether a study abroad experience is positive or negative is often determined by both the availability and the quality of these services.

The efforts of the American Council on Education (ACE) through its Center for International Initiatives and the International Association of Universities through United Nations Educational, Scientific, and Cultural Organization (UNESCO) are innovative, exciting, and promising. But nowhere in these efforts is much attention given to student services as an integral part of planning.[1] What is missing is a coordinated national effort by student services professionals and professional organizations that articulates the goals, objectives,

and policies of international development in the profession for the global future. We hope this monograph will encourage and assist that discussion at this critical juncture.

References

Boyer, E. (1987). *College: The undergraduate experience in America.* New York: HarperCollins.

Christie, R. & Ragans, S. (1999). Beyond borders: A model for student and staff development. In J. C. Dalton (Ed.), *Beyond borders: How international developments are changing student affairs practice* (pp. 79–88). San Francisco: Jossey-Bass.

Dalton, J. (1999). The significance of international issues and responsibilities in the contemporary work of student affairs. In J. C. Dalton (Ed.), *Beyond borders: How international developments are changing student affairs practice* (pp. 3–12). San Francisco: Jossey-Bass.

Nash, R. J. (2002). *Spirituality, ethics, religion, and teaching.* New York: Lang.

Ping, C. (1999). An expanded international role for student affairs. In J. C. Dalton (Ed.), *Beyond borders: How international developments are changing student affairs practice* (pp. 13–22). San Francisco: Jossey-Bass.

Study trend: Foreign students are a boon to U.S. (1997, December 12). *Houston Chronicle,* p. A46.

---

[1] UNESCO published a follow-up publication to its 1998 World Conference on Higher Education titled "The Role of Student Affairs and Services in Higher Education," on which several members of the NASPA International Symposium worked. The major focus of that project, however, was on establishing benchmarks for effective student services.

PART II

INVOLVING STUDENTS AND STAFF IN THE INTERNATIONAL EXPERIENCE

THREE

DESIGNING A STUDY ABROAD EXPERIENCE
ACADEMIC AND STUDENT AFFAIRS COLLABORATION

Tony W. Cawthon, Pamela A. Havice and Jeanine Ward Roof

College students, faculty, and staff from all sizes and types of institutions in the United States participate in study aboard programs all around the world. Also, students, faculty, and staff from all parts of the world come to the United States to experience life on American college and university campuses. The Institute of International Education Open Doors Report 2004 (Institute of International Education, 2005) indicated that more than 174,629 U.S. students studied at foreign institutions. This record number of students studying abroad represented an 8.5% increase over the 2002–03 year, which also saw an increase of 4.4% over the previous year. And it is 145% higher than the number of students who studied abroad in 1991–92. There is also an increase in the diversity of institutions that students are selecting to visit. Of the top 20 sites visited, 7 of the 11 destinations with significant increases were outside Western Europe. Increases in areas outside Western Europe and in locations where English is not the primary language are experiencing increased popularity. According to the report, the most popular locations remain the United Kingdom, Italy, Spain, France, Australia, and México, but there were significant increases in visits to Eastern European locations such as the Czech Republic, Russia, and Hungary (Institute of International Education, 2005).

The report concluded that, despite numerous concerns, students remain strongly interested in study abroad for credit. However, the Open Doors data show that American students prefer study abroad programs lasting eight weeks or fewer, and there is a continued decline in interest in long-term programs. One reason offered is that more programs are being integrated into campus curricula, allowing more students to take advantage of such experiences (Institute of International Education, 2005). There are also numerous organizations and resources available for assisting students in exploring study abroad options. These include: (a) The Electronic Embassy (http://www.embassy.org);

(b) Study Abroad (http://www.studyabroad.com), (c) AIESEC International (http:www.aiesec.org/), and (d) Colleges and University Home Pages-Geographical Listings (http://www.mit.edu:8001/people/cdemello/geog.html) (Dalton, 1999).

Marginson and Yang (2005) stated that global networking within education has a huge impact on participants' ability to educate themselves and others about study abroad experiences, as well as the potential to reshape institutions' practices and habits. Dalton (1999) stated that faculty in most academic disciplines have historically participated in organized exchanges, but only recently have student affairs practitioners realized the significance of international collaborations. He also reported that this same lack of attention to international concerns was evident in our professional association until recently. While the Fulbright Scholars program is probably the most well known organization assisting American scholars to study and conduct research in other countries (Fulbright Program, 2005), participation in this program requires participants have an earned doctorate, be engaged in activities of interest to the host country, and plan to be abroad for an average of a semester. Hence the program is not an option for many student affairs professionals. The Council on International Educational Exchange (http://www.ciee.org/) (2005) is another organization whose mission is to assist individuals in developing skills for working and living in a culturally diverse world. In recent years, organizations such as the NASPA–Student Affairs Administrators in Higher Education and the Association of College and University Housing Officers International (ACUHO-I) have offered international travel and exchanges for their members. In 2007–08, NASPA offered exchanges to China (2007), France (2007), Germany (2007), Ireland (2008), Mexico (2008), New Zealand (2007), Spain (2008), and United Arab Emirates (2007) (NASPA, n.d.), and ACUHO-I co-sponsored an exchange to South Africa (ACUHO-I, n.d.). These programs are more attractive in that most are short, allow for group travel, and allow participants to select sites of interest.

In addition, more international exchanges are sponsored by professional associations, and institutions have study abroad offices offering international exchanges. But on most campuses, these study abroad programs focus on providing undergraduates with extensive learning opportunities. As Americans' awareness of global and international issues has increased, numerous institutions have begun offering international programs/exchanges designed specifically for student affairs practitioners, faculty, and the students they serve. Some examples are: (a) Iowa State University has offered an exchange with the University of Glasgow (Peterson, Briggs, Dreasher, Horner, & Nelson, 1999); (b) Indiana University sponsored a trip to South Africa; (c) Miami University initiated a trip to Germany and other parts of Europe (Judy Rogers, 2005, personal communication); (d) the University of Arkansas sponsored trips to Ireland; and (e) Clemson University has offered trips to England. All of these programs are designed to expose student affairs practitioners to cultural and educational issues. Learning about other countries and how they offer student services allows us to become more effective in our delivery of services and our response to student needs. Dalton (1999) stated that it is becoming more common for student affairs to be an integral component in life on foreign campuses. Despite the long history of student services in our country and its newness in other countries, we each have much to learn from one another.

In the summers of 2004 and 2005, the Division of Student Affairs and the Graduate Preparation Program in Student Affairs at Clemson University collaborated to sponsor a study trip to England, and in summer 2006, Clemson offered a similar trip to five institutions in Scotland. Similar study abroad experiences to Scotland took place in summer 2007, and one to Ireland in summer 2008. Coordinating such a study abroad experience requires extensive planning, coordination, and dedication. The primary purpose of this experience is for students and professionals to learn how higher education institutions in those countries offer and administer student services functions.

For graduate preparation programs that are considering such a program, several questions must be addressed to ensure success. Questions to be explored include:

1. What is the rationale for your travel? What are the goals and purpose of the trip? What do you hope students will learn?

2. What will be the focus of the content of your trip? Will it include both educational and cultural learning opportunities?

3. How will you incorporate this experience into your graduate preparation program curriculum? Will

students earn academic credit for participating in the program?

4. What costs, if any, will your institution incur as part of this trip?

5. What other similar programs are being offered that might affect the success of your program?

6. How will technology be used to enhance this experience?

There are numerous advantages to offering an international study abroad trip for both the graduate preparation program itself and for the students enrolled in these programs. For graduate preparation programs, an effective study abroad program enhances the academic reputation, name recognition, and credibility.

For students, participating in an international exchange program offers unlimited networking possibilities and extensive opportunities for collaboration. These possibilities exist with the international colleagues they encounter and the other students participating in the experience with them. Students can develop and cultivate relationships that can impact their future careers and professional development. They are exposed to career options in other countries and gain contacts for additional professional exchanges.

Successful study abroad experiences also benefit graduate programs by increasing students' cultural sensitivity. Student affairs practitioners have long played key roles in enhancing campus diversity and multicultural efforts. Offering our students the opportunity to study abroad is likely to increase their efforts to become international advocates. These experiences expose our students to different social and cultural environments that enhance their knowledge and understanding of different countries and cultures, as well as global and international issues. These experiences challenge the students' personal stereotypes and biases as they meet individuals from their host country and individuals from their own country. From our sponsored trips, students reported that traveling and studying abroad increased their own self-confidence in addressing diversity issues and also provided them with increased appreciation of their own cultures.

Additional benefits accrue if these programs are co-sponsored by the student affairs division and the graduate preparation program. These programs can be designed as model programs of collaboration between student and academic affairs and can showcase how both organizations enhance student learning and development. Working together, these organizations can design a program that links theory and practice.

Planning a Study Abroad Experience: Considerations

As previously mentioned, in 2004 and 2005, the chapter authors hosted a study abroad trip to England. The trip was marketed to both student affairs professionals and students in graduate preparation programs. The study tour spanned 14 days and exposed participants to six institutions. At each institution, participants had the chance to network with British colleagues engaged in the delivery of student services. Designed as a for-credit course, the program was developed to give participants the opportunity to learn about and compare higher education systems. It is easy to overlook the extensive detail, time commitment, and coordination necessary to ensure a genuine learning experience for participants. The next section of this chapter provides details and issues that planners must address before carrying out a study abroad experience. Specifically, the section addresses issues related to: (a) logistics and partnership, (b) purpose and goals of the experience, (c) perceptions and theory, (d) the academic component, (e) use of travel company, (f) site visits, (g) itinerary, (h) budget development, (i) technology, (j) risk management, (k) marketing and recruitment, (l) communication, (m) evaluation, and (n) follow-up meetings.

Planning Issues

Logistics and partnerships

Logistically, the development of a study abroad program for students can be complex, but with basic programming, networking, and communication skills, the process can be manageable. The authors suggest the program hosts take the following steps:

◊ Decide the purpose of the experience (education, professional development, fundraising) and the target audience for marketing (students, staff, community), as well as the country or countries that will be visited and what will be done during each visit.

◊ Decide whether you want to partner with any other office on campus. For instance, you can establish a strong program by including professionals who have contacts overseas or staff who have access to budgetary or secretarial resources.

◊ Research what relationships already exist between the host institution and institutions in other countries.

◊ Work with staff from the study abroad office to better understand the country's education system, memorable sites to visit, the preparation and completion of proper paperwork for traveling in and out of countries, and overall safety issues.

◊ Assess the overall plan to make sure that objections (relating to finances, participants, etc.) can be responded to.

Selecting a country or countries to visit is an exciting aspect of the logistics. The best place to start is by assessing the networks available in order to uncover any contacts who might make good on-site hosts. Typically, the obligation of an on-site host institution includes a day or portion of a day to educate the participants about their institution; network with faculty, staff, and students; and tour the facilities. It is important to arrange the visits prior to marketing the program as these institutional visits are typically the cornerstone of the experience. If existing networks do not include international faculty or staff, try contacting professional organizations (such as NASPA's International Education Knowledge Community) to meet faculty and staff abroad who are interested in global learning.

Purpose and Goals of the Experience

As mentioned earlier in this chapter, the host(s) must decide the purpose of the experience (education, professional development, or fundraising). If the trip is designated as educational or as professional development, the host(s) must decide if academic credit will be offered and through which department. Securing academic credit may take a great deal of time, so be sure to work through the correct process on campus. Often, courses need to be developed and approved on a variety of levels before they can be offered, and this could take an extended amount of time. If the trip is solely a professional development experience, the facets of the experience need to be identified and outcomes explained fully.

Perceptions and theory

Sometime, study abroad opportunities are considered a means by which many faculty and staff are able to travel and have fun and the opportunities for education and growth are ignored. In order to keep this perception to a minimum, be sure to base the program or course in theory and develop the objectives from that theory. As the program is marketed, the solid theory base will be evident and help set the program apart from mere vacations.

Academic Component

One key item that organizers must address early in their planning is whether or not the trip will be for academic credit. If the trip incorporates an academic component and participants earn academic credit, organizers must ensure that the trip meets departmental and academic standards. Our trip was designed as an independent study course, allowing it to be taken by enrolled students for credit or full-time professionals simply seeking a quality professional development experience. Course requirements might include: (a) extensive reading prior to departure, (b) participation in and attendance at all lectures, (c) maintaining a journal to document the experience and allow participants time for reflection, (d) small group discussions, (e) completion of a research paper comparing some aspect of U.S. higher education with the host country's higher education system, and (f) participation in online chat discussions prior to departure. For the participants' pre-trip reading and learning, we would recommend the use of a formal text, such as the formal guide offered at many book stores, or a compilation of readings. These allow students to understand the historical, social, and cultural aspects of the locations they are visiting. If a formal travel guide does not exist, an effective method for collecting readings is to ask your site hosts for recommendations. We found they offered excellent reading that could be easily obtained via the Internet.

Use of Travel Company or Planning Yourself

Many organizers of study abroad trips plan and coordinate all the details themselves. They feel they have the background, experience, and contacts necessary to navigate the maze of details necessary for a successful trip. Others plan their trip with the help of a travel company. Although travel programs can be created and implemented without the aid of a travel company or agent, these services greatly reduce the stress of the program host(s), but do increase the costs of the overall experience. If a reputable travel company is chosen, the host(s) is freed from the details of securing hotels, ordering meals, arranging for transportation, and having to deal with lost luggage, delayed planes, or some of the details of emergencies. Several reputable companies are available to assist, and prudent organizers will explore the pros and cons associated with coordinating the program alone or with the assistance of a travel company.

Site Visit

As the decisions are being confirmed about the program, it is important to plan a site visit to ensure the hotels, transportation, and on-site host institutions are able to manage the participants. Organizers should schedule a site visit up to a year in advance of the trip. During this visit, the organizers should meet hotel staff, plan appropriate meals, coordinate cultural activities, and plan academic components with the host. If a travel company is being used to plan the main trip, it would behoove the host(s) to use the same company for the site visit.

Itinerary of the Study Abroad Experience

A comprehensive and well-designed itinerary should provide participants with a clear understanding and overview of the trip. Prior to departure, all participants know the length of stay, sites to be visited, and events planned. Initially, participants might be given an overview itinerary but closer to the trip, a more detailed itinerary should be provided. For our trip to England, a sample itinerary follows:

◊ Day 1 – Depart from home city and travel (usually overnight) to destination.

◊ Day 2 – Arrive at location and board touring coach for hotel. Orientation occurs immediately after check-in, followed by a group dinner where everyone can get to know each other.

◊ Day 3 – First lecture and visit to first institution. Travel to next city (typically with a little sightseeing on the way) and check into the hotel for the evening. This is a good night to have a free evening for the group to explore the city, provided it is safe to do so.

◊ Day 4 – Visit the second institution, tour, and listen the second lecture. Free afternoon to explore, shop, or sightsee. Host a group dinner with faculty and staff from the institution visited that day.

◊ Day 5 – Travel to next location (if possible, include some cultural sites) and check into the hotel for the evening.

◊ Days 6 and 7 – Free days to explore the city that you are staying in (we made the weekend a time to explore London and provided the day for the students to do so).

◊ Day 8 – During the evening, we met at a local attraction to enjoy the experience together.

◊ Day 9 – Depart hotel and proceed to next institution. Visit with the faculty and staff, listen to a lecture, and tour the facility. Proceed to the next city and hotel, and enjoy a group dinner with small group meetings following the meal.

◊ Day 10 – Visit the next institution, listen to a lecture, and enjoy a networking lunch with the faculty and staff in attendance. Depart for the next hotel and city; upon arrival, the remainder of the day is free.

◊ Day 11 – Visit the next institution and enjoy the local flavor of the city, with a portion of the afternoon free to explore. Gather for a group dinner with the faculty and staff from the host institution.

◊ Day 12 – Depart for next city and campus visit. Enjoy the campus culture, lecture, and opportunity to meet faculty and staff on the host campus. Gather in the evening for a group dinner with the host institution.

◊ Day 13 – Depart for the airport hotel, visiting interesting sights on the way.

◊ Day 14 – Depart for the airport and for the journey home.

Budget Management

Establishing a budget is a critical segment of program development. Table 3.1 offers a view of a budget from a study abroad program that Clemson University hosted to England.

The type of budget chosen for this program was a zero-based budget that included every aspect of the trip costs. Items that must be considered are transportation costs (air and ground), meals, insurance, salaries, admission to events and sites, tips, guest costs, tuition, gifts, and site visit costs. Another area to consider is that of sponsorship or fundraising. With fixed and varied costs covered by other means, host(s) might be able to include scholarships or added benefits as perks within the program.

An effective way to create a budget is to gather all of the fixed and variable costs and divide those costs by the optimum number of participants desired. The optimum number should be determined by transportation or institution restrictions. Once those numbers have been established the costs for the program can be shared and marketed.

The timing of the program can affect the overall costs. Typically, hosting programs during peak times abroad (June, July and August) will incur the highest costs, as that is when most people from the United States travel abroad. Therefore, hosting programs at non-peak times could save the participants a great deal of money. For example, purchasing a ticket to England in May could cost approximately $550, while purchasing that same ticket in July could cost as much as $1000.

An additional budget item to consider is that of arranging for travel and program needs alone or with the assistance of the travel company. The host(s) can save money if they can make arrangements themselves, but they should consider their level of expertise, network connections, and desired stress levels. Using a travel company will cost money but may be well worth the expense.

Technology

Technology can be a real asset to the overall program, specifically if the participants are not all located at the same institution. Clemson University's program used technology to market the program (listservs and a Web site), offer the participants a basic orientation and opportunities to chat with their group members and facilitator, and give them a way to turn in their assignments, view their grades, and e-mail their professor. In addition, all of the general communications were sent to the students by e-mail, and responses on preferences for roommates, meals, and special needs were solicited and obtained via e-mail. Technology enables the program to be offered to a wider group of participants as location is no longer a barrier. Although technology is certainly an asset, one must remember that there is a negative side also; technology is not always reliable as it "goes down" or networks are offline.

Risk Management

As with any program, risk management practices should be included. It is crucial to work with the Office of Risk Management on campus or an individual insurance company. The world is an uncertain place, and participants can become ill or injured while on the trip. The host(s) must be prepared to deal with these situations. Obtaining insurance is important and relatively inexpen-

Income	Amounts
Tuition	$1,077
Student Land Costs with Air	$2,550
Student Land Costs without Air	$1,645
Application Fee	$50
Administrative Fee	$298
Expenses	
Student	
Land and Air Costs	$2,550
Insurance	$31
University Surcharge	$107
Faculty	
Land and Air Costs	$10,200
Salary and Fringe	$6,850
Insurance	$124
Meals	$2,000
Fixed Costs	
Travel – Bus	$11,310
Guest Expenses	$500
Supplies	$285
Gifts	$750
Site Visit Costs	$4,075

Table 3.1. Sample budget.

sive. In addition, be sure that the participants complete some type of release that enables the host(s) to arrange for medical treatment if the participant is not able to do so for him or herself. This will save a great deal of anxiety if a situation occurs while on the trip.

The host(s) should also register with the U.S. embassies in the countries included in the trip, educate the participants about basic safety issues, and encourage everyone to bring a copy of their passport and wallet contents along with them, as well as leave a copy at home with someone who can assist if items are lost or stolen. Organizers should also give participants laminated copies of hotel addresses and phone numbers in case they become separated from the group. These simple steps lessen the overall risk associated with the program.

Communication

Once the participants have decided to attend the trip, constant communication is needed. Communication patterns and content information should be determined early and communicated to the participants. This is especially important for those individuals who have not traveled widely. The program developed at Clemson University established five main communications that were delivered, beginning the January prior to the July trip. These covered such topics as how to obtain a passport, luggage restrictions, itineraries, contact names and numbers, required readings, course syllabus, insurance information, and myriad other items. Individual communications were numerous and differed for each participant based on his or her needs and questions. In order to keep the information consistent, all communications should be streamlined through one host (if there is more than one).

Marketing and Recruitment

Marketing the program is important, as every program has an ideal number of participants. Use resources on campus to market the program to students or professionals, use professional networks to market the program to others across the nation, and use the many listservs that exist to pique the interest of those students and professionals who might want to attend. Depending on the budget of the program, the host(s) might consider purchasing advertising in conference publications or creating mailings to send to graduate preparation programs or student affairs divisions.

Evaluation

It is important to get feedback from the participants about their experiences. The course that was offered through Clemson University was evaluated by the participants at the closing dinner, and those evaluations were used to make plans for the next year. The overall experience was evaluated highly, and the participants were able to identify what they gained from the experience and to provide constructive feedback. The faculty involved with the program at Clemson University used the evaluations and a pre- and post-test to assess the participants' expectations and experiences.

Follow-up Meeting

In order to encourage the bonds that were developed during the actual trip, professional organizations could host reunion activities such as receptions, programs, or dinners at annual conferences (e.g., NASPA or ACPA-College Student Educators International) where participants can reunite with others who attended the trip with them or who attended other trips hosted by the same institution. This is a good way to help participants remember the events of the trip and an excellent way to market future programs. Past participants in solid, successful programs will be the best marketing agents for future programs.

Outcomes, Results, and Benefits

Assessment is integral to any programming a student affairs professional undertakes. Obviously there are a number of approaches to designing a program assessment. Data collection methods may include surveys,

questionnaires, focus groups, pre- and post-tests, or a combination of these methods. With the study abroad experience at Clemson University, the authors chose to develop two types of evaluation or assessment tools to collect the needed information.

First, we created an in-house pre- and post-survey to give to the participants in order to learn their thoughts, feelings, and beliefs going into the study abroad experience and then, what their perceptions were after the experience. The responses were kept confidential. Both surveys had 10 Likert-scaled questions and 7 open-ended ones. The authors framed the questions around the following areas:

◊ Why they chose to participate in a study abroad program;

◊ Beliefs they had about how they would be treated in England;

◊ Opinions on statements about higher education in England and the United States;

◊ Opinions on cross-cultural issues;

◊ Which preparatory/orientation opportunities were the most useful and which were the least helpful; and

◊ What the primary benefits would be from participating.

The pre-survey was given at the orientation session at the airport prior to departure for the United Kingdom. We distributed the post-survey at the closing dinner at the end of the experience.

We created a second evaluation tool to give the planning committee important information about the logistics of the study abroad experience. We adapted this tool from numerous course and study abroad evaluation tools. Our purpose was to evaluate the organizational and communication processes, as well as the costs of the trip. Furthermore, we gained valuable information about the course offering (i.e., the guest lectures, grading process, and course expectations). The final question gave the opportunity to rate the overall experience.

The faculty team used the information from the first tool, the pre- and post-survey, to gain a better understanding of the perceptions of the participants. The pre-survey allowed us to gain a sense of which students might need additional support during the study abroad experience. Even though the data was collected in a confidential manner, the faculty communicated with the group that we were available for additional support if needed. Several students did reveal that they were apprehensive about the trip. Therefore, the faculty members were able to provide more explanations or one-on-one support for those individuals.

From the logistical evaluation tool, we gained valuable information to improve the experience for the future. Several suggestions included: allow individuals to make their own flight arrangements to and from the host country so they can take advantage of frequent flyer miles, discounts, etc.; continue to provide the opportunity for participants to fly as a group from the United States; provide smaller group orientation sessions online to facilitate communication rather than have the whole group, which comprised more than 30 individuals, meeting at the same time.

Overall, the assessment/evaluation system we designed gave us very important and valuable information. The participants were overwhelmingly pleased with their experiences. Most of the individuals stated they would encourage others to enroll in this study abroad experience.

Lessons Learned

Numerous operational details need to be considered and then executed for a successful study abroad trip. The following are lessons we have learned. We hope they will assist others planning study abroad experiences.

◊ Identify a core planning group or team. Deliberately and purposely identify who has what responsibility for the trip. Planning team members should clearly understand their role and function for this experience. Remember that the number of organizers will directly affect the number of participants that the program can accommodate.

◊ Determine all costs of the trip, observable and hidden. Many trip costs will be obvious, but be prepared for hidden costs, such as gifts for hosts, tips for drivers, and tour guides, and be prepared for unanticipated rising costs such as in airline tickets. In preparing the budget, incorporate a small amount for these hidden costs.

◊ While planning can be done by members of the planning team, we suggest the use an established travel company to assist with the numerous details of travel. There are several excellent companies whose primary purpose is coordinating travel abroad experiences. If you use a good company, you will not to have to worry about detailed logistical issues or about having a contact to call if unanticipated situations arise (and they will). This is worth the extra expense.

◊ Plan, plan, plan; communicate, communicate, communicate. Realize up front that you can never communicate too much information, nor can you over plan. Lack of extensive planning is more likely than any other item to doom your trip and your participants' expectations. Despite considerable planning, preparation, and communication, things will happen and require changes on the trip, and your (and fellow participants') flexibility will be challenged.

◊ If the tour is designed as an academic credit course, select a diverse group of applicants. We found that a diverse group, including full-time professionals and doctoral and master's students, enhanced the sharing of perspectives and allowed for enriched discussions and insights.

◊ Organize a pre-departure orientation. This allows participants to get to know one another and to review the unique elements of the trip. This orientation can be face-to-face at the home institution, on site in the host country, or at the airport of departure. We suggest you organize online discussions and chat rooms for participants prior to departure. Traveling abroad is not like traveling in the United States. For example, in England, hotel rooms tend to be smaller and often do not have air conditioning. Learning about the uniqueness of the country they are visiting will enhance participants' satisfaction with the experience.

◊ Find out which participants have traveled extensively in the United States and abroad. Once the tour begins, organizers can use those individuals to help minimize the apprehensions and fears of less experienced participants. For those individuals with limited travel outside of the United States, organizers should be especially sensitive to their fears, concerns, and apprehensions. We recommend frequent individual contact with those individuals prior to departure.

◊ Incorporate a concluding group activity on the final day of the trip. At the end of the tour, gather the participants and allow them an opportunity to share feelings, reactions, and experiences of the trip. This reflection re-enforces what they have learned about themselves, fellow participants, international colleagues, and the countries and institutions visited.

◊ Be prepared for the trip to be a life-changing event. Whether participants have traveled extensively to other parts of the world or not, a successful study abroad trip impacts them as student affairs professionals and as human beings. It exposes them to new ideas, concepts, ways of thinking, and methods for accomplishing student affairs work. They arrive back in the United States as better student affairs professionals, campus participants, and individuals.

For many participants, this experience was the trip of a lifetime. The participants' perceptions were highlighted in the pre- and post-surveys we conducted. The post-survey revealed that, compared to the pre-survey expectations, a greater number of participants believed they grew personally because of taking the study abroad tour. The pre- and post-surveys also showed that the initial intent of the study abroad tour, to gain exposure to another cultural and educational experience, was achieved. Not only were the participants challenged cognitively and socially, but they also had great fun!

References

ACUHO-I. (n.d.). Events and programs: International tour. Retrieved July 14, 2008, from http://www.acuho-i.org/brEventsbrPrograms/InternationalTour/tabid/204/Default.aspx

Council on International Educational Exchange (2005). A world of opportunity. Retrieved September 15, 2005, from http://www.ciee.org

Dalton, J. C. (Ed.). (1999). *Beyond borders: How international developments are changing student affairs practice. New Directions for Student Services, 86.* San Francisco: Jossey-Bass.

Fulbright Program. (2005). Retrieved August 26, 2005, from http://exchanges.state.gov/education/fulbright

Joseph, C., Marginson S., & Yang, R. (2005). Special issue: International education in the Asia Pacific region introduction by the guest authors. *Australian Journal of Education, 49*(1), 3–7.

NASPA. (n.d.). International exchange dates. Retrieved July 14, 2008, from http://www.naspa.org/communities/kc/page. cfm?kcpageID=83&kcid=8

Institute of International Education. (2005). Open Doors Online: Open doors 2004 data tables. Retrieved September 23, 2005, from http://opendoors.iienetwork.org/?p=49929

Peterson, D. M., Briggs, P., Dreasher, L., Horner, D. D., & Nelson, T. (1999). Contributions of international students and programs to campus diversity. In J. C. Dalton (Ed.), *Beyond borders: How international developments are changing student affairs practice. New Directions for Student Services, 86 (pp. 67–77).* San Francisco: Jossey-Bass.

FOUR

STUDENT STORIES OF INTERNATIONAL EDUCATION

Julie Adkins Nhem, Cathy Stevens and Tony Cawthon

Study abroad can be a career-changing, life-changing experience. The following stories show how two individuals reached their career paths as a result of their own experiences abroad—and came to realize the importance (and difficulties) of travel abroad for U.S. students.

Julie's Story:
México, American Samoa, and Costa Rica

A six-week Spanish course in Querétaro, México, during her junior year changed Julie's life and career path as she responded to "a whole new world that was stimulating me in ways I had not imagined. I became excited about life," she said, "and discovered a thirst for knowledge, culture, and language." She had gone to México as a simple way to fulfill a language requirement; she returned determined to add a Spanish minor to her archeology major. After graduating from the University of Oregon, Julie returned to Querétaro for a year, teaching English to pay the rent. Then she resolved to attend graduate school. "From an undergraduate who had no idea what she wanted to do with her future," Julie said, "I became a graduate student with a passionate goal of becoming an international higher education professional.

"I determined that I wanted to work with international students studying in the United States and American students wishing to study abroad. I knew from my experiences teaching English that I enjoyed working with young adults, but that I did not particularly enjoy teaching. I began researching degrees that would enable me to work on a college campus in a non-teaching position. I found both NASPA-Student Affairs Administrators in Higher Education and NAFSA: Association of International Educators to be very helpful resources. I also wrote to prominent members of both organizations and received many responses. My research led me to apply to graduate preparation programs in student affairs and higher education administration, and I was admitted to the University of Arkansas (UA)."

Costa Rica—Spotlighting a Problem of Study Abroad

"The higher education administration program gave me an opportunity to spend the summer in San Jose, Costa Rica, where I worked as the assistant to the director of international programs at a small, private Costa Rican university," Julie said. "During my time there, I had the unique experience of working with students with whom I was also taking Spanish classes. As I was more often viewed as a peer than as a graduate assistant administrator, I heard candid opinions about the school, the program, the department of international programs and its staff, the professors, and Costa Rican culture"

The students joked about how easy the courses were and complained, sometimes with justification, about problems with their home-stay families. "These comments," Julie said, "helped me to think about how student affairs professionals work with students who study abroad and relate my course work to practical application."

One problem, she said, is, "How do student affairs professionals effectively determine which study abroad and educational exchange programs are of academic and cultural quality? With the plethora of programs offered and limited budgets to work with, how do study abroad offices monitor every program offered? As it is impossible to do a site visit to every program provided outside of the institution, international higher education administrators must work together to effectively share the load by keeping detailed information on site visits made. It would be beneficial to save the information in a public database."

There are some vital resources which can help determine the quality of programs abroad. In their Section on U.S. Students Abroad (SECUSSA), NAFSA offers a forum for professionals in the field dealing with issues faced by U.S. students who study abroad. This section deals with issues such as health and safety; resources and information on various exchange programs; financial aid, grants, and scholarships for study abroad students; passports and visas; and methods for keeping track of students abroad.

"Since September 11, 2001, administrators have increased efforts to scrutinize where their students are studying. Campus and national systems have been created to monitor the location of these students for security reasons. One example is Student Exchange Visitor Information System (SEVIS), a national database for international students studying in the United States. As other public databases are developed, they could be used as resources for professionals in determining the quality of non-institutional programs. Surveys could be administered to students assessing aspects of the program. This input of information into the database could be used to assist prospective students.

Another resource available to help explore study abroad opportunities is the U.S. Department of State Office of Policy and Evaluation Education Division. This office provides impact assessment, evaluation, and results for the Bureau of Educational and Cultural Affairs. Some programs currently being evaluated are the Fulbright Student Program, Partnerships for Learning (P4L) Youth Exchange and Study Program, and Professional Exchanges and Study Programs. Visit http://exchanges.state.gov/education/evaluations for more information about the evaluation process.

This resource only reviews and evaluates Bureau programs, but it can be used as a good example for international higher education and student affairs administrators to review and evaluate popular independent study abroad programs and providers. Even though Julie's first job in higher education does not deal directly with international or study abroad students, "I come into contact with them on a daily basis, and I spend time volunteering in friendship partner programs with international students," she said. "My hesitant decision to spend six weeks in a foreign country completely shaped my personal and professional life. If I had not taken that first step to travel and study abroad, I wonder what career path I would be pursuing."[1]

Cathy's Story

In 2005, Cathy Stevens spent nearly six months in the third world: First, she accompanied her husband, a Furman University history professor, who led a six-week study abroad trip to South Africa and Namibia. Soon after, she went with him on his four-month sabbatical in El Salvador. Among other things, she learned the value of the professional study of student affairs, and she was convinced that the profession must highlight international experience. Here is her story.

South Africa

None of the students stirred as they listened to Heinrich's story. He had been a member of the South African Communist Party's underground during the decades-long

struggle against apartheid. He is now a human rights lawyer and makes it his life's work to fight injustice in the new South Africa.

"So, how do you define injustice," Katie, a junior, asked.

In a powerful and definitive voice, Heinrich responded, "You'll know it when you see it." (Heinrich, personal communication, February 4, 2005).

In Africa, I expected to learn much about South Africa's complex political history and to get to know the students along the way. What I did not expect was how invaluable my one year of master's work in a graduate preparation program in student affairs would be. As a first-year student at Clemson University, I became acquainted with student development theory, learning partnerships, and student identity construction. On the trip, I witnessed these concepts as living, breathing entities and had a roadside seat at a crucial intersection, where first-world students cross paths with the poverty and political struggles of a developing nation. It seems that very few reach this junction and pass with ease. I witnessed personal struggle and identity questioning among the students almost every day and felt similar emotions myself.

Because I was not a peer and not a professor, I was in a unique position on the trip. Students frequently turned to me to discuss their struggles. Most of our discussions revolved around how to process what they were seeing. They were overwhelmed. I was overwhelmed, too. Here are some examples of student reflections.

Dale, a junior from Mississippi, said now that he had seen this, he wouldn't be able to forget. But, he didn't know what to do. How would he ever be able to make a difference in the situation? "Most of the people in the world are impoverished," he said. "Yet, poverty is not an issue that people at home want to address. It's not something that churches study, even though the Bible talks about it a lot." As the son of a minister, he didn't know how to reconcile his religion with the horror of meeting more than 100 orphans who lost their parents to AIDS. More than 40% of the orphans also had the disease, and the orphanage could only afford to feed them three full meals a week. Dale and I spent hours talking about what he could do at home to help. To him, the prospects did not appear good (Dale, personal communication, January 30, 2005).

Laura, a senior who grew up as the child of diplomats and who had lived in Brazil, Russia, and Holland, had seen the world's poverty before, and she found Africa's struggles to be similar to those she had witnessed in other countries. She noted that in many places around the globe, a small population of elite owns and controls the majority of the wealth. "I don't feel compassionate and sad anymore. I'm just angry," she said. "I'm angry at the system that makes things this way. But, I don't know what to do. I want to do something meaningful in life, but I don't know how to help" (Laura, personal communication, January 17, 2005).

---

[1] Julie Adkins Nhem received her master's degree in higher education administration at the University of Arkansas where she focused her studies and training on international education. She has studied, lived, and worked in five different countries in Latin America, Europe, and the Pacific Islands and plans to continue her career and education in the realm of international education and higher education administration. Julie is currently working as a paralegal in San Francisco.

James, a senior from South Carolina, often wanted to go home. It was too much. It was too different, and he simply wanted to go to Macaroni Grill.

I have often heard my husband talk about witnessing student growth while on study abroad, and he was not exaggerating. Away from the comforts of home, the friends they know, and access to cell phones and the Internet, the students delved into their travel experience, tackling issues and discussing differences at length. These conversations lasted for hours, with students challenging each other to answer big questions. What is the meaning of our lives? Why is the world organized like it is? Why would any loving God let people be so poor? How can I make a difference? How does the way we live at home affect the lives of people here? It was at once invigorating and exhausting. I fell asleep as soon as I lay down every night.

What stood out the most to me was the overarching theme of most of my conversations with these students—finding a way to lead a meaningful life. Over and over, I heard them say, "I just want to do something meaningful, I want to make a difference in the world. It seems impossible, but I want to help in some way." They are all in the process of developing their identities and determining the paths their lives will take. I tried to form learning partnerships with them, and we grew together as we tackled the issues. In doing so, each student brought his or her pre-trip worldview to the table, and we melded that with what they experienced in Africa.

I have always been a proponent of undergraduate study abroad, but I now feel that it is a crucial element of college study and identity growth. Change occurred daily, as students grew both academically and personally. In a mere six weeks, students' identities were undoubtedly influenced and constructed. It made me think that student affairs professionals could make a huge difference on study abroad trips—and it made me think that perhaps the academics that lead these trips should be knowledgeable about identity development theory. Being with inquiring students left me excited about international education, identity construction, and the hope of youth. Similarly it inspired me to think about the meaning of my own life and how all my time in the developing world was affecting me. With these issues in mind—and just a week after returning from Africa—I began my journey to El Salvador.

El Salvador

The Peace Accords were signed in 1992 after 12 years of civil war in El Salvador. After 12 years, in a country of only six million people, 70,000 were dead and one million had been displaced from their homes. Of those one million, hundreds of thousands left for the United States, Canada, and México. Others were forced to move within the country. They left their homes because they were no longer safe with bullets flying through their streets and bedroom windows.

In the lakeside village of Viejo Copapayo, or Old Copapayo, we heard a story of the war from Raúl, who was a boy of 10 there in November 1983. The army came into the town and slaughtered men, women, children, and the elderly as they ran for cover. When the firing began, Raúl and a friend dove into a nearby ditch. A tree grew over the ditch where they were hiding, and the soldiers, who cut branches from the trees to cover those killed, never saw them. When they felt it was safe, Raúl tried to pick his injured friend up out of the ditch, but he was too heavy. Raúl didn't want to leave him, but the friend told him he needed to escape. They held each other in a hug for a long time, at the end of which his friend simply said, "Vaya con dios" ("Go well")(Raúl, personal communication, March 20, 2005).

The few people who had managed to survive were refugees in Honduras until they returned in 1987. They requested land nearby their old town and began to build a new Nuevo Copapayo. In the years since, the town has built homes, a cobblestone street, a school, a *tienda*, and a church. Not much has changed since before the war. The people are still poor, but Nuevo Copapayo is a testament to strength and fortitude and evidence of the power of community.

Reflections

As I reflect on my time away and the meaning it has brought to my life, one lesson stands out above the rest: We are who we are and have what we have because of one thing—the lottery that is birth. We are born into situations that largely define where our lives will take us. Who are we really? I believe that I am essentially a construct. My identity has been shaped over the years through my experiences, and it is always changing. More importantly, I am the stories I tell myself. As a result of my experiences in 2005, those stories have changed. Coming into direct contact with poverty, courage, and determination in the developing world muddied my feelings about the first world's role in our global society. I have begun to think differently about foreign policy, human beings, and our moral obligations to love and respect others.

Like the Furman students in Africa, I have asked myself where my world views come from. It may be messy and complex, but we need to challenge our own foundations, and we need to challenge the foundations of the students we work with. It was suggested to me that our views come from a decentralized, unconscious place sometimes called "the marketplace of ideas," where we interact with others and the many variables in our lives. It is what postmodern theorists call a dialogue, and we are part of this dialogue from the moment we are born. It is important for us as individuals and as student affairs professionals that these dialogues with students include an international component and challenge our views of the wider world, including the developing, or third world. Students will inevitably respond in myriad ways to dialogue on international issues, but what is crucial is the exposure to these issues. Lack of knowledge about global concerns can be harmful in today's world, and the key is to help individuals recognize that we are all connected to these issues.

In September 2005, I returned for my second year of master's work in student affairs a changed person. I had stared poverty in the face, and I knew I must be involved in some way to make it better. During my first year of graduate school, I was unsure of my focus, but that is not the case anymore. Because I know that students will grow and learn through knowledge of international concerns, I plan to be a great proponent of that. I can think of nothing that has more impact than a study abroad experience. It is a door to self-reflection and identity formation. International experience, especially in the developing world, helps many students shape themselves and bring meaning to their lives. Even though travel is not possible for all students, they can be exposed to global issues in other ways, through mentors and friends and through dialogue. I can think of few better places for change to begin than on a college campus where thousands of inquiring minds are challenging their identity structures and where student affairs professionals can help them figure out who they are. I hope that my international experiences can be part of that dialogue with students.

My travel experiences have changed me personally and professionally. As an individual, this travel has wrought in me a deep-seated need to consider the needs of others as I conceptualize my own, both at home in South Carolina and in the far corners of El Salvador and South Africa. I want to be able to do something every day, but how? By being a mentor and friend to others and engaging in conversation about our global community, I hope to share the things I have seen. I know at my core that people are people regardless of their station in life and that we have a moral duty to love and care for others.

This travel has also changed who I am as a student affairs professional, giving me more of a world focus and global bent. I am more likely to challenge students about related issues and help develop a global consciousness on my campus. As student affairs professionals, we have an obligation to include international components in our student development programming and relationships. If we fail to do so, we are doing our students and ourselves a huge disservice.[2]

Conclusion

The Institute of International Education in the 2004 Open Doors Report provides information about U.S. higher education students studying abroad and international students coming to the United States to study. The most recent data reported is from the 2002–03 academic year. There has been a dramatic increase of 145% in international education participation from 1991 to 2003. During the 2002–03 academic year, approximately 175,000 students from the United States studied abroad, up from 71,000 in 1992. The majority of the students were female (64.7%) and 50% of the programs were considered short term such as a summer session (Institute of International Education, 2004). Student affairs practitioners should consider how they can help more male students participate in a study abroad experience.

The preceding stories illustrate how everyone's international educational experience is unique. Both Julie and Cathy found new ways to develop their own professional interests based on their experiences. They grew professionally and personally as opportunities allowed them to better relate to the students they work with. In our changing world, international experiences provide student affairs professionals with tools and incentives for broadening their students' educational expectations allowing these students to become better citizens in a global society.

References

Institute of International Education (IIE). (2004). *Open Doors 2004*. Retrieved August 23, 2005, from http://opendoors. iienetwork.org/?p=50138

Cathy Stevens is the associate project director at the Richard W. Riley Institute of Government, Politics and Public Leadership at Furman University. She holds an MEd in counsellor education with an emphasis in student affairs.

FIVE

JOURNEYS OF DISCOVERY IN A "FLATTENED WORLD"

Sandy Hubler and Daniel Mackeben

"Individuals must, and can, now ask, 'where do I fit into the global competition and opportunities of the day, and how can I, on my own, collaborate with others globally'" (Friedman, 2005, p. 10).

In his acclaimed book, *The World is Flat: A Brief History of the Twenty-first Century*, author Thomas Friedman contemplates the enormous challenges and opportunities that have emerged as globalization, fueled primarily by the Internet and new technologies, plays an ever increasing role in world, national, and regional economies and communities. A dominant trend in globalization surfacing in the past few years, according to Friedman, is how these worldwide changes are propelled not by Western countries and businesses, but rather by China, India, and other non-Western regions of the world. Friedman contends that this departure from the recent domination of Western countries has created a great leveling of the world's economic and social structures and has figuratively shrunk the globe "from a size small to a size tiny and flattening the playing field at the same time" (Friedman, 2005, p. 10). This "flattening" of the world will undoubtedly have far-reaching implications for countries, corporations, and individuals, including colleges and universities.

Friedman's reflections on the flattening of the world are especially inspiring as he describes the many benefits for those who embrace the emergence of a "newfound power for individuals to collaborate and compete globally" (Friedman, 2005, p. 10). Great possibilities do exist in this evolving world, but Friedman is equally sobering in describing the disadvantages to those organizations and individuals ignoring the increased competition, new ways of thinking, and complex opportunities that arise from this tectonic shift in world economies and communities.

How can student affairs respond to this new, flattened world? This chapter will explore the value and potential of international exchange programs as one profound way that student affairs organizations and professionals can stay in step, and not be left behind, in this worldwide transformation.

Journeys of Discovery

Friedman's book has relevance to this chapter in a number of important ways, including how he gained his insight related to the world's "flattening." His revelation to write the book came not in the comfort of his home nor while surfing the latest blogs on the Internet, but rather through his travel, through his varied experiences abroad. In fact, an encounter with a college professor in India inspired Friedman to "drop everything and write a book that would enable me to understand how this flattening process happened and what its implications might be for companies, countries, and individuals" (Friedman, 2005, p. 10).

Friedman's journeys throughout the United States, the Middle East, India, and other regions of the globe provided the impetus for his new vision of the world. The idea of the flattening or leveling of the economic and cultural playing field of the world is not entirely new, but Friedman's keen, fresh perspectives on these issues were honed and crystallized through travel, by exchanging information and ideas with others and by observing new worlds and ways of doing things.

Friedman's sojourns and his application of the lessons learned suggests that there is much to be gained by student affairs professionals as they likewise embark on their own journeys of discovery.

The Emergence of Student Affairs Exchange Programs

What role is international travel and exchange playing as student affairs organizations and individuals strive to collaborate and compete in this new, flattened world? Evidence of globalization's impact on colleges and universities abound, such as increasingly diverse student populations, dramatic changes in the needs and demographics of our international students, the vital role that technology plays in student service delivery, and the rapid rise of university partnerships with institutions in other regions of the world. New challenges to the student affairs profession are undoubtedly on the horizon, and complex issues await both institutions and individuals as new programs are added, staffing structures are modified, and resources are refocused.

International exchange programs for student affairs staff have so far played a modest role in the efforts of student affairs departments to proactively respond to globalization. Yet the growing number of student affairs professionals traveling abroad and the application of the lessons learned from these journeys show clearly that there is much to be gained at both organization and individual levels.

The importance of exchange programs is especially apparent in light of the rise in student affairs programs around the world and their far more pronounced influence on the philosophy and practice of student affairs today. Student affairs issues and best practices are no longer just originating in the United States. Trend-setting programs, research, and ideas are emerging from student affairs programs in countries such as South Africa, Germany, New Zealand, Bulgaria, and a host of others (see chapters 8–24 for country-specific student affairs program information). Student affairs has crossed the threshold and truly become an international profession, one that will increasingly rely on global dialogue and on collaborative ventures that will frequently be sparked and generated through international exchange programs.

Increasing Options, More Success Stories

Throughout the past decade, student affairs professionals have increasingly traveled around the globe to enhance their own understanding of the ways globalization is dramatically altering the student affairs field and their own individual role in its evolution. International student affairs organizations, such as the NASPA–Student Affairs Administrators in Higher Education and NAFSA: Association of International Educators, have played an important role in inaugurating programs that have spurred the worldwide exchange of information and people. Student affairs administrators have also increasingly participated in standing exchange programs, such as the Fulbright Scholar program.

Because student affairs professionals have not taken part in these exchange programs for very long, little if any research has been conducted on the influences of these experiences on institutions, professionals, and student service delivery. However, anecdotal information and the outcomes gleaned from the growing number of exchange programs do indicate that they have had, and will continue to have, a profound impact on the personal and professional growth of participants and their knowledge of emerging global trends and issues in student af-

fairs. Furthermore, examples abound of the unique and diverse ways exchange program participants are building on the connections made by applying the lessons learned and integrating them positively into their own work. We will explore several of these success stories in this chapter.

The chapter then closes with resources on how student affairs programs can integrate international exchange programs into their own operations. But first, we profile two organizations, NASPA and the Fulbright Commission, that are leading the way in helping student affairs professionals explore this new, flattened world.

Leading the Way: NASPA and the Fulbright Commission

Throughout the last decade, increased attention has been devoted to the potential value of student affairs participation in international exchange and to engaging student affairs professionals from around the globe in dialogue regarding best practices and common issues in the field. Two major initiatives—one relatively new program from NASPA and the other from the longstanding William J. Fulbright program—have played particularly important roles in this expansion.

NASPA played a lead role in initiating this worldwide exchange of people and information within student affairs, inaugurating the first International Symposium at its 1996 Annual Conference in Atlanta. Since then, the symposium has grown in attendance and influence, with student affairs professionals coming together from virtually every region in the world to participate in its workshops and seminars.

In addition to the International Symposium, NASPA established the International Education Knowledge Community, a cohort of student affairs professionals worldwide that built on the symposium's success and spurred the creation of a number of new initiatives that enhanced international educational opportunities for NASPA member institutions. One such advancement is NASPA's International Exchange Program. Established in 1995, the program offers exchange programs both to and from the United States for NASPA members (NASPA, n.d.b). Another organization that offers opportunities for student affairs sojourns abroad is the longstanding Fulbright Scholars Program. The flagship international educational program sponsored by the United States Government, the Fulbright Program is designed to connect educators from around the globe to participate in an impressive range of international exchange programs (NASPA, n.d. a). The Fulbright Program was established in 1946 under legislation introduced by Senator J. William Fulbright of Arkansas, and in 60 years more than 250,000 scholars from around the world have participated in its diverse array of exchange programs.

The Fulbright Program awards approximately 4,500 new grants annually, with support being directed toward both long- and short-term experiences abroad. Grants are provided to faculty, graduate students, researchers, and, increasingly, to higher education administrators. A growing number of student affairs administrators, including the author of this chapter, have been awarded grants to study student affairs programs in other regions of the world. Fulbright recipients are chosen for their academic merit and leadership potential and are charged with studying and teaching in other countries to exchange ideas about common issues and explore potential solutions (NASPA, n.d. a). More than 50% of Fulbright grants are awarded to international scholars and administrators visiting the United States.

The Fulbright Program and the NASPA International Exchange Program are two examples of organizations and associations offering opportunities for student affairs administrators to connect with existing exchange programs and/or propose their own initiatives that, in some cases, can receive sponsorship and funding. These two programs will be highlighted in the following case examples of best practices in international exchange programs in student affairs. In addition to the Fulbright Program and NASPA, Figure 5.1 details other organizations that offer similar opportunities for student affairs professionals. It also must be noted that a growing number of institutions and individuals are initiating their own exchange programs, with several student affairs organizations even forming job-share programs with student affairs personnel at international universities. Later in the chapter, we present one such "home-grown" program at the University of Florida.

Best Practices: Four Success Stories

The following four stories were selected to show the variety of regions that have participated in exchange programs, the varied impact that these exchange programs have had at both individual and institutional levels, and the multiple ways that participation in these programs have enhanced the world view and professional effectiveness of participants. The stories cover (a) the value of networking connections that student affairs professionals developed on exchange programs, (b) a unique institutional partnership between universities in México and the United States, (c) a young professional's quest to create student connections between Nelson Mandela University in South Africa and George Mason University in Virginia, and (d) the former dean of students' Fulbright experience in South Africa.

A Mutually Beneficial Partnership

International exchange programs in student affairs benefit both professionals and organizations. On the organizational level, for example, Virginia Polytechnic Institute and State University (Virginia Tech) and the Tecnológico de Monterrey of México entered into a unique

agreement between their student affairs divisions. This arrangement was inspired by a 2002 visit sponsored by the NASPA International Exchange and initiated by Landrum Cross, Virginia Tech's former vice president for student affairs and current senior fellow to the provost. The partnership was recognized with the Global Partnership Program award in NASPA's International Education Knowledge Community's 3rd Annual Best Practices in International Education and Learning Awards in 2005 (Harris, 2005).

The program, Tec-to-Tech Connections: Building an International Partnership between Tecnológico de Monterrey in México and Virginia Tech, forged an alliance between the two institutions that, according to Virginia Tech, promotes international competence in faculty, staff, and students through international opportunities in professional development, research, teaching, and cultural exchange. The program promotes exchanges through the student affairs office, through academic areas, and between students of both universities. The partnership promotes staff and student exchanges in food services, student government, resident advising, counseling, community development, higher education, student affairs, and academics.

For example, student government leaders from Virginia Tech participated in a student leadership conference at the Mexican institute; community development and service learning personnel from each school met for an exchange program in México; and residence advisers from both schools likewise gathered for a conference to exchange ideas and participate in leadership training activities. Other activities being pursued between Virginia Tech and Tecnológico de Monterrey include:

◊ an exchange of resources, particularly online resources, between the counseling centers of both institutions;

◊ discussions by higher education and student affairs faculty at Virginia Tech about research and teaching opportunities in México; and

◊ discussion of academic exchanges in business, entrepreneurial leadership, engineering, and hospitality and tourism management.

"Since Virginia Tech's goals include international education and the Tecnológico de Monterrey promotes international competence for organizations and internationally competitive students in their fields, an agreement of exchange between the two institutions is a good start toward international understanding and cooperation and will benefit the faculty and students of both schools," says Landrum Cross, who served as an active participant in NASPA's International Symposium and helped connect with the administration at Tecnológico de Monterrey at the Symposium's annual gathering (Harris, 2005).

According to Virginia Tech officials, the program requires students who participate at the partner institution to be able to speak the language of that institution. Benefits of the program for students include opportunities to develop language and cultural competencies and the possibility of practicing them through exchanges. Bringing the students together under the student affairs purview will also enhance student success both inside and outside of the classroom, improve their contributions to their respective campus missions of global exchange, and provide enriching out-of-class experiences.

Another important by-product of the partnership relates to the possibility of cultivating deeper alliances between student affairs and academic units. Virginia Tech officials note that the agreement emphasizes mutually beneficial programs such as: student exchanges, faculty-staff exchanges, cultural exchanges, and visiting scholars exchanges; cooperative and collaborative research projects; double-degree programs; short-term training programs and projects; and cooperative and exchange lectures, conferences, and seminars.

Fulbright Focus on South Africa

Roger Ludeman, former assistant chancellor for student affairs at the University of Wisconsin–Whitewater, has been a longtime proponent of international exchange programs for student affairs professionals. He co-founded the NASPA International Symposium in 1996 and has been a primary force in forging global connections among student affairs staff. Ludeman was the architect of the NASPA International Exchange Program and the recipient of three Fulbright grants, which involved study tours to Germany, France, Belgium, China, Japan, Australia, New Zealand, and South Africa.

"I have found the exchanges to be so enriching, at both a professional and personal level," says Ludeman, now retired from his post at Wisconsin–Whitewater, but still active as a visiting scholar and lecturer with student affairs programs worldwide (R. Ludeman, personal communication, July 21, 2005).

Ludeman has placed a special emphasis on reaching out to student affairs programs in South Africa. In 2002, he received a Fulbright Commission grant to study in—and work with—student affairs departments in the country on a wide variety of issues. Excerpts from his journal, *Fulbright Focus: South Africa,* offer a glimpse into the breadth of his experiences during his sojourn, as well as the many ways he both contributed to, and learned from, his activities abroad.

"The primary purpose of my Fulbright grant was to develop a teaching schema to integrate a set of professional qualifications for student service providers," says Ludeman (2002, p. 9). "The first task was to update and fine-tune a certificate program aimed at individuals currently working in various student services positions, which we then strived to provide to student affairs pro-

fessionals throughout South Africa and surrounding African countries by distance education with traditional onsite instruction" (Ludeman, 2002, p. 9).

Ludeman was also influential in helping the University of KwaZulu-Natal initiate and advance the first-ever master's degree with a specialization in higher education student services. Through his Fulbright grant, he also provided consultancy on a range of programs and initiatives to the student affairs staff at the University of KwaZulu-Natal, as well as to professional student affairs associations and organizations at other universities in the region. A review of his *Fulbright Focus* journal provides a glimpse into his experience in South Africa, and also sheds insight into the rapid advancement of the student affairs profession in the country. Among other activities, he:

◊ Presented a series of workshops entitled "University of KwaZulu-Natal Students – Do We Really Know Who They Are?" for student affairs departments at the University of KwaZulu Natal.

◊ Spoke on the international nature of student affairs work and presented information on the new student affairs master's program at the University of KwaZulu-Natal at a regional conference of the South African National Association of Student Development Practitioners (NASDEV) in Durban.

◊ Restructured the certificate program for initial training of student service providers in South Africa to ensure compliance with postgraduate and master's degree programs in student affairs offered at the University of KwaZulu-Natal.

◊ Worked with students from the University of Kwa-Zulu-Natal who were engaged in a multidisciplinary research study of the interfaces among university policy development, program and service delivery, and student demographics.

◊ Delivered a workshop on international trends and issues in student affairs for the Border Technikon student affairs department, and another session on student affairs functions and roles in higher education to students in the specialized master's program in student affairs.

◊ Published an article highlighting his perspectives on South African student affairs in the journal *Perspectives on KwaZulu-Natal.*

"My Fulbright experience in South Africa…it provided yet another example of the increasingly global nature of the profession and exposed me to new ideas and possibilities that I applied directly to my work at Wisconsin–Whitewater, and beyond into retirement" (Ludeman, 2002, p. 9).

Ludeman's international connections have not waned since he retired in 2001. He remains closely aligned with both the NASPA International Exchange Program and

International Symposium, and contributes frequently to research and teaching projects related to international student affairs. Ludeman directed a two-year Kellogg Foundation grant in Southern Africa to study South African tertiary education student retention data and develop profiles of the students who persist and those who leave higher education institutions permanently. The project was conducted in cooperation with two South African associations, the South African Association of Senior Student Affairs Professionals (SAASSAP) and the National Association of Student Development Practitioners (NASDEV), and two associations in the United States, NASPA and ACPA–College Student Educators International.

A Cadre of New Colleagues

The experiences of 30 administrators from U.S. colleges and universities, representing a range of academic areas and student affairs divisions, show the value of the networking connections and collaborative ventures that can emerge when groups of educators travel together on international exchanges. Our example was the three-week administrators' seminar hosted by the Deutsch-Americanische Fulbright Commission in the 50th anniversary year of the Kommission's synergistic partnership with the U.S. Department of State. Thirty higher education administrators visited approximately 20 educational institutions, including gymnasia (high schools), universities, and fachhochschulen (universities of applied science). The seminar featured programming for all participants in four German cities (Berlin, Weimar, Erfurt, and Achen) and Brussels, as well as small group travels to Osnabruck, Erlangen, Munich, Bonn, and Trier.

"Our experiences were so varied as to include a glimpse of Germany's unique dual system of vocational education at industrial giant Siemens; a visit to historic Humboldt University, a cradle of the modern research university; and a sojourn to the famous Bauhaus University," says Ann Donovan, program participant and assistant director of sponsored programs at the University of Iowa (Donovan, 2002, p. 14). In addition to visits to schools throughout Germany, the administrators' seminar included a visit to Belgium. Belgium was selected because many recent and forthcoming reforms in European higher education emanate from Brussels, capital city of the new Europe (Donovan, 2002, p. 14).

Donovan says that the group encountered many common educational themes throughout their visit. Most prominent, she says, was the German higher education system's commitment to open its doors and promote international exchange at all levels of the educational system. "Perhaps the most salient of the themes we observed was the fervent desire of institutions [in Germany] to promote themselves as attractive havens for foreign scholars," she reflects (Donovan, 2002, p. 14). "Everywhere we went, German administrators and academics were transforming German academe to surmount language

barriers, streamline degree programs, and overturn a traditional disinclination to recognize credentials earned at foreign institutions" (Donovan, 2002, p. 14).

The visit to Brussels allowed the Fulbright contingent to learn firsthand from some of the creators of the Bologna process, an ambitious initiative to harmonize Europe's higher education systems. The Bologna Declaration of 1999, signed by education ministers from 30 countries, seeks processes to enhance faculty, staff, and student exchanges both among European Union countries and in other world regions.

"It was inspiring to see the EU being such strong advocates for international exchange," commented Charles Rickard, program participant, and associate vice president of student affairs at Kent State University (C. Rickard, personal communication, June 21, 2002). "In terms of student services programs, our Fulbright experience offered many insights and new perspectives. I also found the networking connections made with other Fulbright participants to be extraordinarily valuable, and they are connections that have remained strong since our experience in 2002" (C. Rickard, personal communication, June 21, 2002).

This experience in Germany was part of the Fulbright Commission's expansive international exchange programs for higher education administrators. The Fulbright Scholars on the Germany experience represented not only student affairs divisions, but also a wide range of academic departments and administrative function areas from U.S. colleges and universities.

In addition to the expected lessons learned about other cultures and educational systems, what also emerged from this Fulbright experience were long-term professional connections that have brought the participants great personal and professional support.

Andy Fraher, program participant and director of international student services at Embry-Riddle Aeronautical University, comments, "My Fulbright experience crystallized my view that learning about other cultures and systems is the greatest outcome of such an endeavor. Sharing these values with our students, friends, colleagues, and communities is our duty, especially in today's world" (Fraher, 2002, p. 1). See Figure 5.1 for details on the Fulbright program for higher education administrators, as well as other Fulbright programs.

Another group exchange program—a 2005 NASPA exchange to the United Arab Emirates (UAE)—underscored the value of professional connections made through group exchange programs. The trip, made by four student affairs administrators from the United States, including the author, provided participants with an eye-opening look at the nature of student affairs programs in the UAE and also a look into the complex and unique needs of Middle Eastern students. Since our journey, trip participants have frequently connected to reflect on the lessons learned from the experience, as well as apply these lessons in our own work with international students, both at their home campuses and with partner programs in the Middle East.

Another NASPA international exchange tour—to Spain in 2004—inspired Tom Shandley of Davidson College to create the International Institute in Spain as part of the James E. Scott Academy for Leadership and Executive Effectiveness. Held at the Universidad de Salamanca in June 2005, the Institute brought together 35 student affairs administrators and six faculty members—representing seven countries—for a six-day leadership institute, "Shaping Student Affairs Leadership through Global Perspectives."

"The Institute was truly intellectually stimulating as we learned about higher education in other countries," says Gue Hudson, vice president for student life and community relations at Agnes Scott College (Schierr, 2005). "Participants from South Africa, Costa Rica, Qatar, and Canada so enriched the conversation," The Institute also offered the 40-plus participants opportunities to forge new connections and professional alliances. Future plans are to offer the institute biennially.

Leadership Development and Community Service in South Africa

In the fall of 2004, Chayla Haynes, director of new student orientation and family programs at George Mason University, ventured to South Africa to explore student affairs programs and service delivery there. Under the NASPA International Exchange Program, Haynes visited with student affairs staff and students at Nelson Mandela Metropolitan University. Her exchange was designed specifically to explore concepts of leadership development and civic engagement and their applications in the South African higher education system. She also visited local townships in the country and saw first-hand some of the unique ways South African universities and nonprofit organizations are working together to address community needs. Haynes' exchange was funded through the University Life Division at George Mason (Haynes, 2005).

Promoting leadership development and civic engagement for college students, both at George Mason and in South Africa, remains an important priority for Haynes as she applies the lessons learned from her NASPA International Exchange visit. Immediately upon her return to the United States, she proposed a comprehensive partnership with the Nelson Mandela Metropolitan University through a range of co-curricular program initiatives designed to expose George Mason University students and student affairs staff to South African culture and collegiate environments. The foundation of this new partnership between George Mason and Nelson Mandela Metropolitan University includes service learning, leadership training, and community service components involving both administrators and students (Haynes, 2005).

"I hope that these programs can do what the NASPA International Exchange provided for me," says Haynes "Experiences with our student affairs colleagues in South Africa gave me so many new perspectives on trends and commonalities in student development and learning, and also exposed me to new strategies for engaging college students in community service" (C. Haynes, personal communication, September 2, 2005).

Haynes, who teaches a course on leadership for the 21st century at George Mason, plans to integrate into future courses a cross-cultural leadership development seminar that will feature a series of roundtable discussions between student leaders at George Mason and the Nelson Mandela Metropolitan University campus. Blended education models, using a combination of online discussion groups and video-conferencing, will serve as modules for the seminar (Haynes, 2005).

"I see great value in incorporating discussion groups with student leaders from both universities and building these discussions around leadership theory and concrete experiences," says Haynes (C. Haynes, personal communication, September 2, 2005). Themes that the seminar will explore include community and civic engagement accountability, self-knowledge/awareness and its impact on leadership styles and approaches, and further exploration of working with diverse populations and teams (Haynes, 2005).

In terms of service–learning, Haynes has already begun to work on adopting a township in South Africa and then working with the African Students Association at Nelson Mandela Metropolitan University to identify opportunities for students at both universities to participate in service–learning projects with township residents. Haynes also has designs to connect the educational resources available at George Mason to support AIDS/HIV education in South Africa. This continues to be a monumental issue within the higher education culture and affects the socio-economic progress of South Africa. Staff at George Mason's Health and Wellness Center are partnering with Haynes on this AIDS/HIV outreach program (Haynes, 2005).

Toward a "Renewal" of Global Exchange Programs

The Abraham Lincoln Study Abroad Commission was initiated by President George W. Bush in 2004. This expansive committee of government, education, business, and community leaders was charged with spurring new programs and initiatives for international exchange to encourage a conscious act of national renewal, driven by international education and on par with the Morrill Act of 1862, the GI Bill, and the Marshall Plan (Commission on the Abraham Lincoln Study Abroad Fellowship Program, 2005).The Commission developed a comprehensive report (2005) and interactive Web site recommending far-reaching initiatives to enhance study abroad programs, with special emphasis on studying in developing countries. The commission's report makes compelling rationale for the expansion and renewal of study abroad programs, as well as offers a range of recommendations with regard to new channels and programs for study abroad efforts.

Is the student affairs profession poised to offer similar opportunities to both students and professionals that support a "renewal" of study abroad programs? As future students venture abroad and students in turn come to the United States, how can student affairs professionals proactively respond to the new ideas, new ways of thinking, and new forms of student service delivery that will most surely be required to keep in step with the times?

International exchange programs for student affairs have played, and will continue to play, an important role in helping student affairs keep in step with this call for renewal and also respond to the challenges and opportunities presented by the flattened, dynamic world described by Thomas Friedman.

We conclude this chapter with references to important resources student affairs professionals can access in order to learn more about these exchange opportunities. Opportunities with NASPA and the Fulbright Commission are outlined in Figure 5.1, along with information related to other organization and association resources, concerning both opportunities and funding. Several higher education institutions have actually initiated their own internal programs for student affairs staff. The University of Florida's program is particularly expansive and intentional in creating exchange opportunities for staff at all levels of the organization. Florida's program serves as an excellent model for other institutions. The basic mission and constructs of the initiative are outlined in Figure 5.2.

This chapter has focused on examples of the unique, meaningful ways that international exchange programs are already contributing to this renewal. Each of the cases discussed in this chapter provides a glimpse into the tangible and potential benefits of these exchange programs for student affairs professionals. It is the author's hope that these examples make a powerful case for the value—at both an organizational and an individual level—of these exchange programs, and that they encourage even greater participation in these worldwide ventures in the future.

Figure 5.1. International exchange opportunities for student affairs professionals.

Following are summaries of several major professional associations or government agencies offering opportunities and/or funding support for student affairs exchange programs.

NAFSA: Association of International Educators – Cooperative Grants Program (COOP)
www.nafsa.org
Since 1974, NAFSA's Cooperative Grants Program has provided funding for U.S. campus- and community-initiated enrichment programs that involve postsecondary international and/or U.S. education abroad students. These COOP-funded projects have addressed a variety of issues in international education, including education abroad pre-departure and re-entry, international student and scholar adjustment, cross-cultural communication, volunteerism, healthcare, the environment, and democracy and human rights. Contact the NASFA office for program and application information.

NASPA – Student Affairs Administrators in Higher Education
www.naspa.org
NASPA has initiated a number of cooperative international exchange programs enabling U.S. student affairs professionals to travel abroad and professionals from other countries to come to the United States. Australia, United Arab Emirates, Spain, China, and Ireland are among the exchange possibilities. Exchange programs are possible for both groups and individuals. Application is required; selection criteria include (a) NASPA membership, (b) involvement with the International Education Knowledge Community or other NASPA initiatives, (c) geographic, institutional, race/gender, and professional experience with diversity, (d) agreement to attend future NASPA International Symposia, and (e) agreement to serve as the coordinating venue host for a future delegation from one of the relationships when requested.

People to People International – Professional Ambassador Programs
www.ptpi.org
Ambassador Programs offer scientific, technical, and professional exchanges that bring delegates together with their overseas counterparts in prearranged activities. Both sides benefit from face-to-face contacts during which information, ideas, and experiences are shared. These exchanges include a variety of fields, including medicine, education, social sciences, science and technology, law, arts, agriculture, business, and culture. Application procedures and criteria are available from the organization's office.

Fulbright International Education Administrators Program
www.cies.org/IEA/IEA_contacts.htm
U.S. international education administrators are invited to apply for two- to three-week seminars in Germany, Japan, or Korea. The deadline each year is November 1. The seminars are designed to introduce participants to the society, culture, and higher education systems of these countries through campus visits, meetings with foreign colleagues and government officials, attendance at cultural events, and briefings. Basic requirements include: U.S. citizenship; international education professionals and senior university administrators (e.g., deans, provosts, vice presidents) with significant responsibility for international programs and activities; and applicants should have a minimum of three years of work experience in international education. A PhD is not required for these seminars.

Figure 5.2. Creating an international exchange program for student affairs staff: The Career Resource Center at the University of Florida.

The University of Florida has created its own pilot program to encourage and arrange international exchange programs for junior- and mid-level student affairs staff. Wayne Wallace, director of the University of Florida Career Resource Center, reported on the approach, rationale, and structure for this program in the Spring 2004 issue of NASPA's *Leadership Exchange* magazine. Florida's program is administered under the auspices of the university's Career Resource Center (CRC). Key components of the mission and implementation of the program, which can serve as a guide and model for any student affairs unit or division, are described below. This information is directly excerpted from Wallace's article in NASPA's *Leadership Exchange* magazine.

Mission: The purpose of the Career Resource Center (CRC) staff exchange program is to foster a greater sensitivity and understanding of international difference and similarities in the creation, delivery, and analysis of collegiate career services. Participation in an exchange program with other centers outside the United States will mutually benefit the operations, participants, and fellow staff of all institutions. Student and employer clients, who are engaged in an increasingly internationally focused work world, also will benefit. Exchange participants gain an opportunity to expand their horizons while further developing professional credibility.

Exchange Partners: The Career Resource Center director establishes a working relationship with potential host institutions to ensure compatibility and appropriateness. Quality assurance and relevance are primary considerations for program inclusion.

Expectations of the Host Campus

◊ Negotiated visit dates occur during a reasonable time, ideally two to three weeks, for observation and participation of prime career center activities.

◊ Opportunities exist to engage in a general center orientation with key staff to explore major issues, operational and staff expectations, challenges, and goals.

◊ General assistance with housing, transportation availability, and other related personal maintenance issues is offered.

◊ The visiting participant receives adequate work space, materials, and technology access.

Expectations of the Sending Campus

◊ A reasonable visit date and duration is negotiated with the host campus.

◊ A selection process identifies the appropriate staff participant, and he or she is oriented to role expectations and objectives.

◊ Appropriate financial support for direct air and ground transportation expenses to and from the host site is included.

◊ Lodging expenses and meal expenses are covered with cooperation and advice from the host university.

◊ The exchange is viewed as a regular work-based assignment.

◊ A learning agreement and pre-visit agenda are created.

Exchange Participant Criteria [for University of Florida staff members]

◊ Two and one-half years of full-time work experience with CRC are required.

◊ The participant submits an application, including a statement of interest and reason for consideration, within a prescribed time period.

◊ High-caliber employees who could serve as good ambassadors for the center, the student affairs division, and the university are considered.

◊ Participation in this exchange may be in lieu of financial support for conference attendance during the fiscal year.

Selection

◊ Availability of exchange options fully depends upon the host campus' willingness, funding availability, appropriateness of participant pool, and timing.

◊ A committee reviews candidates' applications and provides recommendations to the director, who makes a final decision.

◊ Upon completion of the exchange, a summary report and a critique offering suggestions for improvement are submitted.[1]

Reproduced with permission from *Leadership Exchange*, Spring 2004, 26–27. Copyright 2004 National Association of Student Personnel Administrators.

References

Commission on the Abraham Lincoln Study Abroad Fellowship Program. (2005, November). Retrieved April 11, 2008, from http://www.nafsa.org/_/Document/_/lincoln_commission_report.pdf

Donovan, A. (2002, Fall/Winter). After the wall. *International Accents*. University of Iowa, 14–15.

Fraher, A. (2002, Summer). A Fulbright for administrators? Yes! *Wide Open Spaces*. NAFSA: Association of International Educators, Region II, 1–2.

Friedman, T. (2005). *The world is flat: A brief history of the Twenty-first century*. New York: Farrar, Straus and Giroux.

Harris, S. (2005, June 13). Virginia Tech partnership wins NASPA award. *Virginia Tech News*. Retrieved September 13, 2005, from http://www.vtnews.vt.edu

Haynes, C. (2005, February). *NASPA international exchange report from George Mason University*. Unpublished manuscript.

Ludeman, R. P. (2002, March/April). *Fulbright in focus: South Africa*. Unpublished manuscript.

NASPA. (n.d. a). *General Resources: Fulbright Program*. Retrieved September 13, 2005, from http://www.naspa.org/communities/kc/resources.cfm?genresID=1&category=Fulbright%20Program&kcid=8

NASPA. (n.d. b). International Exchange Dates: International Exchanges. Retrieved August 1, 2005, from http://www.naspa.org/communities/kc/page.cfm?kcpageID=83&kcid=8

Schier, T. (2005, August). International institute in Spain a success. *FORUM: E-Newsletter*. Retrieved August 20, 2005, from http://www.naspa.org/naspa_forum/forum.cfm?cid=3&fid=285

Wallace, W. (2004, Spring). Creating an international exchange program for staff. *Leadership Exchange*, 26–27.

SIX

COMPETENCE IN STUDENT AFFAIRS ADMINISTRATION

PERSPECTIVES FROM THE UNITED KINGDOM AND UNITED STATES

OLGA RYBALKINA

This chapter presents the findings of a dissertation study examining competencies and professional development opportunities in student affairs administration in the United States and United Kingdom. During the last two decades, student affairs administrators from various parts of the world have sought to improve professional standards, services, and outcomes. A number of international professional associations started to offer recommendations and guidelines on professional standards and to sponsor and accredit a wide range of courses in professional development and training. (These organizations include the Asia Pacific Student Services Association [APSSA], the Association of Managers of Student Services in Higher Education [AMOSSHE] in the United Kingdom, Centre Nationale des Œuvres Universitaires et Scolaires [CNOUS] in France, the Canadian Association of College and University Student Services [CACUSS], and Deutsches Studentenwerk [DSW] in Germany.)

Although many studies conducted by U.S. scholars address professional preparation of student affairs practitioners in the United States, little national or international research is available on professional development of student affairs practitioners elsewhere. Initial dialogues on the importance of a cross-cultural analysis in this area took place among international researchers during the Global Roundtable at the 2002 NASPA Annual Conference; however, no systematic, comparative analysis had been completed until this study.

Although the development of student affairs as a field within the United States and United Kingdom higher education systems has been shaped by specific cultural, political, and socioeconomic factors, in both instances its evolution has been driven by a growing commitment to student support and student learning. Despite the differences in the management systems and types of student services provided, the overall goals of student affairs are essentially the same: to "develop a shared sense of purpose that binds together all teaching, learning and helping into a coherent educational philosophy" (Earwaker, 1992, p. 134); and "to make the formal structures of course and degree programs and the patterns of campus life compatible and reinforcing whole" (Ping, 1999, p. 15). Student affairs/services professionals in both contexts aspire to be recognized as an educated and educating partner supporting the academic mission of higher education and enhancing human learning. As noted by Rowley (1996), a British educator and practitioner, "the skills and expertise of the staff within student support services contribute directly to the total student learning experience" (p. 160).

Student Affairs/Services in the United Kingdom and the United States

Across various national systems, the focus has been on the holistic development of the learner, with a particular emphasis on his or her cognitive advancement. Approaches and attitudes toward fostering this development, however, have differed significantly due to various historical, cultural, and socioeconomic conditions. The earliest British universities were established with clear purposes to develop the sons of gentlemen according to Christian beliefs and to train them initially in logic and natural philosophy based on the works of Aristotle. Those who continued beyond BA and MA levels studied for doctorates in medicine, civil or canon law, or theology. The first residential colleges of Oxford and Cambridge differed from the patterns of university life in the medieval learning centers located in the urban settings of Bologna and Paris (Haskins, 1923), where scant consideration was given to supervision or to arrangement of student life. In England, the young men received guidance from their "moral tutors," ordained clergymen who were to act *in loco parentis*. The living areas, dining halls, libraries, and chapels were integral parts of the colleges "so that the four elements of shared residence, shared scholarship, shared religion, and even shared leisure were practically and symbolically linked" (Earwaker, p. 103). The model was based on the British ideal that teacher–student relationships are formed through informal one-to-one tutorials, and student–student relationships are naturally promoted through shared living and learning.

This so-called Oxbridge philosophy of residential education heavily influenced the development of the first colonial colleges in North America. Among the first immigrants to the Massachusetts Bay Colony were the graduates of Emmanuel College in Cambridge (Rudolph, 1962). Following the Emmanuel pattern, they established Harvard College in 1636. The institution was governed by the clergy; the curriculum resembled that of Cambridge, with a strong emphasis on law, government, medicine, and religion; and the residential arrangement "was suited for shaping immature youths" (Cohen, 1998, p. 17).

Further developments in both the United States and United Kingdom higher education systems could not leave intact the ideal of a close and interconnected residential community. American institutions started to emphasize the pre-eminence of the faculty's intellectual duties above all other tasks, increasingly influenced by the German ideas of the supremacy of research and scholarship. In the beginning of the 20th century, faculty involvement in student life and the provision of student needs (including accommodation, recreation, counseling, and discipline) became minimal and indirect (Fenske, 1989). College presidents began appointing non-faculty staff to assume responsibility for managing student behavior and for attending to student non-academic needs (Leonard, 1956). Starting with an emphasis on student discipline, these new functional responsibilities grew to include personal and occupational counseling, student health, accommodation, recreation, and social programs. The unprecedented growth of the U.S. higher education system formed conditions that made further progress in student services "both possible and urgent" (Nuss, 1993 p. 27). Many factors contributed to the emergence of the student affairs field, including the rise of land-grant colleges, emergence of public higher education, escalating enrollments and greater diversification of the student body, introduction of the elective curriculum (Rhatigan, 2000), a shift from religious to secular missions (Fenske, 1989), and other institutional and societal influences. In the first decades of the 20th century, a greater emphasis on the vocational role of higher education prompted career advising to become one of the key functions of student services units (Nuss, 1993). This function continued to grow in size and levels of responsibility. With the award of the first professional diploma for an "Adviser of Women" in 1914 at Columbia University's Teachers College (Teachers College, 1914), student affairs work became an area of vocational specialization. While vocational guidance and placement were the primary functions of the "personnel bureaus" (Yoakum, 1994) in the

beginning of the 20th century, the student services grew rapidly (Lloyd-Jones, 1994).

During the 20th century, the field of student support services in the United States experienced an internationally unprecedented transformation into a specific area of scholarly inquiry, a multi-layered organization, and made substantial progress toward becoming a profession (Carpenter & Miller, 1981; Carpenter, Miller, & Winston, 1980). This development reflected the process of professionalization of American life in general, which intensified in the 19th century and continued through the 20th century (Bledstein, 1976).

From the 1960s to the 1990s, higher education in the United Kingdom also underwent an intense growth similarly manifested in expanded enrollments, widening composition of the student body, and openings of new types of institutions (Dunne, 1999). Through these changes, "British sense of responsibility for every aspect of the student's life" (Earwaker, 1992, p. 101) remained a prominent feature in the philosophy and character of the U.K. higher education system. The model of the so-called "pastoral care" of the early universities shaped further development of higher education and student support services. Even the universities established in response to the expansion of the higher education system in the 1960s such as Lancaster, Kent, and York were built away from urban settings, with campuses "designed to accommodate, serve, and entertain their students" (Rowley, 1996, p. 167). In secular and religious, public and private, large and small institutions, faculty continued to serve as personal tutors to students, providing them with both academic and personal guidance and support. Although the founding of 30 polytechnics through consolidation of local-authority vocational colleges in the 1960s served as an antithesis to the Oxbridge tradition of the "elite, independent, small-scale, single-sex, religious-foundation colleges" (Earwaker, p. 103), the components of pastoral care were present even in those settings (Earwaker; Rowley). On-site housing, medical attention, tutoring, and chaplaincy remained integral parts of these institutions. The vocational nature of polytechnics required professional career advising within the institution that would develop students' specific competencies related to the profession, direct them in the understanding of their career interests, and develop interpersonal skills, similar to the trend in U.S. higher education earlier in the century. Counseling and career advising became an essential part of student support in all types of institutions. Thus, pastoral or amateur support provided by tutors and professional assistance supplied by counselors in the same institution continued to co-exist, representing "a peculiar British phenomenon" (Earwaker, p. 102).

Astin (1993) found that student–student and student–faculty interactions, rather than the content of academic programs, were the best predictors of positive outcomes in such categories as commitment to helping others, self-awareness, appreciation for diversity, problem-solving, and leadership skills. These results provide clear evidence supporting the argument shared by both U.K. and U.S. student affairs professionals that

> Student support is not just about dealing with problems, but concerns students' ongoing development as individuals and their social relationships; and second, the task of helping students is not just ancillary to what higher education institutions are about, but a central, integral feature of the task. (Earwaker, 1992, p. 129)

Professional Preparation and Development in Student Affairs

Rowley (1996) asserted that "the skills and expertise of the staff within student support services contribute directly to the total student learning experience" (p. 160). The issues of competence and professional development in student affairs have been extensively addressed in the U.S. literature and raised in some U.K. resources. Quality of the student affairs personnel, according to Winston and Creamer (1997), is the most critical factor in determining the degree of success in management of student affairs. This quality is largely founded on relevant formal academic preparation and the appropriateness and quality of ongoing professional development (Creamer, Winston, & Miller, 2001). In the United States, there are more than 80 master's and doctoral degree programs in student affairs (American College Personnel Administration, 1994). About 160 programs specialize in higher education administration and educational leadership, often providing courses in student development, student affairs management, and other subjects closely related to the work of student affairs practitioners (Association for the Study of Higher Education, 2001). Most mid- and senior-administration positions and many entry-level positions require an advanced degree in the related area. Winston and Creamer (1997) found that more than two thirds of chief student affairs officers participating in their study held advanced degrees in student affairs, higher education, or counseling. Although there has not been a clear agreement on the content of graduate education, there is a basic consensus that academic preparation addressing work with students in the out-of-classroom context is necessary for an informed provision of student support.

This consensus regarding the necessity of formal education, however, has only been reached in the United States. In the United Kingdom, as elsewhere in the world, formal academic qualifications in the area of student services are not required for appointments across all levels of responsibility. Except for a few continuing education courses in higher education and programs in counseling, no formal education in student affairs is generally available. While most counselors working in higher education institutions are formally trained, those in other student affairs areas including student accommodation, welfare, substance intervention, student dis-

cipline, and recreation commonly acquire their skills and knowledge through on-the-job training and continuous professional development.

Student affairs in both contexts resists the institutional and societal perception of being merely a service provider and aspires to be recognized as an educated and educating partner supporting the academic mission of higher education and enhancing human learning. The shift, however, in both perception and actual position of student affairs within the institution can only be possible if student affairs practitioners are indeed adequately educated, if they "possess certain knowledge, hold certain values, and execute certain skills" (Winston & Creamer, 1997, p. 360).

Relevant formal education and continuing professional development are the cornerstones of quality personnel. In the absence of formal academic preparation in student affairs, as is the case in the United Kingdom, the emphasis on continuing professional development is even more crucial. The Higher Education Quality Council (HEQC) in the United Kingdom, and the study group appointed by ACPA–College Student Educators International and NASPA–Student Affairs Administrators in Higher Education in the United States expressed a similar view that assessing practitioners' competencies and professional needs and developing training opportunities to address these needs must be integral parts of a quality framework of student support services (Higher Education Quality Council, 1995; Study Group, 1992).

Student affairs within higher education systems in the United Kingdom and the United States have shared a common heritage (Altbach, 1998) and have developed similarly over the years. They have preserved many of these similarities in their contemporary forms. Their historical and cultural closeness allowed for an investigation of professional development of student affairs administrators in both countries. Student affairs in both countries have also developed some differences, particularly in the qualifications and training of persons engaged in student affairs work. In the United States, formal graduate education is a basic requirement, while in the United Kingdom, with few exceptions, specific academic qualifications are not required for appointments at most levels of responsibility. The lack of commonly accepted professional standards prompted a comparative investigation of the essential competencies and methods of their development in the United States and the United Kingdom.

Summary of the Research Process

The purpose of this study was (a) to establish the importance of various competencies conceptually related to student affairs practice as perceived by senior student affairs officers (SSAOs); (b) to determine which competencies were and were not perceived important cross-culturally; and (c) to identify available professional development methods and the degree of their effectiveness in both countries.

The established purposes for the study were accomplished through employing a survey research methodology. As noted in the literature (Drew, 1980; Isaac & Michael, 1987; Lang & Heiss, 1991; Mitchell & Jolley, 1988), survey research is often used to explore areas that previously were not thoroughly investigated. In addition, survey research allows the examination of massive amounts of information and the inclusion of difficult-to-access populations (e.g., U.K. student affairs administrators). The study employed a Web-based survey, which was significantly more cost effective, expedient, and accurate than a paper-based method (Mertler, 2002).

The U.S. sample of 200 SSAOs was randomly selected from the population of 831 SSAOs holding membership in NASPA and working at four-year U.S. institutions. The U.K. sample included all SSAOs (n = 113) whose institutions were affiliated with AMOSSHE, with the exception of two SSAOs representing Dublin City University, Ireland, and Hong Kong University.

All SSAOs were contacted electronically with an invitation to participate in the study and were contacted with several follow-up e-mails. As a result, 52% of U.S. SSAOs and 53% of U.K. SSAOs responded. The data-collecting instrument (available at http://assessment.utoledo.edu/eListen/Surveys/SASD_US/survey_us.html) was developed by Roberts (2003), who adapted a survey initially developed by Kane (1982) and further modified by Fey (1991), Gordon (1993), and Windle (1998). The survey proved to have good validity and reliability when used in the United States. It was sent to five U.K. SSAOs for a review of its content and conceptual and terminological clarity. These SSAOs concluded that, with minor modifications, this survey could be applicable to the U.K. student affairs context. Based on their suggestions, the U.K. version of the instrument was developed reflecting slight changes in the phrasing of competencies and skills.

This comparative research required a continuous monitoring for potential methodological pitfalls in conducting a cross-cultural analysis. These pitfalls (e.g., the challenged credibility of the data source, obscure terminology, and incomparability of the groups) were generally avoided through the use of a carefully designed approach to studying the problem. Another major pitfall, the researcher's bias, was constantly remembered and challenged but could not be entirely avoided, as noted by Trethewey (1976). Cultural differences unarguably influence the researcher's selection, perception, and interpretation of the material.

Major Findings

The study provided the answers to the established research questions concerning (a) competencies perceived

Table 6.1. Response means by competency area in ranked order of importance to U.S. SSAOs.

Competency Area	Mean*
Leadership	1.31
Diversity	1.41
Communication	1.43
Fiscal Affairs	1.56
Legal Affairs	1.58
Human Resources	1.61
Student Contact	1.65
Research	1.83
Professional Development	1.96
Technology	2.06

* The respondents were asked to choose one of the four levels of importance of 72 competencies using a Likert-type scale as follows: (1) Essential, (2) Important, (3) Somewhat important, and (4) Not important.

Table 6.2. Response means by competency area in ranked order of importance to U.K. SSAOs.

Competency Area	Mean*
Leadership	1.42
Human Resources	1.57
Diversity	1.59
Communication	1.59
Fiscal Affairs	1.64
Student Contact	1.76
Technology	1.78
Legal Affairs	1.92
Research	1.96
Professional Development	1.97

* The respondents were asked to choose a level of importance for 72 competencies using a Likert-type scale as follows: (1) Essential, (2) Important, (3) Somewhat important, and (4) Not important.

important by U.S. SSAOs, (b) competencies perceived important by U.K. SSAOs, (c) competencies important/not important cross-culturally, (d) available professional development methods in the United States and the United Kingdom, and (e) the degree of effectiveness of professional development methods in the two countries.

Competencies Perceived Important by U.S. SSAOs

Participants were asked to indicate the level of importance of 71 competencies in the areas of leadership; student contact; communication; human resource management; fiscal management; professional development; research, evaluation, and assessment; legal issues; technology; and diversity. The competencies in the area

Table 6.3. U.S. and U.K. SSAOs' perceptions of importance of competencies (combined essential/important responses).		
Category/competency	**U.S. SSAO (%)**	**U.K. SSAO (%)**
Leadership		
Promoting the academic mission of the institution	98.1	78.3
Working in the institution's political environment	95.2	91.7
Developing the mission and vision of the department/division	99.0	96.7
Communicating the mission and vision of the department/division	99.0	96.6
Developing a strategic plan with realistic goals	99.0	98.3
Following the profession's ethical principles	99.0	100.0
Role modeling behavior to other professionals	97.1	98.3
Implementing appropriate decisions under uncertain conditions	97.1	93.1
Utilizing the expertise of others	98.1	100.0
Gaining the commitment from top leadership	98.1	100.0
Utilizing effective techniques to motivate staff	94.1	96.7
Delegating when appropriate	96.2	100.0
Developing collaborative relationships with another division	100.0	90.0
Student Contact		
Applying student development theories in decision making	81.6	47.4
Assessing student needs	100.0	100.0
Including students in policy-making decisions	89.4	84.5
Advising student groups	80.8	79.7
Providing assistance and services to students	97.1	100.0
Responding to student crises	99.0	100.0
Training students to perform paraprofessional duties	99.0	47.5
Communication		
Writing effective correspondence and reports	97.1	100.0
Making oral presentations/public speaking	99.0	93.3
Accurately interpreting attitudes and needs of others	97.1	98.3
Effectively communicating with the media	98.1	50.0
Maintaining appropriate levels of confidentiality	100.0	100.0
Human resource management		
Applying successful professional staff recruiting techniques	95.2	96.6
Using appropriate staff selection techniques	98.1	94.9
Training staff using appropriate instructional techniques	77.7	81.4
Developing staff through continuing education programs	85.4	89.8
Supervising professional staff	96.1	86.4
Evaluating professional staff	98.1	96.6

Table 6.3. U.S. and U.K. SSAOs' perceptions of importance of competencies (combined essential/important responses).

Category/competency	U.S. SSAO (%)	U.K. SSAO (%)
Terminating professional staff after following due process	90.4	82.1
Mediating conflict among staff	90.3	91.5
Recognizing accomplishments of others	100.0	98.3
Fiscal issues		
Analyzing financial reports	96.2	90.0
Utilizing available resources	99.0	98.3
Applying budget development techniques	92.2	86.7
Projecting future priorities and needs	99.0	96.7
Writing grants and contracts to garner additional resources	54.8	75.0
Understanding the financing of higher education	94.2	91.7
Responding to budget cuts	99.0	88.3
Professional development		
Assessing one's own professional development needs	95.2	93.3
Maintaining a scholarly background in one's discipline	71.2	54.2
Attending professional development activities	94.2	91.7
Keeping abreast of current issues in student affairs/services	99.0	100.0
Writing an article for professional publications	28.2	22.0
Being involved in a professional association	76.0	71.7
Research		
Interpreting research as reported in professional literature	80.8	62.7
Initiating or developing surveys or studies	76.0	76.3
Interpreting/analyzing statistical methods and results	60.2	61.0
Utilizing results of studies	87.5	83.1
Evaluating programs for effectiveness	99.0	96.6
Performing self-studies for accreditation reviews	99.0	75.9
Developing a comprehensive assessment plan	94.2	80.4
Legal affairs		
Keeping abreast of current legislative issues	91.3	96.7
Keeping abreast of current court cases	78.6	60.0
Using proactive risk management techniques	99.0	83.1
Implementing due process concepts	98.1	63.6
Understanding personal and professional liability issues	97.1	84.5
Technology		
Using technology to find information	92.3	95.0
Using technology to develop a professional presentation	64.4	86.7

Table 6.3. U.S. and U.K. SSAOs' perceptions of importance of competencies (combined essential/important responses).

Category/competency	U.S. SSAO (%)	U.K. SSAO (%)
Understanding the use of technology in the marketing/delivery of services	86.5	86.7
Using technology to communicate with the staff	83.5	91.7
Utilizing computer software programs to perform job functions	77.9	78.3
Developing services for distance learners	44.2	60.0
Diversity		
Providing services for under-represented students	99.0	98.3
Understanding needs of under-represented students	99.0	98.3
Applying minority development theories to understand under-represented students	87.5	55.2
Considering needs of diverse populations when making decisions	100.0	98.3
Participating in educational events to understand people different than oneself	96.2	81.7
Working effectively with someone with a different background than oneself	94.2	86.7

of leadership, diversity, and communication were most consistently chosen as essential (Table 6.1). The majority of respondents described as "essential" or "important" all competencies except two: writing an article for professional publications and developing services for distance learners.

Competencies Perceived Important by U.K. SSAOs

The competencies in the area of leadership, human resource management, diversity, and communication were most consistently chosen as essential (Table 6.2). The majority of U.K. respondents described as "essential" or "important" all competencies except three: applying student development theories in decision making, training students to perform paraprofessional duties, and writing an article for professional publications.

A Comparative Perspective on Competencies

The study identified statistically significant differences in responses pertaining to the importance of 29 out of 71 competencies included in the questionnaire. Significant differences were found in responses pertaining to each competency area. On average, U.S. SSAOs perceived 18 competencies to be more important than they were to their U.K. counterparts. The three competencies with the highest mean differences were (a) "promoting the academic mission of the institution," (b) "role modeling behavior to other professionals," and (c) "implementing due process concepts."

On average, U.K. SSAOs perceived seven competencies to be more important than they were to their U.S. colleagues. The three competencies with the highest mean differences were from the area of technology: (a) "developing services for distance learners," (b) "using technology to develop a professional presentation," and (c) "using technology to find information." Nevertheless, the study showed that many competencies were important to both U.S. and U.K. SSAOs (Table 6.3).

Professional Development Methods Available to U.S. and U.K. SSAOs

The questionnaire listed 12 professional development methods (see Table 6.4). The data indicated that while the majority of U.S. SSAOs considered each method as available, the majority of U.K. SSAOs marked two methods as not being available to them: online courses and degree program in student affairs.

Effectiveness of Professional Development Methods as Perceived by U.S. SSAOs

Of the 12 professional development methods listed, only one—professional conferences—was perceived as highly effective by the majority of respondents. Seven competencies were most frequently selected either as highly effective or effective: (a) mentor relationships (b) membership/involvement in professional associations (c) degree program in student affairs (d) divisional/departmental orientation programs (e) books (f) on-campus workshops and (g) professional journals. The four

Table 6.4. Available professional development methods: Perceptions of U.S. and U.K. SSAOs.

Professional Development Method	U.S. SSAOs (%)	U.K. SSAOs (%)
Divisional/departmental orientation programs		
On-campus workshops	94.2	92.7
Online courses	97.1	98.2
Mentor relationships	71.0	49.0
Professional journals	100.0	69.4
Books	100.0	100.0
Membership/involvement in professional associations	100.0	100.0
Professional conferences	100.0	100.0
Degree program in student affairs/services	91.3	32.0
Training courses outside of degree program	92.2	86.3
Internet-based research activities	87.5	82.4
International exchange programs	64.0	51.0

remaining methods were most frequently perceived as only somewhat effective: (a) training courses outside of degree programs, (b) Internet-based research activities, (c) international exchange programs, and (d) online courses.

Effectiveness of Professional Development Methods as Perceived by U.K. SSAOs

None of the 12 professional development methods listed was perceived as highly effective or effective by the majority of U.K. SSAOs. The two methods perceived as the most effective were professional conferences and membership/involvement in professional associations. Five professional development methods were most frequently seen as only somewhat effective: (a) books, (b) professional journals, (c) Internet-based research activities, (d) degree program in student affairs, and (e) online courses.

A Comparative Perspective on Professional Development Methods

The study identified significant differences in the groups' perceptions regarding the degree of effectiveness of five professional development methods. Three of these methods were perceived, on average, more effective by U.S. SSAOs: (a) mentor relationships, (b) profes-

sional conferences, and (c) degree program in student affairs. Two remaining methods, international exchange programs and training courses outside of degree programs in student affairs, were considered, on average, more important by U.K. SSAOs. Although the mean difference in responses pertaining to professional conferences was statistically significant, both groups perceived this method to be the most effective among all methods included in the questionnaire.

Conclusions and Implications for Student Affairs Scholarship and Practice

1. Student affairs administrators in each country have a comprehensive and distinctly identifiable knowledge and competency base fundamental to student affairs practice. This study reaffirmed the competency base relevant to student affairs practice in the United States, which was established previously (Fey, 1991; Kane, 1982; Lundsford, 1984; Roberts, 2003; Windle, 1998; Mueller & Pope, 2001; Pope & Reynolds, 1997). The study was also the first to offer consistent empirical data suggesting the existence of a clearly defined set of competencies relevant to student affairs practice in the United Kingdom.

2. A large number of competencies were established as important to both U.S. and U.K. SSAOs, suggesting the existence of a cross-culturally consistent general understanding of competence in student affairs. For the most part, the instrument that had been developed within the U.S. context proved to be applicable to U.K. student affairs, leading to the establishment of a scholarly foundation for an informed collaboration between the researchers and practitioners in the two nations.

3. The understanding of competence, however, did not emerge as exclusively uniform between the United States and the United Kingdom groups, suggesting that variations in contextual understanding of SSAOs' roles, degree of professionalization, history, and societal conditions might have contributed to differences in perceptions. A variety of political, cultural, and socioeconomic conditions, present realities, and historical developments pertaining to the U.K. and U.S. systems of higher education have shaped student affairs in both countries, and, consequently, influenced the perception of competencies required for a knowledgeable practice.

4. Available professional development opportunities did not emerge consistently as highly effective or effective, particularly in the United Kingdom, suggesting a critical need to address the quality of existing professional development methods and processes. Both U.S. and U.K. literature emphasized that continuing professional development is crucial to a competent student affairs practice (Rowley, 1996; Winston et al., 2001) and even more crucial in the absence of formal academic preparation, as in the case of the United Kingdom.

Implications for Higher Education Scholarship and Practice

Implications for Student Affairs in the United States

As a result of this study, a clearly defined set of competencies important to student affairs practice was identified. This research confirmed the findings of several studies, which had previously established the importance of numerous competency areas. In addition, the study demonstrated the importance of student affairs competence in the areas of diversity, legal affairs, and, to some extent, technology.

An accurate, current understanding of the skills and competencies relevant to student affairs practice is important to all constituencies involved in the professional development process who share responsibility for its success—individuals, departments and institutions, preparation programs, and professional associations. Continuous professional development must be a part of the individual responsibility of every member of the profession (Kruger, 2000), and student affairs professionals should actively pursue opportunities for their professional growth. Continuous self-assessment based on knowledge of relevant skills and competencies is fundamental to a purposeful professional development process.

Woodard and Komives (1990) suggest that student affairs departments create a guiding learning philosophy that incorporates intentional development programs. Departments and institutions should develop professional development plans incorporating the larger organizational goals (Winston & Creamer, 1997) with opportunities to enhance individual competencies in specific job contexts (Bryan & Mullendore, 1990).

Preparation programs should continuously evaluate the relevance of their curricula to contemporary student affairs practice and emphasize the content areas necessary for effective practice. The fact that the competency areas of leadership and diversity emerged as the most essential to student affairs practice must be thoroughly addressed with courses on leadership and multicultural education and by including various aspects of leadership and diversity throughout the curriculum.

This study indicated that attendance at professional conferences was perceived as the most highly effective method of professional development. Professional associations play a leading role in the development of the individual and the profession. Some competencies that emerged as important in this study constantly evolve, so they require continuing education. These areas include diversity, assessment and evaluation, legal issues, and technology (Scott, 2000). Professional associations must ensure that their conferences and workshops address many areas of expertise in student affairs.

Intentional planning for professional development, which occurs at multiple levels (individual, departmental, institutional, and national), must be based on an accurate understanding of the necessary competencies in student affairs. Only then will professional development reach its related outcomes: professional growth of the individual; enhancement of student support, development, and learning; and advancement of student affairs as a profession (Roberts, 2003).

Implications for Student Affairs in the United Kingdom

Although the U.K. literature suggested that "the skills and expertise of the staff within student support services contribute directly to the total student experience" (Rowley, 1996, p. 166), the development of necessary competencies, has been largely unexplored.

One result of this study was to establish the importance of 68 competencies. The resulting comprehensive competency base included the areas of leadership; student contact; communication; human resource management; fiscal affairs; research, evaluation, and assessment; legal affairs; diversity; and technology.

In the absence of formal academic preparation, effective professional development serves as the main means of developing skills and competencies essential to student affairs practice. However, the U.K. SSAOs did not perceive any of the professional development methods included in this study to be highly effective. As noted by Rowley (1996), a staff development program is foundational to the development of quality staff. The established relevance of nine competency areas and 68 skills may become a basis for modifying existing programs and creating new professional development areas at the levels of departments, institutions, and national associations. Assessment of the practitioners' competencies is critical to the development of a quality framework in U.K. student support services (Higher Education Quality Council, 1995). The findings of this study may serve as a scholarly foundation for the development of assessment instruments that are not currently available in the United Kingdom.

Several institutions that offer courses conceptually related to student affairs may re-evaluate their curricula to ensure that critical competency areas are included in the content. In addition, educational institutions and professional associations may consider developing academic courses for student affairs professionals that specifically address critical competencies and skills (E. Bell, 1996; Harrison et al., 2001).

Establishing important competencies and a relevant knowledge base is an important step in establishing national standards (D. Bell, 1996). The findings of this study may prompt professional associations, such as AMOSSHE, to formulate professional principles/standards of student affairs work, including ethical principles, and to commission research exploring theoretical and philosophical frameworks guiding student affairs practice.

Student affairs professionals in the United Kingdom advocate an integrated approach to the delivery of student services (Imerson, 2003; Rowley, 1996). The identification of competencies important to *all* student affairs administrators regardless of their specific job settings is critical to (a) the integration of previously unconnected functions into comprehensive departments of student services, (b) individual professional development, and (c) the advancement of a professional culture of student affairs in the United Kingdom.

Cross-cultural Implications

As noted by Heady (1998), comparative research can identify administrative knowledge that transcends national boundaries. This first comparative study in the area of professional development in the United States and the United Kingdom has established a common knowledge and competency base for student affairs administrators in both countries, leading to important implications for the scholarship and practice of student affairs in both countries and globally. Theoretically, identifying skills and competencies relevant to student affairs practice in both the United Kingdom and the United States suggests that student affairs is evolving as a field—if not as a profession—internationally and is undergoing continuous professionalization. Practically, the study may serve as a foundation for developing educational and professional partnerships among U.K. and U.S. higher education institutions, student affairs divisions, professional associations, and preparation programs.

The knowledge of cross-culturally important competencies and cross-culturally effective professional development methods may be helpful to other countries, particularly where student affairs programs have developed recently. This study may be used as a foundation for identifying the core competency bases for student affairs in these countries and for establishing professional development methods. It also can encourage the creation of training opportunities for student affairs professionals around the world.

A comparative study may not only suggest the potentials but also set "the limits of international borrowing and adaptation" (Noah, 1998, p. 49). The findings of this study suggest that, while general competence in all of the investigated areas was important to student affairs practice in both countries, a number of specific competencies were viewed as culturally specific. These findings imply that international training opportunities (e.g., international exchanges, international conferences, short-term training programs) should be designed carefully to ensure the studied concepts and practices are applicable and to maximize usefulness of professional development experiences.

Conclusion

This comparative study was conducted to establish the importance of various skills and competencies conceptually related to student affairs practice in the United States and the United Kingdom, to determine which skills and competencies are and which are not perceived important cross-culturally, and to identify available professional development sources and the degree of their effectiveness in both countries. The findings suggested that U.S. and U.K. SSAOs perceived the majority of presented competencies as essential or important to student affairs practice and that U.K. and U.S. SSAOs had a common competency base fundamental to student affairs practice in both countries. The study also identified available professional development methods in the United Kingdom and the United States and established the effectiveness of each method. These findings lead to numerous opportunities to improve professional development models and processes in each country, to enhance collaborative programs and projects in student affairs between the United States and the United Kingdom, and to advance the student affairs field internationally. Although this study does not suggest that the established competencies are globally transferable, its results may be helpful to countries where the field of student affairs is in the initial development stage. The precedent of the comparative analysis of competencies and of the effectiveness of professional development methods in both countries can encourage the development of training opportunities in the area of student affairs for professionals around the world.

References

Altbach, P. G. (1998). *Comparative higher education: Knowledge, the university, and development.* Greenwich, CT: Ablex.

American College Personnel Association. (1994). *Directory of graduate preparation programs in college personnel.* Alexandria, VA: Author.

Astin, A. (1993). *What matters in college: Four critical years revisited.* San Francisco: Jossey-Bass.

Bell, D. (1996). Developing occupational standards for the advice, guidance, counselling and psychotherapy sector. *British Journal of Guidance and Counselling, 24*(1), 9-17.

Bell, E. (1996). *Counseling in further and higher education.* Buckingham, UK: Open University Press.

Bledstein, B. J. (1976). *The culture of professionalism: The middle class and the development of higher education in America.* New York: W. W. Norton.

Carpenter, D. S., & Miller, T. K. (1981). An analysis of professional development in student affairs work. *NASPA Journal, 18,* 16–22.

Carpenter, D. S., Miller, T. K., & Winston, R. B. (1980). Toward the professionalization of student affairs. *NASPA Journal, 18,* 16–21.

Cohen, A. M. (1998). *The shaping of American higher education: Emergence and growth of the contemporary system.* San Francisco: Jossey-Bass.

Creamer, D. G., Winston, R. B., & Miller, T. K. (2001). The professional student affairs administrator: Roles and functions. In R. B. Winston, D. G. Creamer, & T. K. Miller (Eds.), *The professional student affairs administrator: Educator, leader, and manager* (pp. 3–38). New York: Brunner-Routledge.

Drew, C. J. (1980). *Introduction to designing and conducting research* (2nd ed.). St. Louis, MO: The C. V. Mosby Company.

Earwaker, J. (1992). *Helping and supporting students: Rethinking the issues.* Buckingham, Great Britain: The Society for Research into Higher Education & Open University Press.

Fenske, R. H. (1989). Historical foundations of student services. In U. Delworth, G. R. Hanson, & Associates (Eds.), *Student services: A handbook for the profession* (pp. 5-24). San Francisco: Jossey-Bass.

Fey, C. J. (1991). *Mid-level student affairs administrators: A study of management skills and professional needs.* Unpublished doctoral dissertation, Texas A&M University, College Station.

Gordon, S. E., Strode, C. B., & Mann, B. A. (1993). The mid-manager in student affairs: What are CSAOs looking for? *NASPA Journal, 30,* 290–297.

Harrison, R., Edwards, R., & Brown, J. (2001). Crash test dummies or knowledgeable practitioners? Evaluating the impact of professional development. *British Journal of Guidance and Counselling, 29,* 199–211.

Higher Education Quality Council. (1995). *A quality assurance framework for guidance and learner support in higher education.* London: Author.

Isaac, S. & Michael, W. B. (1981). *Handbook in research and evaluation* (2nd ed.). San Diego, CA: EdITS.

Kane, N. E. (1982). A comparative study of student affairs mid-level professionals: Characteristics, perceived skill attainment and need for continued development. *Dissertation Abstracts International, 43*(9), 2902A.

Leonard, E. A. (1956). *Origins of personnel services in American higher education.* Minneapolis, MN: University of Minnesota Press.

Lloyd-Jones, E. (1994). Personnel administration. In A. L. Rentz (Ed.), *Student affairs: A profession's heritage* (2nd ed., pp. 19–26). Lanham, MD: ACPA.

Lundsford, L. W. (1984). Chief student affairs officer: The ladder to the top. *NASPA Journal, 22,* 48–56.

Mertler, C. (2002). Demonstrating the potential for Web-based survey methodology with a case study. *American Secondary Education, 30,* 49–61.

Mitchell, M., & Jolley, J. (1988). *Research design explained.* New York: Holt, Rinehart, & Winston.

Mueller, K. H., & Pope, R. L. (2001). The relationship between multicultural competence and white racial consciousness among student affairs practitioners. *Journal of College Student Development, 42,* 133–44.

Nuss, E. M. (1993). The role of professional associations. In M. J. Barr (Ed.), *The handbook of student affairs administrators* (pp. 364–377). San Francisco: Jossey-Bass.

Pope, R. L., & Reynolds, A. L. (1997). Student affairs core competencies: Integrating multicultural awareness, knowledge, and skills. *Journal of College Student Development, 38,* 266–275.

Rhatigan, J. J. (2000). The history and philosophy of student affairs. In M. J. Barr, M. K. Desler, & Associates (Eds.), *The handbook of student affairs administration* (pp. 3-24). San Francisco: Jossey-Bass.

Roberts, D. (2003). *Skill development among student affairs professionals in National Association for Student Personnel Administrators Region III.* Unpublished doctoral dissertation, Texas A&M University, College Station.

Rowley, R. (1996). Student support services. In D. Warner & D. Palfreyman (Eds.), *Higher education management: The key elements* (pp. 166–180). Buckingham, Great

Britain: Society for Research into Higher Education, Open University Press.

Scott, J. E. (2000). Creating effective staff development programs. In M. J. Barr, M. K. Desler, & Associates, *The handbook of student affairs administration* (2nd ed., pp 477-491). San Francisco: Jossey Bass.

Study Group on Quality Assurance Issues in College Student Affairs. (1992). *Quality assurance in college student affairs: A proposal for action by professional associations*. Washington, D.C.: American College Personnel Association and National Association of Student Personnel Administrators.

Windle, L. M. (1998). *Skill performance assessment and need for further professional development of student affairs mid-managers*. Unpublished doctoral dissertation, Texas A&M University, College Station.

Winston, R. B., Jr., & Creamer, D. G. (1997). *Improving staffing practices in student affairs*. San Francisco: Jossey-Bass.

SEVEN

SERVING INTERNATIONAL STUDENTS

Leslie A. Owen

Since the beginning of the student affairs profession in the United States, the role of professionals in the field has been in a constant state of transformation, correlating to societal changes. In the beginning of the 20th century, student affairs professionals were advocates for students' basic rights as higher education became available to a wider population. With the creation of the G. I. Bill after World War II and the massive influx of veterans attending college, student affairs professionals became growth managers. During the social revolutions of the 1960s, they were peace-keepers, working to bring disparate populations together in peaceful dialogue. Now, with the rapid globalization of the past decade, they must become cultural educators.

The student affairs mantra of helping students become successful is a multi-faceted responsibility for current student services professionals who live in a society of globally connected economies, communities, and peoples. Students realize that employers value the ability to function effectively in the global society and that this ability will be marketable after graduation (Carnevale, 1999; Dalton, 1999; Edmond, 1995). If they are to help develop globally competent individuals, student services professionals must recognize the importance of international education.

One major educational resource available to domestic students is the international student population on their campus. Current research further indicates that "institutional diversity emphasis has a positive effect on most students' overall level of satisfaction with college" (Villa-Ipando, 2002, p. 141). International students are invaluable resources for domestic students because they bring diversity to the environment and provide an opportunity for the cultivation of cross-cultural relationships, both in and outside of the classroom.

In addition to creating a culturally diverse environment for domestic students, international students are, in many ways, of great value to the university. In 2004, international students contributed nearly $13 billion to the U.S. economy (Institute of International Education

[IIE], 2004). Given that international students typically pay much higher tuition than do their domestic counterparts, and given that, according to 2004 Open Doors Report, 67% of international students relied primarily on personal and family funds to pay their expenses, the conclusion is that almost 400,000 students paid for tuition and living expenses in the United States from monies originating in their home country (IIE, 2004). This represents a significant monetary influx into the U.S. economy. In addition, international students provide other peripheral economic benefits. For example, many students who return home from studying in the United States will continue to purchase American goods and services, continuing their positive economic impact long after their departure (Peterson, Briggs, Dreasher, Horner, & Nelson, 1999). International students also bring inexpensive expertise to campus. By awarding teaching assistantships to international graduate students, colleges can offer many required undergraduate courses without hiring additional faculty members (Peterson et al., 1999). Also, competitive research universities can benefit from the ideas and skills of international graduate researchers instead of hiring full-time lab technicians.

International students are an integral part of an institution's enrollment and development strategy (Dalton, 1999). Many colleges use international students to increase their enrollment and reap the benefit of their higher tuition requirements. But this recruitment strategy brings with it the responsibility to provide proper support services to help the students succeed and to reduce attrition. For example, higher education has become a major export product in Australia. According to the Australian Higher Education Report for the 2004 to 2006 Triennium there were more than 200,000 international students in Australia in 2003, accounting for 22% of the country's total university enrollment (Nelson, 2004). Offering education as a good or service agrees with what Levine and Cureton describe as the "consumer mentality" of today's college student who wants the same service from their institution of higher education as they do from their bank, "convenience, quality, service, and cost" (1998, p. 50). Creating a consumer relationship between the university and the international student brings with it the obligation to provide effective support services (Edmond, 1995). In fact, if international student services are weak, this fact could be known worldwide within minutes via the Internet, affecting that university's ability to recruit new international students (Peterson, et al., 1999). Conversely, "satisfied international students and alumni recruit relatives, friends, coworkers, and others to the United States" (Peterson et al., 1999, p. 70). The international reputation of an institution is dependant on its standard of international student service (Edmond, 1995).

Although the primary reason for studying internationally is to "achieve a degree and/or professional training" there are a variety of secondary reasons (Furnham & Bochner, 1986, p.38). For example, students may wish to learn or become proficient in another language. Or perhaps the university offers courses in a subject that is not available in their home country. Many times, students will come from around the world to work with a specific professor who is an authority in their area of interest. They are also drawn to universities where they will have the opportunity to work with the most modern equipment and newest technologies. Some students go abroad simply to explore a new culture and develop personally through that interaction (Furnham & Bochner, 1986). Whatever the motivation of international students, it is essential that student services professionals understand the difficulties faced by this special population.

This chapter will discuss the international student experience and briefly explain the concept of culture shock. It will highlight the basic needs of international students by discussing the services currently offered in most universities hosting an international student population. It will also highlight the need to improve services for international students and will provide examples of exceptional programs in the United States, Australia, and England. The general concepts are derived from a broad range of research and practice, and therefore are transferable to all institutions—in any country—that host an international student population.

The International Student Experience

In addition to the typical college student development processes such as "developing intellectual, physical, and interpersonal competence," and learning to become self-sufficient by "moving through autonomy toward interdependence," international students must also struggle with adjusting to a new cultural environment (Chickering & Reisser, 1993, p. 45–47). The difficult process of adjusting to a new country and its customs results in the phenomenon called *culture shock*.

Culture shock was first described by Kalervo Oberg in 1960 as "the anxiety that results from losing all our familiar signs and symbols of social intercourse" (p. 177). When students come from a country whose social customs differ from those of their host country, they will experience culture shock. Social customs are described as "signs or cues" that help us "orient ourselves to the situations of daily life," such as when to shake hands, how to greet someone, and how to interpret facial expressions and body gestures (Oberg, 1960, p. 177). For instance, in the United States, moving one's head from left to right indicates a negative response, or no. In some Asian cultures, the same gesture is an indication of agreement. Oberg (1960) describes the symptoms of culture shock as excessive concerns over basics, such as drinking water, food, dishes and bedding, fear of physical contact with the host culture, an "absent-minded, far-away stare," a "feeling of helplessness," heightened anger over things that would normally produce only minor frustration, and homesickness (p. 178). He described four stages of culture shock: honeymoon, crisis, recovery, and adjustment (Furnham & Bochner, 1986, p. 131). The honeymoon stage is the "initial reaction of enchantment, fascination, enthusiasm and admiration" toward the host society (Furnham & Bochner, 1986, p. 131). In the crisis stage, the students experience difficulties due to the disparity between their home culture and the host culture such as, "differences in language, concepts, values and familiar signs and symbols which leads to feelings of inadequacy, frustration, anxiety and anger" (Furnham & Bochner, 1986, p. 131). The recovery stage sees the formation of cross-cultural understanding, where the student learns to become effective in the host-country culture. In the adjustment stage, the student not only knows how to work within his new environment, but has learned to enjoy it (Furnham & Bochner, 1986). This process—an initial psychological high, a decline due to adjustment problems, and a final rise indicating successful cultural adjustment—was first described as a "U-shaped curve," by Lysgaard in 1955 (p. 51). In 1963, Gullahorn and Gullahorn extended it by describing the "W-curve" (also called the double U-curve) of cultural adjustment, which simply asserts that international students will experience a similar culture shock process when they return home (Furnham & Brochner, 1986; Gullahorn & Gullahorn, 1963, p. 41; Lysgaard, 1955, p. 51).

Cultural adjustment is only one of the problems international students face. According to the literature, the two major problems are financial stress and problems associated with lack of language proficiency, which include but are not limited to academic difficulties. Other problems cited include feelings of homesickness and isolation, difficulties with food differences, housing problems, and discrimination (Anumonye, 1967; Barker, Child, Gallois, Jones, & Callan, 1991; Galloway & Jenkins, 2005; Heikinheimo & Shute, 1986; Lin & Yi, 1997; Maundeni, 2001; Oropeza, Fitzgibbon & Barón, 1991; Parr, Bradley & Bingi, 1992; Schram & Lauver, 1988; Stafford, Marion, & Salter, 1980; Tompson & Tompson, 1996).

International students in the United States are especially susceptible to financial stress because they are not eligible for federal financial aid or social welfare services, and they must abide by immigration policies that restrict their work privileges to on-campus part-time jobs when they are enrolled as full-time students. Because most students must be enrolled full-time, they cannot earn any substantial wage. Also, students who have been awarded an assistantship or a fellowship are not eligible to work. Nor are spouses eligible for employment in the United States. Financial stress can exacerbate culture shock by creating feelings of "loss, grief and resentment" as the student also struggles with cultural adjustment (Oropeza, Fitzgibbon & Barón, 1991).

Language deficiency is considered the "most important determinant of international student problems" because it affects every other problem area (Galloway & Jenkins, 2005, p. 185). For example, in the study by Barker et al.(1991), the students "believed that their lack of English competence hindered their full participation in tutorials and interactions with academic staff" (1991, p. 83). Other studies have found that students "who reported having higher English proficiency were more likely to have a lower level of acculturative stress" (Ye, 2005, p. 160). Given the pervasive nature of the problems resulting from lack of language proficiency, this issue is of paramount importance to service providers for international students.

Services for International Students

Understanding the motivation for international study, the basic process of culture shock, and the major problems facing international students is a very good start in providing appropriate services for this special student population. The main motivation for international study is academic achievement. Maslow (1954) described academic achievement as a self-actualization activity or a higher need in the hierarchy of needs, asserting that, in order to accomplish academic achievement, basic needs, such as food, physical safety matters, and love or esteem requirements must first be satisfied. Many of the essential services for international students address their basic needs, and play an integral part in helping them ultimately achieve academic success (Maslow, 1954). Essential services for international students are pre-departure information, arrival services, accommodation assistance, post-arrival orientation, counseling service for health and welfare issues, academic support services, career counseling, a forum for information sharing such as a newsletter, peer support programs and social activities, spouse and family programming, re-entry information, alumni services, and staff development programs (Edmond, 1995).

An important addition to this list is cross-cultural communication training for new international students. Brein and David (1971) contend that a person's adjustment is a "function of effective intercultural communication which occurs between sojourner and host" (p. 224). The literature agrees that intercultural communication contributes to cultural adjustment and decreases the level of culture shock (Black & Mendenhall, 1990; Furnham & Bochner, 1982; Winkelman, 1994). The domestic student population also needs training in cross-cultural communication training, as well as opportunities for interaction with international students. The lit-

erature indicates that there is a positive relationship between time spent with the host culture and successful cultural adaptation for international students (Heikinheimo & Shute, 1986; Hull, 1978; Surdam & Collens, 1984). By preparing the domestic student body to communicate effectively with the international student population and by ensuring opportunities for interaction, we are helping international students with cultural adjustment.

Pre-departure Information

Winkelman (1994) says that "one can minimize cultural shock by preparing for problems and using resources that will promote coping and adjustment" (p. 123). Pre-departure orientation enables the university to inform students of the complicated process they are facing, the possible difficulties associated with such a sojourn, and resources to help them prepare themselves. Pre-departure orientation also provides important information, such as immigration policies, a basic introduction to the host culture and customs, an overview of the higher education system, university rules, regulations, and policies, financial requirements, and accommodation services (Lin & Yi, 1997). Further, it can offer a pre-departure checklist of essential effects such as immigration documents, letters from the student's department, proper identification documents, and so on. Frequently, this list will include packing tips and information about the complicated check-in process that is required by most colleges.

The University of Melbourne in Australia and the University College London in England take this service one step further and offer in-country pre-departure orientation workshops for the nations who send a significant number of students to their universities (University of Melbourne, 2008a; University College London, 2008). This type of service expresses the institution's deep appreciation for its international student population.

International Student Handbook

Many times, universities will communicate pre-departure information through their international student handbook, a document that is either available online or sent to the students before they depart from their home country.

A comprehensive international student handbook should include much more than simply pre-departure information. Appropriate handbook information includes but is not limited to the following:

◊ a description of the institution's history and mission;

◊ a description of the host country's higher education system;

◊ advice regarding culture shock and cultural adjustment;

◊ pre-departure checklist, including packing tips;

◊ a description of the city in which the university is located, including climate considerations;

◊ transportation information, including bus schedules, bike laws, guidelines for purchasing a vehicle and insurance, obtaining a driver's license, automobile laws, and parking;

◊ information about shopping in the host country, including methods of payment, shopping areas and monetary currency converters;

◊ housing information, including expected price range for rent and utilities, a basic explanation of a rental agreement, and tips for roommate selection;

◊ communication capabilities, including the telephone, print media, radio, television, cell phone, Internet and World Wide Web information, and the postal service;

◊ banking information, including a list of banks in the area, types of bank accounts, how to send and receive money internationally, and different currency options such as travelers checks, money orders, cash, and credit cards;

◊ campus safety, including the role of the police and unacceptable behaviors such as bribery;

◊ healthcare information, such as an explanation of the host country's healthcare system, the role and definition of insurance, institutional insurance requirements, acceptable insurance providers, and healthcare facilities such as an on-campus health care center or the emergency room;

◊ information for families of international students, such as education options for dependants, daycare programs, and programs for spouses;

◊ community resources for entertainment, such as theatres, museums, parks, restaurants, and community programming;

◊ description of host culture characteristics including guidelines for appropriate interaction such as making friends and dating;

◊ academic information, including registration, tuition, grading scale, financial aid, instruction, and evaluation procedures;

◊ student services and on-campus resources, such as the international student office, nationality clubs, counseling center, and libraries;

◊ description of laws of particular interest to students; and

◊ immigration information, including visa regulations, employment restrictions, and tax requirements.

A sufficiently comprehensive handbook will serve as a resource document from pre-departure to home country re-entry.

Arrival Services

Arriving in a different country for the first time can be confusing, overwhelming, and frightening. Suffering from the fatigue of a long flight can make the most basic tasks seem insurmountable. It is very important that arriving international students be aware of their transportation options and short-term accommodation plans. Arrival services help students get to their final destination.

Many universities rely on nationality groups—student groups who represent various nationalities—to provide complimentary arrival services. Although this option is

useful for many students, new international students arriving from destinations without an active student group are excluded from this service. Exceptional arrival services exist in Australia, where a consortium of universities provides an Airport Reception Desk for international students. The reception desk is staffed only for the period preceding the beginning of classes. Depending on the university, the desk offers a range of services including a welcome packet, personalized information on transportation to campus, and temporary accommodation booking services. In some cases, there is a complimentary shuttle to campus, which is arranged through the reception desk.

Accommodation Assistance

The task of finding appropriate housing is an important one. Temporary housing services are particularly important for entering international students, who are seeking to satisfy their basic need for shelter (Maslow, 1954). Many universities offer temporary housing accommodations on-campus for a subsidized cost, and others provide information regarding off-campus temporary housing options.

Permanent living accommodation information is available in most international student handbooks. Thorough handbooks describe all possible options for housing, including on-campus options, and renting or buying off-campus.

Post-arrival Orientation

In the absence of a pre-departure orientation, the post-arrival orientation is vital to achieve a smooth transition into the university. This orientation is often mandatory and provides a captive audience for a thorough introduction to the institution and its rules and regulations. Typically, the post-arrival orientation deals with immigration regulations; housing; health and safety; campus resources such as social clubs, the counseling center, or skill enhancement courses; adjustment issues; resources on developing independent living skills; and academic resources.

The University of Texas at Austin (2006, October) offers an online orientation option . This option is an increasingly popular one. Ye (2005) noted a "negative correlation between cultural shock and English-language Internet"; conversely, "English proficiency was found positively related to hours of English-language Internet use" (p. 160). Ye's findings suggest that an online orientation in the host language could help with the development of English language proficiency, subsequently helping with overall adjustment to the host society.

Counseling Service

Winkelman (1994) asserts that "one's psychological disposition, self-esteem, identity, feelings of well-being, and satisfaction with life are all created within and maintained by one's cultural system. Losing this support system can lead to a deterioration of one's sense of well-being and lead to pathological manifestations" (p. 123). Lin and Yi (1997) describe these pathological manifestations as "anxiety, confusion, depression...nervousness, loneliness, insomnia, and physical illness" (p. 474). The university's counseling service plays a large part in assisting international students who are likely to experience these conditions. It is imperative that counseling staff be properly trained in cross-cultural counseling procedures and be "sensitive to the problems of students immersed in a foreign culture" (Ping, 1999, p. 19).

Academic Support Services

Academic support services aim to help students achieve academic success; key to that success for an international student is language proficiency. More specifically, Heikinheimo and Shute (1986) state that "as a student's use of the English language improves, social and academic adjustment becomes less of a problem" (p. 405). In addition to the typical academic advisory functions, remedial English courses should be an integral part of an institution's academic support services.

Research has shown that "international students generally are more engaged in educationally purposeful activities than their American counterparts are, especially in the first year of college" (Zhao, Kuh, & Carini, 2005, p. 226). Similarly, Heikinheimo & Shute (1986) say that "academic achievement is the highest priority" for international students, and it is "unlikely that orientation programs with purely social themes will attract foreign students, whose main concern is success in their courses" (p. 405). According to this research, by carefully combining academically productive activities with social and cross-cultural training, an institution can help its students achieve academic and adjustment success simultaneously.

The University of Melbourne (2008b) offers a Transition Program for its first-year students that successfully incorporates academic and adjustment programming. The Transition Program offers study groups, peer and academic mentoring, information sessions for new students, introductions to subjects for first-year students, and assistance with adjustment to university life through life-skills training.

Career Counseling

Career counseling requires special knowledge when working with international students. The career counseling staff should be knowledgeable about work visa requirements within the host country and career opportunities that exist in the student's home country and globally. In addition to basic job hunting assistance, international students also frequently require specialized workshops aimed at improving interview skills in light of cultural differences and norms. For the same reason, they also require résumé writing workshops to explain the standards required by host-country employers.

Information Sharing

Information sharing, such as through a newsletter, is very important to international students. This provides a forum for efficient dissemination of critical information such as im-migration policy changes, important deadlines, and social activities. It also provides international students the opportunity to express their feelings and share their experiences.

Parr et al. (1992) found that "international students were most concerned about their extended family" and asserts that "offices of student affairs could increase their efforts to promote family contact" and "to reassure parents that the college welcomes and values international students" (p. 24). A newsletter to the families of international students could perform this function by helping families stay connected to the activities on their student's campus.

Peer Support Programs and Social Activities

Winkelman (1994) says that "managing cultural shock requires that one maintain or reestablish a network of primary relations—family or friends—who provide positive interpersonal relations for self-esteem and for meeting personal and emotional needs" (p. 124). One important way to reestablish a network is to join a student group or participate in social activities.

Most typically, an international student will choose to join a student group whose members are of similar nationality or culture. Furnham & Alibhai (1985) showed that students preferred "co-nationals ... for emotional help, shopping, cinema and party attendance" (p. 720). They also showed that students exhibited a preference "not only for co-nationals but those coming from similar or neighbouring countries which may be similar in religion, language, climate, etc." (Furnham & Alibhai, 1985, p. 721). Taking into consideration that other research suggests that "international students have problems in common and also problems particular to their national groups," these special student groups can function to effectively target a nationality group's particular concerns with the host-culture environment (Perkins, Perkins, Guglielmino, & Reiff, 1977, p. 387).

It is also important to encourage social interaction with the host culture student body. Research indicates that international students who spend more time with the host culture are "better adapted" and more likely to be satisfied with their international experience (Hull, 1978; Surdam & Collens, 1984, p. 243). Encouraging international students to join clubs whose membership consists of the host culture population is a good way to increase interaction between the international and domestic student population.

Spouse and Family Programming

Spouse and family programming can be crucial to the success and happiness of an international student. Galloway and Jenkins (2005) reported that "married students experience fewer [adjustment] problems...than do non-married students" (p. 184). Conversely, Scheyvens, Wild and Overton (2003) reported that "families can certainly provide support for the students, but they can also prove to be a distraction and cause of stress" (p. 319). Families of international students can be a built-in support network, but they can also cause stress and unhappiness if they are not provided with the necessary resources to successfully shift into the host-country's cultural environment.

In the United States, international student spouses are not eligible to work or pursue a degree. Spouses of international students are often professionals in their home country who left behind a successful career. It is important to provide activities and opportunities for these spouses so they will not become isolated and dissatisfied. Typical services for spouses include language enhancement classes, social activities and meetings, counseling sessions to discuss adjustment difficulties, childcare services, and play groups. International student handbooks also provide information regarding education opportunities for dependants of international students and community programs targeted to international student spouses.

Re-entry Information

Gullahorn and Gullahorn (1963) described the problems experienced by international students upon return to their home country. It is imperative that re-entry assistance be offered to prepare the student, again, for culture shock, this time, in reverse. Re-entry information should provide not only information about re-adjustment issues, but also practical information, such as freight companies for shipping personal items back to their home country and terminating accommodation arrangements. Re-entry information is typically available in the international student handbook.

Alumni Services

Alumni services are particularly advantageous for the institution. The network created by international student alumni is worldwide and can be a strong recruitment tool. "Satisfied international students and alumni recruit relatives, friends, coworkers, and others to the United States" (Peterson et al., 1999, p. 70). By building a strong community of alumni through alumni services, both the international alumni and the institution benefit greatly.

Staff, Domestic, and International Student Cross-cultural Communication Programs

Communication is a key to success in cross-cultural adjustment for international students. It is imperative that the institution's staff members, domestic students, and international students have training opportunities to improve their cross-cultural communication skills. Interactions between domestic and international students can be very educational for the domestic student, but only if that student is able to successfully communicate with the international student.

Michigan State University offers an Intercultural Communication Workshop (ICW) for both international and domestic students (http://www.isp.msu.edu/oiss). "One ICW involved 80 students, half international and half American, in a two-day overnight workshop that included role plays, skits, mini-lectures, and small-group discussions" (Peterson et al., 1999, p. 71). Michigan State University also offers a one-day workshop for university support staff that is "de-signed for improving their understanding of international students." (Peterson et al., 1999, p. 71). These types of workshops are essential to create understanding between the host culture and the international student populations.

Quality Assurance

All services offered for international students must be constantly evaluated for quality assurance. "Quality assurance involves concepts such as best practice, continuous improvement, stakeholder feedback and satisfaction, identification of goals, setting performance criteria to assess outcomes, peer and other review" (Edmond, 1995, p. 52). In order to offer the best quality of service to international students, an international student services office must be intentional in its quality control and continually seek to improve its services.

Conclusion

Serving international students is a complex, multi-faceted function. By becoming knowledgeable about the complicated process of culture shock and cultural adaptation and by superimposing that information onto knowledge about the practical necessities of daily life as an international student, one may begin to understand the importance of supplying superior services to international students.

The future of international student services is integral to any university that wishes to be nationally or globally competitive; therefore, institutions must strive to increase administrative support and quality in this area. The 2004 Open Doors report indicates that there are many emerging markets in international education such as China and India, which "continue to expand higher education capacity at home while also sending large numbers abroad" (IIE, 2004, p. 24). These new markets will certainly understand the connection between exceptional international student services and successful recruitment and retention.

The higher education systems currently offering the most outstanding services for international students have done so by establishing a shared commitment among all factions across campus including the president, the provost, faculty members, and student affairs professionals. This united dedication to international student services is the key to providing high-quality, comprehensive services for international students. The list of services suggested in this chapter is based on both research and current practices and is applicable to any college or university dedicated to providing quality services for international students.

References

Anumonye, A. (1967). Psychological stresses among African students in Britain. *Scottish Medical Journal, 12*, 314.

Barker, M., Child, C., Gallois, C., Jones, E., & Callan, V. J. (1991). Difficulties of overseas students in social and academic situations. *Australian Journal of Psychology, 43*(2), 79–84.

Black, S. J., & Mendenhall, M. (1990). Cross-cultural training effectiveness: A review and theoretical framework for future research. *Academy of Management Review, 15*(1), 113–136.

Brein, M., & David, K. H. (1971). Intercultural communication and the adjustment of the sojourner. *Psychological Bulletin, 76*, 215–230.

Carnevale, A. P. (1999, Spring). Diversity in higher education: Why corporate America cares. *Diversity Digest.* Retrieved September 27, 2005, from http://www.diversityweb.org/Digest/Sp99/corporate.html

Chickering, A. W., & Reisser, L. (1993). *Education and identity* (2nd ed.). San Francisco: Jossey-Bass.

Dalton, J. C. (1999). The significance of international issues and responsibilities in the contemporary work of student affairs. *New Directions for Student Services, 86*, 3–11.

Dozier, S. B. (2001). Undocumented and documented international students. *Community College Review, 29*(2), 43–54.

Edmond, M. (1995). Quality support services for international students: AVCC code of ethical practice in the provision of education to overseas students by Australian higher education institutions. *Journal of Tertiary Education Administration, 17*(1), 51–62.

Furnham, A., & Alibhai, N. (1985). The friendship networks of foreign students: A replication and extension of the functional model. *International Journal of Psychology, 20*, 709–722.

Furnham, A., & Bochner, S. (1982). Social difficulty in a foreign culture: An empirical analysis of culture shock. In S. Bochner (Ed.), *Cultures in contact* (pp.161-198). New York: Pergamon.

Furnham, A., & Bochner, S. (1986). *Culture shock: Psychological reactions to unfamiliar environments.* New York: Methuen.

Galloway, F. J., & Jenkins, J. R. (2005). The adjustment problems faced by international students in the United States: A comparison of international students and administrative perceptions at two private, religiously affiliated universities. *NASPA Journal, 42*(2), 175–187.

Gullahorn, J. T., & Gullahorn, J. E. (1963). An extension of the U-curve hypothesis. *Journal of Social Issues, 19*(3), 33–47.

Heikinheimo, P., & Shute, J. (1986). The adaptation of foreign students: Student views and institutional implications. *Journal of College Student Personnel, 27*, 399–406.

Hull, W. F. (1978). *Foreign students in the United States of America: Coping behavior within the educational environment.* New York: Praeger.

Institute of International Education. (2004). *Open doors 2004: Report on international educational exchange.* New York: H. K. Chin (Ed.).

Levine, A., & Cureton, J. S. (1998). *When hope and fear collide: A portrait of today's college student.* San Francisco: Jossey-Bass.

Lin, J. G., & Yi, J. K. (1997). Asian international students' adjustment: Issues and program suggestions. *College Student Journal, 31*, 473–480.

Lysgaard, S. (1955). Adjustment in a foreign society: Norwegian Fulbright grantees visiting the United States. *International Social Science Bulletin, 7*, 45–51.

Maslow, A. (1954). *Motivation and personality.* New York: Harper and Row.

Maundeni, T. (2001). The role of social networks in the adjustment of African students to British society: Students' perceptions. *Race Ethnicity and Education, 4*, 253–276.

Nelson, B. (2004). *Higher education report for the 2004 to 2006 triennium.* Retrieved October 4, 2005, from http://www.dest.gov.au/NR/rdonlyres/6B4F6AD6-13D1-4B69-99EB-EFE95E737EE6/1048/triennium_2004_2007.pdf

Oberg, K. (1960). Cultural shock: Adjustment to new cultural environment. *Practical Anthropology, 7*, 197–182.

Oropeza, B. A. C., Fitzgibbon, M., & Barón, A., Jr. (1991). Managing mental health crises of foreign college students. *Journal of Counseling & Development, 69*, 280–284.

Parr, G., Bradley, L., & Bingi, R. (1992). Concerns and feelings of international students. *Journal of College Student Development, 33*, 20–25.

Pederson, P. (1995). *The five stages of culture shock: Critical incidents around the world.* Westport, CT: Greenwood Press.

Perkins, C. S., Perkins, M. L., Guglielmino, L. M., & Reiff, R. F. (1977). A comparison of the adjustment problems of three international student groups. *Journal of College Student Personnel, 18*, 382–388.

Peterson, D. M., Briggs, P., Dreasher, L., Horner, D., & Nelson, T. (1999). Contributions of international students and programs to campus diversity. *New Directions for Student Services, 86*, 67–77.

Ping, C. J. (1999). An expanded international role for student affairs. *New Directions for Student Services, 86*, 13–21.

Scheyvens, R., Wild, K., & Overton, J. (2003). International students pursuing postgraduate study in geography: Impediments to their learning experiences. *Journal of Geography in Higher Education, 27*, 309–323.

Schram, J. L., & Lauver, P. J. (1988). Alienation in international students. *Journal of College Student Development, 29*, 146–150.

Stafford, T., Jr., Marion, P., & Salter, M. (1980). Adjustment of international students. *NASPA Journal, 18*(1), 40–45.

Surdam, J. C., & Collens, J. R. (1984). Adaptation of international students: A cause for concern. *Journal of College Student Personnel, 25*, 240–245.

Tompson, H. B., & Tompson, G. H. (1996). Confronting classroom diversity issues in the classroom with strategies to improve satisfaction and retention of international students. *Journal of Education for Business, 72*, 53–58.

University College London. (2008, April). Pre-departure briefings. Retrieved April 11, 2008, from http://www.ucl.ac.uk/prospective-students/international-students/pre-departure-briefings

University of Melbourne. (2008, March). Pre-departure briefings. Retrieved April 11, 2008, from http://www.services.unimelb.edu.au/international/planning/predeparture.html

University of Melbourne. (2008b, April). Transition and orientation programs. Retrieved April 11, 2008, from http://www.services.unimelb.edu.au/transition/

University of Texas – Austin. (2006, October). International student and scholar services. Retrieved April 11, 2008, http://www.utexas.edu/international/isss/

Villalpando, O. (2002). The impact of diversity and multiculturalism on all students: Findings from a national study. *NASPA Journal, 40*(1), 124–144.

Winkelman, M. (1994). Cultural shock and adaptation. *Journal of Counseling & Development, 73*, 121–126.

Ye, J. (2005). Acculturative stress and use of the internet among East Asian international students in the United States. *CyberPsychology & Behavior, 8*, 154–161.

Zhao, C., Kuh, G. D., & Carini, R. M. (2005). A comparison of international student and American student engagement in effective educational practices. *The Journal of Higher Education, 76*, 209–231.

PART III
COUNTRY-SPECIFIC STUDENT SERVICE DELIVERY MODELS

EIGHT

SELECTED ASIAN COUNTRIES

Howard S. Wang

I first became interested in the roles of student affairs in higher education, especially in Asian countries, when I was on the team that wrote an International Association of Student Affairs and Services Professionals (IASAS) manual. This manual, edited by Roger Ludeman, was presented in 2000 to the UNESCO Office as a follow-up to the World Conference on Higher Education.

For this book, I have used my involvement as a member of the Asia Pacific Student Services Association (APSSA), asking my colleagues from various Asian countries to help me present an overview of the history and development of university student affairs services and programs in each of their countries. Selection of the countries is based solely on the interest and time availability of the various authors. I hope that in the future, authors from Asian countries not included in this book will be interested in sharing the developments in student affairs in their countries when similar opportunities arise. The four countries represented here are the Philippines, Malaysia, Singapore, and Mainland China and Hong Kong, a Special Administrative Region of Mainland China.

The Philippines

The chapter on student affairs and services in Philippine universities and colleges will give readers a glimpse of the history and traditions of the Philippines as well as a summary of a conjunctural analysis of today's Philippine society. It is important to read about student affairs in Philippines' higher education in the proper context of the country's socio-economic, political, and cultural background. The Spanish and U.S colonial experiences undoubtedly prompted in Filipino educators a strong desire to establish their own unique educational identity and values according to the Filipino national tradition. This meant shedding the influence of the United States, which had established the country's public education system, including higher education. The role of student affairs in the Philippines is very much one of *in loco parentis*, a role codified by law to meet the country's own national need to provide nurturing and tender care to its students, who

are much younger than university students in Europe and the United States. The author calls for the global community to share resources, time, and expertise with developing countries such as the Philippines, yet at the same time, points out that developed countries must respect Philippine's *pagsasarili*, or "being our own person" or "self-reliance."

Malaysia

In Malaysia, the central Ministry of Education exerts great influence over the development of its students into Malaysian citizens who are educated, competent, moral, and capable of contributing to family, society, and the nation. Student affairs began in the 1970s as a way to monitor student demonstrations and activities that were deemed inappropriate. Its role quickly evolved into dealing with students' total development in order to produce "quality graduates" to cater to market needs. The government recognizes that developing human resources for nation building involves character-building and the holistic development of students.

Singapore

Singapore shares with Malaysia a common history of British influence, dating from the early 1800s when the British founded a trading post on the island at the tip of the Malay Peninsula (present day Singapore). The University of Singapore was originally attached to the University of Malaya. However, student affairs did not exist at the University of Singapore until 1980, when it merged with Nanyang University (founded in 1955 with resources pooled from the Chinese community) and became the National University of Singapore (NUS). At that time, nonacademic student matters were handled by the public relations office. In 1980 that office was divided into two departments, one of which was the "new" student liaison office, the predecessor to the student affairs office, which was created in 1998. Unlike the "monitoring" role that student affairs assumed in Malaysia in the 1970s, the mission of NUS student affairs from the outset was to partner with students to provide services and programs to enrich their university experience.

Mainland China

The Chinese educational system is certainly no stranger to educational reforms. Following a long history of importing educational models from foreign countries, as well as political upheavals that paralyzed the country's education system, the most recent reform, which began in 1985, saw the birth of institutional autonomy that enabled nearly 300 single-discipline universities to merge into comprehensive, multi-discipline, and sometimes multi-campus universities. Reforms brought about greater differentiation of student services, as well as expansion of the scope of services provided to a new and more diverse population of students: old and young, single and married, high school graduates and professionals returning to school. With this burgeoning enrollment, student affairs work and practitioners seem to be experiencing growing pains. Challenges include high turnover among student affairs practitioners, lack of prerequisite professional preparation specific to managing students, ambiguous roles between serving as teachers in ideological and political education and as administrators and counselors, and perception by faculty colleagues that their role is secondary or unimportant. These challenges may be the result of a lack of focus or clear direction from the central government, namely, the Ministry of Education, about student affairs and their role in the total and developmental education of university students. Yet dedicated student affairs practitioners continue to seek out best practices from other countries throughout the world and attempt to adapt those practices to meet student needs within China's current socio-economic, political, and cultural context.

Hong Kong

In Hong Kong, as in Singapore, a large proportion of the population places emphasis on the value of education, hard work, and economic wellbeing of individuals. Both Hong Kong and Singapore are confined to a small geographic area. The limited natural resources in Hong Kong propel educators to put greater emphasis on developing its human resources to meet the unique market needs—also a typical trademark of colonial education. Transfer of British sovereignty to the People's Republic of China in 1997 brought about a change in the socio-political environment in Hong Kong, so greater emphasis is placed on the all-around development of students to become a pool of graduates not only with talent and competence in their academic subjects, but also aligned with the socio-economic, political, and cultural context of the People's Republic of China. Student affairs work emerged in the early 1970s, subsequent to the "Student Movement" of 1967, in order to better communicate with students and to understand and meet their needs. Services provided at that time were small scale, focusing mostly on careers and employment. For the next 20 years, student affairs in Hong Kong evolved from a service orientation to a student development orientation that promotes intellectual, emotional, artistic, cultural, physical, social, and career skills. The Hong Kong Education Commission intends to educate students of the former colony to be life-long learners with a stronger sense of civic pride and a global outlook. There is a great deal of collaboration among student affairs practitioners in Hong Kong, sharing best practices among institutions, as well as joint academic efforts with faculty members. Collaboration with teaching faculty varies a great deal from one institution to another.

The Hong Kong Student Services Association (HKSSA) was formed in 1984 when student affairs practitioners of the then four major tertiary institutions gathered together to share common concerns and resolve issues. In 1988, at the conclusion of its first international professional conference on student affairs, the HKSSA took the first steps to form the Asia Pacific Student Services Association (APSSA). Today, APSSA has almost 40 members from nine countries, including the United States and Canada.

Comparisons

In all the countries discussed here, the basic services provided to students are fairly similar, and so are the challenges in student affairs work: limited governmental and/or institutional funding, preferential priority for academic work versus non-academic/professional work at the institutional level, and lack of understanding of the importance or relevance of out-of-classroom experience and skills. These situations result in a lack of respect by some faculty colleagues, as well as lack of collaborative efforts between academic and student affairs practitioners in providing a total education of students. Another similarity is that these countries are moving away from "student services" and "student management" to "student development," although "development" is defined differently, depending on the socio-political context as well as the emerging economic and other needs of the country.

Student affairs practice in each of the countries is indeed unique. However, comparative analysis should not be limited to the technical level. I hope these accounts will generate discussions at the conceptual and philosophical levels.

NINE

MAINLAND CHINA

Heidi Huang Yu and Ouyang Ke-Quan
Concluding remarks by Howard S. Wang

All education laws and regulations in the People's Republic of China are part of the country's constitution. The law focusing on higher education, passed in 1998, covers (a) the general principles of higher education endeavors; (b) the development of higher education institutions, their framework, and functions; (c) rights and obligations of faculties, staff, and students; (d) provisions for input and guarantees in higher education development; and (e) criminal/civil responsibilities in accordance with the Education Law (which covers all education and was passed in 1995) (MOE, n.d. b).

Further regulations were established by the State Education Council (predecessor to the current Ministry of Education) and became effective in 1990, with a revised version taking effect in 2005 (MOE, n.d. b). These regulations set out the general principles governing student affairs administration in higher education, such as (a) regulations related to student status (b) regulations on extracurricular activities, and (c) campus order, including student awards and punishments. In 1989, the State Education Council issued a prototype of the Behavior Code, and the Ministry of Education issued a revised version, effective September 2005. Each university or college has its own administrative regulations regarding the vision and mission of student cultivation (similar to "student development" as the term used in western countries) and the rights and obligations of students in all aspects of college life (e.g., class attendance, credit system, dormitory order, awards and punishments, etc.).

Changes in policies take the form of constitutional amendments. For example, the constitution banned college students from being married[1] and in response to issues and incidents related to this ban, the Ministry of Education has already committed to an amendment to the Constitution that would lift it. In the most recently revised Regulation and Behavior

Code, the "marriage ban" is abolished, making this particular law more reasonable and humane. The Ministry of Education also gave higher education institutions greater autonomy to impose sanctions against student cheating by referring them to a university-level arbitration committee and the student appeals committee.

National Framework of China Higher Education Institutions

Section 68 in the Chinese Education Law dictates that "higher schools" are to include: universities, autonomous colleges, and higher technological academies (which include higher vocational and adult education schools). Other higher education institutions include organizations engaged with higher educational functions and scientific research institutions authorized to provide graduate programs.

Higher education institutions are either public or private. Private institutions will not be discussed in this chapter since they are under different governmental administrative guidance and regulation. Public (also called "common") institutions are either under the provincial government, the municipal government, different branches of the State Council or the military. For example, among universities in Guangdong Province, the Sun Yat-sen University is governed under the Ministry of Education, Jinan University is under the jurisdiction of the Overseas Chinese Affairs Office, Guangdong University of Foreign Studies and Guangdong University of Technology are under the jurisdiction of the Guangdong Provincial government, and Guangzhou University and Guangzhou Medical College are under the Guangzhou Municipal government. The former First Military Medical University, which was a military institution under the jurisdiction of the Chinese People Liberation Army, was transferred to the Provincial government and renamed Southern Medical University.

Although these different types of higher education institutions differ in both functions and governance, they are all influenced and dominated by the central govern-

[1] According to the Chinese Constitution and the Marriage Law, only Chinese male citizens older than 22 and female citizens older than 20 are eligible for lawful marriage; however, married citizens are banned from attending universities or colleges.

Table 9.1. Expansion in higher education enrollment from 1999 to 2003.

Year	1998	1999	2000	2001	2002	2003
No. Institutions	1022	1,071	1,041	1,225	1,396	1,552
Enrollment	1,083,600	1,569,800	2,206,100	2,682,800	3,205,000	3,821,700
Total Enrollment	3,408,700	4,134,200	5,560,900	7,190,700	9,033,600	11,085,600
No. of Graduates	829,800	847,600	949,800	1,036,300	1,337,300	1,877,500

ment. The Higher Education Law dictates that Ministry of Education of the People's Republic of China is the leader and administrator of all national higher education undertakings, with municipal governments functioning as the coordinators of the regional higher education efforts. As regional administrators, they are empowered by Ministry of Education to develop their institutions for the benefit of the region. As the head of national higher education affairs, the Educational Administrative Department at Ministry of Education is in charge of all higher education institutions that focus on developments beneficial to China at the national level. Under the Ministry of Education regulations, other specified departments at the State Council are responsible for public relations and serve as liaisons to higher education institutions.

Impact of Higher Education Institutional Reform on Student Affairs in China

The issue of higher education reform was raised in 1985 when China's central government began to promote and provide greater autonomy to colleges and universities. Since 1992, approximately 300 Chinese higher education institutions have merged and upgraded into comprehensive universities and expanded both the scope of their programs and the size of their campuses. Over the last eight years, higher education has been expanding rapidly under government mandates. In 1994, tuition and employment reforms were implemented. Since then, all students attending higher education institutions are required to pay tuition. Furthermore, students with high scores on the national university entrance examination are now able to select the university and the major of their choice. They will not be assigned to specific jobs or employment after graduation, and they are free to choose their preferred career paths. Such landmark reforms have had major impacts on student affairs work.

Reforms brought about additional responsibilities to student affairs administrators, who now must provide such services as financial aid, career counseling, and employment administration. From 1949 to 1985, the Chinese central government underwrote the total cost of higher education (i.e., it was tuition free) and arranged for or assigned all employment for the graduates. As student affairs administrators were the only officials with employment information, they were fully-empowered to allocate employment to their graduates. However, from 1986 to 1994, tuition reform en-

abled universities to charge a boarding fee as well as tuition, based on students' scores on their entrance examinations. Since 1994, all college students have had to pay tuition, and a proportion of graduates were expected to go job-hunting on their own instead of waiting for an assignment by student affairs administrators (Yao, 1995). In 1997, the Ministry of Education issued the Temporary Regulation of Common Higher Education Institution Graduates Employment, which temporarily abolished the college student employment allocation system and declared that all graduates were now expected to venture into the job market on their own merits.

The reforms also expanded scope of student affairs at the university level. The government's 1999 Decision to Deepen Educational Reform and Boost Quality Education advocated for higher education expansion, by setting the goal of a higher education attendance rate of 15% by 2010, up from 9% in 1998. To achieve this goal, the Ministry of Education encourages expanded enrollment and establishment of new universities and colleges. According to the Ministry of Education, the total number of college students tripled between 1998 and 2003 (see Table 9.1) (MOE, d).

In 2001, the Ministry of Education abolished the restrictions on marital status and age of entering students (i.e., the requirement that university candidates be single and less than 25 years old). This provided the impetus to expand and broaden the range of candidates participating in university entrance examinations. Such expansion has provided a great challenge to higher education student affairs administration (Lin, 2002):

a. Change in Campus Administration and Student Demographics: To respond to expanded enrollment, "secondary" colleges or new (branch) campuses have been established, raising issues related to multi-campus administration. At the same time, the greater diversity of students—resulting from the lifting of restrictions on marital status and age—provides new challenges. Issues include mandatory boarding regulations for single versus married students and behavioral problems from older students, some of whom may have had employment experience prior to entering the universities and who may not necessarily wish to abide by campus regulations as compared with the more obedient and younger classmates.

b. Change in Student Affairs Practitioner to Student Ratio: The rapid expansion of students has not been matched by a corresponding increase in the number of student affairs practitioners. This has raised the crucial question of how to provide quality services under the existing administrative structures now that practitioners are in charge of a much larger number of students in the units of class, major, or faculty division. The ratio of one student affairs practitioner to 250 students, as prescribed by law, has now increased in some universities to 1:400 or even 1:600.

c. Increased Proportion of Underprivileged Students: The increased number of underprivileged students, with more requests for financial assistance, has added to the workload of financial aid administrators.

d. Increased Student Mental Health Issues: Increased enrollment forces students to face differences in lifestyles and clashes in values among the diverse peer groups. Some of the students are far more vulnerable to psychological disturbances and require personal counseling. Student mental health problems have caught the public's attention in recent years, with increased rates of abnormal behavior and suicide.

e. Fierce Employment Competition among Graduates: Since 1999, the first year of expanded enrollment, employment of graduates has been a major political and social issue. The government has taken measures to stimulate the domestic supply of jobs and has issued population mobility measures to compensate for the over-abundance of jobless graduates.[2]

Student Affairs and Services in Higher Education Institutions
Concepts and definition of student affairs work

It is somewhat difficult to find the English equivalent of student affairs work in the Chinese higher education system because student affairs practices include such terms as "ideological and political education (IPE)," "moral education (ME)" and "student affairs administration" or "student work."

Cai (2000) described the origins of the key Chinese terms. The function of IPE has been a predominating force in university/college education since the 1950s and the Cultural Revolution. The term ME surfaced during the post-Cultural Revolution era (1977–1980s) when over-emphasis on political education caused widespread discontent among students, and moral standards were in decline. In the 1990s, the term "Student Affairs Work" was widely adopted as institu-

tional reforms had brought about diversification of practical student affairs work or functions that would not fit the category of either IPE or ME. Cai concluded that "student affairs work" mainly refers to the university's efforts to exert educational influence on its students in non-academic or extra-curricular activities, and suggested a wider adaptation of this term for the purpose of communicating with international colleagues in this field.

Wang (2004) divided the administrative roles of higher education institutions into student administration, which focuses on "regulating students" (e.g., student behavior or conduct) and student affairs administration, which focuses on "serving the students' needs." He shared Cai's definition of "student affairs administration," excluding academic experiences but including daily counseling, extra-curricular activities, medical care, psychological counseling, career counseling, financial aid, campus order, and awards/punishment sanctions.

However, the structure and climate of student affairs administration at both the national and the institutional levels has been and still is determined by the goal of ideological conversion and political unification. In general, the term "student affairs" has been widely used in the title of related university departments. Ideological and political education (IPE), adopted more often in academic writings, was emphasized in Document 16, a benchmark document[3] regarding "student work development" in Mainland China. This document integrated all the concepts and definitions of IPE by including three groups of IPE practitioners:

1. university/college-level administrative staff, Communist Party Committee (CPC) and the Communist Youth League of China (CYLC) committee;

2. student affairs counselors and the head instructors in each class; and

3. instructors of courses in ideological and politics theories and philosophy and social science, which all students must take.

Some scholars associated IPE with "political socialization" by pointing out that the latter is a basic focus of college education (Sun, 2000). Ren & Sun (2002) stated that higher education plays an important role in developing the human socialization in political, moral and other aspects of human socialization. They further defined the goal of political socialization as "to cultivate and train individuals as eligible citizens who are compliant with political codes, laws and, regulations; equipped with righteous world view, life view and values; assuming civil rights and responsibilities; promoting political stability; and serving as role-model in political life." He (2004) maintained that higher education institutions should play an important role in the political so-

[2] According to the previous Registered Permanent Residence policy in Mainland China, a student must register his residency upon enrolling at the university, in the administrative zone of the university. Upon graduation, the student must then register his residency in the administrative zone of his employer in order to be included as a community member of that zone. If a student graduates without a job, his "residency" will revert to his original home residence. In 2002, the central government declared the availability of a two-year extension of residency to relieve the employment pressure graduates faced immediately upon graduation. However, in 2005, this policy was eliminated in Guangdong Province because too many graduates preferred to keep their residency with the university rather than seek employment. Statistics have shown that this practice has led to a lower employment rate for the university than prior to the implementation of this policy.

[3] Document released in 2004 by the Central Committee of Chinese Communist Party and the State Council titled "Opinions of Strengthening and Improvement of College Students' Ideological and Political Education." This document is commonly referred to as Document No.16, named after its serial number.

cialization of college students by strengthening the IPE and promoting political culture on campus.

In spite of the various connotations of IPE, ME, and student affairs administration, they all serve as means of "political socialization" of college students in higher education institutions in Mainland China. Qi Xiaoping, currently vice director of the student affairs office at Sun Yat-sen University, summarized the three characteristics of student affairs work. First, he said, it is politically oriented. Second, it involves (a) education in Marxist theory, ideology, and educational practice; (b) teaching, administration, and service; and (c) family, university, and social education. Third, student affairs is characterized by openness to diverse values and unification of behavior codes (Qi, 2003, pp.4-6). Li Xiaolu[4] prioritized ideological and political education as important aspects, among other student affairs perspectives, in higher education institutions in Guangdong.

The vision and mission of student affairs and services in Chinese higher education institutions can be viewed on two different levels:

Level 1: General vision of student affairs work as prescribed by Chinese Higher Education Laws and Regulations. The Higher Education Law sets out the vision of what a "cultivated student" of higher education should be. This student should be one who abides by all campus and civil laws and regulations; complies with behavior codes; respects faculty and seniors; is assiduous in his or her academic studies and regularly participates in physical exercises; is patriotic, collectivistic, and socialistic; is knowledgeable in Marxism, Leninism, Maoism, and Deng Xiaoping Theory; is compassionate, with high moral fiber; and finally, is capable of mastering advanced scientific knowledge and special techniques.

Section 2 of the Regulation of Higher Education Institution Student Administration of 1990 states that university students should be "correctly directed" in their political pursuits, devoted to socialist China, and supportive of the leadership of the Chinese Communist Party (CCP). Students should participate in social practices; comply with laws, regulations, and university disciplines; be compassionate and moral; behave with civility; and be diligent in their studies and knowledgeable about modern science and culture (MOE, n.d. c).

Level 2: Vision and mission of student affairs work as prescribed by university/college administration. Document No. 16 states that, as part of an overall vision of ideological and political education, the vision of student affairs work is that it contributes to the growth and development of students (Central Committee of Chinese Communist Party and State Council, 2004). This document is used as a guideline for student affairs work in all higher education institutions. The mission of student affairs work, according to Qi Xiaoping (2003), should at minimum include:

◊ cultivation of morality, intellectuality, and physical fortitude;

◊ development of both students and student affairs practitioners; and

◊ service to the university, students, and society (pp. 6–7).

Qi & Tang (2005) illustrated the missions of student affairs work in terms of society, university, and students. To serve the society, student affairs practitioners should aim at helping students:

◊ to familiarize themselves with the history and situation of China;

◊ to understand and persist in the basic course of the Communist Party Committee (CPC);

◊ to accept and respect the workings of a socialist democratic legal system; and

◊ to learn Marxism, Leninism, Maoism, Deng Xiaoping Theory, and the "Three Representative Thoughts"[5] (pp. 6–8).

To serve the university, student affairs practitioners should always:

◊ maintain and interpret the values, vision, and policies of the university;

◊ participate in university administration and take personal responsibility for university decisions;

◊ assess, evaluate, and improve the education received by students and student social practices;

◊ provide student information in university policy or amendments;

◊ create policies and devise schemes for the safety and stability of the campus;

◊ effectively manage human and financial resources concerning students;

◊ embody the university values by executing and improving student behavior codes;

◊ encourage and coordinate student participation in university administration;

◊ promote and facilitate the interaction between faculty members and students;

◊ handle any incidents that would cause harm to students;

◊ engage in academic research and professional activities;

◊ maintain favorable communication and relations with the local community; and

◊ coordinate smooth relationships among student affairs departments, faculty affairs departments, and other departments in the university administration.

---

[4]Li is the vice-director of the Office of Education of Guangdong Provincial Government. He was quoted from his preface of the corpus of Guangdong Student Affairs Practitioners titled "The Education and Management of Students After the Expansion of Enrollment."

[5]The "Three Representatives" require, as first proposed by the former Party leader Jiang Zemin in 2000, that the CPC must always represent the development trend of China's advanced productive forces, the orientation of China's advanced culture, and the fundamental interests of the overwhelming majority of the Chinese people. Information extracted from http://www.china.org.cn/english/features/48642.htm

To serve students, student affairs practitioners should facilitate:

◊ the process of students adapting to college life;

◊ student learning to make sound choices and judgments;

◊ problem-solving ability and interpersonal communication skills and teamwork;

◊ use of financial resources needed by students while in college, such as scholarships, stipends or part-time jobs;

◊ whole-person or "total" development of students;

◊ a healthy lifestyle, including personal hygiene and mental health,

◊ civility among students and between students and faculty and staff; and

◊ career goal-setting and satisfaction with employment.

Typical Organizational Structures for Student Affairs and Services in China

Because higher education institutions vary so greatly, it is not possible to provide a universal depiction of a typical student affairs organizational structure in China. Nonetheless, a basic framework can show a general picture. Figure 9.1 (based on Wany, 2003) illustrates a typical "centralized model" student services organizational structure.

At some universities, departments involved in career counseling, military training, or psychological counseling are under the University Student Affairs Office (SAO); at other universities, such departments parallel the Faculty SAO. Figure 9.2 (based on Wang, 2003) illustrates a "faculty level" student affairs organization model. Unlike the centralized model (Figure 9.1), the faculty level model has the full-time undergraduate students overseen by the Faculty SAO. Ad-

ministrative responsibilities are assigned to the class committee and the head student in charge of dormitory rooms. Students who are in the same year and the same major are grouped into "administrational" classes overseen by the class committee and the China Communist Youth League (CCYL) Branch, which in turn report to the Faculty SAO administration. Campus residency for students is mandatory and students of the same "class" are then assigned by the Faculty SAO to their rooms, with the "Head Student" reporting to the Faculty SAO administration. Although student residents are under dormitory management, they ultimately are the responsibility of the Faculty SAO. Students in one class usually take the same courses and live in adjacent dormitories. Overall, the Faculty CCYL Committee, faculty student union, class committee, and the CCYL Branch are all overseen by the Faculty SAO.

Student Services Delivery Model

The student services delivery model (Figure 9.3) (based on Wang, 2003) at Sun Yat-sen University (or Zhongshan University) represents a combined "centralized" and "faculty-level" student services delivery model, one where the CCYL committee, career counseling, psychological counseling center, and Armed Forces Department each run as independent units rather than as subordinates to the university SAO administration. This student services delivery model is based on a collection of papers published in *The Education and Management of Students after the Expansion of Enrollment* (Tang, Qi and Wong, 2002).

In this model, the university-level student affairs services or functions are placed on the left hand side in the vertical list of boxes, while all faculty-level student services or func-

Figure 9.1. A typical representation of a centralized student affairs administration model (Wang, 2003).

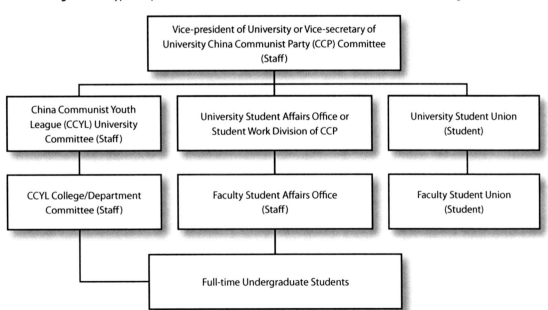

tions are placed on the right hand side. Typical student services provided are listed in the center column of Figure 9.3 (based on Wang, 2003).

Common Approaches and Practices in Student Services

Freshman Orientation. The student affairs staff publishes orientation materials introducing the university and its history, current campus developments, university organization structure, campus amenities, personal guidance services, and other information needed for adjustment to a new college life. That staff also manages all aspects of the registration process, including collecting student archives and personal data such as students' social relations, educational background, and biographical information. The opening ceremony for freshman students is held as part of the orientation, in conjunction with education on personal discipline and military training. At some universities, extension programs are provided to enhance experiential learning during freshmen orientation.

Financial Aid. The National Student Loan program is funded by national banks at no interest if the loan is repaid within the first six years after graduation from college. It is the major mode of financial assistance for students attending higher education institutions in China. Only Chinese citizens are eligible to apply. An eligible applicant is a full-time student 18 years or older. The application must be submitted to the local government, which verifies the completed "Questionnaire of

Student Family Financial Status" to ensure that the average income per person in the family is less than 300 RMB ($43 USD) prior to qualifying for the loan. The Faculty SAO then processes the applications and the University SAO then processes all information and coordinates with banks in signing the national student loan agreement. Approved student borrowers sign their agreements at the Faculty SAO with the office staff endorsing and serving as witnesses to the process. Other types of financial aid include the National Scholarship for underprivileged freshman students. Scholarships are generally funded by individuals, foundations, or stipends. Students also work at part-time jobs. The Faculty SAO provides information about such aid, processes applications, determines eligibility, and coordinates awards.

Rewards and Disciplinary Action for Student Conduct. To encourage the holistic development of students, universities reward outstanding students based on their achievements in several areas: their moral character and their performance in academics, social services, leadership, sports, and arts. For students who violate university regulations (e.g., those who cheat or plagiarize), the school imposes sanctions according to regulations described in the university handbook, as well as the National Higher Education Student Administration Regulations. To respond to students who may have violated the law, the university collaborates with the campus legal department to ensure that education is a priority, and that

Figure 9.2. Faculty-level student affairs organizational structure.

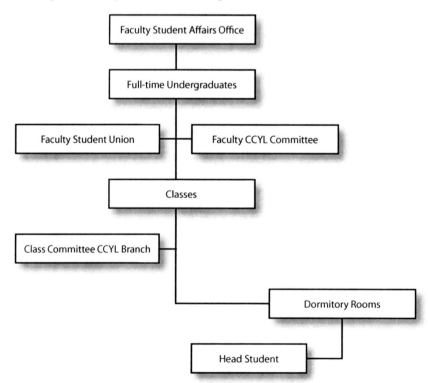

punishment is used as a tool to provide a learning experience for the student.

Graduate Employment. To boost the rate of employment of university graduates, an increasing number of Faculty SAO staff are providing career counseling to students during their college years, as well as introductory courses on employment policies for seniors. The student affairs staff also shares with seniors any employment information it has and provides references if requested by potential employers. Employment contracts, signed by the university, the employer, and the student as the employee, must be endorsed by the university career counseling center.

Service–Learning. The term "service–learning" is being used in this context to describe the student affairs practitioners' role in student societies and student activities. Student affairs practitioners are supervisors, facilitators, and administrators of service learning. The Faculty SAO is in charge of various student societies. The university CCYL Committee is the regulating body for the university student unions and other university-level student societies registered with the CCYL Committee. The Faculty SAO oversees the application process for university-based intensive training on leadership, teamwork, and other personal development skills, as well as exchange programs and activities off campus.

Ideological and Political Education. Student affairs practitioners are responsible for ideological and political education (IPE) of students through individual counseling, teaching IPE courses, developing Communist Party Committee and China Communist Youth League branches, and delivery of promotional information for political socialization. At many universities, student affairs practitioners act as part-time teachers for introductory courses on Marxism and other political theories (Lin, 2003).

Psychological Counseling. In the absence of professional psychological counselors, student affairs practitioners serve as listeners and provide suggestions to students during the preliminary stage of mental health counseling. However, they refer severe cases (e.g., neurosis) to professional psychiatric facilities off campus for further treatment. As mental health problems among students have increased in recent years, a university center staffed with psychologists has been identified as a significant and important need for the campus.

Staffing and Staff Development
Position and titles of student affairs practitioners

Although generally addressed with the title of "teacher," student affairs practitioners are known to have various titles such as "student counselors," "political counselors," "ideological and political counselors," or "political work counselors." Chen (2002) reviewed the historical accounts of this position in China. In the early 1950s, the central People's Republic of China established a mechanism for higher education institutions to cultivate the "political quality" of college students. In 1965, the Ministry of Education issued "The Regulation of Political Counselors," whose

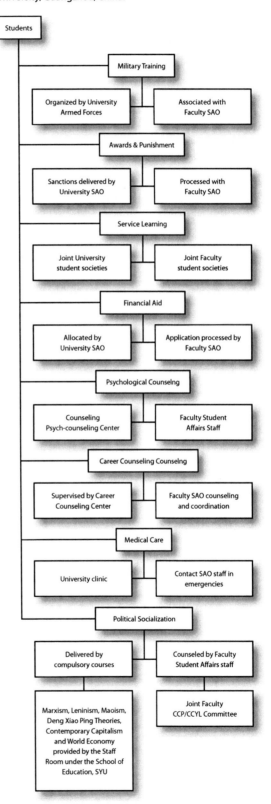

Figure 9.3. Student services delivery model at Sun Yat-sen University, Guangzhou, China.

general mission is to oversee the political education and activities of students. The Higher Education Law of the Peoples Republic of China adopted at the 4th Meeting of the Standing Committee of the 9th National People's Congress on August 29, 1998 stipulates that "Institutions of higher learning should check up the ideological and political performance, professional ethics, professional level and actual achievements in work of teachers, administrators…" implying that teachers, as student counselors or political counselors, are responsible for the development of a socialist higher education as guided by Marxism-Leninism, Mao Zedong Thought and Deng Xiaoping's Theory (MOE, n.d. b).

In addition, Document No. 16 reasserted the political counselor's position as a "teacher" in the context of the university's personnel system. Such assertion is expected to bring more confidence to student affairs practitioners, who, as Chen described, are marginalized in the daily routines of focusing mostly on student crisis management.

The multi-faceted roles of student affairs practitioners.

Qi & Tang (2004) summarized the main roles of student affairs work as being involved in education, administration, service, development, research, and instruction. Being an "educator" involves teaching IPE, counseling students who were required to accept their "assigned" majors and/or universities due to their low scores on the national university entrance examination[6], providing mental and physical health education, cultivating interest and skills in organization and coordination, safety education, instilling Party and CCYL knowledge, and adjusting to college life.

As administrators, student affairs practitioners deal with information management of student archives, employment agreement archives, and financial aid application processing. They also review Party and CCYL member qualification documents, deal with student behavior (such as disciplinary action and rewards, crisis management), attend meetings, and communicate with other campus entities and within student affairs. Services provided include personal counseling, freshmen orientation, student loan processing, providing part-time job opportunities, stipend allocation, processing tuition fee reduction, and offering career counseling and employment services.

Challenges in Staff Development for Student Affairs Practitioners

Chen (2002) wrote that the most significant challenge for student affairs practitioners is the irreconcilable role conflict

between the duties inherent within such roles and the employment trends in modern society. By law, student affairs practitioners as a group are members of the academic division, with the title of "teacher." However, they are often considered and treated, at least among some faculty colleagues, as babysitters of students, as policemen to handle accidents and crises involving students, and as servants of the faculty when extra hands are needed in teaching or administrative tasks. They are also often the group of staff to whom every department in the university can assign tasks concerning every aspect of students via issuing administrative orders (Shi & Zhu, 2002).

On one hand, student affairs practitioners' heavy administrative workload precludes them from doing research or writing academic papers, two essential elements needed for promotion and tenure of teachers. It would be easier to assess the "worth" of research and writing of a faculty member undergoing tenureship to receive recognition. However, it would be difficult to quantify or evaluate the worth of contributions made by faculty members towards students' welfare, co-curricular education and personal development. Many faculty members, therefore, simply shy away from such "administrative" duties even though they are considered as value-added functions. On the other hand, when these value-added functions are just part of the job duties of student affairs practitioners, the latter are not expected to be recognized because of the rigidity of the current personnel system which does not reward student affairs personnel through promotion or recognition. Student affairs practitioners are often discouraged from hoping for a promotion or expecting any recognition in their work.

High turn-over and lack of adequate accumulation of the necessary experience.

Professional development is difficult due to the high turnover rate of student affairs practitioners. They experience role conflicts and become burned out due to demanding workload. According to Shi and Zhu (2002), a majority of student affairs practitioners leave this line of work after only two or three years and then enroll in graduate programs or switch careers entirely.

As Zhan (2004) observed, quite a number of student affairs practitioners enter this profession only to use it as a stepping stone to their intended position of choice in the academic or administrative divisions. Thus, they have little investment in this career and no sense of responsibility or much interest in furthering their career in student services. Zhan also pointed out the difficulty of recruiting new workers with the potential and passion for student affairs work.

Varied educational backgrounds and a lack of any prerequisites for any professional knowledge specific to student affairs.

There are misconceptions among some student counselors who think that they are merely functioning as parents who take care of students' problems; or as operators of a

---

[6] In the existing higher education enrollment system, students are enrolled by their performance in the entrance examination. Those whose scores meet or exceed a pre-determined national standard are enrolled according to their choice as listed prior to the examination, while those with lower scores will be assigned to other majors or universities. Therefore, a number of freshmen not admitted to the university or major of their choice are faced with adaptation problems since they are to study in subjects they are not interested in.

locomotive that leads students in their extracurricular activities (Chen, 2003). It is not surprising that a majority of student affairs practitioners do not regard themselves as specialized professionals when their academic degrees are in irrelevant fields and when professional knowledge in education, administration, and other disciplines is not required.

Yet the diverse roles of student affairs practitioners—educator, administrator and a service provider—render student service work highly demanding and require specialized skills, including extensive experience in working with students as well as professional knowledge in multiple disciplines. The preparatory program most novice workers receive is merely a few days of introductory courses without further in-service training or development. The short tenures and high turnover rate are partly due to a lack of systematic professional development program to provide the necessary knowledge and skills, as well as the lack of a reward system that is essential to make this work more professionalized and recognized by academic colleagues (Shi & Zhu, 2002).

Fortunately, an increasing number of student affairs practitioners and scholars are beginning to emphasize the need for prerequisites in professional knowledge, obtained either through an academic or preparatory program specifically designed for student affairs administration prior to employment.

Concluding Remarks on the Future Prospects of Student Affairs Work in China

As the higher education system in China continues to evolve, develop, and expand, student enrollment will continue to increase. As access to higher education improves, university officials, faculty, and staff must recognize the non-academic needs of students and develop programs and services to meet those needs. Recruitment of student affairs administrators should be among one of the priorities of university administration and human resource planning. Recruitment strategies and standards need to be developed. Decisions need to be made on the academic qualifications and skills needed for student affairs practitioners.

China's most recent reform of its higher education systems began almost two decades ago and has concentrated on academic reform as well as organizational and institutional restructuring, merging single-discipline higher education institutions with others to form multi-discipline, and sometimes multi-campus university "systems"[7]. Reform efforts in the mid-1990s include Project 211, the Chinese government's endeavor to strengthen about 100 institutions of higher education and key disciplinary areas as a national priority for the 21st century. There was no mention in its objectives of any strategic planning for student support services or campus/student life. The main focus of this round of reform was on training high-level professional

man-power mainly for educational institutions, rather than for the broader society and the country. The only mention of "student development" is contained in a summary of Project 211 (CERNET, n.d.). The statement reads: "The reform of education and teaching will be carried out in depth in order to optimize the structure of academic programs (specialties) and to enhance the overall *student development* in moral, intellectual, and physical aspects, thus ensuring substantial improvement in the quality of education" (CERNET, n.d., para. 3). In describing teaching reform in China's higher education, a 1995 statement sought to enhance "...the cultural education of university students... moral and ideological quality, cultural quality, professional quality, and physical and psychological quality..." (Ministry of Education of the People's Republic of China, n.d., p. 4, para. 2). Such references to aspects that pertain to student development suggest that teaching reform is intended to go hand-in-hand with development of the non-academic side of students. However, in practice, student development and support, by and large, is still primarily focused on enforcement of university rules and regulations, organized control of student behavior, and "moral training" (i.e., ideological and political education) of citizenship.

The latest, more ambitious Project 985 (declared at Peking University's centennial celebration by former President Jiang Zemin on May 4, 1998, hence "985") was launched to build up some Chinese universities into world-class institutions. Project 985 encourages specific and further academic and faculty development, including enhancement of research and improvement of the quality of its undergraduate and graduate students. As a result, there has been a steady increase in activities such as international exchange of scholars, Chinese students studying abroad, and international students attending Chinese universities. However, while emphasizing the "quality" of its undergraduates academically, Project 985 fell short in specifically addressing the importance of students' out-of-classroom experiences that support student maturation and personal development. Such co- or extra-curricular experiences would include programs in career planning and guidance, job placement, learning skills, interpersonal skills and relationships, community involvement, leadership skills, health education, ability to be independent as well as interdependent, etc.

Mohrman (2003), in her Fulbright monograph, pointed out that generally the "non-academic side of student life" revolved around academic departments, with the exception of Zhongshan University where there was "expansion of student organizations, extracurricular activities, and counseling, all designed to support students' personal development." (p. 25). Duan (2003) wrote that campus life, in the past, was dull compared with today's "rich campus life" (such as clubs, competitions, performances, and festivals). The author used the term "bookworm" to describe a typical college student 20 years ago; whereas today's Chinese college students can be called "cosmopolitan," with numerous

---

[7]Information on reform efforts and statistics can be found at http://www.edu.cn/HomePage/english/index.shtml

non-academic interests. Campus life today is enhanced with newer "classrooms, libraries, computer labs, auditoriums, gyms, and indoor swimming pools" and "attractive campus landscapes." Duan (2003) indicated that 20 years ago, "six to eight students typically shared a standard single dormitory room" with very poor and simple amenities. But in "some leading universities nowadays, three students share one standard dormitory unit, which has a bathroom, a television, a telephone, and Internet-equipped computers." My visit in 2002 to several science and technology universities, a forestry university, Peking University, and Tsinghua University in Beijing supports Duan's contention that campus life, including student services such as financial assistance and career guidance, has indeed improved a great deal.

However, to fully develop students into knowledgeable and highly skilled citizens for China's future, a university's mission must include a systematic plan of specific goals and strategies based on the country's economic as well as social and cultural needs. This would seem to require a national mandate in specific terms in China's laws governing higher education. At the local level, academicians in higher education should conduct social and psychological research on the personal development of Chinese students. The results of such research could be applied to establishing a theoretical framework within which student affairs programs and services can be based. Academic preparatory programs can then be designed to train and produce graduate students who would become student affairs practitioners specializing in student development, programs, and services. They can then be mobilized to deal with issues and needs of students in contemporary and developing China.

A few student affairs practitioners from Asia Pacific rim countries contend that importing the U.S. concept of professionalization of student affairs management, and its model of graduate student personnel preparatory programs (Wong, 2004) may not be appropriate for Asian countries and their students. But Wong also argued that in order for student affairs practitioners to gain the respect of the faculty and administration in modern China, they need academic preparation and training in specific Chinese student development, including general human development theories, as well as in higher education administration and other relevant disciplines (e.g., psychology, sociology, political science, urban planning, counseling, etc.). This training should be established and administered within the context of the emerging and unique needs of China's university students, and within the context of China's diverse culture and rich history. Chinese student affairs practitioners must consider local community and social needs in implementing their programs and services. They must also collaborate with faculty and other institutions, whether local, regional or international, to share best practices. Finally, all practitioners must adopt a global perspective in order to be seen and treated as educators.

Recently, some Chinese faculty and student affairs practitioners (some of whom have faculty appointments) have begun to do just that. There is no shortage of articles in China on student affairs management, especially with the expansion of enrollment in the Chinese higher education sector. Administrative regulations and the behavior code for students in higher education were established in 1990 to regulate student conduct and campus order, with clearly defined mechanisms for awards and sanctions. However, student affairs practitioners have begun to embrace the concept of "total student development," and they look toward the international community of experts to help shape and orient China's student affairs programs, services, and administration.

Starting with the 1998 Hong Kong international conference on student services, organized by the Asia Pacific Student Services Association (APSSA), there has been a notable presence of delegates from China's higher education institutions at the biannual conferences. In addition, a number of student affairs practitioners from China's universities participated in "shadowing" programs sponsored by APSSA where they could spend up to three months in a student affairs office in Hong Kong and other Southeast Asian countries serving as interns. Informal administrative internships have also begun to gain importance. For example, this author personally received several requests to be "shadowed" at California State University Fullerton from an administrator at the President's Office of Zhongshan University (now known as Sun Yat-sen University).

Exchanges of faculty and students have been part of this international engagement with other countries in Europe, Australia, and to some degree, the United States. A reporter at China Education News, a prominent Chinese newspaper, highlighted 12 U.S. "Presidential Scholars" who were invited to visit China prior to their attending various colleges and universities in the United States. The article not only dispelled some of the myths about U.S. students in general, it also highlighted two Chinese American students in their quests for successful academic careers. All students were shown to be successful not only in the classroom, but also in their involvements in extra- and co-curricular activities such as community work. They showed understanding of diverse religions, languages, and cultures and demonstrated self-confidence and self-discipline. Inviting these scholars clearly attempts to demonstrate the value and importance of total or overall student development.

In addition, as globalization becomes more important for all universities around the world, Chinese university administrators are participating in initiatives such as The China University Administrators' Shadowing (CHUAS) Program, a component of education and training development activities established in 1999 by a formal agreement between the Australian Vice-Chancellors' Committee (AVCC) and the China Education Association for International Exchange (CEAIE) (Universities Australia, 2005, September). Although the Chinese participants mostly expressed interest in general or academic management at the university level, some showed interest in graduate student and international student "management." In the United States, in the absence of a strong central (federal) government interest or leadership, individual campuses or university systems, as well as national professional associations, tend to establish informal agreements or MOUs with individual campuses or associations in China. For example, the Association of Normal University Student Affairs in China (ANUSAC) formed an exchange agreement with NASPA in the United States (NASPA, n.d.)

Although it is uncertain if there are any professional associations in China at the national level specifically created for student affairs, municipal or provincial associations for student affairs and/or for ideological and political education do exist. The Beijing Association of College and University Student Affairs Workers invited speakers from Singapore, Hong Kong, and the United States (Permaul & Wang, 2002) to provide "advanced training" for a group of more than 75 student affairs practitioners at the director level. In 2003, a training conference was jointly sponsored by the Association of Student Personnel Work, the Research Association for Ideological and Political Education in Institutions of Higher Learning, Guangdong Province, and the Student Affairs Office of Sun Yat-sen (or Zhongshan) University. Funded by the Lingnan Foundation[8], the conference featured research papers presented by Zhongshan University faculty (Li & Hua, 2003), a faculty member from Beijing (Li, 2003), and administrators from the United States (Permaul, 2003; Wang, G., 2003; Wang, H., 2003). Fudan University, a sister university with California State University, Fullerton, seems to have an organized professional development and human resource cultivation program in the university's student affairs office. The university also has a counselors' association to provide professional development and support for its counselors.

If exchanges with practitioners from other countries can be encouraged and established, higher education in China will slowly but surely evolve to create its own brand of student affairs work that meets the needs of its students.

References

Cai, G.C.(2000). A comparative study of the concepts and definitions in student affairs administration in China and the United States. *Journal of Yangzhou University, Higher Education Study Edition, 4*(2), 56–59.

Central Committee of Chinese Communist Party and the State Council. (2004). Opinions of strengthening and improvement of college students' ideological and political education (Document No. 16). Ministry of Education of the People's Republic of China: author.

Chen, J. (2003, December). Reflections on position and work of counselors on ideology, theory, and education, pp. 78–80.

Chen, Y.D. (2002, October). The identities, responsibilities and role conflicts of student counselors. *Journal of Xianning Teachers College, 22*(5), 112–113.

China Education and Research Network (CERNET). (n.d.). *Project 211: A brief introduction (II) – The overall goals and mission of Project 211.* Retrieved September 21, 2005, from http://www.edu.cn/20010101/21852.shtml

Duan, X.R. (2003, November–December). Chinese higher education enters a new era. *Academe Online.* Washington, DC: American Association of University Professors.

He, H.B. (2004, November). The purpose of ideological and political education in the political socialization of citizens. *Journal of Si Chuan College of Education, 20*(11), 23–24.

Li, J.H. (2003). *Discussion on the development of student affairs.* Training workshop presented at the Advanced Training Program on Management of College Student Affairs, Guangzhou, China.

Li, P., & Hua, Z.M. (2003). *Research on the development of student affairs.* Training workshop presented at the Advanced Training Program on Management of College Student Affairs, Guangzhou, China.

Lin, J.H. (2003). Reflection on the political counselors' role as a part-time instructor in "two courses" in higher education institutions. *Journal of Zhangzhou Teachers College (Philosophy and Social Sciences), 3*(47), 104–106.

Lin, L. (2002, April). Challenges and methodology in higher education student management subsequent to student recruitment and expansion. *East China Economic Management, 16*(2), 160–161.

Ministry of Education of the People's Republic of China. (n.d.). *Higher education in China.* Retrieved September 21, 2005, from http://www.moe.edu.cn/english/higher_h.htm

MOE (Ministry of Education of the People's Republic of China. (n.d. b). Higher education law of the People's Republic of China. Chapter V, Article 51 and Chapter 1, Article 3. Retrieved May 12, 2008, from http://www.moe.edu.cn/edoas/website18/en/laws_h.htm

MOE (Ministry of Education of the People's Republic of China. (n.d. c). Administrative regulations and behavior code of students in higher education. Retrieved April 25, 2008, from http://www.moe.edu.cn/edoas/website18/info886.htm

MOE (Ministry of Education of the People's Republic of China. (n.d. d). Planning and statistics and Higher education pages. Retrieved September 21, 2005, from http://www.moe.edu.cn/edoas/website18/en/index.htm

Mohrman, K. (2003). *Higher education reform in Mainland Chinese universities: An American perspective.* Unpublished manuscript about the Fulbright Scholar Program, Chinese University of Hong Kong and the Hong Kong American Center.

---

[8]The Lingnan Foundation is a private foundation, formerly the Trustees of Lingnan University, first incorporated in the State of New York in 1893 to support the development of a college in Canton (Guangzhou), China that later became Lingnan University. Its activities are associated with the Lingnan (University) College, Zhongshan University. The Lingnan Foundation's mission is to contribute to the advancement of higher education in the historic Lingnan region of South China.

NASPA. (n.d.). NASPA goes international. Retrieved April 11, 2008, from http://www.naspa.org/programs/exchange.cfm

Permaul, J. (2003). *Education role of student affairs work: A perspective from American higher education*. Training workshop presented at the Advanced Training Program on Management of College Student Affairs, Guangzhou, China.

Permaul, J., & Wang, H. (2002). *Introduction to student affairs and services work*. Training workshop presented at the Advanced Training Course on University Student Affairs Administration, Beijing, China.

Qi, X.P. (2003). (Ed.). *The design and evaluation of student personnel work*. Guangzhou, China: Sun Yat-sen University Press.

Qi, X.P., & Tang, Y. (2005). (Eds.). *Student affairs administration in higher education*. Guangzhou, China: Sun Yat-sen University Press.

Ren, X.X., & Sun, Y.Y. (2002, January). The function of higher education in human socialization. *Journal of Shanghai University, 9*(1), 98–101.

Shi, Y.H., & Zhu, S.F. (2002). Specialization: An essential pathway to the establishment of full-time political counselors group in colleges and universities. *Heilongjiang Researches on Higher Education, 5*(109), 28–30.

Sun, A.H. (2000, November). Socialization of politics: A basic point in collegiate education. *Journal of China Youth College for Political Sciences, 19*(6), 6–9.

Tang, Y., Qi, X.P., & Wong, Z.C. (2002). (Eds). *The education and management of students after the expansion of enrollment*. In Monographs of the Association of Student Personnel Work and Research Association for Ideological and Political Education in Institutions of Higher Learning, Guangdong Province. Guangzhou, China: Zhongshan University Press.

Universities Australia. (2005, September). China and Australia renew agreement to strengthen cooperation and collaboration. Retrieved, April 11, 2008, from http://www.avcc.edu.au/content.asp?page=/news/media_releases/2005/avcc_media_45_05.htm

Wang, B.S. (2003, January). A comparison of student affairs administration between colleges in Hong Kong and Mainland China. *Journal of Northeastern University (Social Science), 5*(1), 70–72.

Wang, G. (2003). *Financial aid in U.S. higher education*. Training workshop presented at the Advanced Training Program on Management of College Student Affairs, Guangzhou, China.

Wang, H. (2003). *Technology in Student Affairs*. Training workshop presented at the Advanced Training Program on Management of College Student Affairs, Guangzhou, China.

Wang, Y. 2004, February). The unforgettable domain: Advances in student affairs work in higher education institutions. *Journal of Technical Higher Education, 23*(1), 9–12.

Wong, S. K. L. (2004). Country report: Hong Kong. *Proceedings of the 9ᵗʰ Asia Pacific Student Services Association Conference*, Bangkok, Thailand, 10–12.

Yao, Z., Zhen, C., & Wen, Z. (1995). A review of tuition and employment system reforms in China's higher education institutions. *Research World, 1*, 61–76.

Zhan, L.P. (2002). Reflections on the establishment of college counselors in Jilin Province in the new era. *Modern Education Science, 5*(185), 109–111.

TEN

HONG KONG
SPECIAL ADMINISTRATIVE REGION, CHINA

Carol Tang and Kwok Hung Lai

Hong Kong, having been a British colony for more than 150 years, inherited much of its political, legal, and economic systems from Britain. The education system in colonial Hong Kong, without exception, was monolithic, elitist, apolitical, and examination-oriented, emphasizing economic and pragmatic values of education. However, in response to the signing of the *Sino-British Joint Declaration on the Question of Hong Kong* and the transfer of sovereignty to the People's Republic of China (PRC) in 1997, there has since been pressure for the government of the newly designated "Special Administrative Region" (SAR) to prepare pupils to become competent citizens, and to develop a politically literate and active population in order to function as an autonomous political and economic entity (Lai, 1998, 1999).

Higher Education in the Era of Change

The transfer of sovereignty accelerated the linkage with China as well as the movement of university graduates in the labor market between China and Hong Kong. Extending Hong Kong's external linkages makes it necessary for Hong Kong to become a regional center that produces an enriched talented pool of graduates. The changing political and social environment also brings increasing demand for graduates to be highly adaptable to change and for Hong Kong to provide life-long education to such graduates. The recently adopted Education Commission report "Learning for Life, Learning Through Life: Reform Proposals for the Education System in Hong Kong" clearly states that the overall goal of education for the 21st century should emphasize the all-round development of students (Education Commission, 2000). Such student development would include solidifying students' abilities and attitudes for life-long learning, nurturing them to become confident, instilling in them a sense of justice and social responsibility, and enabling them to have a global outlook.

Higher education has existed in Hong Kong for nearly a century, beginning with the founding of the University of Hong Kong in 1911. The Chinese University of Hong Kong was established in 1963 by merging three tertiary colleges. Tertiary education in the past decade has expanded rapidly. Two polytechnics have been transformed into universities, another three tertiary education institutes have been upgraded to become self-accredited universities, four teacher training colleges have merged into one university, and two new technical colleges have been established to offer sub-degree vocational training courses. All together, the number of government-funded institutions increased from two to eight. Seven of the eight institutions are universities and the remaining one an institute for teacher education.

The increasing demand for higher education and support from the Hong Kong Government are evident in the escalating percentage of participation in higher education among cohorts that graduate from secondary schools: from about 2% in the 1970s to approximately 18% in 1994. Although in his *Policy Address 2000*, the Chief Executive targeted 60% of Hong Kong's senior secondary school graduates to receive tertiary education by 2010, the latest participation rate of secondary school graduates attending full-time first degree programs funded by the government is unchanged from the 1994 figure of 18%. This is due to budget cuts after the "Asian financial crisis" in 1997 and the economic downturn in the early 2000s.[1]

History of Student Affairs and Services

Student affairs did not emerge as a defined area of work in universities until the early 1970s. The "Student Movement" in Hong Kong in 1967 prompted moves to improve communication between the university and its students so that students' needs could be identified and better addressed. As a result, the University of Hong Kong appointed its dean of students, and the Polytechnic University appointed its head of Student Services Unit in the early 1970s. Under their leadership, small-scale student

---

[1] For the full text of the Policy Address 2000, see http://www.policyaddress.gov.hk/pa00/pa00_e.htm. For highlights of the address, visit http://www.policyaddress.gov.hk/pa00/hlight_ehtm

services began, focusing on careers and employment. Some form of student services were also offered at the Chinese University of Hong Kong.

In the 1970s and 1980s, student affairs offices were established gradually at other universities. At some universities, the functional "sections" within the department were very independent, each staffed with field specialists. However, resources were shared within the departmental structure. Many other universities took a more generalist approach, and staff members, other than those in counseling services, were expected to rotate jobs. For example, in 1998 after restructuring of the technical institutes and technical colleges, the Hong Kong Institute of Vocational Education (IVE) merged its civic education, student counseling, and physical education sections into one Student Affairs Office (Hong Kong Institute of Vocational Education, n.d.).

Student affairs offices in all institutions are funded by the government, either through the University Grants Committee (UGC) or the Education and Manpower Bureau, in about the same way.[2] These offices are responsible, either directly or indirectly, for more or less the same areas of work that include student guidance and counseling, career and employment, financial assistance and scholarships, sports and recreational facilities, student amenities, residence halls, health services, food services, co-curricular activities, students with disabilities, and international students. In short, Wong (2004) simply described "student affairs" in Hong Kong as a "U.S. concept being implemented in a U.K. higher education system."

Student Services Delivery Model

Although all higher education institutions in Hong Kong offer similar student services, student affairs organization, management, delivery systems, concepts and approaches, and methods in measuring outcomes differ significantly. In recent years, however, student affairs practice has evolved from emphasizing service and management to the "total education" of students. The current trend is to enrich the campus life of these institutions to encourage whole-person development.

The scope of student affairs at the University of Hong Kong, the oldest tertiary institution in Hong Kong, covers both undergraduates and postgraduates, and services are delivered by three units under the dean of student affairs, who is considered as one of the officers of the university. The three units are the office of student affairs (University of Hong Kong, n.d.) , the careers education and placement center (University of Hong Kong, 2008), and the personal development and counseling center (Hong Kong University, 2005). While these three student affairs units operate autonomously, each with different emphasis, efforts are now being made to integrate student affairs programs and share

resources and expertise, including the sharing of support staff and accommodation wherever possible (Hung, 1998).

The newly established universities are ready for more radical changes. In July 1998, the president of the City University of Hong Kong approved a request by the student affairs office to change its name to Student Development Services (SDS) to better reflect a change in emphasis from a more service-oriented, remedial, and maintenance-focused office to one that provides activities and programs that are development oriented, proactive, focused on the enrichment of students' educational experiences, and based on the concept of whole person development (Yu, 1998). The Student Whole Person Development Model includes seven areas: spiritual development, intellectual development, physical development, social development, aesthetic development, career development, and emotional development (Student Development Services, n.d.)

The Student Services Centre (SSC) at Lingnan University (n.d.) provides administrative support in implementing the portion of the Integrated Learning Program (ILP) that aims to enrich students' learning experiences, enhance their skills in thinking and judgment, enable them to interact with others, inspire their creative thinking, and expand their cultural horizons. This is done through five areas: (a) civic education; (b) intellectual development; (c) physical education; (d) social and emotional development; and (e) aesthetic development (Lingnan University, n.d.). All undergraduate students are required to take a minimum number of ILP units for all five areas during their study. In keeping with the university's strong liberal arts education tradition, the president meets with all the students over breakfast for dialogue. Student affairs practitioners are responsible for logistic arrangements of this activity, including publicity, recruitment and enrollment, catering, and other related administrative tasks (Wong, 1999). The president himself seems to have taken on the role of "chief" of the Student Services Center when he communicates with the students directly by meeting and discussing with them their future goals.

Student affairs practice at the Hong Kong University of Science and Technology (HKUST) has followed an integrated or holistic approach since the office was established in 1990 (Yuen, 1998). Its mission emphasizes personal growth and development, quality of campus life, and services to students to help with problem solving and support academic learning. It serves as communication liaison between students and the university. The director of student affairs oversees all student services, including personal counseling, career guidance, physical education, amenities, residence halls, and scholarships and financial assistance. (Hong Kong University of Science and Technology (HKUST), n.d. a). Within the HKUST student affairs office, there are three senior staff members: one senior student affairs officer, one senior physical education officer, and one senior student officer (HKUST, n.d. b) . Each officer oversees a few operating units that cover a broad range of work. There is less emphasis on professional boundaries among the units, thus providing

---

[2]For a brief description of UGC, see committee at
http://www.ugcs.gov.hk/eng/ugc/about/secretariat/home.htm or
http://www.ugc.edu.hk/eng/ugc/index.htm. For the Education and Manpower
Bureau, visit http://www.emb.gov.hk

greater opportunities for collaborative efforts and team work. Jobs are rotated.

Various student development services were incorporated into the routine work of the student affairs office. One important function is to provide different kinds of developmental programs, including a compulsory "Key Skills Module" for all first year students (Lai, 2004). With the launching of this mandatory learning module, it seems that the Student Affairs Office is serving in a subordinating role to those teaching departments.

Professional Student Affairs Organizations

In early 1978, student affairs personnel of the four major tertiary institutions in Hong Kong agreed that they should meet occasionally. Subsequently, they met three times a year to share issues of common concern and to help each other with common problems. In July 1982, some practitioners believed that there was sufficient interest to form a professional society, so a formal proposal was presented to all student affairs practitioners in tertiary institutions to form The Professional Association of Student Services. Subsequently, a constitution was drafted, the new organization was named The Hong Kong Student Services Association (HKSSA). The organization was formally constituted in December 1984, and the first executive committee was elected, chaired by Mr. Luke Wong, then senior student affairs officer of the University of Hong Kong. As stated in the constitution, the objectives of the HKSSA are: (a) to advance, develop, and strengthen student service work among members; (b) to assist students in better fulfilling their educational goals through provision of service; and (c) to promote interaction and cooperation among persons in student service work in Hong Kong and abroad (Hong Kong Student Services Association, 2007).

With a small membership and a limited budget, the association had a modest beginning. The major activities were guest speakers at dinners, visits to tertiary institutions in neighboring areas, and social functions. The first major professional event was organized as the first Asia Pacific Student Affairs Conference in Hong Kong in July 1988. The success of the conference led to the formation of the Asia Pacific Student Services Association (APSSA).[3] The association's constitution was confirmed in 1990; its secretariat is based in Hong Kong, where it is served by the HKSSA. APSSA is registered in Hong Kong. Its objectives are: (a) to enhance liaison and cooperation among members in the development of student affairs work and student services in the Asia Pacific region; (b) to assist in the development of student affairs work and to strengthen its role in the development of tertiary education in the region; (c) to promote the welfare of students in tertiary education; and (d) to enhance intercultural understanding and develop intercultural communication skills among members.

Since then, with the rapid expansion of tertiary education in Hong Kong, the number of persons involved in student affairs work increased—and so have resources available to the association. Members of HKSSA include staff members from eight government-funded institutions, two other institutions in Hong Kong, and one university from Macau. As of March 2005, HKSSA had a total of 68 full members, whereas APSSA had 36 institutional members and 26 individual members from seven countries/regions.

Professional Training and Education

Since local universities in Hong Kong do not offer specialized degree programs in student affairs work, an increasing number of colleagues seek to advance professionally through attaining doctoral and postgraduate diplomas/degrees in related fields, such as management, education, counseling, social work, public administration, social policy, law, and sociology. At the same time, the HKSSA and its working groups routinely conduct educational seminars and workshops on areas of concern among colleagues, such as advancing student affairs, law and student affairs, benchmarking and quality assurance, hall life education, and more. During the past few years, the association also organized regular study tours and training programs, often visiting various universities at different cities in Mainland China, such as Beijing, Shanghai, Guangzhou, Jilin, and Xizang.

Aside from activities organized by the HKSSA, colleagues are also actively involved in various training programs conducted by APSSA, such as the bi-annual student services conferences, study tours to the United Kingdom and Germany, and various types of training workshops organized by APSSA's Institute of Student Affairs. APSSA established the institute in July 2000 for the training and development of student affairs practitioners in higher education at the international level.

APSSA also launched the Student Affairs Laboratories project in 1998, which aims to provide cross-institution and cross-country student affairs experiences by attaching student affairs practitioners to other member universities. This is a kind of "campus life laboratory." It is a residential facility on campus intended for a student affairs practitioner to live and conduct systematic studies on student residential and campus life. As in other kinds of laboratories, users are not required to pay for its use. Participants in staff attachment programs only need to pay for travel and food. More than 10 institutions in the Asian Pacific Region are ready to serve as host institutions. They offer dozens of work areas with proven success and documentation, and these can provide significant leaning opportunities for participants. In 1999–2000, an award scheme was launched to encourage staff attachment activities among members. One university in Hong Kong, which has been very active in promoting staff attachment and its student life laboratory, attracted many student affairs practitioners from abroad. Some local student affairs practitioners have also sought attachment

---

[3]For APSSA membership information, member benefits, and current list of executive committee members, see http://home.ust.hk/~sanet/apssa.htm

opportunities in Singapore, the Philippines, Germany, and the United States. For example, an informal staff exchange occurred in 1999 between the student affairs offices at the University of California at Los Angeles and the Hong Kong University of Science and Technology, each spending about one month rotating through various student affairs departments on the two campuses.

Inter-Institutional Collaboration

Hong Kong, with an area of only about 1,050 sq. km., has an excellent communication system and transportation network that promotes collaborative efforts among student affairs practitioners at all levels and from various institutions. They meet each other in person, with frequent formal as well as informal interactions. Joint efforts began on a small scale in the 1970s and have grown significantly over the years in participation and diversity in membership from different student services areas. The student affairs practitioners believe that by pooling their expertise they can provide enhanced services to the student population at large. The achievements of such collective efforts have been remarkable. The importance of cross-institutional collaboration has been recognized. Some of the major collaborative efforts were:

◊ *Joint efforts in the promotion of student activities.* Dating back to 1972, joint efforts between the University of Hong Kong and the Chinese University of Hong Kong began with an inter-varsity debate competition. This was the first program under a commercial sponsorship to promote interest in debating activities and interaction among students of the two universities. The competition was well received by the students and later became an annual event.

◊ *Joint universities creative works exhibitions/other joint projects.* The exhibitions were organized jointly by the two universities in 1983 and 1984 to promote creativity and to develop friendship among students. Also in 1984, the Incorporated Trustees of Hsin Chong – K.N. Godfrey Yeh Education Fund sponsored a Wellness Training Program to promote inter-institutional and interdisciplinary cooperation among four institutions. Successful collaborations in the 1980s included a four-day conference on student affairs and higher education in an era of change, a civic education night, an "interflow camp," and a conference on the role of students' unions in tertiary institutions. More than 50 joint projects of various kinds were sponsored in the early 1990s (Ha and Wong, 1996).

◊ *The China Synergy Program for Outstanding Students.* This program was supported by eight UGC-funded institutions in Hong Kong. It was established in 1998 to encourage and reward outstanding Chinese youths who are residing overseas and in Hong Kong, Macau, and Taiwan. Through participation in exchange activities in Hong Kong, Guangdong, Xian, Beijing and Shanghai, approximately 200 outstanding university students get to learn

more about the socio-economic, technological, and cultural developments in China. Activities included meeting with top government officials and prominent leaders, visiting major universities and participating in exchange activities with local university students, visiting local and foreign enterprises in China, and attending lectures presented by distinguished scholars, as well as sightseeing. The program has successfully brought together ethnic Chinese candidates from all over the world

◊ *Joint Institution Job Information System (JIJIS).* Developed by seven universities in Hong Kong, JIJIS was launched in 1995. This is a database system that provides convenient, efficient, and accurate services to: employers submitting job postings; students seeking employment; and career counselors collecting, retrieving, and organizing job information. A JIJIS Management Committee with representatives from all participating institutions oversees the development of the system and related policies. The system setup was funded by a government grant, and the maintenance cost is shared by participating institutions. While data entry to the system is handled separately by individual institutions, a Joint Information Center, based in the Career Services Unit of the host institution, is responsible for its overall operation. This joint project transcends institutional boundaries in career work and leads to re-conceptualization of employment services. In the 1990s, career counselors from seven universities jointly published *Career Prospects,* a career guide for graduating students. They also conducted a joint study on the career development of graduates in the years 1988 to 1990.

◊ *Outstanding Student Services Award Scheme.* The Hong Kong Student Services Association (HKSSA) established an outstanding student services awards scheme in 1991 to encourage students to develop leadership in community service. Twenty awards annually are given to full-time undergraduates on the basis of students' record of social involvement, their leadership potential, and participation in extra-curricular activities, as well as academic standing. In 1993, 35 previous award recipients formed the Hong Kong Outstanding Tertiary Students' Services Association, whose objectives are to arouse students' awareness of community welfare and to encourage joint efforts in promoting students' participation in social services.

◊ *Jockey Club Summer Internship Project.* With stronger linkage to Mainland China after 1997 and the growing importance of globalization, there is an urgent need for Hong Kong students to gain wider exposure and be able to serve in Mainland China as well as in places all over the world. Student affairs practitioners try hard to provide learning opportunities to students in the form of summer internships so that they may gain first-hand experience working in non-local environments. In 2002, a joint proposal was submitted to the Hong Kong Jockey Club Charities Trust, soliciting sponsorship for a three-year summer internship program for 1,500 undergraduate students from eight tertiary institutions. The organization donated HK$16 million ($2 million USD) for this joint institutional project, and students have been placed in major cities in China such as Beijing, Shanghai, Xian, and the Pearl River Delta, as well as in other countries. Participants are able to gain better understanding of the business operations as well as cultural and social practices in Mainland China and other countries.

◊ *Special working groups.* The desire to promote general health care of local tertiary students brought student affairs practitioners and university medical staff together. In 1991, the Hong Kong Tertiary Institutions Health Care Working Group was established as a special work group under the HKSSA. Currently, 10 institutions participate in the working group, which is chaired by a medical doctor and includes registered nurses, counselors, and student affairs officers. The working group focuses on studying the health profiles of tertiary students, promoting awareness of current health issues among them, and organizing inter-institutional health activities for the students. It has conducted a number of cross-institutional surveys on topics related to health status, sexual behavior, and stress level of undergraduate students. The findings of the surveys informed relevant parties of the needs of students, and directions for the development of health-related programs and services. The working group also launched health promotion campaigns and activities, produced pamphlets and booklets on specific health topics, and organized a series of exhibitions. Thanks to the working group, more proactive rather than reactive measures have been adopted in health education and health care services in the tertiary institutions.

◊ *The Hong Kong Tertiary Institutions Psychological Counseling Working Group.* This group was established in March 2001 to promote and develop psychological counseling services in tertiary institutions in Hong Kong. Its objectives are: (a) to encourage the exchange of professional knowledge and skills among psychological counselors working in local tertiary institutions, (b) to work on issues related to psychological counseling common to all institutions, and (c) to foster professional sharing with counterparts in China and other countries. Activities organized by the working group in the past few years included exchange visits to counseling centers in Taiwan, production of educational materials such as handouts for faculty members on university freshmen, and many professional development discussions and workshops on such topics as counseling for Mainland students, basic solution-focused therapy, and psychological first-aid.

Funding of Student Affairs Services

Currently, eight universities are funded through the UGC and one through the Education and Manpower Branch of the Hong Kong Government. In 2003–04, the approved grants for UGC-funded institutions amounted to 5.5% of the total government expenditure and 23.6% of the total government expenditure on education. Students of UGC-funded institutions pay around 18% of the annual student unit cost, with the remaining 82% funded by the government. Students studying in private universities and colleges pay much more. The government provides financial assistance in the form of means-tested grants and loans to needy students of full-time UGC-funded programs and non-means-tested loans to all needy students irrespective of the source of funding of their study programs. This is to ensure that no student is deprived of the opportunity to study because of financial difficulty.

In tertiary institutions funded by UGC, the student affairs office relies mostly on public funding to support its operations. A one-line budget for non-staffing expenses is allocated to the office on a triennium basis, and the office is free to allocate resources to specific areas of work. Student affairs offices usually put significant resources into promoting campus life and student learning through student development programs. In the past, provisions in terms of space and equipment, staffing, and recurrent expenses have been sufficient, but in recent years, because of serious budget cuts, institutions have allocated more resources to academic work than to student affairs. Student affairs work is considered supportive or complementary in nature. Principles such as "pay for play" and cost-sharing have been adopted, with students sharing part of the operating costs of sports facilities or student development program expenses. Food service and student halls are defined by self-financed items, according to UGC guidelines, and cross-subsidization is not allowed. Much effort is placed upon income generation through external funding sources, such as leasing of student halls during vacation periods.

Student Affairs within the Campus Structure

An Example at Hong Kong Institute of Education (HKIEd)

All institutions have a well-defined student affairs structure. The chief executive in student affairs normally bears the title of director of student affairs. In the early days, the student affairs offices reported to the president, indicating the centrality of students and student affairs. As the presidents became burdened with other priorities, vice presidents were asked to oversee student affairs. Currently, most student affairs offices report to a vice president or equivalent position of the institution. At some other institutions, the director of student affairs reports to the dean of students, which is a concurrent post held by a full-time faculty member. The fact that the student affairs office is placed under the line manager holding an administrative or academic position reflects the different emphasis on student affairs work. In general, the director of student affairs is a member of most of the institution-level committees, including the Senate where academic policies and decisions are made. At one university, the dean of students is a member of the Council, contributing to the governance and development of the university. At this university, only the director of student affairs sits on the student disciplinary committee since it is perceived that the role of the student affairs office is to represent, support, and advise students. At the Hong Kong Institute of Education, the chief executive is currently called the head of student affairs. Previously reporting to the president, the student affairs office of HKIEd now reports to a vice president in charge of academic support services. The head of student affairs is a member of the academic board and numerous committees: estates development and management, resource allocation, non-academic staff development, institutional partnership, student affairs, scholarship and prizes, and student grievances. He or she also serves on institutional advisory groups or work groups, such as the advisory group on strategic planning and equal opportunities work. The head of student affairs is required to attend various formal institutional functions, as well as meetings with media.

Student affairs practitioners are normally classified as administrative staff or staff of academic support units and are remunerated on a pay scale different from that of academic staff. At some institutions, student affairs practitioners bear different functional titles which reflect their work portfolio but not necessarily their rank. For example, some practitioners have titles of director of campus life or head of the Leadership Development Institute to reflect the work areas for which they are responsible. Under the leadership of the director, usually there are section heads, mid-level professionals, and junior professionals. They are supported by a team of executive and clerical staff. Most institutions have a more integrated organizational structure with four basic sections: counseling, physical education, student amenities and administration, and student health. Those putting greater emphasis on student development may have a student development/student activities section. Professional boundaries among the sections may not be as distinct or emphasized as in other countries, and cooperation among teams is encouraged. Some new institutions have adopted an integrated matrix structure. Staff members in sections that require a particular professional background, such as counseling, physical education, and amenities, interact with those in management services, as well as with those having educational and liaison functions of student affairs (Wong, 1999). Staff members are pooled to perform specific tasks without rigid professional or administrative boundaries.

Student affairs practitioners at HKIEd are administrative staff and have the title of officer (e.g., student affairs officer), which does not reflect the functions of their work areas. The office adopts the integrated matrix model and staff members, except for the counseling staff, are expected to be multi-skilled and capable of multi-tasking. Job rotations are normally required. Counselors, on the other hand, are expected to concentrate on specific areas of service. At HKEld, because the student affairs office gives special emphasis to providing non-formal education programs to complement formal curricula in the development of prospective teachers, each of the student affairs practitioners is expected to play a greater role as an educator.

Collaboration among Student Affairs, Other Campus Entities, and Teaching Faculty

The relationship between the student affairs office and the teaching faculty differs from one institution to another. While some student affairs offices play a leading role in promoting all-around development of students, complementing or even guiding the teaching faculty where appropriate, others may play a more subordinate role, providing only administrative support to the teaching faculty in the education of students.

On the whole, there is frequent contact and collaboration with offices of public affairs, alumni affairs, registry, estates office, information technology services, and teaching faculties on matters related to publicity, image building, campus facilities, networking, student record system, admission of students, and student support services. It seems that student affairs offices and the academic departments collaborate in productive efforts to promote the universities' mission and educational goals. For instance, the student services center at Lingnan University collaborates with various units toward all-around development of students (Tam, 2002). It also actively helps to coordinate community services through service–learning projects, (Tam, 2004). At the Morrison Hill campus of the Hong Kong Institute of Vocational Education, the Department of Business Services and Management and the Student Affairs Office are working together to launch peer mentorship and service–learning programs (Lai and Chan, 2004). Also, academic staff members are involved in a research project on campus culture and values (Lai, 2000). At the City University of Hong Kong, academic colleagues and student societies actively collaborate in Total Quality Management (Yu, 2000).

At HKIEd, where the student affairs office is heavily involved in formulating the institute's strategic plan, the student affairs office maintains a close relationship with academic and non-academic staff (Tang, 1999). Student affairs officers at HKIEd present themselves in a multiplicity of roles. They are developers of non-formal curricula, experienced organizers of student activities, skilled trainers for specific student development programs, experts in knowledge of students, facilities managers, and resource persons for supporting and advising students. Each officer is responsible for the liaison work with specified academic program personnel to ensure that the needs of the student groups are met and that the students are aware of the services the student affairs office provides. All staff members are expected to maintain a harmonious working relationship with colleagues of other departments so that collaborative efforts can be made to improve services.

Student Affairs – The Way Ahead

Student affairs and student services in Hong Kong have been making steady progress since the practice was established in the early 1970s. Thanks to the early leaders in the field of student affairs who actively promoted mutual support and cross-institutional collaboration, student affairs practitioners are now able to work together and learn from each other. This is particularly important in the era of change, when student affairs practitioners must face much greater challenges. With joint efforts that transcend traditional professional, institutional, and administrative boundaries, challenges can be transformed into opportunities. Some areas that may require greater attention include:

◊ *Budget cuts.* The resources of student affairs offices have been reduced reduced significantly over the last few years. The budget cuts have led to serious debate, as well as to staff and student protests. Though the government has not yet confirmed further reductions, the extent of budget cuts have already called for a new mind set, new service models, and a new culture. New approaches include increased use of Web-assisted services, collaborative efforts in sourcing external sponsorship for joint projects, and efforts to improve efficiency. New cost-saving strategies have to be developed without compromising service quality.

◊ *Expansion of higher education sector.* With the fast-expanding student population in the tertiary sector and the increased number of self-funded academic programs, there is an increased demand for student affairs practitioners and the need to provide student services at lower costs. While formal training in student affairs is not available in Hong Kong, the Hong Kong Student Services Association extends its support to new practitioners through organizing sharing sessions, seminars, and workshops. In a few cases, new institutions have invited experienced student affairs practitioners from other institutions to serve as consultants or service providers in specific areas. This stimulates more sharing of expertise among institutions and broadening of income sources for some institutions.

◊ *Internationalization.* Internationalization of higher education is one of the targets set by the University Grants Committee. The percentage of international students at each institution is increasing. This brings challenges concerning the medium of instruction at universities, the development of campus culture, and adjustment of students. Student affairs practitioners have an important role to play in helping both local and non-local students to maximize their learning through enhanced interactions.

◊ *Strengthened educator role.* As the educator role becomes more prominent, student affairs practitioners should become more concerned about the quality of the education work offered and the integration of student learning with student life on campus. It has become important to develop systematic quality assurance and improvement processes. The University Grants Committee in Hong Kong adopted six quality principles to measure the education work in tertiary institutions. These quality principles are related to measuring learning outcomes, focusing on the student learning process, ensuring coherence of quality processes, delivering quality education as a collaborative responsibility, benchmarking with good practices, and giving priority to continuous improvement (Tang, 2002). In addition, they are required to work closely with the academic staff to systematically integrate formal and non-formal education programs that improve student learning.

References

Ha, O., & Wong, V. (1996). *Joint effort of student services personnel in developing new programmes for students in Hong Kong.* Paper presented at the Hong Kong Workshop and the International Symposium at NASPA.

Hong Kong Institute of Vocational Education (IVE). (n.d.). IVE. Retrieved April 11, 2008, from http://www.vtc.edu.hk/vtc/web/template/institute_desc_list.jsp?fldr_id=438&lang=en

Hong Kong Student Services Association (HKSSA). (2007). Hong Kong student services association. Retrieved April 14, 2008, from http://home.ust.hk/~hkssa/

Hong Kong University of Science and Technology. (n.d. a). About student affairs office. Retrieved April 14, 2008, from https://www.ab.ust.hk/sao/dir1/saservices.htm

Hong Kong University of Science and Technology. (n.d. a). About the student affairs office: Organization chart. Retrieved April 14, 2008, from https://www.ab.ust.hk/sao/dir1/sastru.htm

Hung, S. (1998). Coping with budget cuts. In *Managing change in student affairs: A collection of papers prepared by members of the Asia Pacific Student Services Association attending the annual meeting of the Association of Managers of Student Services in Higher Education* (pp. 9–12). Brighton, United Kingdom.

Lai, K. H. (1998). A new direction for civic education in Hong Kong SAR. *Journal of Youth Studies, 1*(1): 151–58.

Lai, K. H. (1999). Civic education: A focus on student affairs practice after reunification. *Educational Studies, 25*(1): 141–51.

Lai, K. H. (2004). *Learning resource centre – An attempt to total education.* Paper presented at the Seminar on Student Services, Jilin University, China.

Lai, K. H. (2000). *Staff and student culture orientation: Implications on student affairs services.* Paper presented at the 7th Asia Pacific Student Services Association Conference, Manila, Philippines.

Lai, K. H., & Chan, T. (2004). A collaborative student affairs and department peer mentorship and service learning initiatives. *Proceedings of the 9th Asia Pacific Student Services Association Conference*, Bangkok, Thailand, pp. 181–187.

Education Commission. (2000). Learning for life, learning through life: Reform proposals for the education system in Hong Kong. Education Commission, HKSAR: Printing Department, pp. 1–6.

Lingnan University. (n.d.). Introduction to the integrated learning programme (ILP). Retrieved April 14, 2008, from http://www.ln.edu.hk/ssc/ilp/

Student Development Services. (n.d.). Whole person development award scheme. Retrieved April 11, 2008, from http://www.cityu.edu.hk/sds/wpd/index.htm

Tam, S. P. V. (2004). Community based development and social responsibility from community service to service-learning – The way forward. *Proceedings of the 9th Asia Pacific Student Services Association Conference*, Bangkok, Thailand, pp. 58–61.

Tam, S. P. V. (2002). *Integrated effort in developing all-round students.* Paper presented at the 8th Asia Pacific Student Affairs Conference, Kuala Lumpur, Malaysia.

Tang, C. (1999). Building partnerships in promoting student learning and student success. *Managing change in student affairs: A collection of papers prepared by members of the Asia Pacific Student Services Association attending the annual meeting of the Association of Managers of Student Services in Higher Education,* United Kingdom, Brighton, pp. 13–16.

Tang, C. (2002). *Enhancing the quality of student development programs.* Paper presented at the 8th Asia Pacific Student Affairs Conference, Kuala Lumpur, Malaysia.

University of Hong Kong. (n.d.). Centre of development and resources for students (CEDARS). Retrieved April 14, 2008, from http://www.hku.hk/osa/

University of Hong Kong. (2005). Centre of development and resources for students: Student development and counseling. Retrieved April 14, 2008 from http://www.hku.hk/sdcsc/

University of Hong Kong. (2008). Centre of development and resources for students careers and placement. Retrieved April 14, 2008, from http://www.hku.hk/cepc/NEW/index.html

Wong, S. K. L. (2004). Country report: Hong Kong. *Proceedings of the 9th Asia Pacific Student Services Association Conference*, Bangkok, Thailand, pp. 10–12.

Wong, S.K.L. (1999). Development of student affairs in Hong Kong. In Dalton, J. C. (ed.) *Beyond borders: How international developments are changing student affairs practice.* San Francisco: Jossey-Bass.

Wong, W. M. (1999). The president meets all students over breakfast: Implications on student affairs work. *Managing change in student affairs: A collection of papers prepared by members of the Asia Pacific Student Services Association attending the annual meeting of the Association of Managers of Student Services in Higher Education.* Brighton, United Kingdom, pp. 29–30.

Yu, E. (1998). *Student whole person development – The city university experience.* Paper presented at the 6th Asia Pacific Student Affairs Conference, Hong Kong.

Yu, E. (2000). *TQM in student development services.* Paper presented at the 7th Asia Pacific Student Services Association Conference, Manila, Philippines.

Yuen, P. (1998). *Training for development of a new multi-skill workshop culture.* Paper presented at the 6th Asia Pacific Student Affairs Conference, Hong Kong.

ELEVEN

MALAYSIA

R. Ambihabathy and Mohd Razali Agus

The overall philosophy of education in Malaysia is guided by the National Philosophy of Education.

Education in Malaysia is an on-going effort towards further developing the potential of individuals in a holistic and integrated manner, so as to produced individuals who are intellectually, spiritually, emotionally, and physically balanced and harmonious, based on a firm belief in and devotion to God. Such an effort is designed to produce Malaysian citizens who are knowledgeable and competent, who possesses high moral standards, and who are responsible and capable of achieving a high level of personal well-being [as well] as being able to contribute to the harmony and betterment of the family, the society and the nation at large. (Ministry of Education Malaysia, n.d., para. 1).

The education system in Malaysia starts with preschool, normally from the age of four to six years, followed by six years of primary education and generally followed by five years of secondary education, which culminates with the Sijil Pelajaran Malaysia Examination (SPM) (Wikipedia, n.d.). The SPM is the equivalent of the British General Certificate of Education "O" levels examination. Depending on grades, preferences, support, and financial resources, students are then likely to enrol for Sijil Tinggi Pelajaran Malaysia (STPM) or matriculation courses, A-levels (U.K.-based A-levels offered by private colleges), or pre-professional courses (Wikipedia, n.d.).

Upon successful completion of these courses, the final lap for most students will be tertiary education. Students who enroll at the public universities are predominantly from the Sijil Tinggi Pelajaran Malaysia (STPM) or matriculation courses, whereas private universities and colleges accommodate students from A-level and pre-professional courses. The most recent and quite a widespread development seems to be students enrolling in "twinning programs," where local colleges enter into special arrangements with foreign universities, mostly from the United Kingdom, United States, Canada, Australia, and New Zealand (for additional information on the program, see http://www.rihed.seameo.org). Students either wholly or partly finish their courses in Malaysia and spend the remaining period at foreign universities. Upon comple-

tion, students are generally granted a degree by the foreign university. These are recognized in Malaysia for the purposes of further studies and employment.

Currently, there are 17 public universities and university colleges, and around 670 private colleges and universities. University colleges, unlike universities, are set up by the government to offer specialized courses or training, which at the moment is predominantly in technology and/or engineering. Public and private universities are now being coordinated and monitored by the Higher Education Department, a department within the newly established Ministry of Higher Education. Numerous acts of parliament dictate the way these institutions are governed. The extent of autonomy of the universities, particularly public universities, is subject to the government's direction as the government is the major stakeholder that provides the funding. Universities are duty bound to take into consideration the National Education Philosophy, and university departments of student affairs act to achieve the government's aspirations or agenda.

In this chapter the authors will focus more on student affairs and services in Malaysian public universities, with some discussions on the private institutions. As University of Malaya—founded in 1905—is the oldest, it will be used as a point of reference in our discussion of student affairs and services work.

Development of Student Affairs and Services in Malaysian Universities and Colleges

History of Student Affairs in Malaysia

The first Department of Student Affairs (DSA) was established in 1975 at the University of Malaya, following the University and College University Act 1971 (as amended in 1975). That seems to have been the beginning of the student affairs profession in Malaysia. A deputy vice-chancellor for student affairs was appointed by the Minister of Education for a fixed term, and ever since then, the government—first through the Ministry of Education and now through the Ministry of Higher Education—has had a major say in the appointment of this principal officer, who presumably is the chief architect of student activities on each campus. With a handful of officers, the DSA at the University of Malaya is set up to perform two primary functions: (a) to establish discipline and order on campus and (b) to monitor and regulate student activities on campus. Statutes spell out rules that govern every aspect of student activities such as registration of societies, annual general meetings, elections, and administrative and financial matters.

Some argue that formation of DSAs with the enactment of the 1975 version of the University and College University Act of 1971 was mainly due to the numerous demonstrations by student bodies in the early 70s, most notably the "baling incident" in 1974 (Tze, 2005). During the "baling incident," peasants mostly from small rubber plantations in a northern state protested and demonstrated against price increases on food and other necessities and urged the government to raise the price of rubber. This struggle was strongly supported by students from universities and other institutions of higher learning throughout the country. It sparked numerous student demonstrations. Thus, one may say that the establishment of DSAs was to regulate and monitor student activities and movement.

However, DSAs could not avoid taking on an educational role as they were part of university communities with unique cultures and traditions. The University Council meeting minutes, dated September 16, 1975, stated that the purpose of establishing DSAs was (translated): "...to provide facilities and opportunities for students to be involved in all aspects so that not only they succeed in the academic field but also as capable leaders of the future" (University Council Minutes, personal communication, September 1975). The objective is to foster talents and produce well-balanced students. Similarly, other public universities in Malaysia have DSAs as one of the core departments in their overall organizational structure. More importantly, the overall focus of these DSAs seems to be on "student development" more than anything else. In fact, the department of student affairs at the University of Malaysia is known as the student affairs and student development section. So, while the original purpose of DSAs seems to have been regulatory in nature, Malaysian universities, in line with other university communities around the globe, are aware that they should provide and support an environment that enhances the learning process and students' total education. Thus, student development has slowly gained magnitude and has now taken the center stage.

Evolution of Purposes of Student Affairs

With rising societal and institutional concern for producing quality graduates to cater to market needs, and in the wake of stiff competition among both private and public universities, student affairs departments have now gained importance in university organizational settings. This importance is heightened due to an increase in the number of private and public universities, the need for globalization,

and a deep sense of concern among almost all universities that in order for their graduates to be competitive, they must possess extra skills transferable to the world of work, in addition to paper qualifications obtained through classroom engagement alone. The latest announcement of unemployment among graduates stands at an alarming figure of 80,000. While DSAs in public universities play an integral role in the national economy, numerous private institutions of higher learning have also established DSAs to meet market needs and assist in the holistic development of students. Universiti Tun Abdul Razak (or UNITAR), a private university, declares, "UNITAR is aware that a really 'complete' education cannot be achieved merely through formal education...the university is entrusting its Student Affairs Department (SAD) with the task of providing the facilities and services necessary for the provision of informal education" (UNITAR, n.d., para. 1–2). A survey of most of the organizational structures and missions of DSAs in private institutions shows some similarities as those in public institutions, but the operations of their programs are on a smaller scale. A review of DSA mission, objectives, and implementation strategies at the University of Malaya shows that various initiatives have been launched to promote student development.. At the International Symposium in California, jointly sponsored by the University of California, Los Angeles, and California State University, San Bernardino, Ambihabathy (2002) reported that to reach these objectives, strategies were adopted in a number of areas:

1. Academic and Intellectual – to stimulate critical thinking and leadership skills such that a student becomes knowledgeable both academically ("classroom knowledge") and in non-academic areas through programs such as forums, seminars, symposia, leadership and motivation courses, publications, and similar activities.

2. Welfare and Community Service – to provide community-based student service programs that will open students' minds and hearts to community conditions and prepare them to be better leaders for the future.

3. Spiritual and Ethics – to provide courses, lectures, forums, and festival celebrations that foster a better understanding of various religions and goodwill among various ethnic groups on campus.

4. Art and Creativity – to facilitate students' becoming more refined and cultured by utilizing and incorporating visible art, music, traditional and creative dances, drama, theater, and poetry in student activities.

5. Sports and Recreation – to encourage competitive and noncompetitive, indoor and outdoor, individual and group-based activities that promote physical health, mental health, and social interaction.

6. Uniformed Groups – to instill discipline, leadership qualities, and positive attitude by serving on the Reserves Officers Training Unit (ROTU), an auxiliary of the army, navy, and the latest, the Police Unit which was es-

tablished in mid-2005 as an auxiliary of the army, navy, and the latest, the police.

Role of the Malaysian Government

The government, through the Ministry of Higher Education, plays a major role in setting the agenda on issues related to student affairs and services. The Ministry of Higher Education coordinates and monitors the activities of institutions of higher learning in Malaysia. Various built-in mechanisms are in place, such as periodic meetings with these institutions and issuing of ministerial directives to ensure that national objectives are closely adhered to. In realizing their main focus on student development, most DSAs work with various governmental agencies including the "Biro Tata Negara," the National Civic Bureau, which conducts courses on good citizenship and patriotism.

It is said that the role and practice of a DSA should take into account institutional mission and vision, which should be congruent with the government's requirement, given that the government is a major stakeholder in the education process. Other factors considered in setting the pace and direction of student services delivery and development include sensitivity to the needs of the community, the national economic situation, and the job market. The National Philosophy of Education document also provides direction and goals for student affairs work, such as in "nation building;" "preparing for human resource needs of the nation;" and "character and holistic development of students." In short, DSAs in public universities do not exist in a vacuum; they are deeply embedded in a myriad of political, social, and educational contexts.

Coordinating Body of Student Affairs and Services

In Malaysia, DSAs have a unique feature. The DSAs, particularly at public institutions, have a Secretariat of deputy vice-chancellors/vice-rectors, which provides a forum to deal with student-related issues. The Secretariat was set up in the 1980s to "coordinate, and to encourage the processes of exchange of ideas and experiences for a common benefit." This arrangement is unique in the Asia Pacific Region (Mohaiadin, 2004). The Secretariat has eight Malaysian University councils, each with specific functions: sports, culture, debating, leadership, student housing, discipline, entrepreneurship, and counseling.

The councils are chaired by a deputy vice-chancellor of the university and comprise senior student affairs personnel dealing with each of the functional areas concerned. The tenure of the chair for both the Secretariat itself and the eight councils is two years. A paper presented on student affairs development at public institutions of higher education in Malaysia (Mohaiadin, 2004) explained that the initial reasons for creating these councils under the Secretariat were (translated):

1. To plan and carry out activities and programs involving students in a more systematic and effective manner.

2. To monitor and coordinate student activities and programs for all the universities to minimize overlapping and wastage of resources.

3. To enable sharing of experiences, expertise, and resources as well as experiences between universities in order to improve the quality as well as student performance in the relevant field.

4. To encourage good relationships between staff and students at each university.

Public universities and university colleges have a central body which seeks to coordinate, regulate, and ensure that the stakeholder's (i.e., the government's) aspirations are carried out, alongside its main thrust of student development activities. Similar arrangements in the private institutions of higher education are not specifically available in the student affairs arena. However, national bodies such as the National Association of Private Educational Institutions (NAPEI) and the Malaysian Association of Private Colleges (MAPCU) exist to represent private education.

Recruitment, selection, and training of student affairs personnel

Student affairs personnel or practitioners in all public and private universities and colleges are mostly career administrators, with the exception of the deputy vice-chancellors/deputy rectors and the deans of student affairs, who are from the academy Like any other administrators, student affairs personnel in most public universities are recruited as assistant registrars who are within the purview of the registrar of the university. Officers of student affairs departments are either recruited directly by a recruitment process or by appointing serving officers from various faculties. It has been a practice that the positions of student affairs officers, like any other personnel positions, are subject to posting according to the needs of the human resources department, which is also under the jurisdiction of the registrar. However, recruiting methods are different for the Counseling Unit, as counselors are expected to possess specific knowledge, expertise, and special skills.

In recent years there seems to be a concerted effort by most universities, and notably at the University of Malaya, to recognize that student affairs practitioners need special competencies that include people skills or interpersonal skills, and more importantly, experience as a student leader who understands the needs and wants of students and student societies. At the University of Malaya, young graduates who were themselves former student leaders are groomed to be student affairs personnel. Many of them are recruited as contract officers who, based on availability of positions and their performance, are offered positions as assistant registrars. Professional development and preparatory programs are not conducted on a regular, scheduled basis at most universities. However, student affairs personnel do attend seminars, workshops and even conferences conducted by various councils, under the Deputy Vice-Chancellors Secretariat, and other professional associations such as the Asia Pacific Student Services Association (APSSA) and other overseas universities.

Partnership with the academic community

In the DSA's endeavor to promote student development and total education, it needs to strike a strategic alliance and partnership with various agencies and entities in the campus academic community. Most universities enlist the support of academicians in student-related issues and development. Also, Malaysia has a residential college structure. Each residential college is headed by a master and a number of residential fellows who are mostly from the academy. At the University of Malaya, for example, aside from providing accommodation and food, the main thrust is student development. Various niche areas have been identified for students to participate in. The purpose is to inculcate desirable values in character and skill building, values that are critical for employment and for the overall development of good citizenship that is important in nation building. Some of the niches are: academic and intellectual, community services, sports and recreation, and arts and creativity. Various committees involving the residential fellows and students plan and implement programs related to the niche. The deputy vice-chancellor in charge of student affairs acts as the "captain" in setting the direction and the course to be taken and by inspiring the college masters and fellows to plan and implement student development programs. At the University of Malaya, this dual student affairs and academic relationship is further enhanced by the establishment of the masters committee and also the fellows committee, headed by the deputy vice-chancellor, to work on student-related issues and development.

Funding

At all public institutions, DSAs provide financial assistance and facilities such as rooms, equipment, and communication resources to promote student involvement in activities and in the development of "soft" skills. Through annual government grants formulated at Ringgit Malaysia (RM) 50 per student ($15 USD), the DSAs subsidize almost all activities organized by student societies. Likewise, an amount totaling RM 35,000 ($11,061 USD) is allocated annually to the residential college action committee, comprising student leaders, to plan and organize programs for student development. The distribution of the government grants within each university varies among different DSAs. At the University of Malaya, the DSA has devised its own workable formula over the years to provide student services such as:

1. Financial assistance to the student representative council,

2. Financial assistance to 111 registered student societies,

3. Travel and meeting expenses for student affairs,

4. Cultural and sports activities,

5. Provision of transportation for students and student activities,

6. Secretarial facilities, equipment, and support for student activities,

7. Publication of the student bulletin.

Proposals from student bodies are again vetted when the question of subsidies arises. At the University of Malaya, for example, several factors are given high ratings in considering financial aid for programs: intellectual content, social obligations to the community, multiethnic involvement, and internationalization. In recent years, the university has given additional funding for the sole purpose of training and developing students who are in the pipeline to cater to market and the nation's needs. Some public universities, such as Universiti Sains Malaya, have incorporated as part of the fee structure specific fees to fund extra-curricular activities for the student body. This again serves as evidence that most universities now recognize the fact that student development or holistic learning takes place both in the classroom and in out-of-class settings.

Student affairs organization

The organizational structures of student affairs departments in most public universities are similar, with slight variation to accommodate the needs of each of the universities. A typical organizational chart is given in Figure 11.1.

Four units in particular have now been placed under faculties or the main administration: sports and recreation, cultural, co-curriculum, and industrial training (which caters to work-integrated learning). At one point, these were under the DSA's jurisdiction. However, in most of the "younger" universities, these units are still intact within the DSA.

Using the University of Malaya (UM) as an example, the different sections and units within a student affairs department are as follows:

1. *Student Services Section.* The goal is to assist and render services that enhance students' academic performance and holistic development. Thus, UM has units that look after the welfare of students by providing the following services: (a) transportation, especially shuttle bus services to and from their classes and for attending student activities; (b) student accommodation, both on campus and off campus; and (c) financial aid services offered through the liaison and coordinating office. These services provide linkage between various government and private scholarship/loan agencies and students in need of financial aid.

2. *Student Development Section.* This section conducts and coordinates various strategies and programs that intentionally create the environment that enhances student learning and personal development. At the University of Malaya, this section contains several units:

a. The student relations unit is given the important task of student development.

Figure 11.1. Organizational structure: Student affairs department, Universati Malaya.

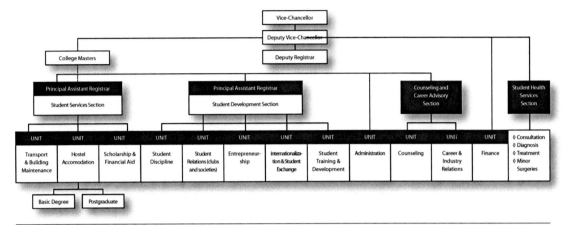

b. The entrepreneurship unit, which provides basic training on business knowledge and skills, prepares students to be entrepreneurs, and also provides the funding and space for students to engage in small business ventures even before they graduate.

c. The student training and development unit selects students from various residential colleges and societies and organizes and plans specific training programs for them to nurture leadership skills and to instill discipline and patriotism. The aim is to prepare them eventually to lead the student body and major programs on campus.

d. The internationalism and student exchange unit places an increasing focus on providing an opportunity for students to spend two weeks at a foreign host university. As a start, the unit is only focusing on South East Asian countries, with future plans to include all other countries around the globe. These exchange programs also open the doors to other foreign universities to send their students to Malaysia for a better understanding of its people and its culture.

3. Counseling Advisory Section. This section's main aim is to provide individual or group counseling to students facing emotional crises or personal problems. An important unit within this section is the career and industry relations unit, which focuses on employment opportunities for graduates, and prepares students for the job market. This unit is essentially a center that matches and links the student with prospective employers.

4. Student Health Service Section. Most universities have a student health service section that renders medical services such as consultations, diagnosis, treatment, and even minor surgeries.

5. Alumni Section. Public universities and colleges are paying attention to establishing an alumni section. This is a current focus of the Ministry of Higher Education.

Changing student demographics

Student services are evolving further with changes in student demographics. The percentage of female students has increased on most campuses. At the University of Malaya, 68% of the student body is female. Intake of postgraduate students has increased following the government's call to make Malaysia a hub or center of academic excellence. As a consequence, more mature and married students, both from Malaysia and from foreign countries, are now enrolled at universities in Malaysia. Housing for married students is a concern for many "older" universities. At the University of Malaya, a separate division within the accommodation unit was created to deal with this issue. Most residential colleges have a number of apartments reserved for postgraduate students. Also, an international relations unit has been set up within the university organizational structure to look after the welfare of these international postgraduate students. At private universities and colleges where competition is the order of the day, many colleges have begun to recruit students from Asian countries such as China and Indonesia. Again, this has placed corresponding demands on student services to provide living accommodations as well as counselors to guide these students who may have initial difficulty in adapting to local conditions.

International collaboration and internationalization

Most student affairs departments at public universities are seeking to establish linkages with foreign universities. International conferences, seminars, debate competitions, and more recently, study tours to other universities around the globe, are gaining importance. It is recognized that for students to be better global citizens, exposure to other cultures, socio-economic situations, and languages is important. At the University of Malaya, a deliberate attempt is being made to ensure the "internationalization of student activities," such as through an exchange program that exposes student to societies, cultures, and languages of countries outside of Malaysia.

This internationalization program was launched in 2005. Likewise, student affairs personnel, aside from attending national conferences, are very interested in collaborating with other universities around the globe to exchange ideas, and learn about new models and best practices. Malaysian universities participate in and have representatives at conferences organized by the Asia Pacific Student Services Association (APSSA). APSSA has also created staff exchange opportunities for its members who wish to gain in-depth knowledge in a particular area of student affairs.

Challenges and Opportunities

The department of student affairs at public universities, which once played a predominantly disciplinary and advisory role, has changed its focus to become more developmental in its services and programs. This strategy is even more important with rising societal and institutional concerns in the wake of stiff competition among both private and public universities in the quest to produce quality graduates. It is also a fact that for graduates to be competitive, they must possess extra skills transferable to the world of work. Graduates must be prepared to compete globally as well as locally. Nation building, preparing for the human resource needs of the nation, and character and holistic development of students to be patriotic citizens are demands placed on universities and colleges in Malaysia.

The departments of student affairs at both public universities and private institutions alike are becoming more relevant than when they were first established in the 1970s due to competition, globalization, and the national agenda. Student affairs work has become more challenging. Opportunities such as international conferences, workshops, and student and staff exchange programs may provide a good platform for preparing students and staff alike to be globally aware of the changes occurring around them. Malaysian universities and colleges would be highly receptive to any form of international collaboration or opportunities with foreign universities or professional bodies. Likewise, Malaysia would be an excellent place for international students to further their interests. Also, it is important for Malaysian universities to pursue international collaboration while the country enjoys very good political stability. Furthermore, Malaysia as a country affords a unique spectrum of culture, with various ethnic groups displaying a harmonious and symbiotic relationship. Malaysia is truly diverse, with Malays, Chinese, Indians, and others. Any form of exchange programs in Malaysia will be an enriching experience for all participating.

References

Ambihabathy, R. (2002). Student involvement: University of Malaya's strategies and experience. Paper presented at the International Symposium on Encountering the Nexus of Student Affairs: Languages, Cultures, and Partnerships, University of California – Los Angeles, and California State University – San Bernardino, CA.

Ministry of Education Malaysia. (n.d.). National education policy. Retrieved October 9, 2006, from http://apps2. emoe.gov.my/tayang.php?laman=falsafah&bhs=en

Mohaiadin, J. (2004). Country report: Malaysia. Report presented at the 9th Asia Pacific Student Services Association Conference (APSSA), Bangkok, Thailand.

Mohaiadin, J. (2004). Hala tuju majlis di bawah Sekretariat TTNC/TR HEP IPTA. Paper presented at the Seminar memperkasakan Hal Ehwal Pelajar (HEP), Sekretariat Timbalan-Timbalan Naib Canselor/Timbalan Rektor Hal Ehwal dan Pembangunan Pelajar IPTA Malaysia, Kota Kinabalu, Sabah, July 2004 (Direction of the councils under the Secretariat of Deputy Vice-Chancellors/ Vice-Rectors. Paper presented at the Seminar to Improve Student Affairs, Secretariat of Deputy Vice-Chancellors/ Vice-Rectors, Student Affairs and Development, Public Institutions of Higher Education, Kota Kinabalu, Sabah, July 2004.)

Tze T. S. (2005, January 23). Student freedom movement in Malaysia – a short overview. ReMag – The ReCom Magazine.

UNITAR. (n.d.). Student affairs department. Retrieved September 20, 2005, from http://www.unitar.edu.my/ student/studentaffairs.html

University of Malaya. (n.d.). Student affairs division. Retrieved September 20, 2005, from http://www.um.edu.my/ccm/ navigator/offices/student-affairs/officesad

Wikipedia – The Free Encyclopedia. (n.d.). Education in Malaysia. Retrieved September 20, 2005, from http:// en.wikipedia.org/wiki/education_in_malaysia

TWELVE

THE PHILIPPINES

Manuel M. Tejido

The purpose of this chapter is to offer readers a description of student affairs and services in Philippine colleges and universities today. It is, however, necessary to do so within the larger context of Philippine history, the Philippine national situation, and the Filipino national tradition, since many readers may be unfamiliar with the Philippines and the Filipino people.

A Brief History of the Philippines

The Philippines is located South of Taiwan and North of Borneo. It is composed of 7,107 islands with a total land area of about 300,000 sq. km, and a population of 88.57 million as of 2007 (National Statistics Office, Republic of Philippines). Filipino is the national language, but English is spoken by most as a second language; there are 111 other indigenous languages throughout the country's 16 regions, 79 provinces, and 115 cities and municipalities. Eight-one percent of the population is Catholic, 5 % Muslim, 3 % Evangelical, 5 % other Christian, and 6 % of other religious traditions (CIA, July, 2008).

On June 12, 1898, the Philippines declared independence after almost 300 years of Spanish colonial rule (1521–1897). In 1898, the Philippine revolution against the Spanish Crown intensified. At the height of the revolution, Spain secretly ceded the Philippine Islands to the United States for $20 million in the Treaty of Paris on December 10, 1898. Thus, the Philippines fell under U.S. domination from 1898–1940.

It was during these years that the United States established the Philippine public educational system (elementary and high school) and patterned it after their own. (Even after independence, many tertiary institutions were established in the 1950s and the 1960s and fashioned similarly in the U.S. way. A notable exception is the Pontifical University of Santo Tomas, which was established in 1611 by the Spanish Dominican, Miguel de Benavidez.)

In 1934, the U.S. enacted a law promising independence for the Philippines in 1946. In 1935, a Commonwealth regime began when the Republic of the Philippines was still under the watchful eyes of the United States. These

were years of relative peace and autonomy. During World War II, the Japanese occupied the Philippine Islands from 1941 to 1945, when the war ended. The Philippine Republic was established in 1946, and five presidents nurtured it until 1964. In 1965, Ferdinand Marcos was elected the sixth President of the Republic. He declared martial law in 1972. The blatantly dictatorial regime continued until January 1986. The dictator and his wife Imelda were ousted in a bloodless people-power uprising in February 1986. Corazon Aquino, the wife of the slain Filipino nationalist, Ninoy Aquino, assumed the Philippine presidency. While President Corazon Aquino succeeded in restoring democracy and freedom in the Philippines, there was much more that needed to be done (U.S. State Department, 1999).

An Analysis of Philippine Society Today

In 1995, Jesuit social activist Fr. Romeo Intengan wrote what he called a conjunctural analysis[1] of Philippine society, which in some measure is still true today. Although somewhat Marxist in his language and a little dreary in his perspective, his insights are still quite revealing for present day Filipinos. The following are summaries from his analyses on:

◊ Economic System: The basic economic structure of Philippine society may be described as a patriarchal, dependent, neo-liberal capitalist system with remaining areas of feudalism.

◊ Social System: Philippine society is extremely divided into social classes—upper, middle, and lower. A diagram of the structure of Philippine society would take the shape of a steep and sharp-peaked pyramid. At the base of the pyramid includes 90% of the population. Of these, 48% are poor peasants and fisher-folk, 42% are proletariat and semi-proletariat. A thin middle

---

[1] "Conjunctural analysis" is a technical term used by social analysts today. It refers to "a meeting point" between different dimensions (social, political, cultural, and religious, etc.) of social reality. Two other terms accompany these: "synchronic" (apart from a timeline) and "diachronic" (across time) social analysis.

layer of the pyramid stands for the petty bourgeoisie who are 9% of the population. At the peak of the pyramid, one finds the middle bourgeoisie and feudal landowners. Together, they make up only 1% of the total population.

◊ Political System: Philippine society is governed by a dysfunctional, patriarchal, liberal democratic framework dominated by 'traditional politicians.

◊ Cultural System: Philippine society has some sound values such as sensitivity to personal needs, strong regard for the family, and resiliency in the face of hardship. At the same time, it is heavily influenced by a colonial mentality and excessive personalism.

More recently, in an issue of Intersect, a publication of the Institute of Church and Social Issues at the Ateneo de Manila University, several authors (Alfonso, 2002; Reyes, 2002; Karaos, 2002; Lim, 2002; and Soco, 2002) described issues related to the "national situations" and different aspects of Philippine's social reality. These issues were published a year after Gloria Macapagal Arroyo became president in January, 2001. Their analyses are, in general, reconcilable with that by Intengan (1995).

The most recent study of the Philippine economic and political situation was published by the faculty of the economics and political science departments of the Ateneo de Manila University in The Philippine Daily Inquirer (March 6, 2005). The article, entitled "View from Loyola Heights: Beneath the Fiscal Crisis," reinforces, to some degree, Intengan's analysis. The study described the present fiscal crisis as a symptom of a deeper developmental crisis. It claimed that Philippine economic growth is narrow and hollow; that the growth in the service sector is accelerating while growth in the manufacturing and forestry sectors is declining. Powerful monopolies dominate the economy and arrest growth; as a result, income inequality among the social classes has worsened. The Philippines suffers from a "low-level equilibrium trap" or "slow economic growth," which prevents steady economic growth that its Asian neighbors have been enjoying since 1980.

The Filipino National Tradition

As a fitting response to this dreary conjunctural analysis of Philippine society and this most recent perspective by Filipino social scientists, it is necessary to review the Filipino national tradition (de la Costa, 2002). It could help readers contextualize student affairs and services in Philippine colleges and universities today, in a more balanced way, and begin to understand how many Filipino student affairs and services practitioners and professionals cope with the economic, social, political, and cultural realities in our country.

There are five dominant values or principles that characterize the Filipino national tradition. First, pagsasarili, or self-reliance (to own oneself, to be one's own person): this is the personalist principle of the Filipino national tradition that rejects both the abolition of private property and the absolute, unbridled ownership of material goods. Second,

pakikisama, or the "partnership principle" of the Filipino national tradition, refers to the equitable sharing of goods and services among all who help produce those goods. Emilio Jacinto, in the Kartilya ng Katipunan (a Handbook of the Filipino Revolution against Spanish colonial rule) demonstrates this ideal. Pagkakaisa is the third principle. It means unus instar omnium, being one for all, i.e., being responsible for one another. It means being free to do good for oneself and for others. Freedom does not mean doing what one simply wishes to do. Apolinario Mabini, one of the Filipino patriots, puts it this way: "Freedom itself demands that we conform our conduct to the guiding light of reason, and the commanding voice of justice" (de la Costa, 1971). Pagkabayani, or patriotism, is the fourth principle. Filipinos are patriots or nationalists not because they wish to separate themselves from the rest of humankind, but because they wish to build up a nation that can make its own distinctive contribution to the general advancement of the human race. Jose Rizal, the Filipino National Hero, lived this ideal unto his own martyrdom. This fourth principle is completed by the ideal of pakikipagkapwa-tao, or to be a friend to fellow human beings, to be equal as persons in relation to others in the world, i.e., inter-human solidarity (de la Costa).

Many student affairs and services programs and projects in Philippine colleges and universities embody these five principles of the Filipino national tradition. They thrive even against the somewhat dreary economic, social, political, and cultural systems that characterize Philippine society, and which adversely affect most Philippine colleges and universities today. The successful programs and projects undertaken amidst many difficulties and against many obstacles constitute our unique Filipino contribution to the enhancement of student affairs and services programs and projects throughout the world. In 1987, a misinformed American writer claimed that ours is a "damaged culture." He claimed that in the Philippines, there is a "failure in nationalism" and that "…Filipinos have a total devotion to those within the circle; a total war on those outside; contempt for the common good and the national ambition to change their nationality (Follows, 1987, pp. 7–12)." This thesis is blatantly false; it represents the views of a few in the upper class of Philippine society, who look down on the Filipino masses (Follows, 1987).

An Overview of Student Affairs and Services in Philippine Colleges and Universities

Villanueva (2000), in her report presented at the Asia Pacific Student Services Association Conference in Manila, indicated that as of 2000, there were 1,403 public and private colleges and universities throughout the Philippine Islands. Of these institutions, 1,173 are private colleges and universities and 230 are public. Metro Manila (with 13 cities and municipalities) has the most colleges and universities (225), and the Autonomous Region of Muslim Mindanao (ARMM) has the fewest (24). The tertiary-level institutions in the Philippines vary in size from as little as 500 students (and even fewer) to as many as 50,000 students.

Government subsidy for public tertiary institutions has been steadily dwindling over the years, while student tuition in private colleges and universities has been steadily rising. Sixty percent of the government subsidy for public colleges and universities is earmarked for faculty salaries. (This is also true for private tertiary institutions, where revenue comes almost exclusively from student tuition.) In theory, student services at all these institutions could be supported from the remaining 40% of the government subsidy. In reality, the bulk of the remainder goes to infrastructure maintenance and the salaries of all non-academic personnel, including student affairs practitioners, with little, if any, left for student service programs and activities.

Among the student services available in all of these public and private colleges and universities are (a) scholarships and financial assistance, (b) counseling and guidance, (c) health services, (d) student learning assistance, (e) food and cafeteria services, (f) living facilities such as residence halls and dormitories, (g) assistance to international students, and (h) supervision of student activities, especially social action programs. All Catholic colleges and universities, of course, have campus ministry offices and offices for social concern and involvement.

Student affairs and services personnel at these schools also vary in number, from just one in smaller schools to 50 in larger universities. The more affluent private universities, and the premier public University of the Philippines in Diliman, Quezon City, of course, offer more and better student services. Some of these (notably those in Metro Manila) are as sophisticated as those offered in developed countries in Asia, Australia, the United States, Canada, and in Europe. Villanueva (2002) reported at an international symposium held in 2002 in Los Angeles that student affairs and services in tertiary-level institutions in cities and municipalities, especially among the more affluent private colleges and universities, have steadily improved over the years in both quality and quantity of service. However, in most colleges and universities in the provincial and remote areas, student services have remained largely unchanged, due to financial and personnel constraints.

The problems and concerns that many Filipino student affairs and services practitioners in typical colleges and universities face today are (a) lack of funds and facilities, especially computer hardware and software to support student services; (b) lack of personnel, resulting in overburdened student services practitioners; and (c) lack of trained staff, as a result of heavy turnover of student affairs practitioners who seek greener pastures in other professions. These concerns are understandable within the larger context of Philippine social and economic realities.

Most student affairs and services offices in these colleges and universities are considered subservient to the academic community. They serve merely as a support system to the academic life of the students. However, a significant number of those appointed to administrative posts related to student affairs and services come from the ranks of the faculty.

Professional Organizations: Growth and Development of Student Affairs

Practitioners in the Philippines

Like U.S. colleges and universities, student services in the Philippines grew mainly as a service and support component of the academic programs in the 1950s and 1960s, when many of these colleges and universities were founded. There are at least six active associations of student affairs and services practitioners and professionals in these Philippine colleges and universities today:

◊ The Philippine Association of Administrators of Student Affairs (PAASA), which began in the 1990s, is a nationwide organization with several hundred active members. The PAASA National Capital Region Chapter meets monthly and has yearly conferences and seminars attended by practitioners throughout the country. Senior members of PAASA offer consultancy services to member institutions.

◊ The Philippine Association of Campus Student Advisers (PACSA) was established in the early 1980s as a response to student activism in the 1970s.

◊ The Career Development Association of the Philippines (CDAP) was born in the mid-1990s.

◊ The Philippine Association for Counselor Education, Research, and Supervision (PACERS) was established in the 1980s.

◊ The Philippine Guidance and Counseling Association (PGCA) was established in the 1960s.

◊ The Philippine International Friendship Organization (PIFO), established in 1954 by Ben Mahinay, is perhaps the oldest student services association in the Philippines. It is an organization of international student advisers and their students, which seeks to promote the welfare of international students in Philippine colleges and universities.

A report presented at the 9th Asia Pacific Student Services Association, Banaynal (2004) noted that these organizations meet regularly and hold conferences, workshops, and seminars aimed at enhancing the competencies of their targeted student services practitioners and professionals. In a profile of student affairs practitioners and professionals in the National Capital Region, Bonnet (2003) reveals two significant characteristics: the presence of a strong vision/mission as student affairs practitioners, and the presence of a positive cultural acceptance and outlook in their institutions. They are committed to their work and their malasakit (tender care) for students.

Student affairs heads and student services providers, including coaches, trainers, nurses, and especially teachers, stand in loco parentis vis-à-vis their students. Education laws in this country require this. This is perhaps the single most important difference between them and their counterparts in Europe, the Unites States, Australia, and some other Asian countries. Some American and German student services professionals cringe at this idea, but they need to remember that college and university students in the Philippines are in their middle adolescence and are at least two or even three years younger than their counterparts in Europe, the United States, and some Asian countries. For us in the Philippines, it is a valid ideal to be like a second parent to our students in school.

In most of these colleges and universities, there are no existing full-blown and in-house programs for the professional growth and development of student affairs practitioners and professionals. However, many institutions have some form of regular in-service training sponsored by the professional associations and subsidized by their respective institutions. The De La Salle University in Manila has an M.A. in student affairs management and development; the University of Santo Tomas is developing one at present. The Catholic Educational Association of the Philippines/National Capital Region Student Affairs Committee has a series of short-term, non-degree courses in student affairs management.

Government Subsidy or Assistance to Student Services in Private Colleges and Universities in the Philippines

In general, the Philippine government gives little student financial aid to most private colleges and universities. What aid there is comes in the form of tuition scholarships like the Merit Scholarships from the government. These are granted to high school students in premier public schools who have graduated with honors. They receive full tuition benefits, book allowances, and even subsidy for room and board at the school where they are accepted. There are also a few outside agencies that offer assistance to deserving but financially handicapped high school graduates attending private colleges and universities.[2] However, it must be noted that the bulk of tuition revenue from these sources (60%, by law, as indicated above) goes to faculty salaries; student services receive a meager amount.

Collaboration with Academic Departments

In most of these colleges and universities, student services practitioners work independently of the academic departments. After all, student services are viewed mainly as support services to academe. However, Banaynal (2002) found there have recently been significant changes in many of these colleges and universities. Many academics now seem open to asking and even requiring their students to participate in co-curricular activities. Some have even redesigned their courses to dovetail with the work of, for example, the campus ministry, and with the office of social concern and involvement, in Catholic colleges or universities. In like manner, at a few colleges and universities, some student activities and services programs and projects have been redesigned to incorporate academic requirements. The Ateneo de Manila University has taken the lead in the development of a holistic curriculum that includes both the academic and the non-academic aspects of the student's total formation (Tejido, 2002).

Campus Structures and Organization of Student Services

In most Philippine colleges and universities, student services are coordinated at the highest administrative level. A dean of student affairs (or an associate dean of student affairs, or a vice chancellor for academic affairs overseeing an office of student affairs) is usually in charge of six or more offices, which are directly involved with a variety of student services. Deans of students or associate deans of student affairs typically report directly to the university vice president. It is not uncommon for the team of student services practitioners to meet monthly under the leadership of the dean of students, who supervises all their activities. In a typical Filipino college or university, the dean of students (or the associate dean of student affairs) has authority over students only in reference to non-academic matters. Thus, they play merely a supportive role in the academic life of students; student affairs and services practitioners have little or no influence on the faculty and the academic curriculum. Close partnerships and collaboration between academics and student services practitioners are rare.[3] In many colleges and universities in metro Manila and the bigger cities and municipalities, school structures such as organization, facilities, human, and financial resources contribute significantly to enhancing student services. However, in less endowed colleges and universities in provincial areas (especially public tertiary-level institutions and a few private colleges), students have to contend with the barest minimum in student services. A few of these schools still use typewriters today. Some lack competent teachers and basic facilities like blackboard and chalk, a decent library, toilets, a cafeteria, and even classrooms.

Change in Student Demographics and Student Services

There are no significant changes in student demography in most of these Philippine colleges and universities. The usual tendency to enroll in metro Manila schools or in major city schools still prevails. There has been a recent decrease in the number of students in tertiary-level institutions among the less popular public and private colleges

---

[2] Alumni, parents, and outside private businesses and agencies also offer assistance to students in private colleges and universities. The Ateneo de Manila University ASPAC (Arts and Sciences Parents Council) offers several full scholarships to deserving students; so do Filway Marketing and many other business establishments.

[3] To see a typical student affairs office as described above, see the Web site of De La Salle University, Manila at http://www.dlsu.edu.ph/offices/sps

and universities even in metro Manila, but statistical data about this decrease are unavailable at this time.

The Social, Political, and Economic Climate in the Philippines Affecting Student Services

The Challenge of Building Justice Locally, and Globally

The social, economic, and political situation in the Philippines was outlined earlier in this chapter, and this climate of structural injustice has adversely affected student services in Philippine colleges and universities. We all know that colleges and universities represent a microcosm of the society where they are situated. However, at the deeper level, this climate betrays the many forms of societal injustices on both national and international levels, in our midst and as a global community. Whether they know it or not, the excessive affluence, wastefulness, and consumerism among students and student services professionals in developed countries adversely affect students and student services practitioners in developing countries. Unless the former give up much of this undue affluence and wastefulness, the scarcity of student services' resources in developing countries will continue. Dismantling unjust societal structures nationally and globally is a major challenge that student affairs practitioners and professionals around the world face today.

Here are some examples of this excessive affluence, wastefulness, and consumerism:

1. The almost incessant upgrading of computer software and hardware leads to so much wastefulness in developed countries. If only these functional and valuable, though "outdated" tools were resold or better still, donated— systematically (and efficiently) to students and student services practitioners in developing countries, like the Philippines, the delivery of student services could significantly improve in these countries. A recent CNN feature presentation based on an article written by Curran (2003) reported that computer software and hardware could be upgraded every two or three months. At universities where computer upgrades are done every two or three months, the discards are in fact potentially very valuable to third world colleges and universities, which simply cannot afford this constant and probably questionable upgrading.

2. The sheer amount of brand new college and university textbooks being sold to students year after year in highly developed countries is staggering, from a third world perspective. However, little is being done to allow students in third world countries to re-use the books after they have been read and studied by their Western counterparts. Instead of throwing away the books or even recycling the book paper, it is the book that should be re-used again and again, elsewhere among the poor

in the world. If students and student affairs professionals in first world countries could see the meager holdings of libraries in poorer colleges and universities in third world countries, they would better understand what structural injustice means.

3. In many colleges and universities in developed countries sporting equipment (balls, bats, gloves, body building equipment, rackets, etc.) is "top of the line." This is also true of office equipment, blackboards, erasers, even wooden panels, etc. Students are given the best that money can buy, and often, they are given more than they need.

Again, what is being suggested here is just a valid ideal: that after using this equipment, institutions in developed countries should share it with those who have little or none at all. They should use these resources sparingly in the first place and avoid any form of waste. College and university students in poorer countries deserve to have more, not for the sake of competing with their Western counterparts, but rather in order to become better persons and better students. When richer students and student affairs and services professionals in developed countries give up these superfluities and excesses, they are not performing an act of charity; they are performing an act of justice.

International Collaboration among Student Affairs Practitioners in the Philippines

Since 1996, the Asia Pacific Student Services Association (APSSA), among other organizations, has given many Filipino student affairs and services practitioners and professionals the chance to collaborate with their counterparts, not just in the Asia Pacific region but also in the United States and Europe. The APSSA staff attachment program is one way this collaboration has become a reality.

There has been significant collaboration among many of the premier Philippine tertiary-level institutions in the area of student welfare. For more than 50 years, the Philippine International Friendship Organization (PIFO) has succeeded in harnessing the energy of international student advisers in some Philippine colleges and universities in promoting the welfare of international students in their respective institutions. In 2004, they pooled their resources and organized a symposium co-sponsored by the University of California, Los Angeles, and the California State University. Fullerton. There they interacted with their counterparts on issues like multicultural counseling and inter-religious dialogue among international students. The Philippine Association of Administrators of Student Affairs, and the Student Services Committee of the Catholic Educational Association of the Philippines/National Capital Region likewise pooled the resources of student affairs practitioners in several Philippine universities and gave them the opportunity to improve their skills and competencies through a study visit, sponsored by APSSA, to the United Kingdom and Germany in 1999.

Challenges for Filipino Student Affairs and Services Practitioners and Professionals

The main challenge that Filipino student affairs and services practitioners and professionals face is the creative work of designing and implementing more programs and projects for the benefit of Filipino college and university students now and in the future. However, these are to be realized amidst the many difficulties that Philippine society faces today. They must also be realized in the context of the enduring values and principles found in our Filipino national tradition. It should be clear to all of us that one of the underlying issues that we need to face squarely today, as student affairs professionals, is the question of building social justice. There are many examples of good practice in student services in the Philippines, and it is interesting to note that the most developed programs and projects concern student involvement in social action. Most public and private colleges and universities in the Philippines have similar programs meant to address social justice issues.

In particular, we face the challenge of speaking the language of our own students in improving and especially in promoting student services in each of our Philippine colleges and universities. This, in effect, means student services practitioners must be more assertive about the role of student services in the total development of students, especially among first year and graduating students who deserve greater care and attention, as highlighted in an interview by Charles Schroeder (2003) with John Gardner on "The First Year and Beyond." We need to push for a seamless curriculum, especially for both groups of college students. Academics in Philippine colleges and universities need to see more than just their academic curricula. They need to see the importance of a carefully prepared non-academic curriculum in tandem with theirs, which could help these students improve their performance in classroom work. This assertiveness on the part of student services practitioners and professionals includes the challenge to do more amidst dwindling financial and personnel resources available in the impoverished milieu of most Philippine colleges and universities. It also includes the challenge to do better (with less) and the challenge to be more Filipino in all student services programs and projects, in the name of social justice. At the same time, however, we need to forge another student affairs language in the company of our international colleagues and counterparts. We need to help them raise their global social consciousness in the area of student affairs and services. We need to help them nurture not an attitude of mere curiosity toward the plight of students and student services practitioners in developing countries but rather an attitude of availability that may lead to active cooperation in improving student services in impoverished countries.

In the same vein, the task of nurturing the Filipino national tradition in our college and university students through our programs and projects must also include in-stilling a growing global social justice outlook among them in the pursuit of academic excellence. Together with their mentors and student services providers, they should see themselves not as beggars but as partners who can also contribute to the enhancement of student learning and student services in richer developed countries.

Student affairs and services practitioners in the Philippines, for instance, could warn some of their U.S. counterparts about the dangers of running student services in their colleges and universities much like the way corporate America is running their businesses: they are often driven simply by market forces. They seem keen on quick financial return and are sometimes unmindful of long-term adverse consequences on student learning. They tend to outsource some student services (as a cost-cutting measure) to the detriment of a more personalized attention that students deserve. In the end, they renege on their responsibility, as student affairs professionals, to enhance student learning and promote the student learning imperative (ACPA, 1996). It would be useful for Filipino student affairs and services practitioners to recast and reinterpret this document in the light of our Filipino national tradition. It would be a useful tool in the work of designing a holistic curriculum for college and university students in the Philippines.

The Role of Student Services Professionals in Developed Countries vis-à-vis Developing Countries like the Philippines

It is somewhat pretentious on the part of a Filipino student services practitioner even to outline the role of student affairs professionals in Europe and the United States vis-à-vis their counterparts in developing countries. Ideally, they should discover this role for themselves. What follows are tentative suggestions for discussion purposes.

1. Help us help ourselves in the work of improving student services. Offer us some preferential assistance. We need this more than other colleges and universities in developed nations in the world. Social justice requires this of you. Respect our pagsasarili (being our own person: the personalist principle). Be reminded that there can be no universal, all-embracing standard of excellence in student affairs and services, applicable to all colleges and universities throughout the world. Do not impose on us your expertise and your own ways of doing things. We respect your American and European standards for excellence in student affairs work, but we need to develop our own. Our development as practitioners can only be done within the context of our own language and culture. Makisama kayo sa amin (join us; be with us: the partnership principle). What is necessary is interpretation of what others do and creative innovation. We need to work with you, but we need to work with you according to the principles and values of our own Filipino national tradition, not yours. We ask you to study and understand these, take them seriously, and measure what we do according to these principles, not yours. Look also into our success

stories and our good practices, and see how you yourselves can interpret and adapt these within the ethos of your own universities, in the spirit of pagkakaisa (united by consensus).

2. Share with us your time and expertise, as well as your material resources. Some Philippine colleges in distant provinces still use typewriters; do not just throw away your outmoded PCs. Donate them to student services practitioners in these colleges (especially in the ARMM, the Autonomous Region of Muslim Mindanao, in Southern Philippines), while you teach them how to use these, in the spirit of pagkabayani (total dedication). Better yet, adopt a few of these colleges and universities as your own. Come visit us and see what we do. In return, we will share with you our Asian and Filipino student affairs and services experience and hospitality. Invite us every now and then to visit you, so that we can see what you do and show you how you could perhaps do even more with less. Our common attitude as partners should be: "Here is our way; show us yours."

In conclusion, we believe that this mutual openness and trust among colleagues will nurture pakikipagkapwa-tao (to be a fellow to one another). You have much to learn from us, as we have much to learn from you. Tell us what you think of what we do; allow us to tell you what we think of what you do. In the spirit of our Filipino national tradition, let us offer constructive criticism of each other's student services programs and projects. Let us allow the "guiding light of reason and the commanding voice of justice" to lead the way in this dialogue, as Apolinario Mabini, the brains of the Philippine Revolution, teaches us.

References

Alfonso, E.L. (2002). Surviving the transition year: The politics of consolidation. Intersect, 17(1), 4–6.

American College Personnel Association. (1996). The student learning imperative: Implications for student affairs. Retrieved April 10, 2008, from http://www.acpa.nche.edu/sli/sli.htm

Banaynal, B. (2004). Country report: Philippines. Proceedings of the 9th Asia Pacific Student Services Association Conference, Bangkok, Thailand, pp. 21–25.

Banaynal, B. (2002). The career development of Filipino students in a trimester system at the De La Salle University. Paper presented at the International Symposium on Encountering the Nexus of Student Affairs: Languages, Cultures, and Partnerships, Los Angeles and San Bernardino, CA.

Bonnet, P. (2003). The profile of national capital region student affairs practitioners and its implications to the practice of student affairs in the region. Paper presented at De La Salle University, Philippines.

CIA. (July, 2008). The world factbook: Philippines. Retrieved July 28, 2008, from https://www.cia.gov/library/publications/the-world-factbook/geos/rp.html

Curran, R. (2003, June 13). Mining gold from computers: Resale, recycling firms, reap "trash" cash. Austin Business Journal, 4–6.

de la Costa, H. V. (1971). The Filipino national tradition. In R. Bonoan (Ed.) The Alay Kapwa Lenten Lectures (pp. 42–56). Manila, Philippines: Ateneo de Manila University Press.

de la Costa, H. V. (2002). The Filipino national tradition. In R. M. Paterno (Ed.), Selected essays on the Filipino and his problems today (pp. 70–87). Manila, Philippines: Kadena Press Foundation-Asia.

Follows, J. (1987, November). A damaged culture. The Atlantic Monthly, 7–12.

Intengan, R. (1995). A conjunctural analysis of the Philippine national situation. Unpublished manuscript, Loyola School of Theology, Quezon City, Philippines.

Karaos, A.M. (2002). A scaling down of numbers. Intersect, 1(1), 10–12.

Lim, E.G. (2002). CARP in Gloria's year. Intersect, 17(1), 16–18.

Manalo, C. (2004). Effective development and management of student activities: The Centro Escolar University experience. Proceedings of the 9th Asia Pacific Student Services Association Conference, Bangkok, Thailand, 130–134.

Melegrito, L. (2004). The Triadic intersection of community-based learning, social responsibility, and community-based development. Proceedings of the 9th Asia Pacific Student Services Association Conference, Bangkok, Thailand, 39–53.

National Statistics Office, Republic of Philippines. (August, 2007). Philippines in figures. Retrieved July 28, 2008, from http://www.census.gov.ph

Reyes, M. (2002). An inextricable link. Intersect, 17(1), 7–9.

Schroeder, Charles. (September–October, 2003). The first year and beyond. About Campus, 8(4), 9–16.

Soco, A. (2002). Declining farm yields. Intersect, 17(1), 19–21.

Songco, E. (2004). Developing social responsibility among students of the University of Santo Tomas. Proceedings of the 9th Asia Pacific Student Services Association Conference, Bangkok, Thailand, 62–66.

Tejido, M. (2002). The student affairs practitioner today. Keynote address presented at the International Symposium on Encountering the Nexus of Student Affairs: Languages, Cultures, and Partnerships, Los Angeles and San Bernardino, CA.

Tirona, A. (2004). Enriching student life: The Kalayaan Residence Hall experience at the University of Philippines Diliman Campus. Proceedings of the 9th Asia Pacific Student Services Association Conference, Bangkok, Thailand, pp. 198–201.

U.S. State Department. (1999). World rover: Philippines. Retrieved July 28, 2008, from http://www.worldrover. com/history/philippines_history.html

Villanueva, B. (2000). Country report: Status of student affairs work in Philippine tertiary institutions. Proceedings of the 7th Asia Pacific Student Services Association Conference, Manila, Philippines.

Villanueva, B. (2002). Partnerships in student affairs work: Status and prospects in the University of Philippines, Diliman campus and selected tertiary institutions in the Philippines. Paper presented at the International Symposium on Encountering the Nexus of Student Affairs: Languages, Cultures, and Partnerships, Los Angeles and San Bernardino, CA.

THIRTEEN

SINGAPORE

Ng Suan Eng

The Republic of Singapore is a small tropical island in Southeast Asia with a total land area of 646 sq km. It is located just one degree north of the equator. It is a young country, having achieved independence only in 1965. Its history dates back to 1819 when the British founded a trading post on this tiny island in the Malay Peninsula. Soon it became a busy sea port, and immigrants from China and India came in search of a new life. It thus developed into a multi-racial, multi-cultural society with a current population of more than four million people, of which about 750,000 are foreign workers. Of the local population, Chinese constitute 77%, Malays 14%, and Indians 7.6%. Other ethnic groups make up the remaining 1.4% (Ministry of Information and the Arts, 2001).

There are four official languages: Malay, Mandarin Chinese, Tamil (a language of Southern India), and English. Malay is the national language, and English is the language of administration as well as the main medium of instruction in schools and higher education institutions. Mandarin is widely used in the community.

Singaporeans enjoy a relatively high standard of living. The per capita income is US$25,000. Ninety-three percent of the households own their own homes. On average, the size of each household is four persons. Even the poorest families are blessed with a television, a refrigerator, and a telephone (Singapore Government, 2008).

Education System in Singapore

With its majority population being Chinese, Singapore is a very typical East Asian society, which places emphasis on the following values:

◊ High savings rate

◊ Economically oriented society

◊ Hard working

◊ Willing to learn and invest in human capital

◊ Law and order above personal freedom

Singapore has no natural resources; education is therefore a top priority as the people are her only resource. It is well recognized that a good education system will prepare the people for the knowledge-based economy and global competition.

Every child in Singapore has at least 10 years of general education. This comprises six years of primary education and four years of secondary education. The entire education system aims to equip the students with the desire and skills for continuous learning beyond the confines of school. Information technology is used widely to develop skills in communication and independent learning. An emphasis on bilingual ability ensures that students learn at least two languages: English and the mother tongue of the ethnic group they come from.

Higher Education

The institutions of higher learning in Singapore include three universities and five polytechnics. The universities are the National University of Singapore (NUS), Nanyang Technological University (NTU), and the Singapore Management University (SMU). The first two are state universities, and the third is a publicly funded private university. A fourth university is now being considered. The five polytechnics are Singapore Polytechnic (SP), Ngee Ann Polytechnic (NP), Temasek Polytechnic (TP), Nanyang Polytechnic (NYP), and Republic Polytechnic (RP).

Higher education began in Singapore in 1905 with the founding of the Straits Settlements and Federated Malay States Government Medical School. In 1928, Raffles College was founded, and in 1949, the two institutions merged to become the University of Malaya, Singapore Division. In 1962, the governments of Singapore and the Federation of Malaya decided that the Singapore Division of the University of Malaya should become autonomous as a national university of Singapore, to be known as the University of Singapore. In 1980, Nanyang University, founded in 1955 with resources pooled from the Chinese community, merged with the University of Singapore to become the National University of Singapore (National

Table 13.1. Number of student affairs staff and staff/student ratios.

Names of Higher Institutions	No. Student Affairs Staff	Student Enrollment	Ratio
National University of Singapore (founded in 1905)	81	32,000	1:395
Nanyang Technological University (established in 1980)	129	23,465	1:182
Singapore Management University (established in 2000)	13	2,200	1:169
Singapore Polytechnic (established in 1954)	35	16,500	1:471
Ngee Ann Polytechnic (established in 1963)	29	14,000	1:482
Temasek Polytechnic (established in 1990)	27	13,000	1:481
Nanyang Polytechnic (established in 1992)	37	15,490	1:418
Republic Polytechnic (established 2002)	4	2,000	1:500

Note: Each team comprises administrators and support staff. During peak periods, some sections may hire student helpers. In student residential life, it is common to appoint faculty or administrative staff as residential advisors and students as residential assistants to help organize activities for residents. These administrators are appointed for fixed terms and are compensated with free accommodation in student residences.

University of Singapore, 2008a).The other two major universities, Nanyang Technical University (NTU) and Singapore Management University (SMU), were established after 1980. Previously, NUS and NTU were "state" (government supported) universities, which are treated as "semi-government" organizations whose polices are subject to review and approval by the government; whereas SMU is a "private" university. All three received funding from the Singapore government. As of 2006, NUS and NTU were "privatized" into non-profit universities; each campus is now governed by a board of trustees that can set its own policies. All three institutions continues to receive government funding, but are now considered autonomous universities.

Most of the tertiary institutions are currently under the purview of the Ministry of Education, with more than 75% of their operating costs being funded by the government.

Student Affairs and Student Services Personnel

The development of Singapore's student affairs programs and management in higher education is relatively recent. Of the three major universities in Singapore, the National University of Singapore was the first to develop and evolve into

the present day student affairs office that provides services and programs for its students. Almost as soon as they were established, the other two major universities, NTU and SMU followed National University of Singapore as a model in establishing their student affairs offices.

NUS, in its early years, did not have a student affairs office. Some of the student non-academic matters were subsumed under the public relations office. In 1980 that office was divided into two separate departments, with a new student liaison office overseeing student services such as accommodation (housing), counseling, and support and guidance for student organizations. In 1998, the office was further expanded and became known as the student affairs office.

The mission of the student affairs office at NUS, simply stated, is "to provide, in partnership with our students, a total University experience that builds a strong NUS spirit" (National University of Singapore, 2008b). This mission statement reflects the goals of all of Singapore's universities and polytechnics.

Currently, the three universities and the five polytechnics together have a total student enrollment of 120,000, supported by about 355 student services personnel. Table 13.1 shows the number of student affairs office staff at each of Singapore's higher education institutions and the staff/student ratio (Ng Suan Eng, personal communications, various April dates, 2005).

Student services personnel are mainly administrators. They all have at least one university degree, and those in counseling and physical education have relevant qualifications specific to their fields of practice. In recent years, a trend has developed among these institutions to appoint academic staff as deans of students and heads of student affairs departments.

Although currently there is no professional association for student affairs personnel in the country, the universities and polytechnics generally enjoy good relations and co-operate fully with each other on major projects. Some of them are members of the Asia Pacific Student Services Association (APSSA). There are no formal academic programs or training, except in areas where specific skills are needed (e.g., counseling).

Scope of Services in Student Affairs Departments

In the universities and polytechnics, the department of student affairs is usually in charge of the non-academic life of students and entrusted with the mission of enhancing students' university experience by providing them with the environment and opportunities for leadership and character development.

Services normally include the following (using examples of services provided by National University of Singapore to provide additional details):

1. Support and guidance for student organizations and student activities: At NUS, it provides guidance and advice to student societies on campus, assists in organiza-

tion of activities, and offers opportunities to participate in local or overseas student activities, as well community service projects.

2. Student Counseling Service: At NUS, it provides personal guidance and counseling that promote students' life skills, with services that include workshops, personal and group consultations, and administration of a host of personality tests and interests inventories.

3. Careers and Employment Service: At NUS, this would include job fairs and recruitment talks, workshops on career planning and resume writing, an electronic "Job Shop," e-Resume Bank, alumni mentor scheme, and walk-in interviews.

4. Student Housing Services: At NUS, in addition to providing housing for 6,000 on-campus students in traditional residence halls, there are 200 on-campus apartments and 545 off-campus housing units for graduate students. Residential life services provides hall activities, social and sport activities, enrichment programs, and resident assistant and "cluster leader" programs to residential students.

5. International Student Services: At NUS, it provides students from more than 40 countries with pre-arrival services and orientation sessions, a host family program, international student welfare services, services related to immigration visa, part-time work permission, and general guidance and support by international student advisors.

6. Sports and Recreation: At NUS, the sports and recreation center provides recreational sports for the campus community, and overseas sports exchange and competitive sports at the institutional, national, and international levels. (National University of Singapore, 2007b)

The student health service (the University Health, Wellness and Counseling Centre) is a separate office and has never been included as a service within the student affairs office at any of the three universities. At National University of Singapore, it provides comprehensive outpatient medical care to all of the NUS community, a resource center for wellness programs for NUS staff, and a dental clinic for all NUS students and staff (National University of Singapore, 2007a).

Organizational Structure in Student Affairs

The organizational chart, as depicted in Figure 13.1, shows the reporting structure at NUS. This structure also reflects typical reporting relationships for student affairs within the university organization (National University of Singapore, 2008c).

Student Profile and Influx of International Students

Singapore students are generally very motivated and focused in their studies. They do not have problems with

drugs, alcohol, or vandalism. They are very driven and generally law-abiding. Attrition rate is low. Most of them would like to complete their course of study in the shortest possible time. Obtaining a first degree is generally regarded as a passport to a well-paying job and a good life.

On the negative side, they are self-centered, uncaring, and indifferent to politics and community issues. Among the undergraduate population, only about 10% to 15% take part in activities outside their curriculum. Common disciplinary cases typically involve the following:

◊ Misuse of computer accounts (e.g., sale of pirated software and use of vulgar language online).

◊ Infringement of copyrights.

◊ Breach of hostel rules.

◊ Plagiarism.

◊ Lack of discipline, e.g., use of mobile phones during lectures; late for meetings and official functions, etc.

In the past, students in Singapore's higher education institutions were mainly local, with a small percentage of international students from the country's immediate neighbor, Malaysia. With Singapore developing into a globally diversified knowledge-based economy, a government policy to attract foreign talent was introduced in 1998, and the universities stepped up their recruitment of international students for undergraduate and graduate courses. Currently international students constitute about 20% of the student population. They come from more than 40 countries, with the majority from China, India, and other Southeast Asian countries. There are also a high proportion of international students from Western countries on exchange programs. This has posed a new challenge to the student affairs personnel, especially in the area of student life and development.

Common Issues and Challenges Facing Student Affairs Personnel

In the past, due to the relatively short history of tertiary institutions in Singapore, senior management did not give student services work much priority. The universities in particular focused more on academic excellence relevant to the nation's needs. Staff at the universities is divided into two career tracks—academic and administrative/professional. Administrators generally receive less recognition and enjoy a lower status. Those in the student services departments have no professional training and have to learn on the job. They can also be re-deployed to other administrative departments.

Funding for student services work is also limited, with student organizations having to seek external sponsorships for many of their major events. For the past few years, when Singapore was affected by the global economic slowdown, the office of student affairs at the NUS, for example, faced budget cuts of 5% to 10% each year. Increasingly, with manpower downsizing and introduction of new student development

Figure 13.1. Office of student affairs' reporting structure at the National University of Singapore.

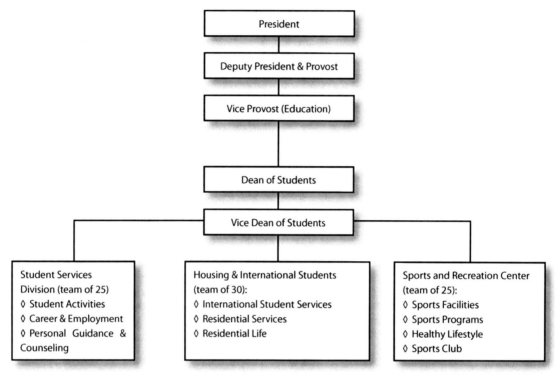

Note: Each team comprises administrators and support staff. During peak periods, some sections may hire student helpers. In student residential life, it is common to appoint faculty or administrative staff as residential advisors and students as residential assistants to help organize activities for residents. These administrators are appointed for fixed terms and are compensated with free accommodation in student residences.

programs, student affairs workers have to multitask, with no new hires. To meet the new challenges of an information technology age and a more complicated student profile, the office of student affairs needs the cooperation of the faculty. Student affairs workers are administrators and not teaching staff, and student leaders tend to respect their faculty deans and teaching staff more than the student affairs administrators. This situation is made worse by the growing trend of student affairs practitioners being regarded as law enforcement officers and given the task of disciplining students instead of being the students' advocates. Therefore, student affairs administrators are now creating new initiatives to collaborate with faculty members, such as encouraging them to appoint vice deans (faculty members) to be in charge of student matters, and to work through the deans to better serve and educate students. At the same time, student affairs administrators are holding more dialogue sessions with the students' Union to discuss student affairs concerns, and involving them on some policy making committees.

The road ahead is still long for student affairs administrators to be respected as professionals in their own right, but they hope to see the day soon when all three parties—student affairs practitioners, faculty, and student leaders—working hand-in-hand as equal partners to develop

Singapore's students, not only in their intellectual potential but also their social and leadership skills.

References

Ministry of Information and the Arts. (2001). Singapore facts and pictures. Singapore: Author.

National University of Singapore. (2007a). University health, wellness, & counselling centre. Retrieved April 15, 2008, from http://www.nus.edu.sg/uhwc/

National University of Singapore. (2007b). Office of student affairs: Services. Retrieved April 15, 2008, from http://www.nus.edu.sg/osa/svcs_main.html

National University of Singapore. (2008a). Milestones. Retrieved April 15, 2008, from http://www.nus.edu.sg/corporate/timeline/

National University of Singapore. (2008b). About us: We are here for you. Retrieved April 15, 2008, from http://www.nus.edu.sg/osa/profile/abt.html

National University of Singapore. (2008c). University administration. Retrieved April 17, 2008, from http://www.nus.edu.sg/corporate/about/offices.htm

Singapore Government. (2008). Singapore statistics: Publications. Retrieved April 15, 2008, from http://www.singstat.gov.sg/pubn/catalogue.html#sib

FOURTEEN

AUSTRALIA

Annie Andrews

Overview

In Australia the term *student affairs* has not been extensively used when labeling or describing student support initiatives or units. The term most frequently encountered is *student services*. In Australia, student support, student services, and student amenities historically and currently remain the responsibility of three distinct agents of service delivery: the Commonwealth government, the universities, and student organizations within the institutions. All three agents have made financial investments in student support, services, or amenities since the middle of the last century.

The Australian higher education sector has evolved in response to government directives and initiatives, been driven by the substantial increase in the nation's population, and greatly influenced by the role that the sector has been required to play in the economic development of the nation. Australia, once the "lucky country," has been urged to become the "clever country" as government policies have been framed around the shift to a knowledge economy and away from the early wealth-generating products of the agricultural and manufacturing industries. This means that "the cap and gown are encroaching on the big end of town," and education services have become an export product of considerable importance in Australia's economy.

Changing Demographics and Developing Services

Student support services offered by universities have evolved primarily since 1914. Development has been somewhat haphazard, and provision of student support services has been managed, with relatively limited funding, to be responsive to the lived experience of the successive student cohorts. From the outset, student services began purposefully to assist commencing students make successful adjustment and transition to the formal university environment. In response to the desire of successive governments to protect financial and policy investment in higher education, universities have provided student services in an effort to reduce attrition and to promote degree completion.

This original government-generated push for the development of student services within higher education focused on helping students adapt to university demands rather than on influencing universities to adapt their processes to fit the needs of the commencing cohorts unfamiliar with university culture and academic requirements. In the last half of the century, student services provided by institutions have increased numerically to include academic support services, childcare services, disability support, careers, employment, counseling, health services, sporting facilities, and more recently, services for international students, among other services. The initial goals of retention and completion have become stable themes informing the provision of centrally funded student services.

During the last 15 to 20 years, student cohorts and student services have benefited from the diversity that has become increasingly evident within the student population. This ongoing change in the student demographic has been, in part, the result of the broadening of the Australian immigration policy since the softening of the White Australia Policy in 1966, and continuing through to the current immigration directions.[1] The worldwide trend toward the internationalization of education has strongly influenced the diversity of the student cohort enrolled at Australian universities, broadening the cohort to include students from at least 80 cultural and language groups. The increasing diversity and weight of enrolled student numbers has had considerable impact on specialization within the provision of student services on Australian university campuses. What has emerged, driven in part by the changing student demographic, has been a gradual increase in the number, type, and specialization of student services.

By the mid-1990s, a common approach to managing the needs of student support within universities had evolved,

---

[1]The current Australian immigration policy is outlined in Multicultural Australia: United in Diversity, (DIMIA, 2003). A tertiary qualification is desirable for a permanent residency application and it is not unusual for international students on student visas to have the achievement of permanent residency in Australia as a tangible goal following completion of a degree from an Australian University.

and the existence of student services had become familiar to the culture of all university campuses. The structure and form of student service provision had evolved with a local emphasis in response to the needs of each university and the resources available (or not) to students in the surrounding community.

Yet despite the increasing presence of these specialized services within each university there has been no nationally endorsed or formally accepted philosophy or overarching framework for the delivery of student services. On reflection, and considering the evidence provided by a review of student service-generated literature, this is surprising, but it does suggest that the major stakeholders in higher education do not yet view student support nationally as an integral player in the broader story of student success.

The most recent years in the development of student services have corresponded with the era of restructuring and rationalization, with a subsequent influence on the institutional structures. In some cases, the resulting structural positioning of student service functions within each institution appears to have been driven more by administrative convenience than by the support needs of student cohorts or the ultimate efficiency and effectiveness of student service delivery.

Budgeting and the "Place" of Social Services

Tensions historically exist on university campuses between different budget units, with the most noticeable division existing between those budget units with predominately general staff and those with academic staff. This divide, while existing as an uncomfortable and competitive under-current in a campus climate, has its origins in the fact that general staff support and underpin the "core business" of the university. There are a number of layers in a campus hierarchy. The most valued work is that conducted by the members of the university research community. Second in importance are the contributions of those who provide the student-focused learning and teaching experiences. The academic staff populates these two areas. Those units that provide the administrative and support functions for both staff and students are generally the domain of general staff, and as such underpin the functions and roles considered more central to the university's core business of teaching and research. In addition to the division of work responsibility, there are different work conditions and salary scales governing these two staffing areas. Adding to the complexity is the possibility that general staff working within the faculty (academic) context may receive higher pay for similar duties and responsibilities as those undertaken by general staff in non-faculty, centrally positioned divisions.

Student support services are frequently caught in a kind of neutral zone without a well-recognized place in the academic/learning environment or the areas of student administration. Residing in this neutral zone, without clear affiliation, student service units can be overlooked in the communication pathways. Others in the formal structure may make judgments about the 'need to know' and 'value in seeking input' in relation to student service personnel and their capacity to contribute to policy and procedure development. The result is a workplace culture that

misses some of the richness available to it and lowers the quality of student support provided. This frequently unacknowledged feature of campus culture means that options for possible improvements and initiatives are sometimes overlooked because expertise and knowledge from all student support units is not recognized, valued, and incorporated.

The university-allocated budgets for student services tend to be drawn from the university operation account. The dollar allocations to student service budget areas have been necessarily restrained by the budgetary demands of the core business areas of research, teaching, and learning. Budgets for the "soft" people-focused services that offer individual support to students tend to consist primarily of salary allocations, with little discretionary funding for new initiatives or responsiveness. The total budget allocated to student services has never been clearly identified, but in the last 15 years budget allocations have been stationary or reduced incrementally as student numbers have increased.

Despite the impact of an era of economic rationalism, a higher education sector marked by periods of boom and catch-up, and the ad-hoc nature of the development of student services, there are surprisingly only minor differences across the sector. The providers of the services have remained resilient by displaying considerable flexibility in response to the institutional variations at the local level and the surges of change that have been the hallmark of the Australian higher education sector at a national level.

Student Organizations Deliver Student Services

Student-run organizations also have a substantial place in the history of provision of programs, services, and amenities designed to enrich the lives of Australian students. The university student unions, associations, guilds, and representative councils; sports associations; and postgraduate student associations have become the centre of student amenities, student life, sports, culture, and representation in governance on Australian university campuses. The Higher Education Support Amendment (Abolition of Compulsory Up-Front Student Union Fees) Bill 2005 banned the collection of compulsory fees levied on students for membership of student organizations. This has affected the non-academic services and student representation provided by these student organizations. It has also resulted in a loss of AUS $160 million ($153 million USD) to the university sector and effectively severed the student organizations and their services from their major income stream. This legislation has had a far reaching impact on the student organizations, the student experience on campus, and on the universities. The ramifications will be ongoing for some years.

The Influence of Research

The ever growing and diverse student communities have complex needs and issues. Programs to help student transition and adjustment to university rules, requirements, and cultures has been influenced by the substantial body of research that now exists on the first year cohorts and their transition and adjustment needs. The early Australian research in this field owes much to the Australian pioneers in student service delivery who conducted, published, and presented the results of surveys designed to shed light on the experiences of students in the university context. Orientation programs, peer mentoring experiments, and programs to encourage "freshers" to survive and thrive were early features of student service provision. They were most often driven by counselors employed in the fledgling counseling services. Currently, these aspects of student service delivery remain and receive broad support within each university.

When a significant budget crisis hit in the mid-1980s, research conducted by psychologists, counselors, and advisors in student services was considered in some institutions to be "not core business," and this area of service activity was pruned for economy, by the need to serve more students with the same or fewer members of staff. For some decades, the development of student-centered research was deemed not appropriate activity for student service practitioners, and regrettably, this active research practice has diminished. In the early 1990s, large-scale inquiries into the first year experience were developed through the activities of a specific research center, the Centre for the Study of Higher Education, based at the University of Melbourne. National conferences linked to the First Year Experience (FYE) movement began at that time, and these contributed to a renewed focus on improving student success via the pedagogical approach applied to first-year teaching.

Practitioner research is thankfully returning as an influential force, as the literature from evidence-based research affects service delivery outcomes and quality service provision via benchmarking and best practice considerations. An area of obvious interest now and in the future is the development of an overarching, cogent, conscious, and nationally accepted philosophy to underpin student services in Australia.

The Government and Peak Bodies Influence the Sector

The Commonwealth government department for higher education has played a very strong role in influencing the sector, including student services. Currently called the Department of Education Science and Training (DEST), it has introduced sweeping reforms following a 2002 inquiry into the Australian higher education sector. Many of these reforms have had, and will continue to have, a direct impact on students.

The Attorney-General's Department also plays a role in relation to higher education via the Commonwealth Disability Discrimination Act 1992 and the Disability Standards for Education 2005. Another significant government department is the Department of Immigration and Multicultural and Indigenous Affairs, which generated strong rules governing the student visa application and associated compliance for international students and the institutions at which they are enrolled (Commonwealth of Australia, 2006).

There are national peak bodies associated with both the student-based organizations and the institution-provided student services. A *peak body* is typically an overarching not for profit association or organization accorded the status as being recognized as representing the views and interests of relevant associations or organizations within a particular sector or user interest group. The peak body provides services and representation on behalf of its members who generally have similar goals, community service foci, or sector agendas. The peak body provides referent power for purposes such as political lobbying or providing a collective response to government legislation, policy, or initiatives.

These peak bodies related to student services provide considerable commentary and critical appraisal on policy, policy implementation, social and cohort changes, and university and government responsiveness to student needs and challenges. They also provide substantial contributions to professional development and career path support for those employed in the sector.

The Australian Vice-Chancellors' Committee (AVCC) also plays an important role across the higher education sector, exerting influence at the political level on behalf of the individual universities and producing sector-wide statements with responses to policy and other sector influences.

Professional Development and Preparatory Programs for Student Services

Viewed historically, it is evident that the role and purpose of student services on Australian university campuses is accepted and recognized. This is evident from references made in a series of reports (1956–2000) that highlight (a) the substantial contribution that student services have made to the quality of students' educational outcomes and (b) the enhanced reputation gained for each institution via the experience of support received by individual students.

Despite this recognition, there remains a lack of formal acknowledgement of student services as a professional career area within the higher education sector in Australia. Education administration and management has more recently gained credibility as a career path. There are substantially more managers employed in post-secondary education in Australasia[2] than people employed in student services. It is estimated that there are fewer than 7,000 staff employed within traditional student support services across the combined higher education sector for Australia and New Zealand. For example, one large university (more than 40,000 students) has approximately 150 staff across student administrative and student support areas. Due to the difference in numbers, the aspiring managers in higher education have a career path supported by postgraduate coursework programs offered by a number of universities. The career path available in student support services is limited and is not afforded such recognition or formal qualification support. A past president of the Australian and New Zealand Student Services Association, Inc. (ANZSSA) has approached various universities to host a postgraduate-level curriculum, written specifically for the sector, and suitable for a flexible mode of delivery, but so far,

---

[2]The term "Australasia" is commonly used to describe the geographical region that includes Australia, New Zealand, New Guinea, and the islands of the South Pacific.

these efforts have been unproductive. As a result, the lobbying efforts required to achieve such a goal have languished.

International Collaboration

International collegiate exchange and communication are facilitated via national associations and institutional affiliations. For example:

◊ Opportunities for interaction between student services personnel in Australia and New Zealand are encouraged within ANZSSA, the International Education Association (ISANA), and the Association for Tertiary Education Management (ATEM).

◊ There are regular "visit" exchanges between ANZSSA and the U.S.-based NASPA–Student Affairs Administrators in Higher Education.

◊ Programs for professional development are offered by the previously mentioned associations and by the Asia Pacific Student Services Association (APSSA);

◊ An international study tour can be taken via an Association of Tertiary Education Managers (ATEM) bursary/scholarship or employer universities.

Student services personnel from overseas institutions regularly visit Australian universities and these visits provide opportunities for dialogue on the similarities and differences that exist in the provision of student services within and across the nations.

Many Australian universities have offshore campuses, and the presence of these in various locations from Asia to South Africa and the Middle East establishes opportunities for international collaboration and exchange.

Into the Future

Student services in Australia are on the verge of discernable reinvention. A plethora of forces for change are now evident within the sector or are noticeably massing on the horizon. Each is likely to carry significant impact be it rapid or evolving.

These forces include:

◊ The outworking of the previously mentioned Higher Education Support Amendment (Abolition of Compulsory Up-Front Student Union Fees) Bill 2005 on the student-run organizations, and via the related budgetary ramifications, on all non-academic and student support services;

◊ the progressive corporatization of university management structures;

◊ the increased competition within the higher education sector for undergraduate and postgraduate coursework and postgraduate research student enrolments;

◊ the differentiation of student cohorts based on level of degree and the tailoring of university relationships with those cohorts based on different needs and circumstances;

◊ the emerging trends in research in particular, cross-discipline studies and collaborations;

◊ the introduction and expansion of full-fee places for both local and international students;

◊ the increasing numbers of international and local students whose first language, educational experience, and culture are different from that of the Australian-born local student;

◊ the continued societal and government-driven desire to see higher education more accessible for indigenous students, young men, and those from backgrounds of disadvantage, or those with a disability, and those from rural, regional, and isolated communities;

◊ the continued expectation from the federal government that a quality learning experience for students be underpinned by a quality learning and teaching environment; and

◊ the shifting sands of funding provision delivered to the sector from government budget allocations that is inevitably reflected in each institution's operating resources and subsequently reflected in budget allocations within the institutions funding priorities.

The cumulative impact of the above forces is likely to provide a noticeable change in both the approach to service delivery and the student support culture. This shift has the potential to produce shock waves of seismic proportion for some of the specialized services or for individual student service workers. It is however, possible that the likely outcome for students will be the provision of support delivered in more systemic, integrated, and seamless ways.

Student Services within the Context of Higher Education in Australia

History of Student Services—The Beginning

It is impossible to discuss the development of student services in Australia without some understanding of the growth of higher education in Australia. Compared with the development of higher education in Europe, Britain, and the United States of America, Australia's higher education sector has a relatively short history characterized by periods of rapid expansion.

The experience of higher education for students in Australia did not begin until the University of Sydney was established in 1850 (University of Sydney History, n. d.) in the British Colony of New South Wales in the pre-Federation days of Australia's colonial history.[3] By Federation in 1901, there were four more universities established, and by 1911 each of the six Federated States had a university located in its capital city. These have become known as the sandstone universities, and together with Australia's national university (Australian National University, established in Canberra in 1946), comprise six of the eight Australian

---

Prior to 1901, Australia consisted of separate colonies reporting directly to the Government of Britain. In January 1901, these colonies formed a federation of states (and two territories included later) within the Commonwealth of Australia.

universities that currently dominate as research-intensive institutions known as the Group of Eight. During the first decades of the 20th century, the Australian universities were strongly influenced by the British model of higher education in structure, ritual, and tradition and provided for the needs of the country's emerging middle class professionals. The class sizes at that time were relatively small compared to current standards, and were filled with white males of primarily British background preparing for careers in law, medicine, and the public service (Anderson, Boven, Fensham, and Powell, 1980; McMullen, 1991; Catley, 2004). Population participation rates in the early 1900s were low and provided a university education to only about 2% of the population. Enrolments from women were low, and they were under represented compared with the percentage of women in the population (McMullen, 1991).

Enrolment Jumps, Demographics Change

Big changes occurred in 1946, after the end of the World War II, when the Commonwealth government funded university places for many of the returning Australian service men and women (McMullen, 1991). This access to university by mature age students from varied academic and class backgrounds was the beginning of a continuing and progressive change that increased the diversity of student cohorts enrolled at Australian universities. In response to increased demand for university places, the number and size of universities grew as they coped with growth in enrolments doubling in size in the years from 1946–1961, and doubled again during the next decade (1961–1971) (Roe, Foster, Moses, Sanker, and Storey, 1982).

In 1987, substantially more university places were provided following the Dawkins Reforms (Dawkins, 1988), which paved the way for the 'massification' of higher education in Australia. These reforms opened the university system to allow for double the number of students drawn from across the breadth of Australian society (Catley, 2004). The Dawkins Reforms accomplished this by creating a Unified National System[4] that permitted the merger of colleges of advanced education and institutes of technology with universities (Moses, n.d.). The dominant objectives of the Dawkins Reforms were to increase numbers of enrolled students, to increase access and equity, to increase the relevance of higher education to Australia's global competitiveness, and to lower costs per student unit, achieved partly through rationalization of institutions (Yerbury, 1996).

Following the Dawkins Reforms, the sector continued the trend of rapid expansion and the national population participation rates in higher education increased significantly. Australian national statistics show that from 1994 to 2004 the proportion of persons, aged 15–64 years, with a postsecondary school qualification increased from 39% to 51% (ABS, 2003).

During the 1990s, the enrolments from an international student cohort within the higher education sector started to climb, and the sector subsequently emerged as a significant national export industry. Between 1994 and 2003, the number of overseas students enrolled at Australian universities rose from 40,000 to 210,000, with offshore campuses providing education to 58,000 of those enrolments (News Review, 2004). By 2003, the total value of Australia's education exports had climbed to $5.3 billion, giving Australia's Education Services a compound annual growth rate of 11% across a brief period of three years (2000–03), and yielding the highest growth of all major commodities for 2003 (IDP, 2005). Currently, international students remain very actively recruited by Australian universities providing a fundamental and valued income stream for higher education institutions as they seek to replace essential funding that has been progressively withdrawn by the Commonwealth government over the same time period.

In overall terms, from 1990–2003, the total number of students enrolled at Australian universities rose sharply increasing from 485,000 to 930,000. By 2004, Australian universities provided access to higher education for just under one million Australian students drawn from a total population of more than 20 million people. (ABS, 2003).

Significant in this increase in university places and enrolments is the high participation rate of mature age students who have embraced the government-sponsored entreaty to participate in "lifelong learning."

Influenced by globalization, the internationalization of education, and Australian Government competition policies, the sector continues to expand rapidly. By 2004, Australia boasted 39 publicly funded higher education providers, 37 with the title of university. The most recent university was established in 1996 (University of the Sunshine Coast). Of these 37 institutions, only three are privately funded.

The higher education sector has become very complex. In terms of Commonwealth government policies, 44 self-accrediting higher education providers (not all have university status) have been approved (DEST, 2005a). Over recent decades, various government reforms such as the Dawkins-instigated Unified National System of 1988 (Yerbury, 1996) have resulted in institution amalgamations that have blurred the boundaries across the postsecondary education sectors (higher education plus vocation education and training), with some universities now providing programs within both sectors.

Changes Coming in Governance?

In relation to governance structures, universities in Australia continue to be influenced by both Commonwealth and State legislation and Commonwealth government policies. Since 1974, the Commonwealth government has been responsible for financial and policy direction for higher education; the State and Territory Governments hold the legislative responsibility. In March 2005, Commonwealth and state responsibilities became the subject of an issues paper (DEST, 2005b). The current Commonwealth government is seeking to influence three major areas of perceived impediment within the higher education sector. These impediments are identified as:

---

[4]Prior to 1988–89 the Australian higher education sector included universities and colleges of education/institutes of technology with distinct roles and profiles, different academic structures, and salaries. This binary system was changed into the Unified National System (UNS).

1. legislative differences that restrict universities from expanding and diversifying their revenue sources via commercial activity;

2. the governance and management requirements of public universities that hamper universities in their effective response to the complexity of the current domestic and international conditions; and

3. the consensus of desire for greater national consistency on the recognition of universities and the accreditation of courses and providers.

The provision of student services in the future will depend on the working out of such fundamental changes to university governance and to university income via (a) the capacity to generate income from commercial avenues and (b) the currently identified reward/bonus funding from the Commonwealth government, a funding source tied to the achievement of reform agendas (DEST, 2005b).

Quality Assurance: Impact on Student Services

Establishing and monitoring of quality in the Australian higher education system is governed by government legislation and policy at both federal and state levels, by the universities themselves, and through independent organizations (DEST, n.d.).

Agencies have been established at the highest level to safeguard the quality of higher education, irrespective of whether the education provider is private, publicly funded, or an amalgamation of both. The quality of those offerings and the levels of qualifications within the Unified National System are governed by the Australian Qualifications Framework (AQF) (AQF, n.d). Since 2000, the university sector has been subject to quality audits. The Australian Universities Quality Agency (AUQA), an independent, not-for-profit national agency, was established to promote, audit, and report on quality assurance in Australian higher education (AUQA, 2004).[5] AUQA conducts a series of quality university audits each year (AUQA, n.d. a). These quality audits include examination of the quality processes used within student services at each institution. AUQA has established the Australian Universities Quality Forum as the peak national forum for the discussion and advancement of quality assurance and quality enhancement in Australian higher education (AUQA, n.d. b).

AUQA has also established a database of best practice within the university sector collated from the university audit process. Included are best practice examples for the provision of student services, which can be located by using the search function within the database (AUQA, 2005). While this is relatively new, it is already exerting an influence emphasizing student adjustment, transition, and overall experience in higher education.

As an agency, AUQA offers strong encouragement for student services to highlight examples of best practice. In drawing attention to best practice, the student services units are able to demonstrate the importance and value of their contribution to the quality of the student's "lived" experience, and the contribution of student services to the quality of educational outcomes for students on the nation's campuses, as well as for those studying at a distance or offshore.

In addition, the Commonwealth government has required Australian universities to participate in performance measures, many of which survey the student experience. These performance management tools include surveys of graduating students, undergraduates, and postgraduate students. Some can provide valuable information for student services to use in planning improvement initiatives and strategic directions (DEEWR, n.d.).

Another organization that influences the overall quality demonstrated by Australian universities is the Australian Vice-Chancellors' Committee (AVCC), comprising the presidents of Australian universities (Universities Australia, n.d.). It has an influence on quality via its aim to seek to advance higher education through voluntary, cooperative, and coordinated action, being non-partisan, and existing exclusively for educational purposes. A recent influential AVCC document that directly addresses the quality of student experience on Australian university campuses is a code of practice and guidelines for the provision of education to international students (AVCC, 2005a). These guidelines were designed to complement the legislative requirements established under the ESOS Act 2000. This Commonwealth legislation has required universities to meet specific standards of education and support services provided to international students, whatever their mode of study within the Australian higher education system. This code of practice and guidelines describes the ethical commitment made by the AVCC member universities to provide a quality educational experience for international students and recommends the provision of "consistent and caring procedures in the recruitment, reception, education, and welfare of international students" (AVCC, 2005a, p. 1). The requirements placed on universities in relation to student support services are quite prescriptive, and the full implications of these specifications are still largely untested. In this document, the AVCC set the expectation that universities should develop appropriate support services, including counseling services, for all enrolled international students (both on and offshore).

The Development of Student Services: Focus on Transition, Adjustment, and Retention

The history of student services in Australia commenced in 1890 with the appointment of a Tutor for Women Students at the University of Sydney. The position was established to assist with academic planning, career choice, and personal problems experienced by the very few female students studying at the university. The next major addition to services for students was the establishment of Appointment Boards (Burke, 1990a). The first Appointment Boards established were at University of Melbourne, 1914 and University of Sydney, 1922. Support for

[5]AUQA was established in March 2000. It operates independently of governments and the higher education sector under the direction of a board of directors. AUQA comprises 25 Territory Ministers for higher education who are members of the Ministerial Council on Education, Employment, Training and Youth Affairs (MCEETYA).

students prior to the mid-1940s was primarily assistance with academic and personal matters offered by the wardens and tutors of residential colleges (Roe, et al., 1982).

Post-World War II proved to be a substantial growth period in higher education, with university enrolments ballooning due to changes in the immigration policies. The resulting shift in immigrant patterns permanently broadened the cultural and social diversity of Australian society, with the children of these immigrants forever changing the nature and diversity of the cohorts enrolled at Australian universities. With the introduction of federally funded university places for many returned service men and women in 1946, the Commonwealth government decided to protect its investment in the education of so many mature age students. Consequently, the government initiated additional support for these students as they negotiated the transition from war experience to university learning. Guidance officers were appointed to support this adjustment and to encourage successful retention and completion of university study (McMullen, 1991). Across the higher education sector, student support services emerged to assist with students' adjustment to the Australian university culture that was still strongly influenced by the British model of higher education.

In time, university management also recognized the support needs of this student cohort. In 1958, the dean of science at the University of Melbourne initiated various strategies in response to the reported loneliness experienced by first-year students. (Hooper, 2005).

Dealing with High Attrition

During the years between 1946 and 1960, various types of student services were established on campuses in response to the concerns raised by the number of students failing at their studies (39%) or dropping out. In 1951, the attrition rate was estimated at 42% (Downes, 1961) and in 1956, the Committee on Australian Universities chaired by Sir Keith Murray reported great concern about the student failure rate at all levels of study. The committee reported, "It is difficult to exaggerate the cost in time, effort and money to students, universities and the nation of this low rate of graduation" (Australia Committee on Australian Universities, 1958, p. 35).

Response to concerns about failing students included a number of student service developments, including establishment of health services. By 1958, some Australian universities had established a range of student services that were designed to support the general well-being of students, including counseling and student advisory services.

By 1955, the Appointments Board of the University of Melbourne was very "concerned with the chronic shortage of graduates available for the essential work of the community" and instigated a "survey to measure the loss of appropriate university material at all levels of education from the post primary onwards" (University of Melbourne Appointments Board, 1960, p. 3). In 1955–56, two student counselors at the University of Melbourne Student Counseling Service conducted a survey of the environmental and personal factors that impacted on the academic progress of first-year students. This research is identified as the first research into the first-year experience conducted in Australia (Hooper, 2005). Many student service units provided the early researchers who investigated the student experience and who contributed significantly to the understanding of student needs, the emerging field of student services, and the first-year experience. In the mid-1970s, studies at the University of Melbourne articulated the importance of an integrated approach to first-year student transition and adjustment.

Williams and Pepe (1983) published research on the early experiences of students on 32 Australian College of Advanced Education campuses. They noted a trend that is still a factor in the student experience: "The satisfaction and quality of experience of the first couple of months clearly affected decisions about continuing or discontinuing" (p. 130).

In 1972, student services were recognized for their role as strong contributors to the quality of student life, when the Commission on Advanced Education Third Report claimed: "Few people these days seriously deny the need for supporting services" (as cited in Burke, 1990a, p. 4). The report also stated that the need for such services was beyond dispute if waste, due to attrition, were to be minimized. Further, it made the suggestion that there was a "need to assist each student to attain his maximum satisfaction in achievement and living" (Burke, 1990a, p. 4). This sentiment was echoed and strengthened a few years later when the Australian Universities Commission in its Sixth Report, reinforced the value of student services in overcoming the ongoing problem of student adjustment and strongly encouraged universities to make good use of student support services as a strategy to reduce attrition and promote retention (Burke, 1990a). This report, delivered in 1975, established that a campus without student services was not providing adequate support for its students.

Offering an Array of Services

In 1980–81, a survey on student services in Australia provided a comprehensive data set on the provision of student services (Burke, 1990a), and established that by the early 1980s, universities and large metropolitan institutes of technology were providing student services in areas of "counseling, careers and appointments, health, housing financial and welfare" (Burke, 1990a, p. 5). The report based on the survey, called the Roe Report (Roe et al., 1982), concluded that universities, including those that had only recently been established, appeared to give student services a relatively high priority, a fact reflected in the proportion of the institution's recurrent budget invested in student services (Burke, 1990a).

The size of the institution and/or campus played a strong role in the type of services provided and how they were provided. Burke (1990b) noted that on campuses where enrolment numbers were relatively small, the providers of counseling services (professionals with degrees in psychology or social work) frequently wore many hats, offering the original one-stop shop for the student seeking assistance.

...counsellors typically deal with a broad range of educational and
personal issues, as well as helping students with immediate crisis.
In many institutions, the counsellor frequently may also provide assistance with accommodation, employment or financial assistance.
(Burke, 1990a, p. 5)

Education Equity Becomes a Concern

The Commonwealth government's white paper Higher Education: A Policy Statement 1988, provided the first indication
that educational equity was a concern for the broader society,
and during the 1980s and 1990s equity and student diversity remained central concerns of the government (Postle, et al., n.d.).
Universities began to respond to the government equity agenda with institutional strategies to improve access and equity.

At the First Conference of the Asian Pacific Student Services Association in 1988, Bryan Burke, then president of
the Australian and New Zealand Student Services Association, clearly identified the need for specific specialist services
to assist with the improvement of student participation
and success.

In November 1988, the Australian Vice-Chancellors' Committee released the results of a survey of language and study skills
support provided by Australian universities. The report makes
it clear that the issue of language and academic skills support
available for students from overseas or permanent residents
whose first language was not English was an emerging issue
with a great variety of strategies and services being provided
across the university sector.

Only a few years later, another government report, A Fair
Chance for All: National and Institutional Planning for Equity in
Higher Education, identified a range of student support services
as important in improving participation and success rates for
disadvantaged students (DEET, 1994).

Contribution Is Recognized, but Funding Is Tenuous (DEET Report)

In December 1993 the Government Department of Employment, Education and Training published a report titled Student
Support Services: Management, Delivery and Effectiveness
(DEET, 1994). This report appears to be the first nationally focused exploration of student services since the Committee on
Australian Universities Report in 1958. It provides a summary of
the role of student support services, the variety and type of services, the integral role that student support services play in a university community, and the university management structures
that assumed responsibility for student services. It identified the
fundamental role of student services as "to assist and enhance
the educational experience and outcomes of the diverse range
of students participating in quality Australian higher education"
(DEET, 1994, p. 1). By 1993, the emphasis for student services on
transition and retention had expanded to include emphasis on
the students' educational experiences and outcomes. Such a focus remains to the present day and is not only reflected in the
operational plans for student services but also embedded in the
strategic plans of universities.

The DEET report (1994), notes that the institutions' funding
of student support services had decreased substantially in the
previous five years at a time when the size of student cohorts requiring support had greatly increased. Evidence from interviews
and focus groups suggested that student support services frequently occupied a tenuous position in the allocation of funding at an institutional level. There was an indication that funding
had declined in real terms while the number of students requiring services had greatly increased. The words of the executive
summary are still applicable today:

...[S]tudent support services provide a wide variety of appropriate
services to university communities. Accordingly, student services
have been recognised as a part of a quality learning environment
which includes other physical infrastructure such as libraries, co-op-
erative administration staff, equipment and a safe place to study....
[Student support] services play a role in the maintenance of diversity
and heterogeneity in the university community by providing support
to students with differing needs, and...where...possible...made productive contributions to university planning and policy development.
(DEET, 1994, p. 1)

The primary providers of student support services at the time
of this report were the university administration and student organizations. The report noted, there were "...various degrees of
centralized management....The primary structural problem...
was the lack of access to key decision making processes" (DEET,
1994, p. 1).

Some structural revision of student support services had
occurred by 1993 due to the arrival of fee-paying international
students and/or the amalgamation of institutions following the
Dawkins Reforms. However, the Report (DEET, 1994) notes that
this restructuring was "motivated by fiscal planning without regard for the nature and the increased efficiency of the service
involved" (DEET, 1994, p. 1).

The DEET Report (1994) provided a number of recommendations for change in the management of student services. These
recommendations can, by and large, be seen as influencing the
current practice of primary student service units. These recommendations were:

1. Use a consultative committee of stakeholders to allow
contributions from services providers, service users, and
other major stakeholders.

2. Implement key structural management practices designed to enable the relevant and efficient use of institutional resources.

3. Undertake adequate performance evaluation processes.

4. Use appropriate qualitative and quantitative indicators to enhance and promote quality service provision.
(DEET, 1994)

The DEET Report (1994) gave additional recognition to the
central role of student services for serving student needs, and
it articulated key performance indicators for use as measures to
test the effectiveness of services provided by student services
units. It also provided a cluster of best practice quantitative and
qualitative performance indicators.

These performance indicators have generally been accepted
within the student services domain and are noticeable in the

way that various student services and specialist units (e. g., counseling services, disability services, and learning centers) gather data and report on their activities.

Quantitative Performance Indicators identified included:
◊ professional/support staff ratios,

◊ student/staff ratio,

◊ length of time on waiting lists,

◊ average time spent servicing each student,

◊ service activity cost,

◊ student access rate,

◊ service product range, and

◊ value-adding services.

Qualitative Performance Indicators identified included:
◊ participation in university policy development,

◊ degree and depth of multi-site servicing,

◊ participation in wider community activities,

◊ student/client awareness of and access to services,

◊ user satisfaction,

◊ student demand,

◊ usage patterns,

◊ flexibility and responsiveness,

◊ innovation and openness,

◊ consistency of quality service delivery, and

◊ noticeable difference (measure of impact on students accessing the service). (DEET, 1994)

This Report recognized factors that had produced increasing pressures on the ability of student services to deliver services effectively. Identified in particular were major reductions and changes in government funding provision, the progressive introduction of full-fee student places, and the large increases in enrolment numbers (DEET, 1994).

The DEET Report(1994) observed that there was a lack of coherence as a result of an absence of a common philosophy underpinning the role of student services across the sector. This lack had inhibited the effective provision and development of student support services in Australian higher education institutions. It was noted that the role of student services goes well beyond service provision for the individual and has the capacity to contribute to the development of the university community through input to university planning and policy development and through providing the human face of the institution (DEET, 1994).

> …student support services play an important part in defining the overall quality of an institution, the education services it offers and the quality of the institution's educational outcomes. (DEET, 1994, p. 15)

To this end, the authors of the DEET Report (1994) recommend a common mission statement be adopted by all service providers and by the institutions in which they serve. The role of student support services was proposed as follows: The fundamental role of student support services is to assist and enhance the educational experience and outcomes of the diverse range of students participating in quality Australian higher education (1994).

The performance of this function requires a commitment to:
1. assist students to equitable access and help them progress in higher education,

2. assist students to continue study despite financial, academic, health, legal, or personal difficulties,

3. enhance the university community's environment and the quality of available education services, and

4. continually improve the quality and relevance of student services. (DEET, 1994)

This statement captures well the understanding that has been held by the majority of specialist, student support services, and student services collectively for more than the past decade. Most, if not all, student service units in Australian universities are now working to operational plans with key performance indicators influencing their planning and associated implementation.

Benchmarking

A publication by McKinnon, Walker, and Davis (2000) on benchmarking for Australian universities contained a section dedicated to student services. It identified lagging, leading, and learning benchmarks across a number of perspectives (financial, customer/student, internal process, and people/culture). Significantly, in this document, student services also included student administrative functions, especially those that incorporated a customer liaison or interaction role.

McKinnon et al. also reinforced the now familiar warning to universities that did not address student expectations in relation to student services:

> …where services fall short of student expectations, in the absence of management action to encourage more realistic expectations, or remedial action to supply additional services, universities lose students unnecessarily, fail to achieve optimal success rates, and/or suffer a lower reputation than may be deserved. (p. 92)

One clear result of this developing institutional role for student services is that, in general terms, student services have also more clearly recognized their role, contribution, and central position within the university environment. More than ever before, they have adopted systemic approaches to student support and are looking for ways to be proactive, being frequently guided by preventative rather than remedial imperatives.

More recently, Garlick & Pryor (2004) suggest that fostering organizational improvement is a five-phase approach requiring collaboration and connectivity across interests, learning and knowledge exchange, and leadership commitment. Their five stages for embedding quality are: (a) review the current environment, (b) agree to a strategy plan to implement initiatives and a performance assessment regime, (c) commit to the implementation, (d) review progress, and (e) invest in learning for continuous improvement.

The Competition for Funds

Student services were initially hesitant to embrace the benchmarking requirements and performance indicators of the corporate sector as these began to influence the university sector. Currently, managers and student service personnel are much more reconciled to the impact of reviews, performance indicators, and routine planning, and they approach it all with a practiced pragmatism. They accept the inherent challenges as now a routine aspect of the workplace. However, there are still the annual battles of budget allocation and justification. The position of student services within the institutional structures is regularly changed, as student-focused portfolios are assigned and reassigned after reviews of line management structures and the subsequent restructuring of executive responsibilities to reflect the rapidly changing environment within institutions that are driven by an imperative to maintain viability within the sector.

Planning, operating to key performance indicators, using performance management, and demonstrating outcomes of service delivery all require resources, and quality processes are worthy of a budget line item in their own right. Student services that report within the university organizational structure have budgets drawn from university operating funds. With the exception of services that receive targeted funds for equity, disability, and Indigenous student support provision, very few services have their own independent sources of revenue. Those that do are frequently required to supplement their university-allocated budgets with commercially generated revenues that are relatively small. Surplus accumulated funds are usually returned to the general operating fund of the institution for distribution in the next budget round. Given the spread of student support initiatives and activities across different budget units within each university, an estimate of the percentage allocation from an institution's operating budget directed to student support, services, and amenities is not available. Adding to the difficulty of arriving at a tally for budget allocation to the whole of student services is the fact that many student services are provided by student associations and organizations that exist outside the university income stream and budget allocation.

Where budget issues are concerned there remains a recurring intra-institutional competition around issues of priority for resource allocation. Cohort support needs provided by student services have, more recently, been low on the pecking order for increases in operating funds. Competition for funding is obvious and includes the resource-hungry demands of emerging developments in systems, policy, and other essential university infrastructure requirements. These include, among others, information technology infrastructure, the development and maintenance of online enrolment environments, the data management systems required to cope with shifts in government requirements, the institutional reporting demands, website management, and the investment in the core business areas of research and teaching.

Universities in Australia are currently negotiating difficult times in relation to security of income streams. They need to investigate ways to generate income that depart even further from the traditional dependence on government funding arrangements. Currently in Australia, some universities are thought to be in a precarious financial position as they adjust to changes in the traditional sources of revenue. These budgetary concerns translate all too quickly to the level of budget allocation for providing student services.

Even though student services are now generally accepted as an area of university investment, student service managers find it necessary to regularly champion the value of student support services. Managers must continue to advocate for recognition that student service personnel can bring valuable knowledge and experience to the formulation of policies and processes that affect students.

Students Providing Services for Students: Is Historic Role Ending for Student Unions?

In parallel to the university provided student services, student organizations on campuses have also evolved into providers of student amenities, support, and activities that enhance the experience of university education. A significant player among the student organizations on most campuses is the student union.

McMullen (1999) points out that the term "union," in reference to student organizations at a university, was originally used by Oxford University (in the 19th century) where it meant, "the union or coming together of the various College student clubs" (p. 87). McMullen also mentions the Macquarie Dictionary definition of union, as a club offering dining and recreational facilities for the members of certain universities (p 87).

As enrolments at universities climbed in the 1960s and 1970s, student unions were already well established on a number of campuses, and they became the obvious vehicle for students' strengthening desire to have services for students that were managed and controlled by students. While the establishment of student unions on university campuses predates the demands from students to be represented clearly in the provision of university life and in the institutions' governance structures, the increased student activism of the 1960s and 1970s influenced the consolidation of student representation in university governance structures (McMullen, 1999).

The University Union of The University of New South Wales (UNSW) established in 1961 by that University's Council "as the primary non-academic service provider on campus,"[6] provides a clear example of the primary function of student unions on university campuses in Australia. The current constitutional mission of the UNSW University Union is "to be the community centre of the University: through its programs, services and facilities the Union seeks to cultivate and nurture the community life of the University" (University of New South Wales Union, 2000, p. 2).

---

[6]Quoted from a University of New South Wales Union Board paper distributed during a UNSW-wide consultation (May 2005, p.1).

Within the Australian higher education context, student unions have historically been funded in part by compulsory fees of membership levied on all enrolled students, with the remainder of the funding derived from the proceeds of sales and services provided on campuses. While the services, amenities, and developmental opportunities provided under the umbrella of student unions vary somewhat from one university to another, the University Union at UNSW can be considered typical in its constitutional objectives. The objectives are to:

◊ develop social, educational, and intellectual interests of its members;

◊ provide facilities and amenities for common meeting spaces and venues for social activity;

◊ provide facilities for the refreshment, entertainment, recreation, and convenience of its members;

◊ encourage cooperation within its members toward furthering the interests of the University; and

◊ generally organize and direct activities considered appropriate for the educational and other interests of its members. (University Union Board, UNSW, 2005)

The first-year-experience literature, the literature on retention, and the reported understanding of the student experience from student service workers, all highlight the importance of social integration and engagement with the university as a valuable tool in arresting unnecessary student attrition (Elkerton, 1985; Andrews & Shortus, 1997; Promnitz, 1997; Huon & Sankey, 2002; Krause, Hartley, James & McInnes, 2005). Much of the non-academic life and infrastructure of Australian university campuses has been provided or maintained under the banner of student unions, operating within formal and informal arrangements with the respective university and the associated council of that institution

Currently within the Australian university sector a compulsory student union fee is normally paid at enrolment. Most students also pay a compulsory university-imposed amenities/services charge levied on all students at enrolment. These fees and charges function in a similar way to local council rates with all members of the community contributing to the provision of all services. Part-time students and distance students would, in most cases, have reduced fees or, in some cases, the option not to pay the charge.

There are a number of national student representative peak bodies in Australia. All contribute actively to commentary and lobbying conducted around the policies and practices in the higher education sector and the impact on students enrolled at Australian universities.

The current federal government has a longstanding agenda (first mooted in 1999) to outlaw the collection of compulsory fees that fund the majority of the activities controlled by student-led unions and associations on university campuses and to outlaw compulsory union membership. This agenda has been also gathering momentum at state level and over the last decade, although hard fought, has been introduced in Western Australia and in Victoria by the respective state governments.

The previously mentioned Higher Education Support Amendment (Abolition of Compulsory Up-Front Student Union Fees) Bill 2005 has resulted in the introduction of voluntary student union membership. The income generated by future voluntarily paid membership fees is estimated to reduce to a mere 10% of the pre VSU revenue. As a result, it is anticipated that the nature of student life on campus will undergo considerable change in relation to the management, funding and provision of services, activities, and infrastructure, that has to date, been student controlled. The pre-2005 compulsory student fees provided a suite of student support services, facilities, amenities, and on-campus cultural life, and support services that were in many cases also available to members of local communities. This particularly applied to university campuses in regional areas where the university is often the cultural and sporting hub of the district. A media release from the Australian Vice-Chancellors' Committee (AVCC) stated:

> In 2005, universities look to collect over $170 million in the student services and amenities charge...Less than 15 per cent of those funds collected by universities will actually go towards political advocacy and representation. Less than six per cent of total funds will go towards clubs and societies. The bulk of the money is directed towards sporting facilities (21 per cent), health and welfare services (11 per cent), non-political services (39 per cent), and computer and study assistance (six per cent). The AVCC understands the Government's concern that the monies collected are directed towards student political activity, but clearly…this is not true in most cases. (AVCC, 2005b)

The VSU Bill prohibits all higher education providers from:

◊ Requiring a person to become a member of a student association (union or guild).

◊ Requiring a student to pay fees for non-academic student services unless the student chooses to use the amenity, facility, or service.

University administrators are prevented, and/or penalized, under the legislation, from charging a student contribution fee, at enrolment, for the provision of non-academic student services. The long-term viability for the provision of these facilities and services will play out over the coming years. If universities are prevented, and/or penalized, as they would be under the proposed legislation, from charging a student contribution at enrolment for the provision of non-academic student services, the long-term viability for the provision of these facilities and services will be challenged.

Government Influences Access and Equity in Higher Education, Student Charges, Fees, Loans, and Income Support

The Commonwealth government has taken a strong interest in arresting student attrition and encouraging progression to graduation. The government-driven changes have also delivered consequences, both positive and negative, to the daily focus required of student support services. Campus-based student support services have primarily taken on the tasks of helping students negotiate and interpret the many iterative changes to the procedures resulting from Government legislation and policy, and assisting in the students' interaction and communication with the government departments that translate the legislation into policy and procedure.

Government attempts to address inequities of access to university began in earnest in the 1970s. Prior to the early 1970s, those university students not in receipt of a Teacher's College or Commonwealth Scholarship, paid tuition fees on enrolment. In 1973, the newly elected government led by Labor Prime Minister, Gough Whitlam, made enrolment at Australian universities free of fees. Although the removal of tuition fees was designed to remove the financial barrier for those on lower incomes, a research group commissioned by a government committee determined that between 1974 and 1977, the policy had only a very small positive effect for those who were from low socio-economic backgrounds or from previously under represented groups of part-time students, women, older students, and country residents (Anderson, et al., 1980). Further analyses for the years 1973 through 1985 told the same story.

The Rise of 'User Pays' Education

These free places for local students continued into the mid-1980s. In 1980, a fee was introduced for overseas students, opening the possibility for full tuition fees. Starting in 1986, local students were required to pay the universally applied Higher Education Administration Charge (HEAC). In 1988, HEAC was replaced by the Higher Education Contribution Scheme (HECS), a universal charge that students could elect to defer paying until their income reached a particular threshold. This allowed students to accumulate a fee debt, while they studied now, but paid later. In the late 1990s, a similar scheme to HECS was introduced for postgraduate coursework students with the Postgraduate Education Loans Scheme (PELS).[7] In 2003, universities were permitted to offer full fee undergraduate places to domestic students.

The Higher Education Reform Initiatives (HERI) 2005[8], introduced by the current Liberal/National Coalition Government Minister, Brendan Nelson, raised the charge to students, furthering the trend toward user-pays education. More recently, HECS and PELS were both replaced by the Commonwealth Supported Place and the Higher Education Loan Programme (HELP) (DEST, 2005c). Together these initiatives ushered in a more complex scheme of user pays options and charges.

These reforms provide further savings for the Government, add a valued income stream for the universities via cost shifting to the student, and will inevitably result in higher levels of student debt. Government spending from general tax revenue and the individual student spending via his or her higher education contribution now share the cost of a university education. The assumption is that both the individual and the community benefit from the investment in a university-educated workforce.

Student Services Focus on Financial Hardship

Because of the significant financial implications stemming from these changes to the student contribution schemes, student services personnel have been particularly active in raising concerns and issues regarding each iteration (Callaghan, 1987; Hastings, Hought, Germein, & Gorton, 1997; Bianco, 1998; Benson, 1999; Seal, 2003). Of particular concern is the potential for considerable student debt generated from increased fees (particularly full tuition fees) and the associated loans that are required to be carried over a lifetime of employment (Seal, 2003).

There are some government income support schemes, but the need for financial support continues to be a substantial issue for low-income students. Scholarships at undergraduate level are limited in number, and commercial loans are not usually a viable option for students. Part-time work options on campus are limited. Because of legislation concerned with employment requirements, institutions in Australia are currently unable to provide work–study programs for university students of low income, such as is often the case at universities in the United States. University students without family or independent financial support do frequently struggle to survive financially and have to obtain employment to cover basic living costs.

Most student services staff members are aware of reports of hardship and academic under-performance from students who find themselves working either full-time or a considerable number of part-time hours while being enrolled full-time (Benson, 1999; Bianco, 1998; McInnis, James & Hartley, 2000). Employment within the general community, when available to students, eases financial tensions but generates others. Fatigue, missing classes because of clashes with work shift times, social isolation due to a hectic work and academic schedule, and other work/study/life imbalances hinder the academic progress and performance of many students.

Helping students navigate the tension between the demands of living and academic effort is a major focus of student support services in Australia. Feelings of frustration and depression are commonly experienced during periods of chronic financial pressure (Bianco, 1998) and low motivation for study in this situation is hardly surprising.

National Student Services Associations

Student services in Australia have been supported sector-wide since the establishment of Australia and New Zealand Student Services (ANZSSA) in 1973, when the Australian and New Zealand Student Health Association (established 1956) and the Australian Association of University Counsellors (established 1965) amalgamated. The combined association was seen as a vehicle to serve the interests of all those involved in providing student services on higher education campuses (Burke, 1990a). But later, specialized groups founded their own organizations. Careers advisors established their own National Association of Graduate Careers Advisors. The International Student Advisor

---

[7]PELS was introduced via the Innovation and Education Legislation Amendment Bill (No. 2) 2001. PELS was an initiative valued at $2.9 billion within the Innovation Action Plan, (Backing Australia's Ability).

[8]HERI (2005) is the outcome of a Government lead consultation process (Higher Education a the Crossroads–A Review of Australian Higher Education) that ran for much of 2002–03 (DEST 2005d). The Minister's report on the major aspects of the reforms Our Universities–Backing Australia's Future (the Nelson Report) was enacted by Parliament as the Higher Education Support Act 2003 (see reference DEST 2005e for more information).

Network Australia began as part of ANZSSA but became an independent organization in 1998. In the early 1990s, changes in the national healthcare system made it unnecessary for medical officers to be part of ANZZSA.

Currently, ANZSSA is organized on both a regional and professional interest group basis. Membership from counselors and heads of student services remain the strongest in numbers. In the area of communications and research, the *Journal of the Australian and New Zealand Student Services Association* is a semiannual peer-reviewed publication. ANZZSA has made, and will continue to make, representation to government and the AVCC on emerging student issues, provide sector-wide communication, career development opportunities and conferences (currently biennially), and sponsor regional and professional interest group meetings, workshops, and seminars. At the instigation of the ANZSSA executive, ANZSSA plus other peak bodies connected to student services in postsecondary education established a Memorandum of Understanding (November 2005) and formed the Post-Secondary Student Services Council of Australia (PSSSCA).

Student Services Today

Current Structures

Most universities have a central "whole" of university administrative services and executive management division that exists in parallel to decentralized faculties that are powerful and relatively independent silo structures within the institutions. This arrangement tends to create a divide between the general staff and the academic staff. Further, administrative functions and services for students are located in the faculties and schools (faculty and school offices or student centers) as well as in centrally provided services, so there can be duplication. These overlaps of function can be confusing for the student, who frequently experiences the revolving door of referral while attempting to get appropriate assistance.

Commonly at any university, a student will find a substantial number of centrally provided support services that seek to enhance the quality of their experience. In addition to the centralized services are the clubs and societies provided within the structures of the student organizations, the sports associations and the various departments of the student associations and student union on each campus (childcare options, welfare and legal services, etc.).

Within Australian universities, all student services have an online information presence and frequently provide online service delivery options. While there is little variation in the range of services, there is considerable variation between universities as to how these services are provided and the way responsibilities are shared between student organizations and the student services more directly under university management.

Currently, in many universities, student services functions have been structured to report to a registrar or deputy registrar. There is often a director of student services, who has line management responsibility for both the academic administration services and a cluster of some of the more traditional student services. Alternatively, there will be different managers for the administrative functions and the student service functions with all reporting to a registrar or a similar position within the university senior management structure.

The more academically related services, such as learning centers and indigenous student support units usually exist in a separate line management portfolio attached to a deputy vice chancellor or a pro vice chancellor with responsibility for learning and teaching. Some faculties provide their own specialized student support units or a staff member with responsibility for student welfare, particularly while the student is on an industry placement such as occurs in medical schools or psychology or social work departments.

Examples of organizational structures shown in Figures 14.1, 14.2, and 14.3 are based on variations of structures that would be familiar to:

Figure 14.1 – Research-Intensive University: Go8

Figure 14.2 – Technology University: ATN

Figure 14.3 – Innovative Research University: IRU.

These models of organizational structures reflect only those aspects of the organization that are relevant to student services. Some universities are moving toward a campus life/community model and have a dean of community or a dean of students. Graduate Research Schools (GRS) are also being created across the sector. The GRS holds all administrative and support structures required by graduate research students. They are typically managed by a dean of research and report in most cases to a deputy vice chancellor, research.

Current Goals, Roles Functions and Specialization within Student Services

The twin goals of adjustment and transition currently remain central to the purpose of student services. To these goals have been added the desire to enhance the students' educational experience, enhance the total student university experience, and assist the student achieve his or her academic potential and emerge imbued with graduate attributes attractive to the best employers. Many student services are offered centrally and increasingly, student services that focus on academic advising, academic administration, and academic support are replicated within the faculty structures. Faculties with large enrolment numbers frequently provide dedicated services for their students.[9]

Much has changed over time with regard to the number of specialist student services. Each service area has adapted differently to the increasing demands of the multiple stakeholders (students, government, and the university) and to changes in government policy. Currently, the different services offer developmental and remedial services designed to assist the individual

[9] See UNSW Faculty of Commerce and Economics Student Services Web site: http://www2.fce.unsw.edu.au/nps/servlet/portalservice?GI_ID=System.LoggedOutInheritableArea&maxWnd=_Staff_StudentServices and Monash University Faculty of Art and Design Student and Administrative Services Web site: http://www.artdes.monash.edu.au/sas

with specific needs and/or campuswide systemic interventions and activities designed to impact on the university learning environment and culture. Some examples of the width and depth of service delivery are provided in the comments below.

Learning Centers. Once rare, learning centers are now commonplace, and while offering one-on-one assistance they also act as change agents. They provide learning skills and language support to students via individual consultation, workshops, and seminars. They provide extensive online services, including hints for managing the transition and adjustment to university. They are also an influence for guidance in the way academics integrate and develop appropriate learning tasks within the curriculum, tasks that are designed to stimulate academic skill development in the first and subsequent year. Professional staffing in learning centers across the sector varies considerably and staff-to-student ratios reflect this difference (one learning advisor [effective full time] per 1,500–6,000 students). Typically, the professional staff in learning centers would have a master's-level qualification in a related area such as linguistics. In addition to centralized learning support, some faculties also provide specific learning assistance for their students.

Counseling Service. It is common for a counseling service to provide, in addition to individual counseling and therapy, a selection of prevention strategies offered via systemic interventions, student volunteer programs, campus care programs, or early intervention programs. They also offer workshops and seminars that help develop students' social skills, communication styles, personality type awareness, leadership skills, creativity, and psychological resilience skills. Counseling services are frequently the coordinators of campuswide programs designed to assist the transition and adjustment and the successful progression of students such as O-Week (orientation week for commencing students just before the classes start for a session or semester), peer mentoring, and academic progress support.

Students arrive for counseling with a wide variety of presenting issues, and counselors across the sector are noting the increasing prevalence of serious presentations of depression, disabling anxiety, performance anxiety, perfectionism, eating disorders, chronic procrastination, relationship problems, cultural adjustment issues, life balance issues, severe and chronic stress, internet overuse, computer gaming overuse, and alcohol misuse. Students presenting with the first occurrence of psychotic symptoms are not uncommon. Self-harming behaviors are increasing, or at least are becoming more evident in the student population than in previous decades. At a few campuses over the last three decades, there have been instances of a disturbed student harming other individuals, with very sad and traumatizing outcomes. This has tended to make campus communities a little cautious, if not reactive toward students with mental health histories, who behave differently from others in class. Counselors provide consultation and assistance to academic staff when this different or difficult behavior is present. They also provide appropriate supportive strategies for the student and work, together with the disability officer, to ensure that students with a disability are not the subject of discrimination or other forms of disrespect or disadvantage. Provision of assistance at crisis situations is also part of the role of a university counseling service. Some services also provide counseling for university staff.

Counseling services will aim to work to best practice standards proffered by professional associations, state psychologists' registration boards, and the evidence-based literature. Counseling services in universities in Australia reflects a stepped care model of service delivery (Bower and Gilbody, 2005) with some adaptation for the university environment. Staffing ratios vary from campus to campus and range from 1 counselor (EFT) per 2,000 students to 1 counselor (EFT) per 6,000 students.

Health Services. Health services currently offer most of what would be found in a general/family medical practice. Additional health services available also include dental, physiotherapy, psychiatry, podiatry, and optometry. University students and staff and members of the public from surrounding communities all use these services.

Accommodations/housing. Accommodations/housing offices are probably the service areas currently undergoing the most dramatic change. Although most Australian universities are predominantly commuter universities, with the minority of students residing in accommodation on campus, most do provide a range of accommodation options on or in close proximity to their various campuses. An exception is the University of New England, which has a large number of distance students to whom it plays host during summer and winter schools and has a considerable proportion of its students in residence halls. Many universities are building new college accommodations and providing additional accommodations on or near campus for student rental. There is a trend for these ventures to be outsourced, placed in the hands of a specialist developer. A welfare office or the student service association is likely to take on roles previously managed by housing offices, such as independent rental options (home stays and share houses), and advice on rentals and tenant rights.

Disability Services. Disability services have seen rapid growth in the last 10 to 15 years. The introduction of State and Federal anti-discrimination laws provided new pathways for students with disabilities to attend university. Services provided to students with disabilities include reasonable adjustment to enable access, participation, and educational success. Disability services are required to report on their activities and their use of specific government funding. The Disability Standards for Education (Attorney-General, 2005) requires universities to take reasonable steps to ensure that a student is able to access and participate in the educational experience and use facilities and services on the same basis as a student without a disability.

Universities are also required to develop and implement strategies and programs to prevent harassment or victimization of students with a disability.

Equity Services. Equity of treatment (also covered by antivilification and anti-discrimination legislation) and cultural awareness and exclusivity is also expected. Equity services are dedicated to developing educational processes and policy that promote equity of opportunity for both students and staff. Equity planning and reporting is also required to be public and

Figure 14.1. Student services structure – G08 Sandstone University.

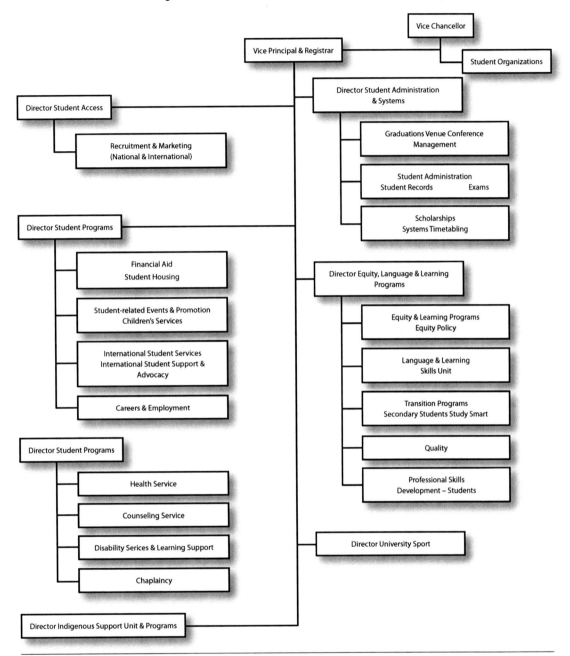

transparent in ways that do not apply to other services. Some universities combine their equity services with other service delivery areas such as equity, language and learning or equity, diversity and disability

Careers and Employment Services. Careers and employment services are actively engaged in developing generic graduate attributes via workshops and seminars and through employment preparation for students. Career services develop strong links with prospective employers, and campus employer markets are commonplace. Interview programs are still held on some campuses, although these are less common than they were 10 years ago. Most universities operate an online part-time work notice board that posts job advertisements placed by businesses and individuals in the surrounding community.

Indigenous Student Support Units. Indigenous student support units are located at nearly all universities and receive specific enabling funding to support the access, engagement, progression, and success of indigenous students in the university en-

Figure 14.2. Student services structures at an ATN University.

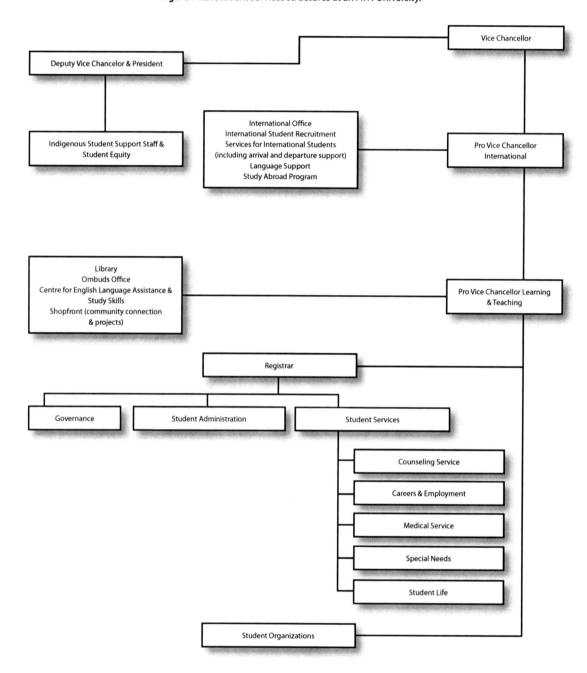

Figure 14.3. Student services at an ATN University.

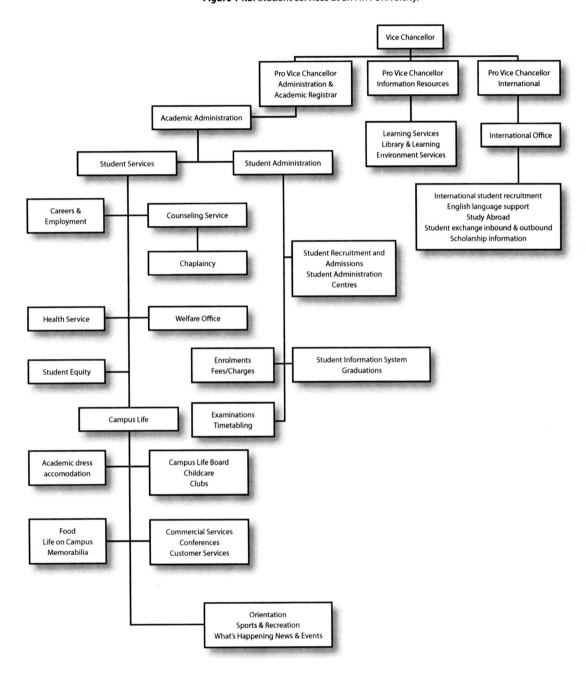

vironment. Where possible, the staff members of these units are indigenous, and there is a strong focus on developing pride in cultural heritage and promoting awareness of indigenous culture within the student and general university community.

First-Year Experience. Underpinning many of the current developments in student services and support is the recently intensified focus on the first-year experience (FYE). FYE initiatives usually offered within the faculty include orientation programs for commencing students, peer mentoring programs, adjustment and transition planning, and peer tutoring programs known as PASS (peer assisted support scheme), as well as support for the tasks of the first-year teacher and course coordinator. PASS programs are offered by paid tutors drawn from advanced year students who have done well in particular course content areas. They are trained in basic tutoring strategies and have the support of an academic who oversees the PASS program.

With greater support from faculty, FYE has a broader base of support than it did previously, when it was dominated by traditional student service initiatives offered by a counseling service or learning center. Peer mentoring programs are frequently operative universitywide, and sometimes within a faculty or school. They rely on student volunteers. Counselors most commonly conduct the training for the mentors.

Looking Ahead

Environmental Scan

Since the mid 1980s, successive Australian Commonwealth governments, both Labor and Coalition, have followed a policy of "economic realism," which has meant that government funding of higher education opportunities has been constantly re-evaluated. The financial burden has shifted from the central government (funding from tax revenues), to individual universities and to individual students, with a much more limited overall subsidy being maintained by government. These policy shifts have redefined and relocated education as a commodity, and forced universities and students to negotiate access and participation within a competitive marketplace. While risking over simplification, it is possible to characterize these changes within the higher education sector, as indicative of a profound change in the way higher education is perceived and addressed. The provision of higher education as a national good that is provided by the state has made higher education an important commodity, purchased by individuals, from corporate universities that negotiate with education consumers.

While they have lowered their financial contribution, Australian governments have increased their regulatory stance by requiring universities to be accountable for the funding they receive and for the services they provide. Accountability measures emphasize performance and include teaching, learning, and research outcomes. Quality assurance processes applied at both national and state levels demand routine external audits and a high degree of transparency in relation to business behavior.

Further, the homogenization and the internationalization of education have shifted the boundaries of the university corpo-

ration, to embrace not only the local but also the national and the international market ground. Public/private partnerships are now encouraged and in some cases even required, and knowledge that can be used within the commercial domain is accorded privileged status. Increasingly, research proposals seeking to attract government allocated research grants are more and more likely to be assessed in terms of their commercial prospects, and the potential to contribute, in the short term to commercial gain and to the knowledge economy.

This mix of government policies, specifically the push for improved university efficiency, performance and accountability; the longstanding emphasis on improving access and equity in participation; the continued provision of student income support; the capacity for students to delay payment of fees; and the introduction of user-pays and cost realignment options can indicate that the government is searching for sustainable social and financial responsibility.

Trends within Universities

For the most part, universities individually, and the higher education sector generally, view growth and expansion favorably. University size has been equated with increased efficiency, and expansion with increased status, particularly when taking the university more convincingly into the international marketplace.

To enable universities to compete more effectively, marketing and development functions have gained an important role in the life of universities and have been most visible in the enormous push to recruit students overseas. A substantial income stream is generated from full-fee paying international students, somewhat counterbalancing the lower government funding.

On the one hand, universities collectively protest such cuts as compromising their ability to respond to student need and demand and, on the other hand, most have established adjunct organizations that operate on a commercial basis. Most universities have also chosen to increase student fees by the maximum allowed by government regulation, thus escalating the process of cost shifting from government to the provider, the university, and then to the purchaser, the student.

Within this cost-conscious context, the proposed outlawing of compulsory student union affiliation/fees is being argued primarily in terms of increasing the cost for universities to support students and campus life, with little thought being given to the implications and consequences of the potential loss of a vital student point of reference within the organization.

Trends in Student Support, Student Services and the Student Experience

Student support services have also needed to accommodate the consequences of these sector changes. One significant change is evidenced in the way that Australian universities understand and respond to the student experience. The current approach to student support service provision is strongly influenced by (a) an increasing number of full-fee paying students looking for an exemplary educational experience, (b) the need to increase retention and in-time completion rates within all student cohorts, and (c) the accumulation of research data on the adjustment, transition, and affiliation experiences of students during their first year of university. During the past five to six years, the findings of this research have captured the attention of politicians, policy makers, and the press; generated increasing expectations from parents; influenced thinking within the academic community, and been of great interest to university marketing departments and student administrators. This attention on the first-year experience in particular, and the quality of the student experience in general, has contributed to a significant shift in the understanding of what is required to deliver relevant and effective student support services.

Another significant factor contributing to a shift in the way that students are viewed and supported within the university is the emphasis placed on corporate culture. This has generated a movement toward a customer service approach, especially within student administrative services. Being student-focused is an essential attitude/stance for those engaged in student administration, as is providing a friendly face or the human touch in response to student enquiries and concerns. Increasingly, the student administrative officer is one of the most significant points of direct contact and interaction between the student and the university. They help to interpret the university to the student and facilitate referral for non-administrative student support needs. However, the student-focused and friendly university administrative officer is sometimes placed in a difficult situation when the demands/needs of the student compete or conflict with those of the other stakeholders within and beyond the university.

But responding to individual and collective student needs is but one part of the student administrative officer's role. The officer must maintain compliance with legislative and policy requirements and must engage with the business/revenue needs of the university. Additionally, strategies are required to achieve increased student access, increased equity, and a satisfying educational experience, all balanced against the need to minimize complaints and grievances.

Reflecting the escalating accountability requirements of government, student administrative departments are increasingly required to operate more explicitly as an extension of various government agencies. This requirement to devote time to meeting central government accountability requirements is not only another form of cost-shifting; it complicates the relationship that exists between student administration staff and their student customers. However, in a more positive sense, the need to adhere to legislative privacy and grievance requirements has forced a review of procedures and policies, to ensure student privacy, to enhance decision-making transparency, and to re-shape and publicize grievance procedures.

A further significant strand of change in the way that student administrative services are interacting with students involves the exponential growth of online services. Increasingly, students are demanding more use of online services for information delivery, enrolment processing, financial statements, and invoicing. The expectation is that the university will be available 24/7.

In developing a customer/student focused function, student administrative services are reinventing their identity and ethos, interacting with students in new ways and adjusting their approach to the required administrative work to more easily balance the tensions created by the increasing needs of students, the university, and central government bureaucracies.

Collaboration and Integration—Benefits and Challenges

Another significant aspect of the reinvention process has been a trend to re-badge student administration as student services, and in doing so incorporate the traditional student services into new student services structures. Central to this reinvention has been the articulation of the need to collaborate rather than compete with various units, previously distinct but now coalesced within the new student services groupings. The challenge and reward of this restructuring is to work with colleagues in new, exciting, and different ways in order to bring about a cohesive and integrated approach to the delivery of support services to students and the enhancement of the student university experience. Forming these new structures has incurred a necessary blurring of functions between work units that previously had little to do with each other. This change will continue to pose challenges for some time.

The challenges faced by these increasingly integrated student service units need to be answered thoughtful planning and strategy implementation at all levels within student services. Steps include:

◊ Develop and establish a cohesive student service paradigm, identity, and ethos.

◊ Balance increasing accountability requirements while at the same time remaining student focused.

◊ Establish more inclusive and effective communication across functionally different areas of student service delivery.

◊ Demystify the different functions carried out by functionally distant units within the new aggregated groupings.

◊ Develop within the new student services amalgamation respect for all aspects of the student services remit.

◊ Manage direct competition for shrinking resources within student services without compromising the effectiveness of service delivery or creating an unsustainable work burden over the longer term for all staff, but particularly for those in specialist professional services where multi-tasking and staff rotations are not feasible.

Within an integrated-collaborative model of student service delivery is the potential to offer a seamless service to students in response to requests for information, assistance, and support. Also inherent within such a model is the need for effective communication and collaboration between the various service delivery areas, which will result in a greater understanding of the student perspective. This integrated, student-centered model will enhance service delivery in a way that could not be achieved by smaller specialist services in a more disconnected student administrative and student service operating environment. Importantly an integrated-collaborative model that includes respect for the important student confidentiality and privacy requirements holds the possibility of bridging what has historically been considered an organizational and values divide between those who have been involved in direct student advocacy and support (the "bleeding hearts"), and the traditional keepers of the rules and standards (the "hard hearted bureaucrats"). Sharing the goals, sharing respect and understanding, sharing the work, sharing the recognition—this could well be the motto of those working in these new and integrated student support and administrative service groupings.

The new student services groupings recognize (as was understood in 1956) that successful adjustment and transition begins at the first point of contact with the prospective student. What is different now however, is the understanding that transitions occur at regular and predictable points in the journey of the student through an undergraduate degree and in the leap from undergraduate to postgraduate coursework enrolment or employment. The concept of the student life cycle, together with the emerging recognition of the benefit derived from engaging with the student across the total university experience is not yet truly integrated within university business culture. However, these concepts are currently influencing the thinking and planning of the specialist services and business units as they engage with the priority to develop a positive interactive relationship between the student and the university. This can occur in the way the services and units provide access to pre-enrolment information, provide support for early career decision-making, simplify the challenges of an enrolment process, smooth the jolt of independent engagement in learning and class participation, and facilitate the student engagement with the joys and challenges of the total university experience. The support for the students' transition to the world of work currently is also on the cusp of reinvention as the role of the alumni association becomes more pronounced in the life of the student. The need for lifelong affiliation with the university is gaining greater emphasis. There is a desire emerging in the institutions for the university to be experienced as a companion, traveling with the students into the next phase of their lives, perhaps in the guise of a university crested credit card or an alumni employment and career development service.

The effective and integrated support of students across the total university experience has the potential to promote this now highly valued student affiliation with the institution. Integrated, quality-focused services will strengthen of the students' affiliation with the university and help forge an ongoing and lifelong link. This continuing affiliation benefits both the student and the university. For the university, each graduating student is a potential lifelong learner, to be encouraged to return to the alma mater to improve career options, support a career shift, or undertake a substantial career reinvention with top-up education via postgraduate coursework. The graduating student venturing into the world feels safe in the knowledge that his or her university is there to support and guide the brilliant career as it unfolds over time.

The university's desire to foster a positive relationship with students as they move thorough the student life-cycle could become an extremely potent ingredient in the total campus system and it could well influence the provision of student support and student service initiatives into the future. For example, one university has reassigned the responsibility for student recruitment and specific student orientation and induction initiatives to the university marketing and development unit. This new arrangement, together with ongoing collaboration and effective communication with the various student support services and student organizations that previously held the coordination role, could improve the commencing students' induction, adjustment, and early affiliation. That induction process would be woven into the early marketing communication with the prospective student.

A Reminder of the Student Voice

It is quite clear that students want personalized support and opportunity to engage in discussion with university personnel and teaching staff. They want flexible access to everything from a distance and "whenever I want it," as well as a friendly in person service provider. Students want to feel the value of social involvement in the university community while they are engaged in the learning, and they want to feel proud of their achievements. As students, they can feel burdened by the cost of the education in psychological, emotional, and dollar terms. This is particularly true of the international students, who are frequently indebted to family or employers for subsidizing the financial cost of the qualification. The university's reputation could be undermined if the institution does not deliver an experience that meets expectations and therefore show it is worth the investment.

Australian universities would appear to be moving, albeit slowly, to embed student support within the business and administrative processes and structures and to ultimately weave student support into the fabric of the learning and teaching culture. Student support may indeed become embedded in the very campus ethos and attitude conveyed to the student by the institution.

References

ABS (Australian Bureau of Statistics). (2003). *Measures of a knowledge-based economy and society. Human capital indicators. Proportion of all persons aged 15–64 with a non-school qualification.* Retrieved July 9, 2008, 2005, from http://www.abs.gov.au/AUSSTATS/abs@.nsf/2f762f95845417aeca25706c00834efa/6ea1328abcae05beca257062000378f3!OpenDocument

ABS (Australian Bureau of Statistics). (2003). *Measures of a knowledge-based economy and society, Australia Human Capital Indicators: Participation in secondary and tertiary education.* Retrieved July 9, 2008, from http://www.abs.gov.au/AUSSTATS/abs@.nsf/2f762f95845417aeca25706c00834efa/23b7b83a21e13ac7ca2571960016b713!OpenDocument

ADCET (Australian Disability Clearinghouse on Education and Training). (n.d.). *Networks/Organisations.* Retrieved July 23, 2005, from http://www.adcet.edu.au/default.aspx

Anderson, D., Boven, R., Fensham, P. J., & Powell, J. P. (1980). *Students in Australian higher education: A study of their social composition since the abolition of fees* (Education Research and Development Committee Report No. 23). Australian Government Publishing Service.

Andrews, A., & Shortus, L., (1997, July 6–10). *Peer assisted learning and other support options for adult learners in distance education.* Paper presented at the Australian and New Zealand Student Services Association (ANZSSA) Tenth Biennial Conference, Bardon, Qld., Australia.

ANZSSA (Australian and New Zealand Student Services Association). (2002). *Incorporation higher education at the crossroads–A review of Australian higher education, response from Australian and New Zealand Student Services Association Incorporation (ANZSSA, Inc.).* Retrieved May 10, 2005, from http://www.anzssa.org

AQF (Australian Qualifications Framework). (n.d.). *AQF Qualifications.* Retrieved July 9, 2005, from http://www.aqf.edu.au/aqfqual.htm

ATN (Australian Technology Network). (n.d.). *Australian technology network of universities homepage.* Retrieved July 9, 2005, from http://www.atn.edu.au/

Attorney-General's Department NSW. (2005). *Disability standards for education 2005.* Retrieved May 10, 2005, from http://www.dest.gov.au/sectors/school_education/publications_resources/profiles/disability_standards_education.htm

AUQA (Australian University Quality Agency). (2004). *AUQA web site.* Retrieved July 9, 2005, from http://www.auqa.edu.au/index.shtml

AUQA (Australian University Quality Agency). (n.d.a.). *AUQA quality audit.* Retrieved July 9, 2005, from http://www.auqa.edu.au/qualityaudit/index.shtml

AUQA (Australian University Quality Agency). (n.d.b.). *AUQA quality enhancement.* Retrieved July 9, 2005, from http://www.auqa.edu.au/qualityenhancement/index.shtml

AUQA (Australian University Quality Agency). (2005). *AUQA good practice database.* Retrieved July 9, 2005, from http://www.auqa.edu.au/gp/index.php

Australia Committee on Australian Universities. (1958). *Report of the committee on Australian universities September 1957.* Canberra, Australia: Government Printer.

AVCC (Australian Vice-Chancellors' Committee). (1971, August). *Student health services.* Canberra, Australia: Author.

AVCC (Australian Vice-Chancellors' Committee). (1988, November). *Language and study skills support services for students from non-English speaking backgrounds.* Canberra, Australia: Author.

AVCC (Australian Vice-Chancellors' Committee). (2005a). *Code of practice: Provision of education to international students.* Retrieved May 22, 2005, from http://www.avcc.edu.au/content.asp?page=/policies_programs/international/cofpractice.htm

AVCC (Australian Vice-Chancellors' Committee). (2005b). *Media releases 2005.* Retrieved July 2, 2005, from http://www.avcc.edu.au/content.asp?page=/news/media_releases/2005/avcc_media_31_05.htm

Bamford, P. (1988). *A survey of perceptions of users of the university counselling service.* New South Wales, Australia: The University of Newcastle, Counselling Service.

Bayne, R. (2003). You and your personality type at university. *The Psychologist, 16*(10), 529–531.

Benson, R. (1999). Motivation or money? A study of University of Ballarat student finances and performance 1998. *Journal of the Australian and New Zealand Student Services Association (JANZSSA), 14,* 27–42.

Bianco, M. (1998). An evaluation of support services offered to and desired by students from low socio-economic status at Flinders University of South Australia. *Journal of the Australian and New Zealand Student Services Association (JANZSSA), 12,* 29–47.

Bower, P., & Gilbody, S. (2005). Stepped care in psychological therapies: Access, effectiveness and efficiency. (Narrative literature review.) *The British Journal of Psychiatry 186,* 11–17. Retrieved July 21, 2005, from http://bjp.rcpysch.org/cgi/content/full/186/1/11

Burke, B. (1990a, June). Student services in higher education in Australia. *Australian New Zealand Student Services Association News, 35.*

Burke, B. (1990b, June). A proposal to restructure ANZSSA. *Australian New Zealand Student Services Association News (ANZSSA), 35.*

Business Council of Australia. (2002, August). *Higher education in Australia: Developing a new data framework and international comparison and issues.* Retrieved June 26, 2005, from http://www.bca.com.au/content.asp?newsID=87770

CAPA (Council of Australian Postgraduate Associations). (2005). *About CAPA.* Retrieved July 23, 2005, from http://www.capa.edu.au/frameset.html?./papers/index.html

Catley, B. (2004). The recuperating universities. *Quadrant, XLVIII,* 5. Retrieved July 9, 2005, from http://www.quadrant.org.au/php/archive_details_list.php?article_id=775

Centre for Study of Higher Education University of Melbourne. (2005). *CSHE.* Retrieved July 2, 2005, from http://www.cshe.unimelb.edu.au

Clarke, J. R., Postle, G. D., & Bull, D. D. (circa 1997/98). Management and planning structures for equity in the Australian higher education sector. In G. D. Postle, J. R. Clarke, E. Skuja, D. D. Bull, K. Bartorowicz, & H. A. McCann (Eds.), *Towards excellence in diversity: Educational equity in the Australian higher education sector in 1995: Status, trends and future directions.* Australia: USQ Press.

Committee for Quality Assurance in Higher Education. (1993). *Quality assurance program: Guidelines for higher education institutions.* Canberra, Australia: AGPS.

Commonwealth of Australia. (2006). *Disability standards for education 2005.* Retrieved July 9, 2008, from http://www.dest.gov.au/NR/rdonlyres/482C1E4B-9848-4CC3-B395-067D79853095/15406/DisabilityStandards_004_screen.pdf

Croker, S. (1991). *Students and the future of higher education: A comparative report on the status of student affairs in Australia and overseas.* Sydney, Australia: University of New South Wales Student Services.

Dawkins, J. S. (1988). *Higher education: A policy statement.* Canberra, Australia: AGPS.

DEET (Department of Employment, Education and Training). (1990a). National Board of Employment, Education and Training. A discussion paper: *A fair chance for all: Higher education that's within everyone's reach.* Canberra, Australia: AGPS.

DEET (Department of Employment, Education and Training). (1990). *A Fair Chance for All: National and Institutional Planning for Equity in Higher Education: A Discussion Paper.* Australia: National Board of Employment, Education and Training/DEET.

DEET (Department of Employment, Education and Training). (1994). *Student support services: Management, delivery and effectiveness: Student services Australia: Tertiary research for the National Union of Students.* Canberra, Australia: AGPS.

DEET (Department of Employment, Education and Training). (1995). Discussion paper: *Equality, diversity and excellence: Advancing the national equity framework.* Canberra, Australia: Higher Education Council/DEET.

DEEWR (Department of Education, Employment and Workplace Relations). (n.d.). *The role of the Australian Government.* Retrieved July 9, 2008, from www.dest.gov.au/sectors/higher_education/policy_issues_reviews/key_issues/assuring_quality_in_higher_education/the_role_of_the_australian_government.htm

DEST (Department of Education Science and Training). (2005a). *All Australian providers.* Retrieved July 9, 2005, from http://www.goingtouni.gov.au/Main/CoursesAndProviders/ProvidersAndCourses/HigherEducationProviders/ListAll/Default.htm

DEST (Department of Education Science and Training). (2005b). *Commonwealth-state responsibility for higher education.* Retrieved July 9, 2005, from http://www.dest.gov.au/sectors/higher_education/policy_issues_reviews/key_issues/commonwealth_state_responsibility_higher_ed.htm

DEST (Department of Education Science and Training). (2005c). *Want to know about changes to HECS & PELS? Paying for your studies (HELP loans).* Retrieved July 9, 2005, from http://www.goingtouni.gov.au/Main/Quickfind/PayingForYourStudiesHELPLoans/Default.htm

DEST (Department of Education Science and Training). (2005d). *Higher education review process department of education science and training: Our universities backing Australia's future.* Retrieved July 9, 2005, from http://www.backingaustraliasfuture.gov.au/review.htm

DEST (Department of Education Science and Training). (2005e). *Our universities backing Australia's future.* Retrieved July 9, 2005, from http://www.backingaustraliasfuture.gov.au

DEST (Department of Education Science and Training). (n.d.). *Partners in quality assurance.* Retrieved July 9, 2008, from www.dest.gov.au/sectors/higher_education/policy_issues_reviews/key_issues/assuring_quality_in_higher_education/partners_in_quality_assurance.htm

Devlin, Y. (2002, June). *Submission to the higher education review: Addressing access on an equitable basis,* Submission 228. Retrieved July 2, 2005, from http://www.backingaustraliasfuture.gov.au/submissions/crossroads/crossroads3.htm

DIMIA (Department of Immigration and Multicultural and Indigenous Affairs). (2003). *Multicultural Australia: United in diversity policy 2003.* Retrieved July 10, 2005, from http://www.immi.gov.au/multicultural/australian/index.htm

Downes, H. F. (1961). *Build your own bridge between school and university advice to secondary school students.* Melbourne, Australia: University of Melbourne, Appointments Board.

Elkerton, C. A. (1985). *A survey of overseas postgraduate students' satisfaction with life and study in Australia* (Res.& Dev. Paper No. 8). Sydney, Australia: University of New South Wales, Student Counselling and Research Unit.

Furnham, A. (2004). Foreign students education and culture shock. *The Psychologist, 17*(1), 16–19.

Gardner, H. (2003). Higher education for the era of globalization. *The Psychologist, 16* (10), 520–522.

Garlick, S., & Pryor, G. (2004). *Benchmarking the university: Learning about improvement.* Retrieved May 19, 2005, from http://www.dest.gov.au/NR/rdonlyres/7628F14E-38D8-45AA-BDC6-2EBA32D40431/2441/benchmarking.pdf

Go8 (The Group of Eight). (2005). The group of eight universities homepage. Retrieved July 9, 2005, from http://www.go8.edu.au/index.html

Hastings, G., Houghton, R., Germein, M., & Gorton, C. (1997). Pawning the future; The social and educational impact of student loan schemes. *Journal of the Australian and New Zealand Student Services Association (JANZSSA), 9,* 4–15.

Hooper, C. (2005). Afterword–The first year experience fifty years ago. In K. L. Krause, R. Hartley, R. James, & C. McInnis (Eds.), *The first year experience in Australian universities: Findings from a dcade of national studies.* Available online at http://www.dest.gov.au/sectors/higher_education/#The_First_Year_Experience_in_Australian_Universities:_Findings_from_a_decade_of_national_studies. Melbourne, Australia: Centre for the Study of Higher Education, University of Melbourne. Department of Education, Science and Training.

Howe, C. (2004). All together now. *The Psychologist, 17*(4), 199–201.

Huon, G., & Sankey, S. (2002). *Transition to university: Understanding differences in success.* Sydney, Australia: University of New South Wales.

IDP (International Education in Australia). (2005). *Fast facts: International education in Australia.* Retrieved June 25, 2005, from http://www.idp.com/research/fastfacts/article405.asp

ISANA (International Education Australia). (2005). ISANA homepage. Retrieved July 23, 2005, from http://www.isana.org.au/Default.aspx

James, R., Baldwin, G., Coates, H., Krause, K-L., & McInnis, C. (2004). *Analysis of equity groups in higher education 1991–2002.* Retrieved June 25, 2005, from http://www.dest.gov.

au/sectors/higher_education/publications_resources/ summaries_brochures/analysis_of_equity_groups_in_ higher_education_splitrtf.htm

Jones, B. T. (2003). Alcohol consumptions on the campus. *The Psychologist, 16*(10), 523–525.

Kemp, R. (2001). *Greater access for students to postgraduate study.* Retrieved July 9, 2005, from http://www.dest.gov.au/archive/ ministers/kemp/august01/k205_300801.htm

Krause, K. L., Hartley, R., James, R., & McInnis, C. (2005). *The first year experience in Australian universities: Findings from a decade of national studies.* Retrieved June 23, 2005, from Department of Education, Science and Training Web site: http://www. dest.gov.au/sectors/higher_education/#The_First_Year_ Experience_in_Australian_Universities:_Findings_from_a_ decade_of_national_studies

Leman, P. (2004). "And your chosen specialist subject is…" *The Psychologist, 17*(4), 196–198.

Martin, L. M. (1994). *Equity and general performance indicators in higher education: Volume 1 equity indicators.* Canberra, Australia: AGPS.

Martin, Y. M., & Karmel, T. (2002). *Expansion in higher education during the 1990s: Effects on access and student quality (Draft).* Retrieved June 25, 2005, from http://www.dest.gov.au/ sectors/higher_education/publications_resources/other_ publications/expansion_in_higher_education.htm

McInnis, C., James, R., & Hartley, R. (2000). *Trends in the first year experience in Australian universities.* Canberra, Australia: Department of Education, Training, and Youth Affairs (DETYA).

McKinnon, K.R., Walker, S. H., & Davis, D. (2000, February). *Benchmarking a manual for Australian universities.* Retrieved July 26, 2005, from http://www.dest.gov.au/sectors/ higher_education/publications_resources/profiles/archives/ benchmarking_a_manual_for_australian_universities.htm

McMullen, D. (1991, January 21-25). *Student services in the "Dawkins Universities."* Paper presented at the Australian and New Zealand Student Services Association Triennial Conference, University of Sydney. Sydney, Australia.

Mitchell, K. R., White, R. G., & Piatkowska, O.E. (1975, April). The treatment of underachievers: Current status and comment. *Australian and New Zealand Student Services: Counselling Monographs* (No.2). Adelaide, Australia.

Mitchell, K. R., & Piatkowska, O.E. (1975, August). Some aspects of student failure: Characteristics associated with failing underachievers. *Australian and New Zealand Student Services: Counselling Monographs* (No.3). Adelaide, Australia.

Moses, I. (n.d.). Unified national system or uniform national system? The Australian experience. Retrieved August 13, 2005, from http://www.dest.gov.au/higher_education/ policy_issues_reviews_reviews_building_diversity/ documents/uni_new_england_info_pdf.htm

NBEET (National Board of Employment, Education and Training). (1997, March). *A review of institutional use of commonwealth higher education funding for indigenous Australian students.* Retrieved May, 19, 2005 from http://www.dest.gov.au/

sectors/training_skills/publications_resources/indexes/ documents/97_03_pdf.htm

NBEET (National Board of Employment, Education and Training). (1992). *Higher education council report: Achieving quality.* Canberra, Australia: AGPS.

NBEET (National Board of Employment, Education and Training) Committee for quality assurance in higher education. (1993). *Quality assurance program: Guidelines for higher education institutions attachment E: Guidelines for the preparation of institutional portfolios.* Canberra, Australia: AGPS.

News Review. (2004, May 7–8). From free to squeezed: Where the money comes from. *The Sydney Morning Herald*, 32.

Newstead, S. (2004). Time to make our mark. *The Psychologist, 17*(1), 20–23.

Olohan, S. (2004). Student mental health: A university challenge? *The Psychologist, 17*(4), 192–194.

Postle, G.D., Clarke, J. R., Skuja, E., Bull, D. D., Bartorowicz, K., & McCann, H. A. (n.d. circa 1997/8). Towards excellence in diversity: Educational equity in the Australian higher education sector in 1995: Status, trends and future directions. Australia: USQ Press.

Promnitz, J., & Germain, C. (1996). *Student support services and academic outcomes: Achieving positive outcomes.* Retrieved May 8, 2005, from

http://www.dest.gov.au/archive/highered/eippubs/student/ eip96-10.htm

Promnitz, J. (1997, July 6–10). *Attrition and the role of student services.* Paper presented at the meeting of the Australian New Zealand Student Services Association (ANZSSA) Tenth Biennial Conference, Bardon, Queensland, Australia.

Roe, E., Foster, G., Moses, I., Sanker, M., & Storey, P. (1982). *A report on student services in tertiary education in Australia.* Commonwealth Tertiary Education Commission, Evaluative Studies Program, Higher Education Institute, University of Queensland, Brisbane, Queensland, Australia.

Seal, P. (2003). *The likely financial effect of budgetary measures (in particular the expansion of full fee places) on students.* Student Financial Advisors Network (SFAN) ANZSSA, Inc., Australia.

Scelly, B. (2000). A lifetime of debt: The long-term impact of the student loan scheme in New Zealand. *Journal of the Australian and New Zealand Student Services Association (JANZSSA), 15,* 38–49.

Schwartz, S. (2004). Time to bid goodbye to the psychology lecture. *The Psychologist, 17*(1), 26–27.

Scott, A. J. (2004). Why I study…student debt. *The Psychologist, 17*(1), 24–25.

Universities Australia. (n.d.). *Welcome.* Retrieved July 9, 2008, from http://www.universitiesaustralia.edu.au

University of Melbourne. (n.d.). Orientation and transition. *University of Melbourne, university assembly report 1.* Melbourne, Australia: Author.

University of Sydney History. (n.d.). Retrieved June 24, 2005, from http://www.usyd.edu.au/about/profile/pub/history.shtml

University of New South Wales Union. (2000, December). *University of New South Wales union constitution.* Retrieved

August 13, 2005, from http://union.unsw.edu.au/website/documents/AboutUs/constitution.pdf

Walker, B. (1982). Correlates of vocational indecision in first year university students. *Student counselling and research unit research and development paper (No. 5)*. Sydney, Australia: University of New South Wales.

Williams, C. (1982, March). *The early experiences of students on Australian university campuses*. Sydney, Australia: University of Sydney.

Williams, C., & Pepe, T. (1983). *The early experiences of students on Australian college of advanced education campuses*. Sydney, Australia: The University of Sydney.

Willis, H., Stroebe, M., & Hewstone, M. (2003). Homesick blues. *The Psychologist, 16*(10), 526–528.

Yerbury, D. (1996, November 28-29). *Ten inter-related trends in the last decade which make participation in APHEN a natural, highly desirable—and necessary—development for Australia.* Paper presented at the Second UNESCO UNITWIN APHEN Conference at Macquarie University. Paper retrieved July 9, 2005, from http://www.mq.edu.au/Aphen/staff/yerbur.htm

FIFTEEN

CANADA

Robert Shea

The past 15 years have provided a renewed focus on the history of student services in Canada. For example, a student services archives was developed at Simon Fraser University in British Columbia and is now housed at the Memorial University library in Newfoundland & Labrador. Also, the Canadian Association of University and College Student Services (CACUSS) developed a video series. Yet CACAUSS has not commissioned a detailed history that is readily available to the future cadre of student services professionals. Axelrod and Reid said it best when they stated, "Studying the university's past deepens our understanding of issues and themes current in social and intellectual history" (p. xii, 1989).

Student services began with the first university in Canada. Those early faculty who were student-centered were our true leaders; they recognized the importance of creating environments that were supportive, and focused on the development of the whole student. Many of those early pioneers were hired because of their involvement in student activities and their ability to "coach" students.

Prior to the beginning of formal national and regional organizations, and prior to a significant investment by the federal government, universities relied entirely on various positions, such as deans of men and deans of women, to attend to the varied needs of their students. The registrar and various housing personnel were also involved in the delivery of student services. As the number of individuals directly responsible for the social welfare of students on Canadian campuses grew, so did the need to focus on a system of organizing these individuals.

In 1946, the Canadian government made funds available to universities to reintegrate returning war veterans into society so that they could attain an education and continue as contributing members of society. This investment by the federal government signified the beginning of a substantial investment in the career and employment needs of university students. The recruitment and selection of career counselors were organized under the title of the University Advisory Services Association. These counselors were truly generalist as there respon-

sibilities ranged from financial advising to career and personal counseling.

In 1952, the University Advisory Services Association was renamed the University Counselling and Placement Association (UCPA). It had three autonomous divisions, dealing with student affairs, career planning, and counseling. (CACUSS/CUCCA, n.d.).

In the late 1960s another division was added dealing with student health.

By the 1960s, with the passage of legislation on technical and vocational training, and on adult occupational training, the community college concept was gathering momentum, with its mission to provide access to postsecondary education for all. (In Canada, "college" refers to community college, while in the United States, the words "college" and "university" are often used interchangeably.) The college system in Canada is a vibrant and learner-centered organization with burgeoning enrolments and a strong career-centered mandate. The history has included a strong connection with government, the labor market, and industry. Reflecting the two facets of higher education, the umbrella student services organization changed its name in 1970 to the Canadian Association of College and University Student Services (CACUSS).

By that time, the career planning group had left the organization and formed an independent association, known today as the Canadian Association of Career Educators and Employers (CACEE, n.d.). In 1979, financial aid administrators joined CACUSS as an autonomous division but became an independent association in 2001. In 1999, CACUSS established a new division, the Canadian Association of Disability Service Providers in Postsecondary Education (CADSPE), indicating that colleges and universities recognized issues connected with the increasing number of students with disabilities on their campuses and the need for services for those students. In 2003, CACUSS added the National Aboriginal Student Services Association (NASSA). This new division has as its core purpose to empower institutions of higher learning to become welcoming environments where Aboriginal peoples can successfully pursue educational goals while maintaining their cultural identities (CACUSS/NASSA, n.d.).

One anomaly in the development of the CACUSS organization is the parallel development of the Atlantic Association of College and University Student Services (AACUSS). This Atlantic organization represents the interests of student services professionals in Nova Scotia, Newfoundland & Labrador, Prince Edward Island, and New Brunswick. AACUSS evolved from the Association of Atlantic Deans of Men and Women, which represented the professional development needs of student services professionals in the Atlantic region of Canada. This is the only regional association of student service professional in Canada.

Student Services Delivery Model

The Canadian model for student services has essentially embraced an American structural model. This represents a structured model that focuses on student support within the context of the larger organizational model for universities and colleges. Student services units are found in every university and college in Canada. Yet, the model and its constituent parts will differ with each university and college campus. While there are many different models those outlined below exemplify some of the more common ones.

Areas of Responsibility

Traditional areas of students services includes housing, food services, counseling, career development, disabilities, Aboriginal and native student services, financial aid, health services, student success, student development and leadership, scholarships and awards, and orientation. In some cases, the registrar and office of recruitment are also included.

Organizational Models

It is important to note that most universities in Canada operate under a bicameral model of university governance, that is, the academic affairs of the institution are governed by the senate and the financial affairs of the university are governed by the board of governors or board of regents. This system has significant impact on the models of student service. It is here that the model of governance exerts influence on the model for student services. By its very nature, the model requires the chief student affairs officer (CSAO) to be a member of the senate. This is required, given the fact that the senate is the final arbitrator of student grades.

On many campuses the chief student affairs officer (CSAO) is an associate vice president and reports to a vice president of academic. In a growing number of universities, there is a move to create vice presidents of students positions. All models embrace a collegial model of administration. Sitting at the senior executive table certainly opens doors to the presidential suite. Yet being a component of the academic portfolio also has benefits for collegiality and cooperation. It appears that the models that work best are

those which embrace the four pillars of universities: cultural, environmental, political, and structural.

In some universities, the CSAO reports to a vice president of administration, and the service is seen more in light of an ancillary service model. This view of student services is often embraced as a revenue-generating model, and some would say it reflects a lack of commitment to the development of students rather than a focus on students as generators of revenue.

Government Involvement within the Scheme of Student Services

While the early work of student service deans of men and women and of student-centered faculty and administrators cannot be under valued, the formal development of student services in Canadian universities and colleges reflects the funding support provided by the federal government for placement and counseling services in the 1940s. This impetus led to a mass of professionals supporting students and to the development of conferences and professional development opportunities. In a more focused way, the federal government operated placement offices on a significant number of university and college campuses in Canada. These offices were independent of the university and college but had a crossover relationship with many student services professionals. In the early 1990s, the federal government disbanded their system of funding employment centers on campus and entered into funding arrangements with universities to transition these federal government offices off campus.

Provincial Government Involvement

Provincial government involvement in higher education is significant. Canada's system of funding higher education is based on a system of transfer payments from the federal government to the provinces and territories. This system lumps together funding for health, social services, and education. It is up to the provincial government ministries of postsecondary and advanced studies and education to decide how much to invest in universities and colleges. Each province enacts its own university and college legislation that establishes the powers of universities and colleges, which govern the financial and academic affairs of those institutions. There is no federal or national department of education or higher education. Provincial governments can change the legislation within their own government legislatures.

The provincial governments can exert much greater influence on colleges than on universities. Recent movements by the provincial governments in Ontario and Newfoundland witnessed a significant commitment to provincial governments becoming more involved in higher education.

Federal Government Involvement

Federal government involvement is limited to the provision of program-specific grants to the administration side of the academy and funding research to the academic side of the academy. The program grants are specific to an area of interest to public policy, and academic investment is limited to funding academic research. There is little direct influence on the provision of student services except on a macro scale, where the federal government may change the student loans act or may invest in a project specific to the institution. The federal government funds a significant amount of research on university campuses across Canada through two distinct organizations, the Social Science and Humanities Research Council and the Natural Sciences and Engineering Research Council. Research grants are highly competitive.

Professional Development and Preparatory Programs within Student Affairs and Services

There currently exists only one program in Canada devoted to the development of student services professionals. This is a master's degree in postsecondary studies, which is housed at Memorial University of Newfoundland. The courses include the administration of student services, adult education, student development theory, and teaching and learning.

The majority of programs in Canada at the master's and doctoral levels focus broadly on higher education. Courses include the foundations of higher education and research and design courses. The Canadian Society for the Study of Higher Education, a learned academic society, produces the peer-reviewed Canadian Journal of Higher Education, to which student services professionals can submit articles.

Higher education programs are currently offered at the Universities of Alberta, British Columbia, Calgary, and Manitoba, McGill University, and the Ontario Institute for Studies in Education at the University of Toronto.

The majority of practicing administrators in Canadian universities and colleges have acquired their education through a myriad of discipline-specific degrees. These degrees span the continuum of education itself. Counselors generally have master's and doctoral degrees in psychology or social work; health practitioners have degrees in nursing and medicine. There is a growing recognition of the need for master's and doctoral degrees to attain senior administrative positions in student services.

The Campus Climate

It is safe to say that faculty and student services are beginning to work closer together. The age-old problem of university silos has at times created a chasm between the two entities. As more and more student services professionals are attaining master's- and doctoral-level qualifications, they will gain credibility within the academy, and the relationship between student services and the academic faculty will be enhanced.

Funding of Student Affairs and Services – Where does the Money Come From?

Revenues

A system of federal transfer payments to the provincial governments and any additional funds that the province allocates make up approximately 75% of campus revenues. Tuition payments make up the rest of the costs of university administration and teaching. Some universities charge a special student service levy. On most of these campuses, students have a direct say in the administration of these monies through special committees that decide where the monies will go in the next fiscal year. All universities and colleges in Canada also have student representation on their board of governors and university senate.

For the most part, the university and college provide the core operating budget for student services. This budget is provided through combined sources of funding. The core budget will cover basic salaries and infrastructure costs. Tuition has been steadily increasing especially in the area of professional schools. There has been a corresponding increase in student demands for student services.

A New Learning Agenda?

It is not surprising that, as products of society, universities were, "reflecting and contributing to social change while at the same time helping to ensure that dominant ideologies retained their primacy within the rapidly developing nation" (Axelrod & Reid, 1989, p. 21).

The concept of experiential learning is not reserved for the classroom. In fact, it is experiencing a birth of sorts within student services in Canada. The terms experiential learning, work-integrated learning, alternation education, practice-oriented education, cooperative education, and internships are being discussed from coast to coast. I believe these concepts will bring a renewed focus to the provision of student services on college and university campuses to the same degree that technology affected the centers' services in the 1990s. The concept of experiential learning will create challenges to the four pillars of universities and college career centers. The environmental, cultural, political, and structural pillars will undergo significant challenges as the concept of experiential learning is embraced. As the lines between formal and informal learning blend there will be a blurring of boundaries between the academic side of the academy and the support side. If this happens, there will be a greater opportunity to join the forces of student learning inside and outside the classroom. This new approach will allow a greater emphasis on how learning occurs, where it occurs, and how we measure that learning.

In speaking about the community college, Levin (2001) envisioned "an adaptable institution...largely unfettered by tradition or by its own bureaucracy, and it is free in many ways to pursue a virtuous and historically idealized path in which students as people, not as economic entities, are paramount to institutional purposes"(p.182). A new learning agenda for student services will allow a return to human capital as the raison d'etre. This new approach to learning will connect the world of work and skill development. The approach will be monitored through the principles of experiential learning, which include reflection and learning contracts.

Service Learning

The creation of the Canadian Association for Community Service Learning in 2005 signaled a formal approach to the coordination and professional development of those interested in service learning in Canada. Service–learning has grown exponentially in the past five years. The concept of integrating service as a co-curricular or curricular experience has gained a great deal of momentum on Canadian campuses. The momentum will surely continue, given a recent announcement by the J. W. McConnell Foundation, a private family foundation based in Montreal, that it would invest significantly in a number of Canadian service–learning pilot projects. An investment in educating students who have an understanding of and commitment to community service indicates that postsecondary institutions are cognizant of the need to educate students to become "citizen leaders." By embracing this form of experiential learning and the principle of reflective learning, our students are attaining citizenship skills and an ability to communicate shared learning.

Demographic Changes on Campus

The profile of the university and college campus has changed dramatically over the past 10 years and continues to change at a frantic pace. In addition to those students we consider traditional, we now have increased numbers of older adult student, single parents, international students, part-time students and full-time workers, distance students, and an increased number of students with physical and emotional disabilities (Crozier, Dobbs, Douglas, & Hung, 1998). Each of these cohorts will present challenges and opportunities for career development and employment centers.

International Students

Over the next 10 years, the face of campuses in Canada will change. This change will occur gradually but will be indicative of a more open immigration policy, and more importantly, a continued assertive and focused recruitment of international students to universities and colleges in Canada. This recruitment and resulting changing demographic will challenge student services as never before. It is anticipated that there will be cultural issues associated with a student's preparation for the labor market. The potential lack of oral and written English skills will provide a challenge for student services to be more understanding and sensitive to international students. Also, the varying comfort levels of these students in approaching student service professionals will change how we deliver workshops, group, and in-

dividual advising and support for students. The experience of some of our more ethnically diverse universities and colleges will be critical if university and colleges are to embrace the continuing internationalization of our campuses.

Aboriginal Students

An increase of Aboriginal students will provide a wonderful opportunity to understand a distinct way of life and approach to the world of higher education and life in general. This will also provide a challenge to student services professionals to understand the cultural and work issues of our Aboriginal students. The creation of a new division within CACUSS, the National Aboriginal Student Services Association, will allow us to build upon their professional expertise. Norm Amundson, a professor at the University of British Columbia, has completed a great deal of work in the area of Aboriginal career counseling, which can provide a foundation for greater work in the area of career information advising and employment counseling, but much remains to be done.

Further Research

There is a significant void in the Canadian literature on student services on university and college campuses. Specifically, a void exists on the impact and outcomes of student services interventions on the students themselves. Canadian research effort will focus on the impact of co-curricular learning on student retention. Themes will include (a) the ability to make a strong connection between the various forms of experiential learning and debt load and (b) whether certain interventions in housing are more successful in assisting students to make a successful transition to university or college. More research is needed on the competencies and skills required for student services leadership. Future focuses should include proposal writing, human resources administration, and leadership styles.

On a national level, there should be more focus on the demographic indicators of student services. These indicators will allow researchers and practitioners to see trends and establish service-level benchmarks. Indicators include resource allocations, revenue generation, educational levels of staff, and future concerns of career professionals working in the career and employment field on all university and college campuses. Questions may include: Is there a ratio of professional staff to students? What are significant caseloads for staff?

Conclusion

As Cobban (1975) indicated, the foundation for our modern universities may be found in the vocational predisposition of the medieval universities. Since that time, the importance of preparing students for a utilitarian purpose has wavered but appears now to be on the increase. This trend is propelled by (a) government influence such as performance indicators tied to graduate employment rates; (b) parents, who are concerned about the student's ability to make the transition to the world of work and start a career; and (c) students, who need to pay off student debts and begin their transition to the world of work.

Student services on Canadian college and university campuses will become more important as universities embrace a new learning agenda that validates what happens outside the classroom as important to the university mission. As the role of student services on Canadian campuses is enhanced, the need for well prepared professionals who understand the theory and embrace the history of our profession will further enhance the importance of what we do. Canada's is a history rooted in the great work of those who have come before us. Canada's is a future that is bright, and a future that will accept the challenges placed before it and continue to develop creative and innovative programs and services for our students.

References

Axelrod, P., & Reid, J. (1989). Youth university and Canadian society: Essays in the social history of higher education. McGill-Queens University Press. Montreal.

CACEE (Canadian Association of Career Educators and Employers). (n.d.). Main page. Retrieved June 3, 2005, from http://www.cacee.com

CACUSS/NASSA (Canadian Association of College and University Student Services National Aboriginal Student Services Association). (n.d.). National Aboriginal Student Services Association: Welcome to the NASSA website. Retrieved August 3, 2005, from http://www.cacuss.ca/en/18-nassa/index.lasso

CACUSS/CUCCA (Canadian Association of College and University Student Services/Canadian University and College Counselling Association). (n.d.). Welcome to the CUCCA Website. Retrieved June 3, 2005, from http://www.cacuss.ca/en/13-cucca/index.lasso

Cobban, A.B. (1975). The medieval universities: their development and organization. London: Methuen & Co. Ltd.

Crozier, S., Dobbs, J., Douglas, K., & Hung, J. (1998). Career Counselling Position Paper. Canadian University and College Counselling Association. Canada.

Levin, J. (2001). Globalizing the community college: Strategies for change in the twenty-first century. Palgrave. New York.

SIXTEEN

FRANCE

Françoise Bir

Centre Nationale des Œuvres Universitaires et Scolaires – CNOUS (National Center for Student Services)

CNOUS, the Centre National des œuvres Universitaires Scolaires (National Center for Student Services) runs the network of Centre régional des œuvres Universitaires Scolaires (CROUS - Regional Centers for Student Services) under the supervision of the French Department of National Education, Higher Education and Research. The objective of the network is to ensure that all students have equal access and equal opportunity for success in higher education by providing them day-to-day support.

The student services network arose out of a student initiative and was established in its current form by the Law of March 16th, 1955. Celebrations were held throughout 2005 to mark the 50th anniversary of CNOUS.

The major milestones in its development follow:

◊ 1918: Student associations organize themselves to set up halls of residence (foyers).

◊ 1936: Minister Jean Zay establishes the Committee for School and University Student Services.

◊ 1946: Establishment of the centers for school and university student services at the national and regional levels as nonprofit organizations.

◊ 1955: CNOUS, the Centre National des œuvres Universitaires Scolaires, is given the status of public establishment with administrative character by the Law of April 16th.

◊ 1987: The Decree of March 5th defines the mission and the organization of student services.

The student services network has forged a strong identity based on a social mission and the values of friendship, fairness, and solidarity.

In France, many players are involved in the student welfare system (including the state, local authorities, and foundations). The student services network plays a primary role among them, running services for students on a local basis: grants, accommodation, welfare benefits, meals, support for cultural projects and initiatives, and opening up to the rest of the world. These actions are implemented by the regional centers (CROUS).

The network of school and university welfare services is made up of three levels. The Centre national, CNOUS, established by the Law of April 16th 1955, is at the head of a network comprising 28 regional centers (CROUS), 16 local centers (CLOUS), and more than 40 branches that provide local services to students in the field. The second level is CROUS, or the centre régional for school and university welfare services. CROUS are public independent bodies linked to CNOUS. They deliver services to students and manage all the student services in their region. Some of the larger CROUS units have a third level of support known as CLOUS or centre local. They deliver the same services as CROUS but are not independent; they depend directly upon CROUS.

There is one CROUS per administrative region in the country, each serving several universities. CNOUS and CROUS are public administrative establishments. They are managed by a board of directors made up of representatives of the state, union organizations, and student associations. They carry out their activities in close collaboration with the universities and local authorities, within the framework of locally developed site policies.

While they are independent from the universities, CROUS regional centers work in close collaboration with them, providing support in the form of practical services for students. Academic issues are the exclusive domain of the universities.

This mission of providing student services and support is accomplished within the framework of a 2004–2007 action plan approved by the French Department of National Education. The development of this action plan is the first time that French higher education entities have collaborated on a project to improve higher education and the services provided to students. The agencies involved are the Ministry of Education, universities, CNOUS, and

CROUS. The plan provides for indicators that will be evaluated in 2007 and will impact all student life affairs (grants, social help, housing, dining services, and cultural life).

Student Affairs in France

The way student affairs is organized in France differs from the rest of the world, where student affairs departments are usually the responsibility of the universities. In Europe, only Germany has a comparable system.

The student services network is the primary body with responsibility for student affairs in France. The Higher Education Division of the French Department of National Education, Higher Education and Research sets the policy guidelines in this domain and establishes the regulations in force across the country.

Professional Development

There are no university programs in France to train people to become professionals in student affairs. Within the student services network, the 12,697 staff holding positions are civil servants recruited through competitive examinations. They learn the specifics of the profession on the job. However, at its specialized center in Tours, CNOUS runs an extensive training program, aimed in particular at new personnel appointed to the network. Of the network's total staff, 5,727 work in catering, 4,084 in accommodation services, and 2,886 in administrative services.

CNOUS/CROUS Budget

The student services network has had to adapt to major changes in French higher education, in particular the opening up of higher education in the 1980s. It also has provided support for the two student welfare programs set up in 1991 and 1997. It has established new forms of university catering. It also provided the initiative for developing the extensive student housing refurbishment and construction program approved in 2002.

The network's budget, excluding grants, is approximately €9.75 million EUR ($1.96 billion USD), of which two-thirds are the network's own resources and one-third comes from state subsidies (see Figure 16.1). It also manages the student welfare grants, which total €1.3 billion EUR ($2.6 billion USD).

Student affairs is organized in the same way across the country. A certain amount of infrastructure is adapted to the needs of people with reduced mobility. Personal problems fall within the competence of the social workers appointed to the CROUS regional centers, whose job focuses entirely on providing assistance and support to students in difficulty.

The student services network has the affairs of France's 2.2 million students in its care. CNOUS manages 500,000 student grants and 150,000 residence hall beds and serves more than 50 million meals a year in its 800 university restaurants. (CNOUS/CROUS, June 2004)

In the 1980s, the opening up of higher education led to a significantly increased need for student services and support

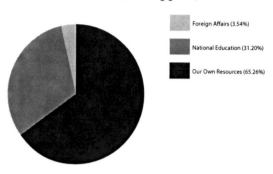

Figure 16.1. CNOUS-CROUS global budget 2005, 974 million euros (excluding grants)

- Foreign Affairs (3.54%)
- National Education (31.20%)
- Our Own Resources (65.26%)

in France. Since that time, the regional centers (CROUS) have been under considerable pressure with regard to the provision of student accommodation. This led the supervisory authorities to launch a program for refurbishment and the construction of 50,000 new rooms by 2012 (CNOUS/CROUS, June 2004). In conjunction, an anticipated population decline should result in the progressive easing of student accommodation pressures.

Conclusion

Education is a sensitive issue in France. To date, the state has been extremely cautious in its higher education-related reforms. Higher education is open to anyone in France. Selectivity varies according to the type of establishment and the educational level provided.

There is a longstanding history of frequent international exchange and discourse on the subject of student affairs between student affairs organizations and professionals. European cooperation is the strongest, particularly between France and Germany. This cooperation is focused on the exchange of staff and the lobbying of the European education authorities to have the student affairs aspect taken into account in the Bologna process. The French student services network is also an active member of the European Council for Student Affairs (ECStA, http://www.ecsta.org).

The European Commission in Brussels is, without a doubt, the authority that will have the greatest influence on French higher education in the years to come. The importance of student affairs and services, long seen as ancillary to universities, has received greater recognition from academic authorities in recent years. Over the next decade many changes will take place in French higher education, and with the collaboration between French agencies, students are expected to be the winners.

References

Centre National des Œuvres niversitaires Scolaires (CNOUS) & Centre Régional des œuvres Universitaires Scolaires (CROUS). (2004, June). The network of school and university student welfare services for 2004–2005. Paris, France: Author.

SEVENTEEN

GERMANY

Achim Meyer auf der Heyde

Development and Change in German Higher Education

Challenges to Higher Education Institutions

The development of higher education in Europe and especially in Germany is characterized by the following three aspects: a growing number of students as a result of demographic developments and national efforts to increase participation in higher education; the internationalizing of European higher education institutions, with the aim of increasing the European Union's competitiveness and opening institutions to the worldwide education market; and The Bologna Process, aimed at establishing a European Higher Education Area with a system of comparable degrees.

These three aspects define new challenges to higher education institutions, and the organizations responsible for student services.

Growing Number of Students

The number of students in Germany has steadily grown from 1,793,945 in 1996–97 to 2,019,831 in 2003–04, i.e., more than 12%. In the same period, the number of first-year students has grown by nearly 50%, from 256,000 in 1996–97 to 377,000 in 2003–04 (Isserstedt, Middendorff, Weber, Wolter, & Schnitzer, 2004). The standing conference of Ministers of Education and Cultural Affairs of the Länder (the 16 Federal States) of the Federal Republic of Germany estimates a continuous increase, reaching half a million students by 2013.

Internationalizing

One reason for the increased student enrolment is the opening of higher education institutions to foreign students. As a result of several political decisions and strategies, Germany has slowly become a host country for international students. In 2001, a joint international marketing initiative was launched to promote study, research and training in Germany. This initiative is a col-

laborative effort among national and federal ministers, research organizations, higher education institutions, academic exchange services, student service organizations, employers associations, and trade unions. In fact, the share of foreign students has grown from 1996–97 to 2003–04 from 150,000 (8.3%) to 246,000 (12.2%), and it is projected that by 2010, the number of foreign students will reach 270,000 (Deutscher Akademischer Austauschdienst [German Exchange Service], 2005).

The Bologna Process

On June 19, 1999, the ministers of education from 30 countries met in Bologna to set forth a joint declaration called the Bologna Declaration[1] in an effort to establish a European area of higher education by 2010 (EUROPA, n.d.). The Bologna Process set out to bring sweeping changes in European higher education. The principle aim of the process is to "make higher education systems in Europe converge towards a more transparent system… whereby the different national systems would use a common framework based on three cycles – Degree/Bachelor, Master and Doctorate" (EUROPA, n.d.).

To achieve this end, the Bologna Process proposed these six actions:

◊ A system of academic grades which is easy to read and compare, including the introduction of the diploma supplement (designed to improve international transparency and facilitate academic and professional recognition of qualifications).

◊ A system essentially based on two cycles: a first cycle geared to the employment market and lasting at least three years and a second cycle (master's) conditional upon the completion of the first cycle.

---

[1] Bologna Process – Wide-ranging reform of higher education in Europe. The ultimate aim of the Process is to establish a European Higher Education Area by 2010 in which staff and students can move with ease and have fair recognition of their qualifications. An important goal of the Process is to move higher education in Europe toward a more transparent and mutually recognized system of awarding degrees. For more information refer to Appendix A – Terminology for the Student Affairs and Services Profession.

◊ A system of accumulation and transfer of credits.

◊ Mobility of students, teachers, and researchers.

◊ Cooperation with regard to quality assurance.

◊ The European dimension of higher education.

In 2005, the ministers added the doctoral cycle to the Bologna reforms, thereby bringing the area of research in European education closer to the area of higher education. As of 2005, many of these ambitious aims had not been reached.

Challenges to Higher Education Institutions

German higher education institutions have to resolve many challenges to realize the ambitious goals of the Bologna Process, including new study courses and changing from the diploma or magister degree to the new bachelor's and master's degrees. All this is involved in realizing the main aim to get higher education institutions competitive.

This development is accompanied by a public financial crisis. With the changing government leadership, politicians and administrators are trying to decentralize competencies and responsibilities by transferring them to the shoulders of the higher education institutions. The government promises the institutions more autonomy, and forces universities to achieve Bologna Process changes alone by decreasing public financial support. As a direct result of the reduced funding from the government, some Länder have proposed introducing tuition fees. However, there is a strong fear that with the added fees there will be fewer students and the overall diversity of students will be impacted These challenges to the universities naturally also affect the organizations responsible for student services.

Student Affairs in Germany: Structure and Tasks of the Studentenwerke

The Studentenwerke

The Studentenwerke in Germany have existed since 1920, when after World War I local associations were founded to overcome the lack of food, housing, and clothing. They were student help associations composed of students, lecturers, professors, and representatives from local businesses and industry. Currently the local Studentenwerke perform public responsibilities related to the economic, social, health care, and cultural support of all students (Deutsches Studentenwerk/DSW, 2003).

Today there are 61 local Studentenwerke, which offer their services to more than two million students at 300 higher education institutions. The local Studentenwerke are responsible for several universities within the region each serves. The various Studentenwerke have within their regions both large and small universities, and as a result the Studentenwerke can offer all students the same services no matter the size of the university. This ensures that costs will be similar at all institutions within the region.

Contrary to the system of student affairs in universities or colleges in the United States, the responsibility for student services in Germany is shared by different partners. The job of the universities is education and research, whereas the German Studentenwerke (STW), as the local service organizations, are responsible for the economic, social, health care, and cultural support of all students, by order of the Federal Länder.

The Studentenwerke are autonomous from the higher education institutions they serve. In their mission they contribute substantially to the realization of equal opportunities for the students they serve. The competence for cultural affairs and the competence for providing student services in higher education area lie with the federal states, the Länder. As a result the sovereignty of the Länder and the individual Studentenwerke are comparable but not equal from Land to Land.

Legal Foundation

The legal basis for the Studentenwerke is defined in laws and bylaws, and regulations of the Federal Länder. This leads to individual statutes of the Studentenwerke, and as a result to several differences among the 61 Studentenwerke with regard to legal form, supervision by the ministers for education, research in the Länder, and the structure and tasks of the decision-making bodies.

Tasks of the Local Studentenwerke

The primary tasks of the Studentenwerke are catering, accommodation, and student financial assistance. Currently there are approximately 700 dining halls and cafeterias that are under the supervision of various local Studentenwerke. In 2004, students seeking accommodation (housing) could select from approximately 176,000 rooms in student residence halls, with an average rent of €169.32 EUR ($266 USD). The third primary task for each Studentenwerke is to distribute financial assistance to students. In order to finance students, the Federal Länder passed the Federal Education Assistance Act (BAföG) and distributes the funds to the local Studentenwerke, which in turn distributes them to the students. Approximately €1.4 billion EUR ($2.2 billion USD) was distributed in 2003 to about 367,000 students. Students qualify for funding based on the income of their parents.

Studentenwerke provide a variety of services.

◊ Advisory services deal with psychological problems, social, and legal counseling.

◊ Students with disabilities can find answers to their questions at the guidance and counseling centers.

◊ Students with children have access to 159 day-care centees. There is space available for approximately 5,000 children.

◊ Some Studentenwerke offer health services and insurance for students.

◊ Foreign students can use specific support schemes and counseling.

◊ Some Studentenwerke offer various cultural activities for students.

Funding

The local Studentenwerke are nonprofit organizations under public law. The overall budget in 2003 amounted to €1.1 billion EUR ($1.7 billion USD). The income is derived from different sources (ECStA, 2005):

◊ 63.8%—Income from catering and accommodation

◊ 15.4%—Länder subsidies

◊ 12.0%—Student contributions

◊ 6.6%—Refunds for administration of BAföG

◊ 2.2%—Other (childcare income)

Organizational Structure

Due to its funding structure and the legal situation, the organizational structure of the Studentenwerke has to meet specific requirements from the government, university, and students. Students are, by their status, members of the Studentenwerke and are involved in the business decisions and strategies of the local Studentenwerke. The Länder administrations are involved as supervisors, and the universities are involved as a direct result of their role as the principle users of the services provided by the Studentenwerke. Finally, some laws of the Länder define the participation of external experts. Generally speaking, the local Studentenwerke organizations have three governing bodies: the executive manager (Geschäftsführer), the board (Vorstand), and the administrative council (Verwaltungsrat). Represented on the board and the administrative council are the various groups (students, university faculty, and local members of the business community), and here the students often hold the position as chair of the board.

Deutsches Studentenwerk (DSW)

In 1921, the 61 Studentenwerke founded the Deutsche Studentenwerk (DSW) as their national association for student affairs. The DSW is a nonprofit organization and holds a neutral position toward political, religious, and ideological groups (DSW, 2003). The DSW fulfils four major tasks:

◊ Supports and promotes its member organizations;

◊ Represents and safeguards the social-economic interests of students;

◊ Maintains close cooperation with institutions and organizations in the higher education sector which serve the same or similar purpose; and

◊ Executes projects on behalf of the federal government or Federal Länder (States).

One of the special projects the DSW is responsible for is the survey on Economic and Social Conditions of Student Life in the Federal Republic of Germany, which is published every three years. This long-term study started more than 50 years ago and provides an excellent overview of changes in the life of students in Germany. (To review the information in the latest survey, the 17th Social Survey, published in 2004, go to http://www.studentenwerke.de/se/2004/Kurzfassung_engl.pdf/).

Executive Bodies of the DSW

Similar to the local Studentenwerke, the DSW is governed by three executive bodies: the members assembly, the executive board, and the secretary general.

The members assembly is comprised of representatives from the 61 local Studentenwerke. Based on the number of students they represent, each local Studentenwerke representative (director) receives one vote for every 4,000 students, limited to a maximum of 10 votes. The member's assembly elects the executive board, which is comprised of nine members (three professors, three directors of the Studentenwerke, and three students). The third executive body of the DSW is the secretary general, who assumes the executive responsibility and heads the national office and staff within the DSW.

In addition to the executive bodies, there are a few counseling bodies such as the board of trustees, the council of the directors (comprising the speakers of the Länder), and the council of students (whose members are delegated by the regional Studentenwerke). The Council of Students was established in 2003 with the goal of involving the students in the strategic discussions on and development of the umbrella organization DSW.

The board of trustees holds an important position in that it supports and promotes the objectives of the DSW. The board of trustees consists of 21 representatives from agencies and relevant areas within the field of education. The chair is the president of the German Rectors Conference, with other members from student organizations; trade unions; national employers organizations; the German Association of Municipal Authorities; the German Academic Exchange Service (DAAD); the Conference of the Federal Ministers of Education, Science and Culture; the national minister for education and research; and members of the German Parliament (Deutscher Bundestag).

Current Challenges and Future Perspectives of Student Affairs in Germany

With the projected developments and changes in the European and German higher education system come new challenges to student affairs in Germany. Some of the concerns and challenges that student affairs will face in the future are (a) financing of study, (b) student accommodation, (c) internationalization of higher education, and (d) the relationship between universities and the agencies responsible for student services.

Future Development of Student Services

The Länder have placed new demands on student services in light of (a) the emphasis on the individual profiles of the universities in a worldwide competitive area of higher education, (b) the decentralizing of competencies from the state to autonomous public organizations, and (c) new study structures with a strict management of study time. As a result of the increased demand upon student services, the DSW organized a symposium in 2004, Studying Successful Perspectives in Cooperation Between Studentenwerk and Universities. Topics included the role of the state and the demands and expectations of the universities and the students. The symposium also addressed how universities, students, and Studentenwerke are cooperating more and more and the need to continue to do so. At the beginning of the symposium, the question was asked whether it would not be better to integrate all student services into the universities. The answer of the symposium was very simple: There is no reason to integrate, but there are many reasons to cooperate to successfully realize the tasks and goals of all parties.

As a result, a redefinition of the future role and tasks of the Studentenwerke will be necessary. In the future, the Studentenwerke will have to address the needs of universities along with the demands of the students and to offer services to universities looking for more ways to become competitive higher education institutions.

For the Studentenwerke this will mean a balancing act. They will have to change from a student help organization to a business-oriented organization that sees universities as customers with specific demands.

Study Financing

With the Federal Constitutional Court decision of January 26, 2005, the system of financing higher education institutions can change from public to partly private subsidies. In the future, tuition fees can be levied for a first degree. In fact, study costs will increase if the federal Länder enable universities to levy tuition fees.

Curently, parents finance approximately 51% of the monthly living costs of the students, while the remaining funds come from various sources: 26% from part-time and full-time employment, 13% from the BAföG grants, and 10% from several other sources. Increasingly, the topic of educational costs raises questions about new sources like loans if parents do not provide their own contribution. For the Studentenwerke, such a process means that they have to widen their portfolio of financing opportunities and work with banks. In this way, the order of the Federal Constitutional Court guaranteeing equal access to higher education can be complied with, even when tuition fees are introduced. Originally, financing was a responsibility of the Federal Länder; now it falls to the DSW and the Studentenwerke. As nonprofit organizations, they can arrange financing that would allow access to higher education for students from lower socio-economic backgrounds. In this way they also can avoid social exclusion caused by the introduction of a variety of diverging tuition fees and financing models in the 16 Länder. There is a feeling among DSW staff that the increased fees would be a strong barrier to student mobility in Germany.

Accommodation of Students

The DSW and the German Association of Municipal Authorities have joined forces and recognized that the demand for student accommodations is on the rise. It is estimated that there is a national shortfall of approximately 21,000 student rooms in Germany, though the problem is greater in some regions than in others. Where has the increase in demand come from?

◊ Increase in the number of international students studying in Germany.

◊ Short-term demands by researchers.

◊ The introduction of the new bachelor's and master's degrees requires a greater presence by students at university sites.

All this comes along with a reduced public subsidy. In the future, as a result of the reduced public subsidy, the Studentenwerke will have to look for joint ventures with new partners, especially with private housing enterprises.

Internationalization of Higher Education

The efforts of the Ministers of Education to enable more student mobility through the Bologna Declaration have brought into focus the fact that student mobility depends not only on sufficient financial support but also on an economic and social infrastructure in the host country that allows immediate integration into the university and into the student body.

Consequently, as part of the Bologna Process, the DSW also promotes the recognition of the social and cultural dimension of the student As a result, the Studentenwerke will have to establish a social infrastructure that guarantees accommodation, food service, intercultural offerings, counseling services, and more to students. In order to achieve this change, they will need to involve various national umbrella organizations in the strategic planning and political discussion.

To achieve such a network, the individual Studentenwerke will be encouraged to cooperate more with responsible institutions for student affairs from different countries. On the one hand, this means training of staff; on the other hand, it means creating a voucher system that guarantees accommodation in the case of acceptance by the foreign university. It also means a reciprocal offering for foreign students in the form of a common service package. The challenge for the Studentenwerke will be to change from their individual approaches and be ready for the development of a common product. In this way, they can also contribute to the ongoing development of the universities.

Future Perspectives

The attractiveness of a particular country for students depends on the academic, social, and cultural conditions. Therefore, in the future it will be necessary to establish transparent and compatible infrastructural conditions for studying. In this regard, an efficient and expressive database is of utmost importance. A step toward this goal is the new Eurostudent Report 2005 (Federal Ministry of Education and Research, 2005) (Social and Economic Conditions of Student Life in Europe 2005), which gives a view of the different conditions of student life in several Bologna states. In the future, the database and list of the participating countries will be widened.

The realization of these plans depends on an improved networking or interaction among the relevant student affairs organizations. For that reason, the DSW and other European student affairs organizations promote the restructuring of the European Council for Student Affairs (ECStA). This council is an autonomous and independent European umbrella group which aims to promote the social infrastructure at universities and all higher education institutions in Europe (ECStA, n.d.).

In order to exchange knowledge on different methods for achieving successful student affairs programs, DSW, ECStA, and other student affairs organizations will need to strengthen their relationships and work cooperatively with overseas student affairs associations such as NASPA–Student Affairs Administrators in Higher Education, ACPA–College Student Educators International, NAFSA: Association of International Educators, CACUSS (Canadian Association of College and University Student Services), ANZSSA (Australian New Zealand Student Services Association), and APSSA (Asia Pacific Student Services Association).

References

Deutscher Akademischer Austauschdienst (German Exchange Service). (2005). Wissenschaft weltoffen: Facts and figures on the international nature of studies and research in Germany. Retrieved July 25, 2005, from http://www.wissenschaft-weltoffen.de

Deutsches Studentenwerk (DSW). (2003). Student services in Germany. Seminar presented at a meeting of Fulbright Scholars, Germany: Author.

European Council for Student Affairs (ECStA). (n.d.). Aims of the Ecsta. Retrieved July 9, 2008, from http://www.ecsta.org/sam/

EUROPA (n.d.). Education and training: The Bologna process – next stop Bergen 2005. Retrieved July 14, 2005, from http://europa.eu.int/comm/education/policies/educ/bologna/bologna_en.html

European Council for Student Affairs (ECStA). (2005, June). Comparison of the student service organisations in Europe. Berlin/Paris: Author.

European Council for Student Affairs (ECStA). (n.d.). Aims. Retrieved July 21, 2005, from http://www.ecsta.org/main/index.html

Federal Ministry of Education and Research. (2005). Eurostudent report 2005: Social and economic conditions of student life in Europe 2005. Retrieved July 9, 2008, from http://www.his.de/abt2/ab21/Eurostudent/report2005/Downloads/Synopsis%20of%20Indicators/SY

Higher Education Information Systems (HIS, Hochschul-Information-System GmbH). (2005). Eurostudent report 2005: Social and economic conditions of student life in Europe. Hannover, Germany: Author.

Isserstedt, W., Middendorff, E., Weber, S., Wolter, A., & Schnitzer, K. (Eds.). (2004). Economic and social conditions of student life in the Federal Republic of Germany 2003: 17th social survey of the Deutsches Studentenwerk conducted by Hochschul-Information-Systems (HIS). Bonn, Germany: Federal Ministry of Education and Research (Bundesministerium für Bildung und Forschung).

EIGHTEEN

IRAN

Sharon M. Karkehabadi

The Islamic Republic of Iran has the second youngest population in the world after Jordan. Of the total population, 69,515,000, over 70%, are under thirty (United Nations, 2002). Thirty-four percent of the population (22,583,637) is between the ages of 15 and 29 (National Youth Organization in the Islamic Republic of Iran [NYOIR], 2004). The youth population presents a significant concern for policy makers and social and economic planners.

Government Policy toward Higher Education and Student Affairs

The Ministry of Science, Research, and Technology (MSRT), along with the Ministry of Health, Treatment, and Medical Education, organizes and supervises higher education in the Islamic Republic of Iran. Government policy toward higher education and youth reflects the importance of education and the personal development of the youth in sustaining the Islamic Republic of Iran.

After the Revolution in 1979, many changes took place in the higher education system. In spring 1980, the Islamic Republic began what it calls the Cultural Revolution. One of its first goals was to restructure the system of higher education in Iran and institutionalize the values of Islam within the universities. In order to do this, the Council for Cultural Revolution of the Islamic Republic of Iran closed the universities to remove anti-Islamic academics, "reform" the curriculum, and generally Islamatize university environments (Talattof, 2000). The universities remained closed for two years (Spring 1980 to September 1982). The Unity Consolidation Office (UCO) was established to oversee all student organizations during this reconstruction period.

From the early 1990s, the government of the Islamic Republic has introduced national policy aimed at addressing the situation of the youth in Iran. The Supreme Council for the Youth was established in August 1992 to achieve four primary goals (United Nations, 2002):

1. to support the overall and natural growth of the personality of youth;

2. to meet mental, social, physical, and spiritual needs and to guide the emotional wants of youth;

3. to provide the grounds for youth participation in social activities and effective implementation of the social affairs and to defend the homeland of Islamic Iran; and

4. to preserve and strengthen youth joyfulness toward the development of the country and glory of Islamic Iran.

In March 1999, the National Youth Organization was established as the executive body of the Supreme Council for Youth, and it is the only official body "responsible for strategy-making, planning, coordinating, and monitoring all youth-related activities and implementing a national cross-sectoral management of youth affairs" (Ebadi, 2004, p. 4). A recent report by the National Youth Organization (NYOIR), "Youth Employment in Islamic Republic of Iran," described the youth as "the most important human resource and social asset" (NYOIR, 2004), and as such has high priority in the national development plans (e.g., the Economic, Social, and Cultural Development Plan (2005–2009). Major objectives of the five-year plan are: "[c]reating job opportunities, supporting economic enterprises [and] innovation…improving technically and intellectually talented people, increasing the employment rate, developing new technologies growth, stabilizing a trustable atmosphere for employers and businessmen, [and] paying attention to the people, especially the youth participation in economic activities" (NYOIR, 2004).

In order to gain political support of youth for the Islamic Republic of Iran, the government has acknowledged that it must meet their developmental, social, and economic needs. Demographic, social, economic, political, and educational factors are all converging to influence Iran's policy toward its youth.

Factors Influencing Higher Education and Student Life

The Political Context

The youth in the Islamic Republic of Iran have tremendous political power based on their number and level of activism. In Iran, the voting age is 15. The success or failure of previous and current regimes have been in large part due to student activism. The election of President Khatami in 1997 on the reformist party platform was due in large part to the support of the youth, who came out to vote and encouraged their parents to vote as well.

Since Khatami's presidency, the Office to Consolidate Unity or Daftar Tahkim Vadat (DTV) originally a fundamentalist Islamic student organization formed after the 1979 Iranian Revolution, began to represent the face of a new generation of students more critical of the Islamic Republic. Some groups have also split off from the DTV. The Student United Front is an example of such a group that organized student activities between 1997 and July 1999. The DTV, however, remains "Iran's largest national student union" with "individual Islamic student associations from over 60 of the country's universities" and has become one of the most vocal critics of the current regime (Atri, 2006, p. 1).

Leading up to the most recent election for president in June 2005, many students demonstrated against their choices and called for a referendum to revise the constitution. At a rally for a presidential candidate at Isfahan University on March 6, 2005, students sang the Nationalist Anthem over the Islamic Republic Anthem as it played and held placards saying, "Referendum Yes, Elections No." At another university in Mashdad on the same day, students removed the Health Minister from the podium and expressed similar demands (Azarmehr, 2005, p. 1).

Since the election of President, Mahmud Ahmadinejad in June 2005, 35 students have been sentenced to prison for political activism and another six students are awaiting verdicts. During the 2005–06 academic year, six students were notified by the Ministry of Science, Research, and Technology (MSRT) that they are no longer eligible to pursue their higher education. Currently, a new crackdown on students has begun since September 6, 2006, when Ahmadinejad made remarks that "universities should be rid of liberal and secular influences" (Esfandiari, 2006, p. 2). In the current academic year, so far at least 11 students have been barred from higher education. "Another 54 students (and possibly many more) have been registered on the condition that they cease their political activities. Also, since July 2005 university disciplinary committees have suspended at least 41 students for up to two semesters" (Human Rights Watch, 2006, p.1). Besides denying students access to higher education based political beliefs or opinions, "university supervision committees have also banned 19 student publications, and suspended or dissolved Islamic Students' Associations in 15 universities" (Human Rights Watch, 2006, p.1). Ali

Nekunesbati, a spokesperson for DTV said, "The government has made some promises but has not been able to fulfill them in the least. Instead of overcoming its weaknesses it has begun a crackdown on critics; and because students, professors, and the student movement are among the most critical, it's acting against them." DTV believes this could be the beginning of "a new 'cultural revolution'" (Esfandiari, 2006, p. 2).

Social Forces

For many Iranian youth ages 15 to 18, their rebellion is existential, not political. A recent survey of Tehran high school age students ages 15 to 18 shows their attitude to be more apathetic. They neither believe in the clergy "who have stolen their lives away, nor in the secular intellectuals whom they don't understand" (Gozlan, 2003, p. 3). According to this survey, only 4% of these students call themselves nationalists. Their world is satellite TV, the Internet (Persian is the third most commonly used language on the Internet after English and Chinese) and Western music, particularly rap (Molavi, 2005).

Iranian youth are pushing the boundaries on civil liberties and individual rights. Most youth do not remember the Islamic revolution or were born after it. Many Iranian youth do not believe in Islamic revolutionary virtues. These youth believe in freedom to do as they please.

So why don't they revolt? Why don't the women and girls remove their scarves? It took a bloodbath to remove the Shah from power in 1979, followed by a decade of war with Iraq. A common saying in Iran is: "We aren't ready to shed anything—not even a tear!" (Gozlan, 2003, p. 7). However, 44 % of youth surveyed, ages 15 to 29, do wish to leave Iran (Dawn, 2005, p. 1) and emigrate to the West.

Economic Forces

Much of the youth's sentiment toward the government is augmented by Iran's troubled economy. Iran has the highest rate of brain drain among developing countries. Every year 150,000 Iranians leave their country. Some four million Iranians now live abroad (International Monetary Fund, 2004). Iranian university students and professors cite the main reasons for brain drain in the country as lack of scientific and technological resources, including inadequate libraries and lack of credentialed graduate professors; lack of job security; low income; restriction of freedom; limited jobs to choose from; and lack of professional development in their field (Loh, 2000). Of the students that study abroad, 40% do not return to Iran. The overall unemployment rate in Iran currently is 15.7% (CIA, 2003). The unemployment rate for youth ages 15 to 29 increased from 14.8% in 1996 to 22.6% in 2002 (NYOIR, 2004).

The Educational Context

Since the 1979 revolution, admission to universities has been extremely competitive and very difficult. The admissions exam is so challenging that it has been nicknamed "the monster." Universities are at capacity; still, demand for postsecondary education exceeds supply. For example, of 752,343 applicants in 1989–1990, only 61,000 or one-twelfth were admitted to postsecondary institutions (The Embassy of The Islamic Republic of Iran, Ottawa-Canada, 2003).

To partly alleviate the problem of access to higher education, Iran has taken three measures. First, in 1982 the Islamic Azad (Open) University (IAU) was established with branches throughout the country. It does not rely on government funding; instead it charges students tuition and fees. In 2006, there were one million students at 220 branches enrolled in this university studying single subjects or taking full-time day or evening courses (Karaj IAU, 2006). To enter this university, applicants do not have to produce specific educational certificates, but its entrance examinations are similar to those of other universities. The certificates issued by this university are recognized by the Ministry of Culture and Higher Education (IAU, 2002).The second way Iran has tried to alleviate the access problem has been to establish distance universities. The Payam-e-Nour University was set up in 1987. It also charges tuition and fees. It principally aims to provide continuing education opportunities for teachers and civil servants. Courses are given through television and correspondence, and students write exams at local university offices. In 2006, Payam-e-Nour University (PNU) had 74 programs with 257 study centers and units, and 467,000 students (PNU, 2006)). Third, in January 2001, the first virtual university was established at the University of Tehran. Courses taught in this program include: computer sciences, energy conversion, applied design, and algorithm and computations (UT, 2004).

The past decade has seen a major change in student demographics as many more women have been admitted to institutions of higher education. Women now make up approximately 60% of university students. "Iranian women are using university studies as a way to leave home, postpone marriage, and generally earn greater freedom and social respect" (Esfandiari, 2003, p. 3). Dr. Said Peyvandi, a professor of sociology, said that ironically the Islamic Republic made it possible for girls from traditional or conservative families to go to school. "The traditional families who had not sent their girls to school before—because the teachers were men or the school was not Islamic—these were the girls that took the greatest advantage from the Islamization of schools, or the fact that schools were no longer mixed, as a way of justifying their presence out of the home" (Esfandiari, 2003, p. 6).

Duties and Authorities of Student Affairs Administrators

The University of Tehran, established in 1934, is the oldest public university that remains open today and is considered the mother university. The duties and authorities of student affairs administrators at the University of Tehran reflect the objectives of Islamic governmental policies. They include the following:

◊ monitoring the implementation of students' welfare services plans, non-educational and outside activities;

◊ developing and extending different sport branches in the university and establishing the necessary facilities;

◊ monitoring student housing;

◊ providing jobs for students in financial need;

◊ supervising the counseling and guiding of students in academic, career, and private fields;

◊ monitoring the cultural, political, and social activities of the students; and

◊ providing cultural and artistic facilities.

The director general in Shahed (Veterans) Affairs is also affiliated with student affairs. The establishment of counseling centers is a particularly new area to student affairs in Iran. Formed in 1996, the centers are presided over by the head of the Supreme Council of the Youth. Part of counseling services involves mental health counseling for students, marriage counseling, and measures to prevent drug abuse among students.

Conclusion

The large youth population in Iran is a major concern for Islamic Iran. The Islamic Republic must satisfy its population of young people for their own and for the nation's well being. National policy as seen in national development plans, legislation, and governmental organizations all address the importance of the social, economic, political, and educational issues facing Iran's youth. Is it possible to address their concerns within the current framework of the Iranian government? Or are these issues a reflection of the current government? Up to now, the government of Iran has not been successful in changing the political, economic, or social situation of the country's youth. It remains to be seen whether the Islamic Republic of Iran can create policy that satisfies the youth and solves the country's continuing economic crisis.

References

Atri, A. (2006). "The urge for democracy." The Journal of International Security Affairs. No. 10. Retrieved October 19, 2006, from http://www.securityaffairs.org/issues/2006/10/atri.php

Azarmehr, P. (2005, March 7). Referendum not elections. Iran va Jahan. Retrieved October 2, 2005, from http://www.iranianvoice.org/article1565.html

CIA Factbook. (2003). Retrieved March 3, 2005, from www.populations.com

Dawn Group of Newspapers. (2005, March 9). Majority of Iranians want to emigrate. Retrieved March 11, 2005, from http://www.dawn.com/2005/03/09/int6.htm

Ebadi, R. (2004). Youth employment, empowerment and participation: Securing the future. XV Malente Symposium, YEN Roundtable, October 19–20, 2004, Lubeck, Germany:

International Labour Organization. Retrieved January 10, 2005, from http://www.ilo.org/public/english

The Embassy of the Islamic Republic of Iran, Ottawa-Canada. (2003). Education system in Iran. Salam Iran. Retrieved on September 30, 2005, from http://www.salamiran.org/Embassy/Embassy/StudentAdvisory/Iran_education/Iran_Education_system.html

Esfandiari, G. (2003). Iran: Number of female university students rising dramatically. Radio/Free Europe Liberty. Retrieved January 6, 2005, from http://www.parsitimes.com/women/women-universities.html

Esfandiari, G. (2006). Iranian government increases pressure by banning student activists. Radio/Free Europe Liberty. Retrieved October 17, 2006, from http://www.payvand.com/news/06/sep/1335.html

Gozlan, M. (2003, November 13). Iran: The liberation won't come from America but from women. Marianne. Paris: France. Retrieved January 18, 2005, from http://www.worldpress.org/article-model.cfm?article-id=1800&don't=yes

Human Rights Watch. (2006). Denying the right to education. http://www.hrw.org/backgrounder/mena/iran1006/iran1006web.pdf

International Monetary Fund (IMF). (2004, September). IMF Country Report No. 04/307: Islamic Republic of Iran—Statistical Appendix. Retrieved March 11, 2005, from http://www.imf.org/external/pubs/ft/scr/2004/cr04307.pdf

Islamic Azad University (IAU), Khorasgan Branch (2002). Higher education in Iran. Retrieved on September 30, 2005, from http://www.khuisf.ac.ir/Highe %20 Education%20in%20Iran/higher_education_in_iran.htm

Karaj Islamic Azad University (Karaj IAU). (2006) About Islamic Azad University (History). Retrieved on October 19, 2006, from http://www.kiau.ac.ir/english/about/htm

Why Iranian students going abroad for higher education refuse to return home? (2000, January, No. 7). Loh Monthly Magazine, pp. 20–23.

Molavi, A. (2005, March). The regime may inflame Washington, but young Iranians say that they admire of all places, America. Smithsonian, 5(12), pp. 54–63.

National Youth Organization in the Islamic Republic of Iran (NYOIR) Presidency. (2004, October). Youth employment in Islamic Republic of Iran. Department of International Affairs. Retrieved on March 3, 2005, from www.ilo.org/public/english

Payame Noor University (PNU). (2006). About Payame Noor University. Retrieved on October 19, 2006, from http://www.pnu.ac.ir/engilish/htm/about.htm

Reporters without Borders. (2006). Independent news website closed, blog platform briefly blocked. Retrieved October 18, 2006, from http://www.rsf.org/article.php3?id_article=19016

Talattof, K. (2000). The Politics of Writing in Iran: A History of Modern Persian Literature. NY: Syracuse University Press.

United Nations. (2002). Islamic Republic of Iran: National youth policy. Country Profiles on the Situation of Youth. Retrieved on March 11, 2005, from http://esa.un.org/socdev/unyin/country

United Nations, Population Division of the Department of Economic and Social Affairs (ESA). (2003). World Population Prospects: The 2004 Revision and World Urbanization Prospects: The 2003 Revision. Retrieved March 11, 2005, from http://esa.un.org/unpp

University of Tehran (UT). (2004). Administration: Center for E-Learning. Retrieved October 17, 2006, from http://ut.ac.ir/en/main-links/e-learning.htm

Yaghmaian, B. (2002). Social change in Iran: An eyewitness account of dissent, defiance, and new movements for rights. New York: State University of New York.

NINETEEN

IRELAND

BARRY KEHOE

The History of Student Services and Student Affairs in Ireland

The third-level education system (college and university) in Ireland comprises seven universities, fourteen institutes of technology, eight colleges of education (all the aforementioned are largely state-funded), and a small number of private colleges. The colleges of education are now either incorporated into universities or closely linked to them.

The Seven Universities

In the universities, there has been a gradual evolution of student services. Up to quite recently most of the universities had a dispersed model of student services, whereby the services existed in relative isolation, typically answering to different members of senior management such as the registrar, bursar, or secretary. Typically, the services included counseling, health, careers, chaplaincy, accommodation, sport and recreation, and in some cases, a dean of women students.

In the mid-1970s, the National University of Ireland, Cork, created the position of head of student services and appointed one of its professors to the post. However, when the incumbent retired the position lapsed. Then, in 1980, the newly-created National Institute for Higher Education, Dublin (subsequently re-designated Dublin City University), decided to create a comprehensive integrated student affairs unit responsible for student services, policy, facilities, and recruitment. Since 2002, most of the other universities have moved toward integrating student services and affairs under one senior or relatively senior manager. At the time of writing, the titles of the managers vary from institution to institution.[1]

The Confederation of Student Services in Ireland (CSSI) was founded in the early 1980s and has helped considerably in supporting all those involved in providing student services in Irish higher education and in making the case for resources. In 2005 a network of those involved in managing student services and affairs in the seven universities was formed: the Irish Universities Student Services Network (IUSSN).

Three other initiatives deserve a mention:

1. The Higher Education Authority (HEA) published Guidelines for the Development of Student Support Services (1998);

2. Since 1996, significant funding has been provided under the HEA targeted initiative scheme. (This has led to growth in inter alia, disability services and services for non-traditional students such as students from low socio-economic backgrounds).

3. In 2004, the Irish Universities Quality Board began a sectoral project on student support services in Irish universities, which was completed in 2006. The publication *Good Practice: In the Organisation of Student Support Services in Irish Universities* is available at www.iuqb.ie.

The Fourteen Institutes of Technology

Eleven of these institutes began as regional technical colleges in the 1969–72 period, and were re-designated as institutes of technology in 1997–98. The development of services at these new institutions was quite slow, and in many cases the chaplaincy service and perhaps a sports officer were the only ones that existed for a number of years. In time, other services were added (careers, counseling, health, etc.). The growth of student services in these colleges received a boost in the mid-1990s by the introduction of a registration charge for all third-level students (also called the non-tuition fee), as the money generated from this charge was used in these colleges (much more so than in the universities) for funding student services. Many of the colleges at this time appointed a student services officer to coordinate student services and cooperate with the students' union. However, this was generally a "catalyst" and co-coordinating role rather than a managerial one. In more recent years the majority

[1] The following posts currently exist within the Irish universities: Vice President, Students; Vice President for Student Services and Human Resources; Director of Student Affairs (2 institutions); Director of Student Services; and Dean of Students.

of the institutes of technology have appointed an academic administration and student affairs manager at a reasonably senior level, reporting to the registrar. The exception is the very large Dublin Institute of Technology (DIT), which was established informally in 1978 from six pre-existing third-level colleges and was given statutory recognition in 1992. For a while during the 1990s, student services in the DIT were integrated under a head of student services, but in recent years the structure has reverted to the "dispersed" model.

Student Services Delivery Model

As indicated earlier, there is no uniform management structure for student services in Ireland. However, in recent years there has been a trend toward integration of the various services under a senior (or relatively senior) member of staff responsible solely for the area, with a corresponding trend away from what have been referred to above as the "dispersed" model and the "catalyst" model.[2]

Thirteen of the fourteen institutes of technology now have an integrated student services structure under a relatively senior member of staff who is also responsible for academic administration: the academic administration and student affairs manager. In some cases there is also a student services officer at middle-management level. The remaining institute, the Dublin Institute of Technology, has a rather dispersed model at the moment, but this may change in the near future, particularly since this is a very large multi-campus institution that is due to move to a single new campus within the next five years.

Student service delivery in Ireland is similar to that in the United Kingdom There tends to be largely the same range of services, with the same variety of management structures. Indeed, historically speaking, many of the professional groupings in Ireland (e.g., careers services, counseling services) had strong links with, or were subgroups of, their U.K. counterparts. There has also been U.S. influence, particularly with regard to best practice and to management structures (e.g., appointing the chief student affairs officer at a senior level).

If we categorize approaches to the delivery of student services along a spectrum extending from student dependency to student empowerment, Ireland would, in common with most European countries, be more toward the empowerment end of the spectrum. Students are viewed as adults, and student government, student clubs, and student societies are the primary agents in the organization of student life. By the same token, in Irish student affairs there is not the same emphasis on the organization of residence life as in the United States.

Governmental Groups/Outside Agencies/ Professional Associations

Student services (like every other section of the university or institute) receive the bulk of their funding from the government or a government agency. However, there is no government agency that provides significant direction and support to the universities and colleges on the issue of student affairs and student services. Granted, the Higher Education Authority published guidelines in 1998, but these have not had very much influence, as it is up to each college to manage its own affairs. Indeed, in recent years the government has put the universities and colleges under increasing financial pressure, with the result that support services generally, in common with their academic colleagues, have been finding it difficult to maintain their level of service.

The Irish Universities Quality Board, which is quite a new body, has been supportive of student services in the universities and is currently overseeing a project to encourage, disseminate, and implement good practice in university student services. This has led to the creation of the Irish Universities Student Services Network (IUSSN), consisting of the senior student affairs officers (where they exist) of each of the universities. The IUSSN is a recognized subgroup of the Irish universities' umbrella group (The Conference of Heads of Irish Universities: CHIU).

The professional representative association of student services and student affairs in Irish higher education is the Confederation of Student Services in Ireland (CSSI). Founded in the mid-1980s, it promotes student development and student support services, facilitates the exchange of ideas and research, and seeks to influence national policy on matters related to student welfare and student development. It organizes a biennial conference and, in each intervening year, a one-day seminar. However, unlike many of its counterparts, it does not have a full-time or even part-time secretariat, and it depends entirely on volunteerism on the part of its officers and committee members.

The individual services also have their national networks and associations, which are quite active and also hold conferences and seminars. These include the Association of Graduate Careers Services in Ireland and the Irish Association of University and College Counselors, and there are similar organizations for those who work in health, sport, chaplaincy, accommodation, access, and disability services.

Professional Development and Preparatory Programs

In Ireland, there is no preparatory program specifically to prepare students to be professionals in student affairs, nor are people normally employed on the basis of such qualifications. Indeed, the concept of student affairs as a profession is not very prevalent, and one suspects that most

---

[2] In summary, the seven universities have the following structures: (a) one vice president for students; (b) one vice president for student services and human resources; (c) two directors of student affairs, reporting to the registrar (= vice president for academic affairs); (d) one director of student services, again reporting to the registrar; (e) one dean of students, who has a policy rather than a managerial role—most of the services report to the college secretary (= vice president for administration); and (f) in the remaining university, the various services report to one of two senior officers of the university, and discussions are taking place about creating a senior student affairs officer post, possibly at the level of dean or vice president.

people (both within and outside student affairs) would see student affairs as a cluster of professionals (from different professions) who share a common mission and set of objectives rather than as a profession in itself. Thus, medical staff members have professional medical training, counselors are trained in psychotherapy, and so on. The staff members working within student affairs in Ireland are generally highly qualified within their own fields, and there is normally a commitment within institutions to ongoing professional development (which can include many of the areas covered in student affairs preparatory programs in other countries).

The Campus Climate: Relationship with Faculty

In general, student affairs divisions in Ireland enjoy a good relationship with their academic colleagues, and there are many examples of cooperation and cooperative ventures (peer mentoring schemes, workshops in study methods, cross-referral of students). However, the emphasis on research output, and its importance in academic promotion, tends to lead to a climate where good teaching, the academic advising role, and involvement in student development on the part of academic staff can be undervalued. There can also be resentment on the part of student affairs staff that their academic colleagues enjoy more favorable work conditions (e.g., sabbatical leave, career progression structures, time for research).

The Evolution of Student Affairs and Services

Because each institution has evolved its own structure, the evolution of student affairs can be influenced by a particularly significant, capable, or powerful individual, whether this be the president, the chief student affairs officer, or some other senior officer such as the registrar or head of administration. Institutional politics can play a role, as can the perceived usefulness of student affairs to the organization in terms of student recruitment, student satisfaction, student retention, and/or fee income.

Funding

Student services in Irish higher education are funded mainly either from the institution's core government grant (this is particularly true in the universities) or from the student registration charge of €800 EUR ($1,259 USD) per year (this is more the case in the institutes of technology). In some institutions one or more of the student services or student facilities are funded by means of a student levy. Certain services (e.g., health service, sports facilities) may impose charges to meet their costs, while college-owned residences are normally expected to be entirely self-funding. Considerable funding for access programs, mature student support, disability services, and student retention initiatives has been provided to the universities over the last nine years through the Higher Education Authority targeted initiatives scheme.

However, this funding is now being progressively mainstreamed into the core grant of each institution. This has led to some fears regarding the net effect of this change on the services involved. Finally, monies for disbursement directly to students are drawn down by both the universities and the institutes of technology from the European Social Fund (ESF) under two headings: a fund for students with disabilities, and a "student assistance fund" for students who are experiencing particular or unexpected financial hardship.

Campus Structures

There is some inconsistency within Irish higher education institutions regarding what services are provided for students and which of these falls under the remit of the student services division. Generally speaking, both the universities and the institutes of technology offer the following services to their students, normally through the student services/student affairs division: counseling, careers, health, sport, chaplaincy, access, disability, student financial support, accommodation, student activities, orientation, and tutoring/mentoring. Normally, international student support is provided by an international office outside the student affairs structure. Likewise, campus accommodation is often run by a campus company, and catering is also run as a commercial operation outside the student affairs remit.

The organizational chart for Dublin City University gives an indication of the range of services offered in an Irish university, staffing levels, and the vocabulary we tend to use. The chart (Figure 19.1) is untypical in that student recruitment is included in the brief and disability support has been moved elsewhere.

Description of Individual Student Services

Counseling services. These exist in all institutions and are normally separate from careers services. Generally, the institutes of technology have one counselor, while the counselor/student ratio in the universities (and the Dublin Institute of Technology) is a very unsatisfactory average of one counselor to every 3,800 students. Some counseling services are situated within the health service, but most prefer to be a separate entity in order not to have their work "pathologized" by association with the medical model. Counselors work both on a one-to-one basis and with groups, and frequently offer workshops in areas such as stress management, self esteem, study methods, etc.

Careers services. These services provide career counseling and career education, liaise with employers, and facilitate graduate placement. In a small minority of institutions the careers service is not within the student services remit but is situated within the division that liaises with business and industry.

Health services. The health services in Irish third-level institutions vary in the range of services provided. The institutes of technology usually have a nursing presence with part-time doctor attendance, while the universities gener-

Figure 19.1. DCU student affairs organizational chart.

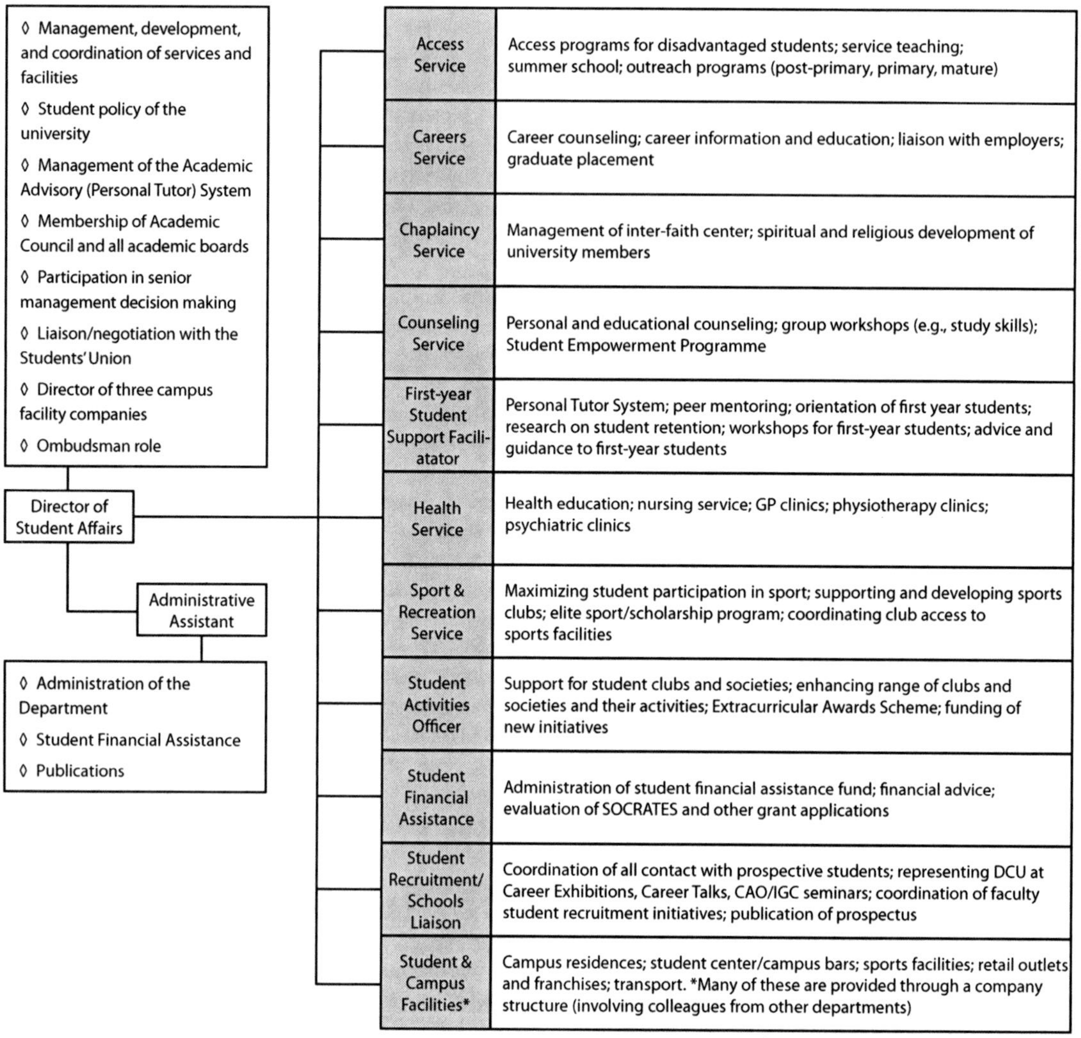

◊ Management, development, and coordination of services and facilities ◊ Student policy of the university ◊ Management of the Academic Advisory (Personal Tutor) System ◊ Membership of Academic Council and all academic boards ◊ Participation in senior management decision making ◊ Liaison/negotiation with the Students' Union ◊ Director of three campus facility companies ◊ Ombudsman role	**Access Service**	Access programs for disadvantaged students; service teaching; summer school; outreach programs (post-primary, primary, mature)
	Careers Service	Career counseling; career information and education; liaison with employers; graduate placement
	Chaplaincy Service	Management of inter-faith center; spiritual and religious development of university members
	Counseling Service	Personal and educational counseling; group workshops (e.g., study skills); Student Empowerment Programme
	First-year Student Support Faciliator	Personal Tutor System; peer mentoring; orientation of first year students; research on student retention; workshops for first-year students; advice and guidance to first-year students
Director of Student Affairs	**Health Service**	Health education; nursing service; GP clinics; physiotherapy clinics; psychiatric clinics
	Sport & Recreation Service	Maximizing student participation in sport; supporting and developing sports clubs; elite sport/scholarship program; coordinating club access to sports facilities
Administrative Assistant	**Student Activities Officer**	Support for student clubs and societies; enhancing range of clubs and societies and their activities; Extracurricular Awards Scheme; funding of new initiatives
◊ Administration of the Department ◊ Student Financial Assistance ◊ Publications	**Student Financial Assistance**	Administration of student financial assistance fund; financial advice; evaluation of SOCRATES and other grant applications
	Student Recruitment/ Schools Liaison	Coordination of all contact with prospective students; representing DCU at Career Exhibitions, Career Talks, CAO/IGC seminars; coordination of faculty student recruitment initiatives; publication of prospectus
	Student & Campus Facilities*	Campus residences; student center/campus bars; sports facilities; retail outlets and franchises; transport. *Many of these are provided through a company structure (involving colleagues from other departments)

ally have a wider range of services. Generally, health services are funded from the institution's own resources rather than participating in the national provision of health services to the whole community, and they seek to supplement rather than replicate these services. By and large, they emphasize occupational health issues relevant to the third-level student population, such as stress management, sports injuries, and sexual health and contraception. Some of the health services are involved in health education initiatives, and in some colleges health services have combined with other services (e.g., sport, counseling, catering) to jointly mount holistic health promotion initiatives (e.g., the "health-promoting campus").

Sports services. All Irish third-level institutions provide a sports service or a sport and recreation service. This service is generally responsible for promoting sport, developing sports clubs, administering sports scholarships, and organizing access to sports facilities. In some cases, the service is also responsible for the management of the indoor and outdoor sports facilities (with perhaps considerable public membership), while in other cases this latter function is carried out by a separate division, perhaps under a company structure. Some of the universities have outsourced the management of their fitness suites to a commercial operator.

Chaplaincy services. The arrangements for the provision of chaplaincy services vary within Irish higher education, but all institutions do have chaplains who see to the spiritual and religious development of the college community. Some chaplaincy services have purpose-built chaplaincy centers, while all colleges at least provide office accommodation. Almost all chaplains in Ireland are paid by the higher education institution.

Access services and disability services. Access services normally provide a range of pre-entry and post-entry supports for applicants and students from low socio-economic backgrounds and for other nontraditional and under-represented groups (mature students, minority ethnic groups). Support for students with disabilities is sometimes within the remit of the access service and sometimes provided by a separate disability service. Both of these areas have developed significantly since 1996 as a result of being included under the Higher Education Authority Targeted Initiatives Scheme. These initiatives are now being mainstreamed by each college; it remains to be seen if staffing and resources will come under more pressure as a result. It might also be noted that disability legislation in Ireland is not yet fully rights-based, although it has improved recently.

Student financial assistance. Each higher education institution in Ireland is given a student financial assistance fund to help students experiencing serious financial difficulty. This money comes from the European Social Fund (ESF), and is a useful means of supplementing the very inadequate national system of student financial support (small means-tested grants). The fund given to each college is based on the number of full-time registered students, and the amount is currently calculated on the basis of €50 EUR ($79 USD) per student. Typically, the student financial assistance service also gives advice on budgeting, eligibility for higher education grants and other awards, and tuition fees. The Irish government abolished tuition fees for first-time Irish and EU full-time undergraduate students in the mid-1990s, so the financial difficulties of most undergraduate students in Irish colleges are related to maintenance (i.e., daily living expenses such as rent, food, transportation, etc.) rather than tuition fees.

Accommodation. Thanks to tax breaks encouraging the development of student accommodation over the last 15 years, there has been considerable growth in both college-owned and privately-owned student residences. Typically, these would consist of apartment blocks, each apartment consisting of a number of study-bedrooms (about four to six) plus a communal area (sitting room, kitchen). There is hardly ever any catering provided within the residences, and there is no tradition of residence life activities organized by the college. Some of the colleges have developed their residences jointly with a commercial developer, while others have developed them and manage them themselves, frequently under a college company structure. All such residences operate on a commercial basis and do not receive any state or college subsidy. In addition, most colleges also provide information and advice to students on off-campus accommodation (apartments, houses, lodgings, etc.). Finally, quite a few Irish third-level students commute to college; the proportion varies from about 30% to 60%.

Student activities /student life. It must be emphasized that much of student life and student activities in Irish colleges is devolved to the students themselves and is organized by the societies, sports clubs, and student government (students' union). This is the "empowerment" model referred to in the section on student services delivery model, which is probably the outcome not only of educational philosophy but also the relative lack of resources. Typically, the student affairs division would seek to create a framework in which student clubs, societies, and activities can flourish, and would provide a certain level of staffing (for example, the staff of the sports service plus, perhaps, a societies officer or a student activities officer). In at least one university there is now formal accreditation of extracurricular activity, and other colleges are considering similar schemes. Most of the funding for sports clubs, societies, and student government comes from the capitation fee paid by each student as part of the student registration charge. The student registration charge is €800 EUR ($1,259 USD) each year, and the capitation fee element of this varies from €90 to €140 EUR ($142 to $220 USD).

There is a rich and vibrant tradition of student activities on Irish campuses, although this can be affected by the need many students have to engage in part-time employment, by the rigid structure of degree programs (allowing for little or no self-pacing), and in some cases, by relatively high numbers of commuting students.

Student government. Typically, each college has a students' union, and each year the student body elects its officers (both full time and part time). A typical scenario would be for a college to have three full-time student union officers (president, education officer, welfare officer) and a number of part-time officers who would continue to be full-time students. Normally, the president and at least one of the other full-time officers would be members of the governing authority of the college. Indeed, there is normally student representation also on academic councils and all academic committees. The students' union is the representative body for all students and frequently also runs a number of services (e.g., shops, ticket agency, entertainments, sometimes the campus bar or bars). There is a national umbrella organization (The Union of Students in Ireland), but not all the unions in the colleges are affiliated with this body.

Student Demographics

Traditionally, access to third-level education in Ireland has been very competitive, and for school-leavers (secondary school graduates) has been regulated by a points system based on grades obtained in the schools' Leaving Certificate examination. The percentage of the age cohort that proceeds to full-time third-level education is currently about 55%, which is quite high by European standards. The intake into third level has also been biased toward the higher socio-economic groups, particularly in the university sector. However, in the past 20 years or so there has been a fall in the birth rate, and this has now affected the third-level sector. Enrollment figures have leveled off (and in some cases dropped), and the institutions have more proactively sought to recruit nontraditional students such as mature students and international students. The latter group has an added attraction to colleges as international students pay high full-cost tuition fees. The changing demographic has also given an additional motive to colleges (over and above the equity reason) to recruit students from low socio-economic backgrounds. (The ability of such students is assessed by broader criteria than grades alone). Finally, there is the significant phenomenon in Ireland of immigration from eastern European countries and elsewhere (the "new Irish"), and there are also many nationals of non-EU countries who have acquired or are seeking asylum or refugee status. Ireland is rapidly becoming a very multicultural society, and this is both a challenge and an opportunity for the third-level sector and for those working in student affairs.

Politics and Higher Education

The political climate and political decisions and legislation have affected higher education and student affairs in a number of ways. Recent legislation on the universities, on equality, and on disability has moved the equity agenda forward, although much still remains to be done. The political climate and the legislation emphasize accountability and quality assurance, which has led to good quality assurance initiatives within the higher education system. In the university sector, the quality agenda is driven by the Irish Universities Quality Board (IUQB), which oversees a system under which each division in each university is subject to periodic quality review. On the more negative side, the Irish system of student financial support is still very inadequate ("if you're poor enough to qualify for a grant you're too poor to live on it"), and over the last three or four years the government has significantly reduced, in real terms, its funding to higher education. There is perhaps a perception that higher education is quite well off and that the needs of primary and secondary schools have a greater claim on the education budget. All this has led to an even greater emphasis within colleges on revenue generation, and reservations have been expressed in some quarters about a perceived overly business mentality and an all-embracing economic rationalism and utilitarian reductionism.

International Collaboration

Irish people have always been outward-looking and have strong international connections. This is true of those working in student affairs. Many Irish student affairs staff members have undertaken study visits to their counterparts in other countries and have hosted visits by them. Some visits within the European Union have been subsidized by EU grants. Many of the professional groupings within student affairs have had strong connections with their counterpart organizations in other countries (particularly the United Kingdom). At the level of national student affairs organizations, a number of individuals within Irish student affairs have been members of Association of Managers of Student Services in Higher Education, NASPA—Student Affairs Administrators in Higher Education, and the Australian New Zealand Student Services Association, and have attended conferences and other events organized by them. In 2004 the Confederation of Student Services in Ireland (CSSI) entered into an exchange agreement with NASPA, and the first exchange visit took place that year. CSSI has always welcomed international delegates to its conference and normally has a keynote presenter from abroad. International exchange opportunities and internships are a matter for individual contact and agreement rather than having an existing agreed framework.

Conclusion

There is much to be optimistic about regarding the future of student affairs within the Irish higher education system. For example:

◊ Those working in student affairs are enthusiastic, highly qualified, professional and innovative.

◊ The movement in Ireland towards integrating student services under a senior student affairs officer will give student services greater critical mass and more influence on policy.

◊ A better understanding of how and where learning takes place and of the importance of transferable skills and competencies will serve to integrate student affairs more into the educational enterprise.

◊ As institutions better appreciate the importance of student recruitment, student satisfaction, student retention, and graduate loyalty (if only for financial reasons), they will also better appreciate the contribution that student affairs can make to these factors.

◊ Greater internationalization of student affairs (of which this book is a good example) will assist us in identifying best practice and adapting it, where appropriate, to our needs.

We in student affairs in Ireland are always glad to learn from, and to welcome, our counterparts from abroad. We look forward to increased contact and to the further internationalization of student affairs, to the benefit of our students, our institutions, and our own professional development and renewal.

TWENTY

UNITED ARAB EMIRATES

Jennifer Hanson and Dala Farouki

A Brief History of Higher Education in the United Arab Emirates

The United Arab Emirates is a federation with powers given to either the federal or the individual emirates' own governments. Seven emirates compose the United Arab Emirates: Abu Dhabi (the capital), Ajman, Al Fujairah, Sharjah, Dubai, Ras al Khaimah and Um al Quwain. The country, originally a protectorate known as the Trucial States, the Trucial Coast, or Trucial Oman, gained independence from Great Britain on December 2, 1971. The year 1971 also introduced the federal court system, which was adopted by all emirates except Dubai and Ras al Khaimah. The current population of the United Arab Emirates is 94% Muslim. The remaining 6% includes Christians, Hindus, and those of other faiths. The two main languages spoken in the country are English and Arabic (AMIDEAST, n.d.). The United Arab Emirates enjoys one of the world's top per capita incomes. The country has the financial resources and capital for a powerful higher education system (http://cia.gov/cia/publications/factbook/geos/ae.html).

Higher education is much needed for this country's population. It will allow U.A.E. nationals to become more self-reliant, with the government making efforts toward Emiratization. Emiratization is the government effort to increase the percentage of U.A.E. nationals in the country's workforce, which is currently made up of more than 70% expatriates. The United Arab Emirates is known in the Middle East as being at the forefront in modern higher education due to its massive expansion and its dedication to education in terms of infrastructure and financial support (Shaghour, 2000). It differs from the rest of the Arab world in that is has a larger variety of educational models on which its institutions are based. American, British, and Australian models of higher education coexist with the national institutions. This unique combination provides students with a wide range of choices for their education. The coun-

try's higher education institutions work toward making students more marketable in the global business world. Career-focused initiatives such as job-oriented courses, leadership programs, and internships allow students in the United Arab Emirates to hone their job and people skills. The Western higher education models that are applied in several U.A.E.-based universities are useful for preparing the national students to work alongside expatriate workers in order to further develop the country.

The Ministry of Higher Education and Scientific Research, founded in 1992, defined higher education through Federal Law No. 4, which stated that "higher education is a place where nationals are prepared in respect both of scientific education and outlook to meet the needs of the country and from which the state can assume its position on the road to modern development and can ascertain its ability to adopt modern technologies" (Al Suwaidi, 1997, p. 124).

In higher education, the term "American" can have many meanings. At the American University in Dubai, it is used to describe the method of teaching, the language of instruction and application (American English language versus British English language), the emphasis on a holistic development of the students, and the focus on students' rights and privileges (W. Atiyah, personal communication, March 2003). The American University in Dubai follows the standards and regulations set by an accreditation agency in the United States, thus guaranteeing the education and mission of the university as acceptable by Western, and "American" standards. "Globalization" is a term that is being increasingly connected to higher education in the Gulf (Ali, 2001). Altbach (2002) states that globalization refers to trends in higher education that have cross-national implications. These include mass higher education; a global marketplace for students, faculty, and highly educated personnel; and new Internet-based technologies. Globalization requires a set of standards and expectations for students and graduates worldwide.

The first higher education institution, the United Arab Emirates University, was established in the emirate of Al Ain in 1976. The three largest national universities are the U.A.E. University, Zayed University, and the Higher Colleges of Technology. Other national (public or government-funded) universities include the Dubai Police Academy, Etisalat University College, Ittihad University, the Khalifa bin Zayed College, and the Naval College. U.A.E. University has eight faculties and is the most popular university choice for U.A.E. national students. Zayed University (ZU), a prestigious national university for women, was founded in 1998. ZU has campuses in both Abu Dhabi and Dubai (Zayed University, n.d.). The Higher Colleges of Technology (HCT), established in 1988, has two campuses in each of the emirates of the United Arab Emirates, 12 in total, with separate campuses for men and women.

U.A.E. University, Zayed University, and the Higher Colleges of Technology, admit only U.A.E. nationals in an attempt to offer the option of in-country quality higher education. Before the U.A.E. University was established, students had to seek higher education abroad. The country provides free higher education to Emiratis in national universities (http://mohe.U.A.E..gov.ae/indexe.html). English is the language of instruction for all the institutions, although several teach Islamic religious studies and other traditional degrees in Arabic as well. The United Arab Emirates' national establishments are not always open to national students; therefore, an expatriate would have fewer options for pursuing higher education. In most cases, expatriates wishing to attend a "brick-and-mortar" (physical) campus must either attend a private university, within the United Arab Emirates, or go abroad (P. Coles, personal communication, February 2003).

The growing number of higher education institutions in the United Arab Emirates has created a "higher education boom." Within the last 10 years, more than 20 establishments have opened their doors. These institutions vary from having a brick-and-mortar campus to having offices with online correspondence as a major component of the education. They may offer certificates and diplomas, or they may be entirely undergraduate, both undergraduate and graduate, or entirely graduate. Offering diplomas of completion in addition to a university degree is more common in the public universities such as Zayed University or the Higher Colleges of Technology. Institutions such as the brand new, privately-operated, British Open University offer only graduate programs in an effort to cater to working professionals through concentrated programs and evening and late afternoon classes.

There are many private, foreign institutions of higher education. The institutions promise education based on older, foreign education models such as British, Australian, American, and Indian. The education institutions are "going global and making partnerships" (Maksoud, 2003).

Educational Hub—A New Concept in Higher Education

Educational hubs in the United Arab Emirates are modeled on other similar clustered landmarks in Dubai such as the Dubai Internet City and the Dubai Media City. The educational hub in Dubai, Knowledge Village (KV), has branch universities from Australia, the United Kingdom, India, Pakistan, Belgium, and Ireland.[1]

The list of higher education institutions in the United Arab Emirates is developing rapidly. Tables 20.1 and 20.2 provide a list of most of the institutions established within the last 15 years.

The KV has made it easier for private investors to establish learning centers in this prominent location without having to worry about health services, activities, or transportation since the KV operates with these services available to institutions located within its grounds. The KV institutions may share facilities with each other such as the cafeteria, performance rooms, and classrooms. There are no residential facilities in the KV; thus, students must find their own accommodations elsewhere in Dubai. Other offices in the village are rented out to adult and distance-learning companies. This makes a huge difference in the character and image of the educational institution. The KV concept is in contrast to the traditional image of a university. For example, the American University in Dubai and the new Abu Dhabi University, located in both Abu Dhabi and Al Ain, have brick-and-mortar self-contained campuses with student dormitories.

The KV and the University City in Sharjah, currently being duplicated in Dubai and called Academic City, are new phenomena to the rest of the world but not to the United Arab Emirates. The nation has seen the emirate of Dubai create several "cities" within the past 10 years that house similar businesses or services in order to increase its business presence in the world. For example, Dubai is home to Dubai Media City, Dubai Internet City (where businesses such as Microsoft and IBM as well as CNN and Reuters are located), and Dubai Medical City. Medical, education, technology, and business companies are being offered state-of-the-art locations next to each other in order to foster competition and collaboration.

The KV is "the world's first free zone for IT, e-business and media, and already a regional hub for many multinational organizations as well as home to smaller, start-up

---

[1] The Knowledge Village includes the following universities: Birla Institute of Technology and Science (BITS)-Pilani; British University in Dubai (BUID); Islamic Azad University; Manipal Academy of Higher Education; Shaheed Zulfikar Ali Bhutto Institute of Science and Technology; University of Wollongong in Dubai; Mahatma Gandhi University Off Campus Centre; University of Southern Queensland in Dubai; Middlesex University; Dublin Business School; European University College Brussels (Knowledge Village, n.d.); and George Mason University in the United States.

Table 20.1. Private higher education institutions in the United Arab Emirates.

Name of Institution	Website
Abu Dhabi Petroleum Institute	www.pi.ac.ae
Abu Dhabi University	www.adu.ac.ae
Al Ghurair University	www.agu.ae
Al Hosn University	unknown
Al Khawarizmi University	www.khawarizmi.ac.ae
Al Quds Open University	www.qudsopenu.edu
American College of Dubai	www.centamed.com
American University in Dubai	www.aud.edu
American University of Sharjah	www.aus.ac.ae
Beams International Education Institute	unknown
BITS: Birla Institute of Technology and Science	www.bitsdubai.com
British Open University	www.open.ac.uk
Dubai Pharmacy College	www.dpc.edu
Dubai University College for Applied Studies	unknown
Emirates Academy of Hospitality Management College	www.emiratesacademy.edu
Emirates College for Management and Information Technology	www.ecmit.ac.ae
Emirates Institute for Banking and Financial Studies	www.eibfs.com
International College of Law and Business Administration	unknown
Mahatma Gandhi University Off-Campus Centre	www.mgudxboc.com/aboutmgoffcampus.htm
Middlesex University	www.mdx.ac.uk
National Institute of Fashion Technology	www.niftindia.com
Preston University Ajman	www.preston.edu/affiliated.html
Skyline College	www.skyline.ac.ae
University of Southern Queensland in Dubai	www.usqindubai.com
University of Wollongong Dubai Campus	www.uowdubai.ac.ae

companies" (BUID, n.d.). It has recently announced plans to open Knowledge Village Universities, to be located in the Academic City and house several international education institutions. The Academic City differs from the KV since the institutions will all be located in a nucleus of education, but they will have independent campuses that supply facilities to their students without much assistance or dependence on the Academic City itself.

Links Abroad

The private institutions in the United Arab Emirates are usually branch or satellite campuses of foreign-based universities. Both public and private establishments in the country regularly establish memorandums of understanding (MOUs) with foreign establishments located in places such as the United Kingdom, the United States, Australia, or India. These MOUs are partnerships between the two institutions involved, on varying levels of assistance from one (foreign, more developed) institution to the other (located in the United Arab Emirates, develop-

ing). It is similar to a mentor relationship. Several U.A.E. institutions have decreased development time by creating business agreements with other, foreign establishment. For example, the Abu Dhabi Petroleum Institute (Abu Dhabi Petroleum Institute, n.d.) has an MOU with the Colorado School of Mines; the American University of Sharjah (American University of Sharjah, n.d.) has an MOU with the American University in Washington, D.C.; and Zayed University has one with the British Open University (Zayed University Web site, n.d.).

The American University in Dubai (AUD), a private institution, has a relationship with both the Georgia Institute of Technology, for the development of its engineering department, and the American Inter-Continental University. These MOUs and mentoring relationships enable U.A.E. institutions to work more efficiently in forming and developing the university and its different departments. Thus, many public and private institutions in the United Arab Emirates have opened student services departments and been able

Table 20.2. Public higher education institutions in the United Arab Emirates (Arabiancampus, n.d.).

Name of Institution	Website
Ajman University of Science and Technology	www.ajman.ac.ae
Dubai Aviation College	www.dac.ac.ae
Dubai Police College	unknown
Dubai Medical College for Girls	www.dmcg.edu
Etisalat College of Engineering	www.ece.ac.ae
Gulf Medical College	www.gmcajman.com
Higher Colleges of Technology	www.htc.ac.ae
Ittihad University	www.ittihad.ac.ae
Khalifa bin Zayed College	unknown
Naval College	unknown
Sharjah College	www,shjcollege.ac.ae
The Islamic College	www.islamic-college.ac.uk
United Arab Emirates University	www.uaeu.ac.ae
University of Sharjah	www.sharjah.ac.ae
Zayed University	www.zu.ac.ae

to outline missions, expansion goals, and ideals for their departments.

For example, AUD could look to the American Inter-Continental University for guidance on how and what to develop for students and classes. The importance of developing well-rounded students who show leadership and active management skills through extra-curricular activities and events is also transferred from the Western-based institutions that help or mentor the U.A.E. universities that are developing under the MOUs (Rao, n.d.).

An immediate goal of new private higher education institutions is to build up student numbers to become economically viable. After an institution has reached its projected enrollment goal, it begins raising its admission and educational standards. The emerging universities in the United Arab Emirates are still in the first phase of this development and will have to accomplish their goals while competing with universities that have already moved onto the second phase of improving quality.

Student Demographics and Emiratization

There is a rising population of students wishing to enroll in private universities within the United Arab Emirates. In 2001, the number of national secondary school graduates seeking admission to higher education institutions through the National Admissions and Placement Office was at an all time high. More than 95% of female and more than 80% of male secondary school students chose to pursue higher education (Kazaa, 2001). This demand will spur further development in quality, as well as the quantity, of higher education institutions. Projections indicate that there will be more than 20 new institutions within the next 10 years (U.A.E./MOHE, n.d.). Non-nation-

al students can choose among private institutions while the nationals can choose from either free national universities or fee-based private ones (Swaroop, 2004).

The huge dependence on a non-national workforce has resulted in the recent move toward *Emiratization*. This is the U.A.E. government's effort, through imposed rules and regulations, to create a strong presence of U.A.E. nationals in both the public and private workplace. Universities, both national and private, have taken an active role in Emiratization efforts (U.S. Central Intelligence Agency, n.d.). A government or administratively imposed quota for Emirati students is established in several private universities (Shaghour, 2000). National universities educate national students and are free of charge, thus encouraging education and achievement in the United Arab Emirates youth. The University of Sharjah is an exception in that it accepts non-national students. If expatriate (mainly non-U.A.E. Arab nationals) are accepted, they must pay for their education (Farouki, 2002-2003).

The U.A.E. government pays particular attention and gives generous funding to national universities. Its goal is to promote the growth of a U.A.E. national workforce that is self-sufficient and highly educated. There are currently government-regulated quotas for private companies to hire a certain percentage of U.A.E. nationals. Over the past decade, the country has realized its dependence on imported manpower and knowledge; Emiratization is the government's effort to rectify and improve the situation (Shaghour, 2000).

Among the private universities, demographics differ from one institution to the next. Although they accept and enroll students of virtually any nationality, some have a particular target population, For example, the

Mahatma Gandhi University Off-Campus Centre attracts Indian students and would tend to have fewer U.A.E. national students than the more international institutions. The American University in Dubai (AUD) has approximately 16% U.A.E. national students. There is no imposed national student quota at AUD (American University of Dubai, n.d.). The American University of Sharjah has an imposed minimum national U.A.E. student quota of 20% for each entering class (Ministry of Higher Education and Scientific Research, n.d.).

It is no surprise that only a small percentage of U.A.E. nationals are enrolled in private universities. At national universities they are promised more attention and free education. Private universities are funded mostly through tuition, which all students must pay (Farouki, 2002–03).

In terms of gender, female students outnumber males. This is evident particularly in regard to Emirati. At the U.A.E. University, in the 1997–98 academic year, 21% of the students were male students while 79% were female (United Arab Emirates University, n.d. b). Female graduates also outnumber male graduates at the U.A.E.. For example, in 2001 the Higher Colleges of Technology college campuses, 56% of the graduating class were women and 44% were men (Coles, personal communication, February 2003). What is being done to rectify this situation, if it has been deemed problematic, is not known at this point.

In contrast at AUD, a private university, the female/male student ratio rarely weighs heavily one way or the other. Currently, AUD has approximately 49% male and 51% female students. The reason for the difference between national and private university student gender demographics may be that education is not free at private universities while it is at national institutions of education. Thus, parents of female students may be less willing to enter their children in private colleges due to financial restrictions. On the other hand, female Emirati students are not entering the workforce in large numbers, even if they are graduating with more degrees. For Emirati women, education is sometimes seen as something to accomplish before moving on to marriage or something to do as an investment of time, as opposed to in preparation to enter the workforce (Altbach, 1991).

Career Services

Student services must be sensitive to such demographic variances and seek to cater to all students within the university while supporting the government Emiratization campaign. For example, career services in private institutions need to take care regarding the job advertisements and placements of their graduates. Some jobs and positions are open only to U.A.E. nationals and some only to Arab or expatriate nationals. In national higher education institutions, the career services can look for opportunities in government offices and agencies, since

the government hires mainly U.A.E. nationals. Recruiting from national universities furthers the government's Emiratization plan.

U.A.E. and U.S. Accreditation and their Influence on Student Services Programming

Private, "entrepreneurial" educational institutions that want to locate in the United Arab Emirates must be licensed and accredited by the U.A.E. Ministry of Education (U.A.E. Ministry of Higher Education and Scientific Research, n.d.). Higher education institutions must receive permission from the U.A.E. Ministry of Higher Education and Scientific Research. The Commission for Academic Accreditation (CAA) was established in 1999 to address the quality concerns of higher education professionals and the U.A.E. government. The CAA grants accreditation to higher education institutions, although public institutions are already governed and established by the government itself. Field visits are a requirement of the accreditation process, and this has helped maintain and identify quality standards in the U.A.E. higher education scheme. The CAA is also addressing the problem of "diploma mills."

But the U.A.E. accreditation program is still young. In order to ensure quality to potential students and their families, many higher education institutions in the United Arab Emiraets seek accreditation from foreign accreditation agencies in addition to gaining recognition from the Ministry of Higher Education and Scientific Research. For example, the American University in Dubai is accredited by Southern Association of Schools and Colleges (SACS) since its mother campus is located in Atlanta, Georgia. The Higher Colleges of Technology's Engineering Technology program is accredited by the U.S. Accreditation Board for Engineering and Technology and the American University of Sharjah's Engineering program is associated with Texas A&M University (L. Blank, personal communication, February 25, 2003).

However, there is no one accreditation agency that caters to all U.A.E. higher education institutions and their specific needs and interests. International accreditation agencies differ in their requirements and standards, resulting in different expectations and understanding of accreditation and quality from each higher education institution in the United Arab Emirates. There are plans for a regional Arabian Gulf accreditation agency, which would standardize accreditation in the region (Al Bakry, 2001).

The accreditation of an institution or university in the United Arab Emirates directly affects the department of student services within that institution. For example, AUD is required by SACS to "provide appropriate academic support services" (AUD Student Handbook, 2004). Each institution, with its own unique demographics, disciplines, origin, mission, and accreditation agencies, will require its unique blend of student services departments and services.

Funding of Student Services

Public universities naturally have more money earmarked for students than private universities. Education at government institutions is free for U.A.E. nationals; thus, student services are also free. Services include free books, housing, meals, bus services, athletics, health services, and activities. Students pay for very little, if anything at all. Money for student facilities, student events, activities, and club support is readily available. Budgets are large, and student services are not lacking in monetary support.

On the other hand, private universities such as the American University in Dubai are dependent on tuition fees, corporate sponsorships, or outside donations. All requests for budgets must be approved and justification must be provided for budget requests. Fact-driven and outcome-based annual budget planning guide yearly financial decision making. Money is allotted for AUD traditional events and programming such as orientation, the international/intercollegiate sports tournament, and certain university festivities. Other events require student ingenuity and creativity to obtain funding. Students often seek corporate sponsorship for their events and programs, thus practicing their business and leadership skills. At AUD, all areas of student programming are fully funded.

Development of Student Services in the United Arab Emirates

The area of student services in the United Arab Emirates has developed slowly compared to other departments of institutions of higher education institutions. Divisions of academic services were the first departments established in new universities, and student services departments were added on as the universities matured. In an effort to help students become more well-rounded, institutions in the United Arab Emirates have cultivated student services, with departments of residential life, health services, academic advising, counseling, cultural and social activities, athletics, and career services.

There are clear differences between the institutions regarding management, funding, composition, student extracurricular activities, and atmosphere. But they do have some similar academic concerns. Many of the high schools in the United Arab Emirates and abroad may not adequately prepare a student to operate fully at high levels of English academic reading, writing, and speaking. This is a problem that was addressed by the Ministry of Education, and many institutions, both public and private, as well as language centers, by offering English as a Second Language (ESL) remedial programs (Al Kady, 2001; S. Al Taei, personal communication, February 16, 2003).

University student service departments may encourage specific aspects of activities or student life or behavior according to their student clientele. The oldest university in the United Arab Emirates, the U.A.E. University, has established the Department of Youth Care and Students Activities, with approximately nine employees solely for the purpose of encouraging students to participate in extracurricular social, cultural, and academic activities (U.A.E.University Web site, n.d.).

Attention to Parental Concerns

Student services or student affairs departments of public higher education institutions tend to give more attention to parents' concerns than do private, Western-based universities. Universities such as Zayed University have a specific department and Web page dedicated to parents of students. The ability and right of a parent to check on a student's progress is encouraged by public U.A.E. institutions. On the other hand, private institutions such as AUD neither encourage nor discourage such parental oversight. Although both Azyed and AUD incorporate the Western model of higher education they also provide parental inclusion due to the regional and cultural expectations of the country and the Emirati families whose children attend the public universities. For example, at Zayed University students are not allowed to leave the campus in between classes and may only leave with pre-approved (through parental permission forms) transportation (P. Coles, personal communication, March 2003). At AUD, parental permission is needed to extend curfew for students who live in residence halls, but otherwise students are free to leave or enter campus as they wish. Responsibility is placed on the student. Private institutions cater more to the international student clientele, so there is not the same parental oversight of social and academic behavior.

"Western-style" Student Services

Promising students a Western education denotes Western academic standards, as well as Western standards (or as close to it as possible) for activities and student services. Private universities using Western models have developed heavily their student services departments and involve students in many of the decision-making and organizational processes for extracurricular student life. Student services in private institutions generally have many social activities, as opposed to purely academic or educational activities, when compared to the public institutions.

This sort of socializing does not occur at public universities because many are single-gender or have gender-separated campuses. For example, there are separate HCT (Higher Colleges of Technology) Abu Dhabi Women's and Abu Dhabi Men's campuses. The University of Sharjah has separate mirror-image campuses within one university located in the same location. The genders are kept separate by cultural custom.

Another difference between many public and private institutions is the role and range of student events and activities outside of the classroom. Public education establishments tend to collaborate on more events than private universities do. For example, the HCT branches regularly work together or compete against one another in activities and sports events. National universities also include Islamic or religiously oriented events and competitions such as a religious competition in the recitation of the Holy Koran (the Holy book of Islam). The University of Sharjah states that it is an "Islamic, gender-segregated institution." It offers student activities with the mission stated as helping "strengthen the sense of religious and national belonging" (University of Sharjah, n.d. a).

Private institutions do advertise such Islamic events for students who are interested, but do not usually host such events, as they aim to be unbiased and neutral.

Many institutions in the United Arab Emirates have public relations personnel to cover their activities. Public relations are beneficial for the university and the students' perceptions of their institution. The active university is the ideal university. Well-rounded students, showcased through media coverage, is very appealing to students and their parents while promoting the university as a place that will provide one with both quality academics and quality enjoyment outside of the classroom. Student services of both private and public universities encourage student voices to be heard, to some degree, in the management and development of the institution. Student government associations, or student councils, are common extracurricular organizations. Events are promoted as ways to interact with other students and learn how to manage and plan projects while still receiving guidance and assistance from student services administrators.

The KV (Knowledge Village) has created a student association for planning events and activities for several universities and higher education institutions located on its premises. Representatives from the member universities cooperated this year to produce the first inter-collegiate competition that the KV has hosted.

The issue of public versus private higher education institutions does not affect athletics as much as the issue of gender segregation does. The female-only institutions do not allow male coaches or spectators during competitions, thus limiting the interactions between teams and institutions in athletics (S. Khoury, personal communication, March 23, 2005).

The United Arab Emirates has seen significant growth and attention in the field of student services during the higher education "boom" that has taken place in the country within the last 10 years. The coming of new universities gives students more choices. Student services are an essential factor in characterizing a university and its ability to attract potential students.

The U.A.E. Student Services Delivery Model: A Model to Fit the Cultural Context of an Islamic Country

While provision of student services in the United Arab Emirates takes its direction from the traditional models of the United States, Britain, Australia, India, and other countries, there are some major differences between, for example, AUD and a liberal arts campus in the United States. Rules and regulations governing student behavior at AUD are precise. Students are required to abide by a dress code and adhere to a detailed Code of Conduct and a campuswide curfew of midnight. Students must have parental permission to stay out beyond midnight. (Parents can extend student curfews by writing a permission letter for a general open curfew, for restricted curfew, or for single events.) Behavior, dress, and conduct are highly influenced by the location of AUD in an Islamic country.

AUD also requires its students to maintain "conduct integrity," defined in AUD's Student Handbook (2004–05) as:

> …demonstrating courteous behavior and professional conduct at all times. Students are expected to maintain an exemplary level of maturity, displaying behavior and dress that do not violate in any way UAE norms, practices, beliefs or expectations of personal conduct. AUD students are subject to all local and national laws. (p. 66)

The handbook goes on to provide detailed examples of unacceptable attire. In addition, no alcohol is permitted or served at university functions, on or off campus, and students are not permitted to keep alcohol in their residence hall rooms regardless of their age or religious affiliation. Any student living in a residence hall who is found with alcohol is immediately permanently dismissed from the residence hall. The punishment for theft is even more severe. Students who are found guilty of stealing are immediately permanently dismissed from the university. Students who are caught plagiarizing or cheating face the Honor Council. Punishments range in severity, but could be as serious as permanent expulsion from the university.

Even though there are strict penalties for violations of AUD's Code of Conduct and Honor Code, there is a highly defined process for judicial hearings. A student who violates specific rules faces the Conduct Council or Honor Council where there is both faculty and student representation. Once a decision is made by the council regarding the student's punishment, the student can submit an appeal to a higher authority, either the provost (academic matters) or the president (conduct issues). This process holds true for all of AUD's various councils—Grade Appeal, Honor Council, Conduct Council, Grievance Council, and Academic Standing. Appeal processes are fully out-lined in AUD's extensive student handbook.

Residence Halls at AUD are segregated by gender; males and females are not permitted to visit each other in the residence halls. In fact, no females are permitted to enter the male residence halls and no males are per-mitted to enter the female residence halls. This includes relatives and friends.

Another major difference between student services programming in the United States and the United Arab Emirates is the emphasis on multicultural programming. Current student activities programming in the United States focuses on multiculturalism in the broadest sense of the word. At a typical U.S. college campus, one would find religious organizations, organizations that focus on particular genders or sexual inclination, or student soci-eties that are oriented toward race or ethnicity.

At AUD, clubs focus on departments, interests, or culture related to national origin. There are no clubs that focus on sexual preference, gender, or religious af-filiations other than Islam. Fraternities and sororities also do not exist. All clubs and organizations must respect U.A.E. law.

The Higher Colleges of Technology have segregated male and female colleges in each of the seven emirates, although the faculty members are mixed. Dubai's Wom-en's College states its mission as follows:

> Student Services creates and sponsors programs, activities, events and plans services based on principles of teamwork and excellence that foster student development. We equip students with professional, ethical, and tolerant behaviors that enable them to be positioned as highly qualified and depend-able graduates in the local and international communities. We actively change and modify our programs, activities, events, and services to assist students in overcoming academic bar-riers, becoming fully functional family members and keeping pace with the changing global environment. (Higher Colleges of Technology, n.d.)

Naturally, at a women-only institution, all programs and activities are for females only.

The U.A.E. University aims to offer "a balanced devel-opment in the student's personality with all the sports, cultural and social dimensions" (United Arab Emirates University, n.d.).

On the social and cultural side, U.A.E. University's Youth Care and Student Activities Department concentrates on developing the abilities and talents of students, and us-ing their potentialities in ways that would benefit them and their country, as well as preparing them to represent their university and community at local and international cultural conferences and symposiums. Students are of-fered courses and workshops in computer applications, administration and leadership, in addition to scientific, cultural, social and religious lectures and seminars.

The department has a Student Care Fund, and uses clear criteria to locate students in difficult living condi-tions and who are willing to benefit from the financial aid offered by the fund. The department also offers ser-vices to students with disabilities and special needs by facilitating their study and admission to the university in coordination with the appropriate authorities.

The department is committed to upgrading the physi-cal fitness and the general health conditions of its stu-dents and expanding sports participation by athletic students, with a view to spotting the talented students and adding them to the teams and groups that represent the university in the different games. The department is deeply concerned about making such representa-tion effective and honorable during participation in the local, Gulf, and international sports events. The de-partment also supervises the scouting movement in the university.

In short, the U.A.E. University's Youth Care and Student Activities Department works to develop activities that align with the modern realities on the one hand, and with our religion, customs, and traditions on the other hand (U.A.E.University, n.d.).

In summary, there are seven key indicators of student services in the United Arab Emirates in general.

1. U.A.E. student services are culturally and religiously conscious. Campus rules, regulations, punishments, sanctions, student organizations, programming, and residence hall living all are intrinsically linked to the fact that universities and colleges are located in a country with an Islamic government. During the most holy month of Ramadan, all students, even non-Mus-lims, are required to refrain from eating, drinking, and smoking in public.

2. Student services in the U.A.E. follow a belief that is fundamentally grounded in the "in loco parentis" doc-trine (Hoekema, 1994)**.** This means that an institution has the authority to direct the behavior of students, the authority to punish rule violations, and the re-sponsibility to care for students by having rules, regu-lations, and programming that best address students' interests. Also, the institution is exempt from limits on room searches carried out in conjunction with the enforcement of school rules. All of the above are practiced to some degree in the various institutions described above.

3. Student services clubs and organizations closely mirror the cultural composition of the United Arab Emirates. At most universities and colleges, clubs are cultural and national in organization or are interest-based. Certain clubs and organizations do not exist in the United Arab Emirates because certain student issues have not yet emerged at various institutions. Other issues are consid-ered taboo, such as those that focus on LGBT (lesbian/gay/bisexual/transgender) programming; still, others are not allowed in an Islamic country such as a Jewish student organization.

4. Student services in the United Arab Emirates can be considered as emerging. With the country still developing and evolving and universities still being establishing in this emerging economy, it is no surprise that student services in the United Arab Emirates are still not fully developed.

5. Student services at major U.A.E. universities and colleges share some key features. Most student services departments have student activities, interest-based and departmental student clubs, student academic support services, housing departments, health centers, and athletics (some women's-only institutions only participate in intercollegiate tournaments with other women's-only institutions). Most student services departments have a holistic view of student development and focus on the development of the total student through various programs, services, and opportunities. Activities, however, could be gender segregated.

6. Student services at any given U.A.E. college or university are based on the institution's mission and goals. At some colleges or universities student services are more structured and protective given the mission of the university; at others, the student is considered more independent. Student services vary based on location, affiliation (public, private, internationally linked), and so on. Titles, job responsibilities, and possibly even gender of student services staff also reflect these differences.

7. Certain universities and colleges possess accreditation of the U.A.E. Ministry of Higher Education. This accreditation in turn governs the operation of all facets of the university including student services. Like accreditation agencies in the United States, the U.A.E. Ministry of Higher Education prescribes a set of practices that all institutions seeking accreditation must follow.

Student services in the United Arab Emirates is a hybrid firmly grounded in a country governed by Islamic law, traditions, values, and practices, yet open to providing quality student programming for the multicultural, international youth populace of the country. U.A.E. student services programming is an example for other countries who seek to seamlessly blend western practices with holistic student education and student life grounded in Islamic values. Islamic law must be always recognized and valued and never contradicted.

A Closer Look at one U.A.E. Institution: Student Services at the American University in Dubai

Provision of student services at the American University in Dubai (AUD) is based on the traditional model of student services used by a majority of U.S. colleges and universities. This model includes specific departments

within the division of student services: offices of the dean of student services, student activities, student athletics, career services, health services, academic support services, and counseling. Each department is staffed by a director, manager, or coordinator depending on the size and composition of the particular division.

AUD's student services operate on an evolving, need-based philosophy. The department was formed in 1995 when the university was established and was staffed by a dean of student services who handled all operations of the division. By December 1996, the university was accredited by the Southern Association of Colleges and Schools (SACS). An assistant dean of student services was added in January 1998 to oversee all student activities, athletics, and housing.

In the fall of 1999, anticipating the first graduating class, the department added a career services manager, as well as a housing manager. A nurse, contracted through the American Hospital Dubai, joined the department in spring 2000 when the campus moved to its new, state-of-the-art premises including student residence halls. At the same time, the university received its licensure from the United Arab Emirates Ministry of Higher Education. An athletics director was hired in fall of 2001, and in December of 2002, SACS reaffirmed AUD's accreditation.

In spring 2004, the director of external affairs began to offer part-time additional support to the career services manager by developing new job opportunities with multinational companies for AUD's graduates and additional public relations support. A student support manager joined the department in fall 2004, and in winter 2005 a personal counselor was hired. AUD's 2004 fall enrollment was slightly more than 2,000 with 500 students residing in the on-campus residence halls. Figure 20.1 shows the current organizational structure of the division.

Student services personnel at AUD comprises multiple departments, due to the philosophy of need-based evolution. Table 20.3 describes the particular responsibilities of each area.

A clearly defined mission statement helps guide student services at AUD.

> Student Services supports the University's Mission and Purpose by providing support and resources for the orientation, transition, retention, and graduation of AUD students, so that they may be prepared both personally and professionally throughout their University experience and their careers. (AUD Student Handbook, 2004–05)

The student services department relies heavily upon and has internalized the principles of best practices in student affairs delineated by the publication *Principles of Good Practice for Student Affairs* (ACPA/NASPA, 1997). Here is how the department has responded to the seven principles:

Engages students in active learning. All AUD student services activities and events in all divisions have clearly

Figure 20.1. AUD student services organizational chart.

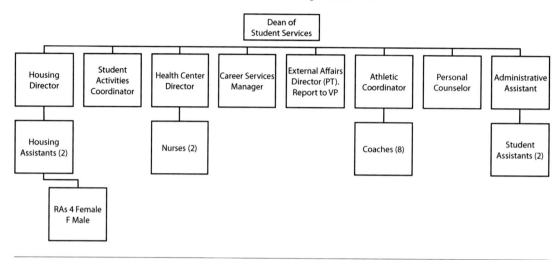

defined and articulated measurable learning objectives. Student clubs are expected to develop yearly plans, mission statements, and goals and objectives. Student services believes that its activities are part of the total university learning experience and looks for opportunities to merge learning outside the scope of the academic classroom with learning within the classroom. This is done through intentional application of skills and competencies acquired in classes.

Helps students develop coherent values and ethical standards. AUD student representatives serve on all Honor and Conduct Councils. All AUD students sign an Honor Pledge during their orientation program. All student government officers take an oath of office at the official inauguration ceremony at the beginning of their terms of office. Monthly meetings with the Student Activities Coordinator are required for all student club and organization presidents.

Sets and communicates high expectations for student learning. Non-negotiable standards and clearly defined principles are two of the hallmarks of the AUD student services department. Students who apply for leadership programs fill out applications, undergo interviews, obtain references, and sign letters of commitment. Failure to abide by the letters of commitment results in dismissal from the various programs. Clubs and student organizations have articulated missions and goals. Students who excel in service to the university and community are given special recognition and awards at the annual AUD Gala Dinner and Awards Ceremony. For the past three years, less than 2% of the total AUD student population has been selected for student awards. Selectivity is important in order to promote quality service and leadership.

Uses systematic inquiry to improve student and institutional performance. A systematized evaluation and insti-

tutional research plan has been in place for the past five years. Findings and recommendations are acted upon in order to improve the division and its major activities and services. Evaluations are conducted on orientation, housing, and various aspects of student services. In addition, all students who graduate from AUD complete an exit survey and individual interview. A follow-up alumni survey is conducted two years after graduation. Annual student surveys investigate student satisfaction with various aspects of student life at the university. Event reports are required for all student-organized events. At the end of the year, the SGA and all student clubs and organizations complete a SWOT (strengths, weaknesses, opportunities, threats) analysis of their progress through their annual report.

Uses resources effectively to achieve institutional missions and goals. The department's and the university's evolving, need-based philosophy dictates a judicious use of resources. Positions are added based on student need and the increase in the number of students. Budgets are produced individually by staff and collaboratively within the division, with final divisional approval resting with the dean of student services. Rationale and support for budget requests are part of every budget. Support for budget requests is provided through results of student surveys and other institutional effectiveness results. Student services also enlists financial support through corporate sponsorship; various local and multinational corporations generously and gladly support an array of student activities and events.

Forges educational partnerships that advance student learning. AUD's student services division has worked with most academic divisions within the university. The instructors who offer an Introduction to University Life course have collaborated with the student activities office to develop service-based learning projects. The student activities office has provided guidance to departments developing professional departmental clubs and organizations. The career services manager works extensively with deans and program chairs to develop new internship opportunities and professional experiences in governmental agencies and in local and multinational businesses in Dubai.

Builds supportive and inclusive communities. AUD's open club memberships give all students the opportunity to be involved in various cultural, artistic, athletic, and departmental clubs. AUD support services provides academic support for students through peer tutoring, individual academic support conferences, personal counseling, disability support services, and academic support workshops. Career services offers individual appointments for students seeking positions as well as a series of career-focused workshops. These services are offered to all students as well as to alumni. AUD focuses on team-based learning both within and outside of classrooms. Students plan, obtain funding for, market, and orchestrate events.

In addition to AUD's commitment to best practices in student services, AUD also has a number of key identifiers that make its student services unique.

Strategic prioritizing. AUD student services identifies key priorities for each year. These priorities are created by members of staff with overall direction and support provided by the dean of student services. Goals and objectives of each area of student services are reviewed annually to ensure that visions are clear and revised as the university grows, develops, and matures.

Self-reflection. Student Services staff are encouraged to reflect on their accomplishments and areas of challenge. Staff reflect on various initiatives, day-to-day practices, beliefs, and programs in order to improve their services, present a positive image of the student services department, and meet the needs of the university community.

Professional development. Professional development is encouraged. On a rotating basis, staff members are provided with professional development time and financial support in order to attend an international professional conference biennially.

Student-centeredness. AUD student services is student-centered, and staff keep their office doors open whenever possible to be readily accessible to students.

By students, for students. Whenever and wherever possible, student services programs are designed in collaboration with students. One example is the annual new student orientation program where students and staff consider carefully the comments and evaluation reports from the previous year as they revise and plan the next year's orientation. Students are also directly involved in the planning of most student campus events and activities.

Accreditation-guided. AUD receives guidance from the Ministry of Higher Education (MOHE) in the United Arab Emirates and the Southern Association of Schools of Colleges who have both accredited AUD. Specific standards and guidelines are offered by both accrediting bodies to the university at large, including student services. Having the guidance of two accrediting bodies helps to ensure that AUD student services is American in substance yet cognizant of the Islamic cultural terrain of the United Arab Emirates. Programs, policies, procedures, and standards carefully consider cultural norms, practices, and beliefs.

Emerging Professional Associations in the United Arab Emirates

At the time of the writing of this chapter, very few professional organizations for higher education professionals exist in the United Arab Emirates. Discussions are currently underway by a group of professionals from several U.A.E. universities to start an affiliate of NASPA–Student Affairs Administrators in Higher Education.

The fields of counseling and English as a Second Language (ESOL) have established professional organizations: Counselling Arabia and TESOL Arabia.

Counselling Arabia is an annual conference begun in 2003 and organized by counseling practitioners from different organizations in the U.A.E. The goal of the conference is to establish a national network of practitioners in the field of personal, career, and academic counseling in both the public and private sector. In 2004, the conference aimed to extend its goals to include practitioners in the counseling field from different countries in the Arab world. This group includes, but is not limited to employer-based practitioners, such as human resources and organizational development, personal and social counselors, career development practitioners, and practitioners in the education system.

The goal of TESOL Arabia is to establish a network of communication among professionals who use English as a medium of instruction, in order to promote and maintain a standard of excellence of their teaching and administration (TESOL, n.d.). A not-for-profit organization begun in 1992, TESOL Arabia aims to stimulate the growth of professional development through the encouragement of both practical and theoretical scholarship; the use of available technologies; the adoption of the instructional methodologies that best meet the needs of students; the promotion of the English language teaching profession as a career; and the provision of a forum for discussion and support. Membership is estimated at more than 1,800 professionals from all across the Gulf region and more than 30 other countries around the world. TESOL Arabia has nine special interest groups, offers annual workshops and conferences, and publishes a free newsletter three times a year. Future plans include the creation of a TESOL Arabia journal.

The U.A.E. Higher Education Sports Council (HESC) was founded in 2000 under the patronage of His Highness

Table 20.3. Functions of student services at the American University in Dubai.

Dean's Office	Academic Support Services	Athletics	Career Services	Counseling	External Affairs	Health Services	Housing	Student Activities
Overall management of leadership of division	Academic Support	Intercollegiate Athletic Programs	Alumni Affairs	Awareness Workshops	Development of Employment Opportunities	Health Education	Housing Discipline	Residence Life Programming
Budgeting	Academic Advising	Intramural Programs	Career Fairs	Personal Counseling	Public Relations	Preventive Health Care	Housing Grievances	Student Activities
Grievances	Disability Services	Sports Tournaments	Career Services			Urgent Health Care	Housing Management	Student Clubs
Graduation Support	Support Workshop		Job Placement				Resident Life Programming	Student Government Association
Honor Societies	Tutoring Programs						Supervision of Resident Assistants	Student Life Programming
Institutional Research								
Judicial Affairs								
Leadership Programs								
Orientation Programs								
Strategic Planning								

Sheikh Nahyan Bin Mubarak Al Nahyan, Minister of Education in the United Arab Emirates. The goals of the HESC are to develop athletics at higher education institutions, improve and enhance the individual skills and talents of university students, and create university sports teams that will participate in Arabian Gulf, Arab, and international sports competitions. Sister organizations are the Arab Universities Sports Federation and the Arab and Asian Universities Sports Federation.

Clearly the need exists in the United Arab Emirates for additional professional organizations in student services for professionals in the fields of housing, student activities, athletics, health services, support services, and general student services. Professional organizations exist in both Europe and the United States, and both groups could serve as models. Among the benefits that could be gained from the establishment of student services professional associations are enhanced professionalism of the field, partnerships with universities abroad, exchange programs for student services personnel, student services area conferences, and support and recognition from established organizations.

The NASPA/U.A.E. International Exchange Program

In February/March 2005, the United Arab Emirates partnered with NASPA for the NASPA/U.A.E. Exchange Program. Four delegates from the United States, including two vice presidents of student affairs from Bellarmine University in Kentucky and George Mason University in Virginia, visited six institutions in the United Arab Emirates during a 10-day period. These delegations visited the American University in Dubai, the United Arab Emirates University, Zayed University, Dubai Women's College, Dubai Men's College, and the University of Sharjah. With the exception of AUD, all universities are governmental, public institutions.

This was the first NASPA exchange program in the Middle East. The four participants visited with student leaders, toured student residence halls, met with student affairs and campus administrators, attended student presentations, and experienced various aspects of cultural life in the United Arab Emirates. The delegates engaged in purposeful discourse on a wide variety of topics related to student life and development at area universities. The four visiting delegates also had the opportunity to share their expertise with student affairs professionals in the United Arab Emirates through a series of specially designed presentations that focused on student apathy, student engagement, and service–learning.

The Future of Student Affairs Programming in the United Arab Emirates

The possibilities for student services in the United Arab Emirates are wide. Opportunities exist for inventive student programming that fosters integration of culture, religion, and student life. Programs could be gender-specific or open to both sexes. Cross-university programming would lead to events that cater to all nationalities and cultures. Both private and public universities must make more efforts to develop activities that are open to all students of all universities. Barriers between the private and public universities must be reduced. Healthy competition and culturally-sensitive student events would guide the way for opportunities for all. The United Arab Emirates' mosaic of cultures should not be ignored but decisively integrated into programming.

The establishment of an independent student services organization or an affiliate of NASPA could guide student services expansion governed by best practices and professional standards. This next stage of development is needed immediately. Given the rapid expansion of education in the United Arab Emirates, this is the prime time for developing standards and guidelines for student affairs.

Programs that are currently the norm in universities in Europe, the United States Australia, India, and other countries could guide programming and initiatives that are clearly unique. An interesting mix of programs and activities that are practiced in Europe, Asia, America, and the Middle East would form the backbone of a different type of student servicing. The hybrid identity of student services in the United Arab Emirates could lead to the creation of a rich, culturally appropriate, distinctive model that could be used for other Gulf universities.

The opportunities for development are endless, but the time is now. Unless steps are taken soon to develop student services at a countrywide level, student services will continue to be a muddle of cultures and models that work against each other. The multitude of cultures must complement and enhance life for the growing student populace of the United Arab Emirates.

References

Abu Dhabi Petroleum Institute Web site. (n.d.). Retrieved April 26, 2005, from http://www.pi.ac.ae

Abu Dhabi University. (n.d.). Retrieved April 26, 2005, from http://www.adu.ac.ae

American College Personnel Administrators (ACPA). (1997). *Principles of good practice for student affairs*. Available at http://www.acpa.nche.edu/pgp/principle.htm

Al Bakry, A. (2001, October 19). Website on accredited programs. *Gulf News*.

Ali, Arif. (2001, February 5). GCC universities 'need greater interaction'. *Gulf News*.

Al Kady, M. (2001, June 27). FNC finds education curriculums wanting. *Khaleej Times*.

American University of Dubai Web site. (n.d.). Retrieved April 26, 2005, from http://www.aud.edu

American University of Sharjah Web site. (n.d.). Retrieved April 26, 2005, from http://www.aus.ac.ae

Al Suwaidi, K. (1997). Higher education in the U.A.E.: History and prospects. In Shaw, K.E. (Ed.). *Higher education in the Gulf: Problems and prospects*. Exeter, United Kingdom: University of Exeter Press.

Altbach, P. (Ed.). (1991). The Arab World. In *International higher education: an encyclopedia*. (Vol. 2). New York, NY: Garland Publishing, Inc.

Altbach, P. (2002, Spring). Perspectives on internationalizing higher education. *International higher education journal*. Available at http://www.bc.edu/bc_org/avp/soe/cihe/newsletter/News27/text004.htm

American College Personnel Association (ACPA) and National Association of Student Personnel Administrators (NASPA). (1997). *Principles of Good Practice for Student Affairs, Statement and Inventories*. Washington, DC: Author.

AMIDEAST. (n.d.). *U.A.E. information*. Retrieved March 14, 2003 from http://www.amideast.org/offices/uae/default.htm

Anderson, C.H. (2005, February 28). George Mason University of USA to open campus in RAK. *AME Info*. Available at http://www.ameinfo.com/54828.html

Arabiancampus.com. Available at http://www.arabiancampus.com/studyinuae/universities/uclist.htm#ajm

AUD Student Handbook. (2004). Dubai, United Arab Emirates: American University in Dubai.

British University in Dubai (BUID). (n.d.). Retrieved July 25, 2005, from http://www.buid.ac.ae

Contreras, A. (summer 2003). A Case study in foreign degrees (dis)approval. *International Higher Education Journal*. Available at http://www.bc.edu/bc_org/avp/soe/cihe/newsletter/News32/text004.htm

College Student Educators International (ACPA). (1997). *Principles of Good Practice for Student Affairs*. Retrieved April 26, 2005, from http://www.acpa.nche.edu/pgp/principle.htm

Dubai Healthcare City announces joint venture with Harvard Medical School. (2003, Summer). *Arab Health Magazine*.

Expenditure on projects put at Dh2.5billion. (2001, March 20). *Gulf News*.

Farouki, D. (2002–03). [How U.A.E. and U.S. universities compare]. Unpublished raw data conducted while a Fulbright Student Scholar.

Goals of NASPA Exchange Programs. (n.d.). *International Education Program*. Retrieved April 26, 2005 from http://www.naspa.org/communities/kc/uploads/IEProgram.ppt

Hanson, J. (2005). [evaluation form of NASPA exchange program between the U.S. and the U.A.E.]. Unpublished raw data.

Higher Colleges of Technology. (n.d.). *Student services*. Retrieved July 10, 2008, from http://www.hct.ac.ae/student_services/aspx/student_services.aspx

Hoekema, D.A. (1994). *Campus rules and moral community: In place of "in loco parentis."* London, United Kingdom: Rowman & Littlefield Publishers, Inc.

Kazaa, Aftab. (2001, August 6). Flood of university applicants sets record. *Gulf News.*

Knowledge Village main Web site. (n.d.). Retrieved April 26, 2005, from http://www.kv.ae

Maksoud, C. (2003, February). Globalisation conference conducted at the American University of Sharjah, Sharjah, U.A.E..

NASPA. (n.d.). *International education program.* Retrieved July 25, 2005, from http://www.naspa.org/communities/kc/uploads/IEProgram.ppt

Rao, S. (n.d.). US education model still popular. *Gulf News.*

Shaghour, T. (2000, December 19). Need for Emiritisation 'is growing critical.' *Gulf News.*

Swaroop, S. (2004, December 27). Adopting a progressive approach. *Gulf News.*

TESOL Arabia Web site. (n.d.). Retrieved July 26, 2005, from http://www.tesolarabia.org

U.A.E./MOHE (Ministry of higher education and scientific research). (n.d.). Retrieved July 25, 2005, http://www.moe.gov.ae/English/Pages/Default.aspx?Silverlight=0

Ministry of Higher Education and Scientific Research. (n.d.). Retrieved July 10, 2008, from http://www.mohesr.ae/

United Arab Emirates University (U.A.E. U) Web site. (n.d.). *Student affairs.* Retrieved July 25, 2005, from http://www.uaeu.ac.ae/apds/index.shtml

United Arab Emirates University (U.A.E.U.) (n.d. b). *Facts and figures.* Retrieved July 10, 2008, from http://www.uaeu.ac.ae/about/facts_figures.shtml

University of Sharjah Web site. (n.d.a.). *Campus life.* Retrieved July 25, 2005 from https://www.sharjah.ac.ae/English/Campus_Life/Pages/default.aspx

U.S. Central Intelligence Agency. (n.d.). *The World Factbook: U.A.E.* Retrieved March 14, 2003 at http://www.cia.gov/cia/publications/factbook/geos/ae.html

U.S. Department of Education. (n.d.). Retrieved June 2005 from http://www.ed.gov/admins/finaid/ accred/accreditation_pg2.html#U.S.

Zayed University website. (n.d.). Retrieved April 26, 2005, from http://www.zu.ac.ae

TWENTY-ONE

SPAIN

The Kingdom of Spain is a parliamentary monarchy with a population (in 2003–04) of 41 million and with a GDP per capita income of €27,000 EUR ($42,600 USD) (2006). The life expectancy of the population is 82 years, and 99% of the Spanish are Catholic. The official language is Spanish; however there are numerous co-official languages in the local areas (Catalan, Basque, Galician, Valenciano) (Go Spain, n.d.). There are 17 autonomous regions as well as five other offshore autonomous areas.[1] Spain has 72 universities, of which 51 are public institutions and 21 are private. Within the universities, there are 165 colegios mayors, which will be discussed in the following pages (Ministry of Education and Science, 2003–04).

History of Colegios Mayores

The Colegios Mayores are University Centres that are integrated in the University, they provide residence to the students and they promote the cultural and scientific education of the residents, directing their activity to the service of the university community. (Boletín Oficial del Estado, 2001a)

This quote is from the Ley Organica de Universidades (Constitutional Law of the University) which is the Spanish Law for the Universities that established the current nature and mission of the colegios mayores within the Spanish university.

However, the colegios mayores are institutions with a long tradition in Spanish university life. Their origins date back to the 13th century, when in a society of guilds, students and masters felt the need to live together in groups to make teaching easier and to be provided with accommodation and food. In time, these residences acquired a

much greater importance. In some cases, they became the basis of the university; in other cases, they became cultural entities more important than the university itself.

The word collegium was first used to denote the corporation of masters and scholars, which provided a study-center and accommodation for students—mainly poor students, although rich students were also among them. Originally, the students had to go where the masters were teaching, sometimes far from their collegium. But very soon the masters went to live in the colegios along with the students. Thus the various subjects were taught at the colegios and a new vision of a unity of knowledge and life was developed for both master and scholar. In this way the colegios became teaching centers. From the start, nearly all of those centers were ruled by the teaching body.

Development of Universities in Spain

The first Iberian universities were established in the Kingdom of Castile and Leon in the 13th century and were often linked to existing cathedral schools. Between 1208 and 1288, various kings established universities at Palencia, Salamanca, Valladolid, Lerida, and Lisbon.

The first Spanish Colegio Mayor was founded in Bologna, Italy, in 1384 under the name of Colegio Mayor San Clemente of the Spaniards in 1384. Between 1401 and 1521, others followed in Spain, in Salamanca, Valladolid, Cuenca, Alcala, Oviedo, and Arzobispo. (Martinez, 1978, p. 12). The colegios mayores prospered, and many more were founded in Salamanca, Alcalá, Granada, etc. to meet the needs of the growing number of students coming to these universities.

But from 1566 until 1812, the colegios fell into decline due to the decadence of the universities itself. The quality of the universities worsened and the quantity of students dropped markedly. For instance, in 1812 at Salamanca University only 50 students were enrolled in the course (Martinez, p. 17). Many colegios were closed, but some have survived to the present day. In 1942, after the Span-

---

[1]The regions in Spain are Andalucia, Aragon, Asturias, Baleares (Balearic Islands), Canarias (Canary Islands), Cantabria, Castilla-La Mancha, Castilla y Leaon, Cataluna, Communidad Valencian, Extremadura, Galicia, La Rioja, Madrid, Murcia, Navarra, and Pais Vasco (Basque Country), and there are also five places of sovereignty on and off the coast of Morocco (Ceuta and Melilla are administered as under direct Spanish administration) (Instituto National de Estadistica [INE], 2003–04).

ish Civil War, the colegios mayores were restored to Spanish university life by the Ministry of Education by a special law. By the academic year 1962–63 there were 122 colegios mayores. Currently there are 165.

Colegio Mayor as a Model of Delivering Services to Students

Today, the colegios mayores continue to maintain their original ideals. They do not restrict themselves to providing lodgings, but provide a complete spectrum of activities. In fact, for many years, most of the cultural and sport activities in the Spanish universities have been carried out by the colegios mayores in each university.

The variety of interests, knowledge, and the geographical origins of the residents allow a strong interdisciplinary dialogue that enriches the education given in the lecture rooms. From this springs an atmosphere of conviviality among the residents; customs and traditions grow up and create the history of each colegio. The students live, work, study, and socialise together as a community. In this community one of the benefits the students emphasize most is that they develop close friendships that usually last forever.

Not all undergraduates belong to one of the colegios mayores. However, many students live there and take their meals there; some courses, free configuration credits, and many extracurricular activities are organized by the colegios. A great deal of socializing with classmates, faculty, and others is centered in the colegios. The colegios mayores founded by religious institutions offer the students their religious services too.

Activities in a Colegio Mayor

Besides the accommodation, food, and a life in common, the students living in a colegio mayor participate in a very active way in all kinds of sports, academic, and cultural activities. Further, the students (colegiales) are in charge of the different departments of the center. Figure 21.1 shows the organizational structure common to all the colegios mayores in Spain.

Other National Models of Student Affairs and Services

Under Spanish law, the state has transferred all the powers with regard to education and science to the different autonomous regional governments and to the universities. Thus the universities enjoy a great deal of autonomy and self-government.

In recent years, laws dealing with university reform and autonomy have helped the universities deal with the challenge of looking after the social, cultural, and recreational life of the students. Thus, most of the services that had been provided by the colegios mayores are now being offered by the university authorities through the vice rectors (vice presidents) and other departments or offices.

The Spanish system, therefore, has parallel tracks for rendering services to the university community. The difference is that the colegios mayores also offer accommodation and the values that result from actually living together, with the shared project of university life.

The University Track: Vice Presidents of Students

The university-track student services try to help the students in their academic life as well as in their social needs.

Service is provided in several areas: grants and other economic aids; enquiries and documentation; legal advice; welfare center; general affairs; counseling centers; disability services; health service, which is widely covered by the national health system; student associations; and sports. Colegios mayores are under this vice president (or another) or directly under the rector of the university. In many universities a special Commission of Colegios Mayores is chaired by the rector of the university, who oversees all functions related to student affairs.

Although Spanish universities offer a variety of colegios mayores located in areas around the city or on the campus, there are unfortunately not enough available for all who apply. As a result, the universities support an off-campus listing service on a computerized database

Complementing the syllabi and teaching curricula, the students are also offered a wide range of support services to make life more agreeable and profitable during their stay at the university: orientation, advice and psycho pedagogic services, social assistance, and grants where applicable. Students have access to libraries, computer services, cultural and sporting activities, lodgings services and so on, and before they leave they can get help finding employment at the Centre for the Promotion of Employment and Practice in Industry.

Cultural Activities and Cooperation to Development

Universities are very involved with their environment and organize many kinds of social and cultural activities, while at the same time encouraging the public in general to engage in these events and contribute to the cultural development of the environment as a whole. Funding comes from a few sources but the university voluntarily coordinates contributions to this dynamic. With regard to social needs, the university is committed to attacking injustice and defending human rights at both local and international levels.

At Granada University, for example, as at others, there are several programs that are worth mentioning:

a. Programs for students with disabilities are aimed at eradicating all barriers obstructing admission to the university and at helping the students to study in a normal way. The programs include such services as interpreters for sign language, different aids to blind students, and transportation to the study centers.

b. Sports programs for poor children from the city slum areas are designed to help them achieve better academic results.

Figure 21.1. Organizational chart of a colegio mayor.

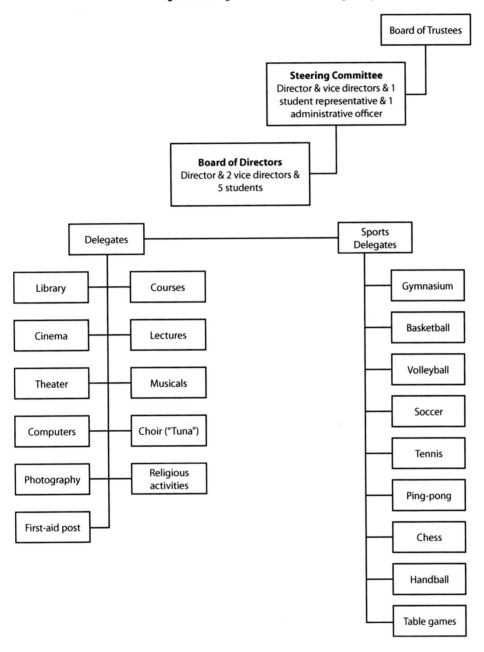

c. Students in the sports program conduct swimming and therapeutic rehabilitation programs for city residents with disabilities.

d. Under an alternative accommodation program, the elderly or persons with disabilities offer accommodation to students in their homes in exchange for company and collaboration in leisure activities. The general aims are to open the university to society, to encourage solidarity between generations, and to partly solve the student accommodation problem.

These are only brief descriptions of but a few of the many services rendered by the universities.

The Government and Student Services and Affairs

As part of their extensive autonomy, universities are responsible for their own student affairs policies. There was a need for a united voice for students services, and the only recognized authority is the Consejo de Colegios Mayores Universitarios de España (CCMU).

The CCMU is a legally constituted association whose members are all the colegios mayores of Spain, whether from public or private institutions. The CCMU safeguards the nature and role of the colegios mayores and is the liaison for communication and cooperation among the country's colegios mayores. CCMU represents the interests of the group before various organizations (courts, governments, labor organizations), and at conferences and national or international meetings.

Further, CCMU works (a) to develop the social infrastructure of the higher education centers for the exchange of students and faculty and (b) to collaborate with the university projects of national, autonomous communities (regions), local, public or private entities. Finally, CCMU collaborates on these matters with Europeans and other institutions and produces programs, projects, surveys, and research on these issues (Ministerio del Interior, 2000).

CCMU is governed by the general assembly, the board of colegios mayores, and the steering committee of the board. The board of colegios is composed of a representative from each university, and the steering committee is composed of five members elected by and among the board of colegios mayores.

Professional Programs Within Student Affairs and Student Services in Spain

In the Spanish university, there are no special professional programs specifically aimed at the training of professional student affairs administrators. Directors (or rectors) of the colegios mayores are elected or appointed by the rector (president) of the university and his government from among the faculty of the university. At colegios founded by private institutions, the rector appoints the director from among the candidates presented by the institution. But in any case the candidates must have a university degree.

The remaining vice presidents and directors of offices or departments related to the student services are appointed by the rector (president) from his team; all the administrative staff members working in the offices of the student services are civil servants of the state. One point to note is that the rectors of the Spanish universities and their governments are elected from among the faculty by all the university members—both students and faculty.

The Campus Climate

There is no gap between faculty and student services because both are one and the same. All the lectures and courses organized by the colegios mayores, not only for their residents but also for all the students, are delivered by faculty, who unselfishly collaborate. All the faculty members are open to suggestions and to regular invitations from the colegios mayores for their academic or cultural activities. These are free of charge for the students living in the colegio (known as colegiales mayores) and for all the students.

Colegios mayores are open to all students irrespective of race or nationality. On the other hand, each colegio mayor has its own set of conditions for admission. Application forms are available on request. In addition to the normal work of the academic year, some colegios have residential facilities and organize various courses during the summer vacation. Some colegios mayores offer associate memberships for those students who do not live in the colegio mayor itself. These students take part in the activities and are allowed to use all the facilities and services that the colegio mayor offers.

Funding of Student Affairs and Student Services

Most of the cultural activities are provided free by the university or faculty. All the student services provided by the vice president's office are totally funded by the university budget, as with other departments. The average budget of a colegio mayor is shown in Figure 21.2.

Students' fees are almost the only source of annual income for a colegio mayor. At three or four universities, some colegios mayores directly founded by those institutions are subsidized through the general budget of the university, and as a result their prices are a bit lower than the private ones. The rest have prices directly corresponding to the actual costs of the services, with no attempt to make a business of it. As nonprofit institutions, the colegios mayores must have their incomes equal their expenses.

Campus Structures

The model of student services (Figure 21.3) delivered by the University of Granada is an excellent example of the administrative hierarchy of the student affairs functions for the majority of the Spanish universities with few variations. Usually student services is under a vice president of student affairs. Although in some universities the title for the vice

Figure 21.2. Incomes and expenses of colegios mayores.

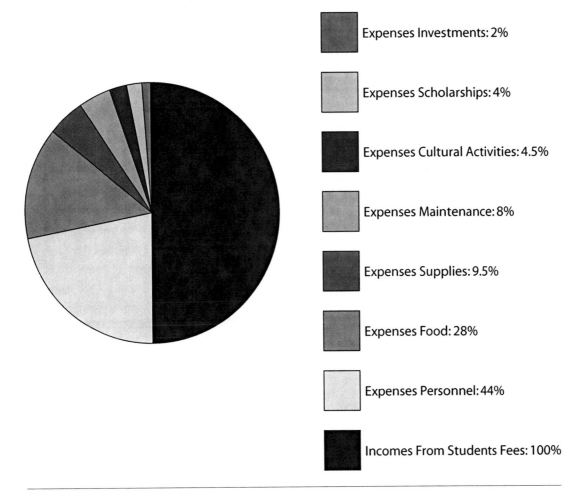

Expenses Investments: 2%

Expenses Scholarships: 4%

Expenses Cultural Activities: 4.5%

Expenses Maintenance: 8%

Expenses Supplies: 9.5%

Expenses Food: 28%

Expenses Personnel: 44%

Incomes From Students Fees: 100%

president in charge of this service could be different. The directors of the colegios mayores report directly to the rector of the university or to one of the vice-presidents.

Health Care

For student citizens of Spain, health care is free. Students from the European Union and from countries within the European Economic Union who have the right to public healthcare in their home countries qualify for the same level of healthcare as any Spanish national and should bring their European health card or the European E111 or E128 form with them to Spain. Non-EU students on an exchange or international program will need to have their own international medical insurance, except in those cases where the university they are coming has agreed to provide such coverage.

Student Demographic Changes

In 1985 there were 788,000 students in Spain. In 1998 the figure exceeded 1.5 million (Hildalgo, 2004). The L.R.U.

(Law for the Reform of the University, 1983) established a special exam for access to the university. At the same time it established "numerus clausus," which limited the number of places for certain studies, due to the lack of space in the classrooms. Many, but not all of the universities and the colegios mayores were crowded.

More recently, major disparities resulting from the simultaneous founding of many new universities, both public and private, have changed the mobility of the students. Many chose to stay at home, studying at their local new universities. As a result, applications dropped at some colegios mayores. Only the old and highly reputed universities have continued to attract students from all across the country. In these universities, the colegios mayores still attract a large number of applicants.

In addition, the Spanish population is decreasing. The country has the lowest birth rate in the world and the highest life expectancy in the European Union: 82 years (Pfizer, n.d.). Projections for 2010 show a drop in the number of students to less than one million.

Figure 21.3. Administrative hierarchy for the student affairs component at the University of Granada.

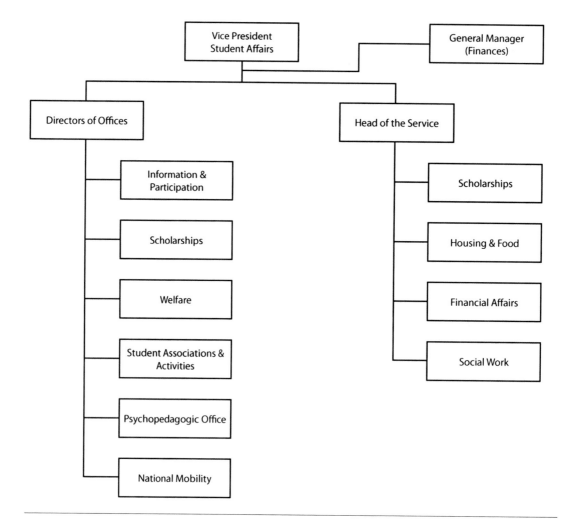

It is the opinion of this author that in the future, some of the new universities will have to close or else be transformed into colegios universitarios, which are university centers where only the first years of certain majors are taught; in other cases they will be turned into faculties forming part of one main university. The colegios mayores founded in those new universities have few students, most from the same city, so they will be facing serious problems of survival.

On the other hand, the decreasing student population is going to have a better opportunity to get the degree they prefer because the "numerus clausus" will disappear and the entrance exam will become nearly symbolic (Puyol, 1999). Therefore the possibility of getting a place in a colegio mayor will be greater.

Politics and Higher Education

Whichever political party is in power, there are no great differences with regard to student service affairs. The party of the left (Socialist Party) always tries to produce laws more in favor of student services, more grants for students, etc. Both parties, when in power, have been very supportive of the colegios mayores and of the way services are delivered to the students.

International Collaboration

The Consejo de Colegios Mayores Universitarios de España (CCMU) has signed an Exchange Agreement with NASPA–Student Affairs Administrators in Higher Education in which both parties agree to organize and provide exchange visits to each country for the purpose of studying the student affairs delivery systems and student issues. The annual visits will alternate between the United States and Spain. As a result of this agreement, CCMU and NASPA organized an international institute for senior-level administrators: "Shaping Student Affairs Leadership through Global Perspectives," held at Salamanca University in 2005.

Occasionally CCMU has contracted with European colleagues to provide exchange opportunities. These exchanges and visits have afforded opportunities for learning about student services systems in other countries. Similarities in student services systems are especially strong between CCMU and the Conferenza dei Collegi Universitari of Italy (CCUI). As a result of the Bologna Process, European communities now share the same educational policy, and CCMU is applying for European projects of excellence in education with CCUI and also with some British colleges. The CCMU is always open to all kinds of exchange opportunities for staff and for students, and university administrators are encouraged to contact the CCMU in order to develop and exchange programs.

Conclusion

In the Spanish university there is a long tradition of colegios mayores and the implementation of student services. This is a very deep-rooted tradition, and as a result it likely will not disappear due to the economic approach imported from some other European countries.

New winds are now blowing and new student service's approaches are cropping up among us, coming from private companies or private groups. The main issue with the private companies and groups is that they are profit based and do not necessarily have the interests of the students as a priority. For this reason, "residences for students" are spreading across the country, while the colegios mayores are not growing as much as would be desired. The "economic vision" of globalization is reaching student services as well. From this point of view, the student is considered not as a person to be educated but as a consumer.

In other European countries, the student services components have developed in a different style from Spain. They have evolved a practice not as holistic as ours, splitting up, if not always completely, the accommodation and food from the rest of the educational tasks. Even education itself has been reduced to mere information or communication of knowledge implemented at the colleges or faculties.

The CCMU preserves and will maintain a more holistic and comprehensive practice and theory of the education of the human being. For this reason, the CCMU will defend at all costs the principles cultivated by the colegios mayores, as centers where the students live together and where values and knowledge are taught to develop the character of the person in a university community as a reflection of the society as a whole.

References

Dancausa, C., Guindos Jurado, L., Moraleda, E., Galvan, J., Viedma, A., Cervera, S., et al. (2001). *España: Los retos de una sociedad envejecida*. Madrid, Spain: Fundación Pfizer.

Instituto Nacional de Estadistica (INE). (2003–04). *España en cifras*. Madrid, Spain: Author.

Boletín Oficial del Estado. (2001a, 6 de 24 de Diciembre). Ley Orgánica de Universidades (LOU). Spain: Author, 1 y 2.

Boletín Oficial del Estado. (1983, 209/83 de 1 Septiembre). Ley de Reforma Universitaria (LRU). Spain: Author, 209.

Go Spain. (n.d.). Spain facts and figures. Retrieved July 10, 2008, from http://www.gospain.org/facts/index.htm

Hidalgo, E. (2004, March). *Council of Colegios Mayores Universitarios Spain*. Paper presented at the annual NASPA International Symposium, Denver, CO.

Martinez Ferrol, M. (Ed.). (1978). *Radiografia del colegio mayor*. Madrid:

Ministerio del Interior. (20 de Julio, 2000). *Estatutos de la Asociación Cultural Consejo de Colegios Mayores Universitarios de España* (article 2). Asociaciones, Madrid: Author.

Ministry of Education and Science. (2003–04). *Estadistica universitaria*. Retrieved January 31, 2005, from http://www.mec.es

Pfizer. (n.d.). *Report on the ageing of the population*. Retrieved January 31, 2005, from http://www.pfizer.es/sala_prensa/notica_66.asp

Puyol, R. (1999, July 19). Demografía y universidad. Madrid, Spain: *ABC Newspaper* (n.d.).

Rodrigues San Pedro Bezares, L. E. (1995). Las universidades de Castilla (ss. XIII-XX). En Agustin Carcia Simón (Ed.), *Historia de una cultura: La singularidad de Castilla*, (vol. II, pp. 409–459).

TWENTY-TWO

UNITED KINGDOM

The landscape of student services in the United Kingdom is complex and varied, and a book chapter cannot expect to do it full justice. The aim is thus not to be comprehensive, but to select areas and issues that provide some flavour of U.K. provision. My approach is inevitably somewhat personal to the extent that it is both colored and limited by my own background, experiences, and aspirations for student services. I shall attempt to indicate where I may be describing provision or developments that are not necessarily nationwide, or experiences that may for some institutions be atypical. I have also had to be selective in what I have chosen to address in detail, sketch in outline, or ignore completely; I apologize in advance to any U.K. colleagues who feel that I have omitted or misrepresented matters particularly important to them.

In order to keep the length of this chapter within reasonable bounds, I shall have to largely ignore what are usually, although not always, relatively minor differences between England, Scotland, Northern Ireland, and Wales, and universities of different types and sizes. I shall also focus on the provision for students studying honors degree and postgraduate courses, although many U.K. higher education institutions (HEIs) also offer sub-degree level, certificated, and short courses.

Background: Higher Education in the United Kingdom

There are currently approximately 170 higher education institutions in the United Kingdom. Most of the undergraduate degrees they offer are awarded after three years of full-time study (four is common in Scotland), or its equivalent part-time, although some professional courses including medicine are longer. The majority of these institutions can also award postgraduate qualifications up to doctoral level. British universities range from institutions with 30,000 or more students to small specialist colleges with fewer than

1,000 students, with a mean of just more than 9000 and a median of 8,000 (Universities UK [UUK], 2004).

The variation in size is matched by a diversity of focus, mission, and history. Some institutions date back to the Middle Ages—Oxford, Cambridge, and St Andrews are perhaps the best-known—but most others followed much later, particularly from the turn of the 19th century onward. These include the late Victorian civic universities (e.g., the Universities of Manchester, Bristol, Leeds, Cardiff, and Birmingham) established in industrial cities with large populations and a need for an educated workforce, and the "red brick" universities (e.g., Nottingham, Leicester, and Reading). Many of these latter grew from colleges that, although founded in the late 19th or early 20th centuries, were teaching the degrees of institutions that had been established much earlier, until they finally attained university status in the mid-20th century. In the 1960s, there was a new wave of expansion stimulated by the rising post-war population of young adults; a number of new universities were founded as modern, even overtly anti-traditional, campus-based institutions (e.g., UEA, Sussex, Lancaster, and Warwick). Although with very different characters, histories, and locations (city center, suburban, or semi-rural), all these universities were, and remain, similar inasmuch as they were teaching institutions but had very strong academic research missions.

During the second half of the 20th century there was a parallel development of other types of teaching institutions that became known as polytechnics. Most of the polytechnics grew from smaller colleges of technology, commerce, art design, and education, often by amalgamation. Although some were engaged in research, particularly applied research, they were primarily teaching institutions with a focus on vocational rather than academic courses. Unlike universities, polytechnics did not themselves hold degree-awarding powers, and their degree-level courses had to be validated by a national external body, which ensured they adhered to strict standards. In contrast, universities had a great deal more independence, and quality of their degrees was assured by peer review through an external examiner system.

Some polytechnics and colleges were awarded independent degree-awarding status during the 1960s expansion (e.g., Strathclyde and Loughborough Universities). However, in 1992, the conservative government abolished the division between the university and the polytechnic sectors. At a stroke the number of U.K. universities, that is, institutions with their own honors degree-awarding powers, was significantly increased, providing a much greater capacity for higher education expansion. Some of the universities created from former polytechnics at this time were the University of Central England and Nottingham Trent, Manchester Metropolitan, and Napier Universities. Although they theoretically have the same status and now the same independence, universities and former polytechnics are still respectively referred to as pre-1992 and post-1992 institutions, or more colloquially, old and new universities.

A further element of the HEI sector is just more than 50 colleges of higher education, including several institutions that offer the majority of their courses in only one or two subjects, such as the arts or music. The HEI colleges do not hold independent degree- awarding powers, and while given a great deal of autonomy, they must have the degree courses that they deliver validated by a university. Not surprisingly, the different histories and backgrounds of the different types of institutions within the HEI sector are often visible in individual cultures, missions, and to some extent, the roles and priorities of their student services.

The History of Student Services in Higher Education

The mosaic pattern of growth within the U.K. higher education sector has inevitably impacted on the way that student support has developed. One of the drivers for the initial establishment of pastoral care systems in HEI was a tradition, particularly in England, for students to go away to university rather than attend their local institution, even when there was a very good university close by. Until 1970, young people did not become legally adults until they were 21, so universities were considered to be in loco parentis—in the place of parents—for their students younger than 21, and thus responsible for their well being. This is reflected in the ways in which some provision has developed.

In Oxford and Cambridge and other universities established on their model, the university consists of a number of semi-independent colleges bound together by an overarching teaching, research, and administrative infrastructure. As originally conceived, the college was a "home" where students lived, received some of their teaching, and were provided with a pastoral care system delivered by what were known as "moral tutors," now more commonly called personal tutors or personal advisers, within their college. These tutors were teaching and research staff who additionally took on the pastoral role for a small group of students. Other staff in the colleges had responsibility for the academic guidance of these students, and an important principle was established of separation of academic from non-academic personal guidance.

The non-collegiate universities established from the late 19th century onward also included extensive student accommodation known as halls of residence. Until the 1990s, it was common practice for each hall to be run by a warden, who was usually an academic member of staff who also had a teaching and research role. Wardens were responsible for the welfare of students living in their hall, ate with them in the evenings, and ensured discipline and good order. All teaching was delivered centrally, and most students also had personal tutors within their academic departments.

The earliest student support systems in the United Kingdom were thus primarily delivered by faculty who, in addition to their academic roles, had quasi-parental responsibilities in relation to a defined group of students. Changing circumstances and political, economic, and social pressures, together with shifts in students' expectations of what they might gain from a university education, highlighted the need for more specialized support and guidance than could be provided by staff whose primary role—and often whose skills— were in research and teaching. Gradually, new services were established centrally to provide a greater range of more professional information and guidance for students.

Some of these services are more than a century old— the Oxford and Cambridge Careers Services were founded in 1892 and 1902 respectively—and in many institutions, careers advice and placement services were the earliest of the central services to develop. The other area where central provision developed at a relatively early but nonetheless much later stage was student counseling. A young lecturer at the University of Leicester with pioneering ideas about the need for psychological help with personal problems and educational guidance (Swainson, 1977) began to offer personal counseling to her students in 1946. She established a *Psychological Advisory Service* that was finally formally recognized by the university's academic body in 1955; this was almost certainly the first university counseling service in the United Kingdom. Other institutions followed these early leads very much at their own pace, but today, all but the smallest U.K. universities have their own careers and counseling services, or equivalent facilities, and a range of other services. Exactly what each institution provides, how it is delivered, and who is responsible for its development and delivery varies widely.

The concept of linked or integrated student services—as opposed to individual, often almost autonomous single service units like the early careers and counselling services— began to be developed in some 1960s HEIs, but more particularly in the 1970s in what was then the polytechnic sector. It was often those working in counseling services or in teacher education, whose job brought them into very close contact with the realities of student life, who recognized that in order to thrive, students needed advice and guidance in a very wide range of areas to help them to address the personal and practical difficulties that might prevent them from completing their studies or achieving their potential.

The Development and Scope of Student Service Provision

Student services staff members pride themselves on being responsive to student need in the face of changing external and internal pressures. A number of external factors have had a very significant impact on the pressures facing U.K. students, the environment in which they study and live, and on their expectations of a degree course. All but one of the universities in the United Kingdom are publicly funded, thus, although the proportion of overall income that is derived from government varies by institution, successive government policies have had a major impact across the sector, particularly on the teaching and student support functions.

One key change has been the reduction in the government per-capita funding stream to universities and to individual students. Between 1989 and 2003 the average amount contributed annually by government to universities for teaching each full-time undergraduate student dropped from £7500 to £4900 GBP per year ($14,900 to $9,800 USD per year). Additionally, students studying at U.K. universities in the 1960s through to the late 1980s paid no fees and were entitled to a means-tested, non-repayable grant that was sufficient to meet all their normal study and term-time living costs. These changes have had a demonstrable impact on the student experience. Little more than a decade ago, many students lived in university accommodation offering cooked meals and overall pastoral care provided by a warden; they were taught in small groups that made it easy to establish a good working relationship with academic staff and their personal tutor. Students graduated without significant debts, and were almost always able to find graduate-level employment or places on postgraduate courses for which again financial support was often available.

Today, all but the poorest students and those in Scotland are paying just more than £1000 GBP ($2,000 USD) per year in fees rising to £3000 GBP ($6,000 USD) from the 2006–07 academic year) and must fund themselves though a mixture of low-interest but repayable loans, bank overdrafts, parental contributions, and part-time employment, and, only if they can demonstrate real financial hardship, small non-repayable grants from government or institutional funds. While this may seem a very generous system by U.S. standards, there is still a widely held view in the United Kingdom that higher education courses should be free and that students should still receive grants. The government view that higher education should be paid for by those who derive the most benefit from it, the graduates, is taking some time to bed into the culture of the United Kingdom. The reality, however, is that today's students frequently graduate with large debts and also find it more difficult to obtain a job at graduate level.

The drop in per capita funding levels has affected the student experience in many other ways. Students are now taught in much larger groups than previously, making it more difficult to establish friendships with fellow students and professional relationships with the staff who teach them. Where previously students lived in catered halls of residence, the vast majority are now living in private accommodation or in university halls of residence where they have to cook for themselves, with only rarely an adult warden to look out for them. Many more are now living at home and attending a local university, and perhaps missing out on some of the social, recreational, and developmental opportunities of student life.

These changes have stimulated many developments in U.K. student services. Responses to the increasing financial pressures faced by students include establishing financial advice centers or advisory functions that also administer the university hardship funds. In many universities there are also employment bureau—often known as "job shops"—whose remit is to help students find part-time work. Part-time working alongside full-time study was very unusual, and indeed prohibited in some HEIs, until the abolition of grants and the introduction of fees. However, a recent survey indicated that more than 40% of students now work in term time, for an average of 14.4 hours per week (UNITE, 2005). The academic demands of degree courses have remained the same, and many students find it hard to balance the competing demands of study, part-time work, and the social life that they expect also to be able to lead as part of student life.

Another driver for change over the last decade has been the government's aim to increase participation rates. Up until the 1990s, the proportion of the U.K. population that went to university and graduated with honors degrees was, by European and North American standards, extremely low. At the beginning of the 1980s only around 10% of those between 18 and 21 years old were in higher education. Successive governments have pressured universities to increase participation rates, and the expansion of the HE sector has been achieved in two ways: first, by increasing the number of higher education institutions, and second, through an increase in the number of students that existing institutions have admitted. By 2002, the proportion of those under

21 years old in higher education had risen to more than 35%. The present government's target is for 50% of 18 to 30 year olds to be in higher education by 2010, but it seems unlikely that they will increase their funding to the sector *pro-rata*.

Until the 1980s, higher education was largely the privilege of the children of middle class and professional families, and all but a very few HEI students had been educated in one of the U.K.'s private schools or in selective state schools. The current Labor government has very laudable ambitions to create a fairer society, and one of its strategies is to make higher education available to groups who had in the past missed out on this opportunity. Widening participation initiatives have resulted in a student cohort that includes more women, more mature students, more part-time students, more students from ethic minorities, more students who come from families or social groups with no previous history of higher education, more students from families that are not able to support them financially through university, more students whose prior education was less intensively academic, and more students with disabilities than ever before.

The development of provision for disabled students provides another example of the ways in which tat universities have responded to recent political and social changes. In this instance, there was a further driver for change: disability discrimination legislation, which makes it illegal to discriminate against anyone with a disability and requires universities to make "reasonable adjustments" to enable students with disabilities to participate in higher education. Furthermore, it is no longer appropriate to make such changes only when a student presents him or herself at the beginning of term; there is now an anticipatory duty. Over the last decade, the English, Scottish, and Northern Irish university funding bodies have offered resources, on a competitive basis, with the aim of stimulating and "pump priming" the improvement of provision for students with physical or sensory disabilities, specific learning difficulties such as dyslexia, and long-term physical and mental health conditions. Those institutions that were successful in obtaining such grants had a duty to disseminate to the rest of the sector the results of the projects that they undertook with their funding (see, for example, Higher Education Funding Council for England [HEFCE], 2002).

Most institutions' student support provision now includes facilities, resources, and individual support for such students. Specialist advisers aim to help students to develop their own strategies to minimize the impact of their disability or difficulty and to put in place the appropriate resources or practical arrangements to help them gain maximum benefit from their higher education experience. These might, for example, include special arrangements for access to accommodation and teaching buildings and adjustments to the teaching environment for those with mobility difficulties. Hearing loops and other aids for students with hearing impairment are provided. Students with visual impairments are provided note-takers and translation of course materials into Braille, onto audio tape, or into electronic format. Students with dyslexia are provided with specialized individual study guidance, and, in some institutions, mental health advisers help the growing number of students who present with, or develop on course, some degree of mental ill-health; they may also play an important role in liaising, on behalf of the student, with the appropriate medical or psychiatric services.

Not surprisingly, the driver for some of the changes in the student population is income generation: the United Kingdom, in common with many Anglophonic countries, now recruits a large number of international students. Although neither the motivations nor the benefits are entirely financial, such recruitment is particularly important as government strictly controls the number of U.K. undergraduates that publicly funded institutions can admit. U.K. HEIs are funded to teach a set number of students, and the national funding bodies impose fines if they admit more than their allocated number. If a university wishes to grow in numbers and generate additional income from teaching, there are essentially only two options. First, it can recruit international students who pay unsubsidized, and therefore higher and unregulated fees (the level of fees that publicly funded institutions can charge for undergraduate courses is restricted by government). Second, it can develop postgraduate courses, as neither their fee levels nor student numbers are controlled. The main recruitment of international students to the United Kingdom is to postgraduate level courses, although there are also many students studying at undergraduate level and on preparatory English language courses. The increase in international recruitment has stimulated the development of specialized provision for non-U.K. students, which may include pre-sessional orientation courses, additional language support, help with visa renewal, and the organization of a range of social activities and visits to places of historical and other interest.

This gives a flavour of some of the ways that student service provision has developed in the United Kingdom and of some of the drivers for change. The range of services across the higher education sector is now very broad; many if not most institutions offer the following services or at least some level of provision:

◊ career information advice and guidance;

◊ counseling for those with significant personal difficulties;

◊ disability and mental health support;

◊ learning skills advice to help students who are experiencing difficulties with their academic work;

◊ learning support for students with dyslexia or other specific learning difficulties;

◊ financial support and advice;

◊ specialist advice for international students;

◊ personal advice to help with practical and personal problems, sometimes including legal problems;

◊ multi-faith guidance and prayer facilities, including appropriate facilities for Muslim students;

◊ employment bureaux, to help students find suitable part-time jobs;

◊ pastoral care systems for students in university accommodation, often delivered by trained students but coordinated by student services staff;

◊ accommodation services to help students find private accommodation;

◊ student health centers, which often develop particular expertise in health areas relevant to young adults, including sexual health;

◊ postgraduate centers, providing specialist facilities for students studying at postgraduate level;

◊ nurseries, to look after the pre-school age children of students who are parents;

◊ sports facilities—sport has traditionally been an important aspect of U.K. university life.

Not every head of student services will necessarily have all these responsibilities. In some HEIs the responsibility for some of the above areas falls within the remit of other administrative units, and in others there may be no central support provided. Table 22.1 summarizes data from the 2002–03 Association of Managers of Student Services in Higher Education (AMOSSHE) member survey in respect of some of the core areas of provision.

Counseling, student financial advice, and disability provision are the areas that most frequently fall within the overall remit of AMOSSHE members, together with provision for international students, spiritual and faith support, and health. Accommodation and sports facilities are often separately managed as they have the capacity to raise their own income and may be run on business lines.

Other areas listed, particularly learning support/study skills development, are relatively new areas that have yet to be provided universally. This latter is another example of development in response to changes in the characteristics and expectations of the student body. Prior to the recent expansion of higher education in the United Kingdom, in what was then a very competitive environment, most students began their degree courses well prepared for the demands of academic study by the work that they had undertaken at school for the state "A-Level" examinations; these were the required qualifications for university entrance. Today, students' prior educational experience is far more varied, and students gain admission to university with a much wider range of qualifications; A-Level syllabi have also significantly changed. In con-

Table 22.1. Percentages of AMOSSHE members with managerial responsibility for, or significant input to, key student service areas (response rate: 37%).

Area of Responsibility	%
Accommodation	38
Careers	64
Childcare	43
Counseling	95
Disability	93
Spiritual and faith support	79
Student finance	90
Welfare advice	81
Health	74
International students	73
Sports/fitness	30
Learning support/study skills	43
N	**42**

trast, the expectations of academic teaching staff have remained very high. The result is that new students now find themselves far less well prepared for higher education than previously, and services offering generic study skills guidance have developed even in institutions that recruit some of the most academically able entrants.

Student services staff may also have other duties, including responsibility for student discipline or at least, and advisedly, disciplinary policy. They are also frequently involved in universitywide activities, such as championing equal opportunity initiatives. Other areas of responsibility include complaints procedures, widening participation, access and lifelong learning support, mature student support, student volunteering, educational guidance, legal advice, graduation arrangements, and cultural activities (Grant, 2005).

In some HEIs, a students' union or student association may provide some of the services available to students. Students' unions are quasi-independent bodies run by students, often with their own premises on university-owned land. Typically, they are partly funded by a grant from their university, but they also raise a significant amount of additional income by means of a range of commercial activities. They provide recreation and entertainment facilities for students, including bars (in the United Kingdom the legal age for drinking alcoholic beverages is 18) and venues for music, but they also play an important role in organizing student representation and supporting and advocating for students in dispute with the university when their independent position is vital. In some universities, they take on some of the advice functions that may in other institutions be provided by student services staff, although there is an expectation that where this happens, there will be good collaboration and liaison between both providers. Heads of student services frequently play a formal role in the management of students' unions through, for example, membership of its management committee, but in some institutions there is only an informal link.

It is in the student profile where some of the differences between the pre- and post-1992 sectors can be most sharply defined. In general, and there are inevitably exceptions, undergraduate students in the pre-1992 institutions are more likely than those in post-1992 HEIs to be studying full-time, be under 25, and be from a professional or middle class background. Although there have been changes to student profiles across the sector—indeed the national funding bodies have set widening participation targets for all HEIs—the post-1992 HEIs have been more successful as a group in widening access to HE. But they have also had some of the greatest demands placed on their student services personnel and have had to develop new areas of provision in response.

Models of Organization, Provision and Delivery

Not only has the scope of central service provision expanded, but there have been significant developments in models of delivery as well. Student services aim to be student-centered, with provision tailored to an individual's needs, but this model of delivery is limited by resources. Typically, a range of approaches to delivery will be taken ranging from self-help papers and Web-based resources through workshops (offered centrally or in-course) to individual guidance and counseling. All information, advice, and guidance will aim to be sensitive to the diversity of the student body in respect of age, gender, ethnicity, sexual orientation, prior educational experience, and family background and religion, and so on. There is now an increasing focus on the development of Web-based resources. This has been driven by an increasingly IT literate student population and a rise in the proportion of students who are part-time or who commute to university to attend lectures, seminars, and tutorials. These latter may be neither able nor willing to spend additional time on campus to visit student services in person. Requests for information and advice are increasingly being made by e-mail, and some initiatives to provide e-mail guidance and even counseling are currently under way (Goss & Anthony, 2003).

In some areas, there may be good integration with teaching. For example, careers advisers may deliver workshops tailored for students studying particular subjects, and some academic courses now have a careers development component integrated into the course, delivered or co-delivered by careers advisers. Staff members who offer study skills advice may also work closely with academic colleagues to ensure that courses integrate the development of academic learning skills into the curriculum.

Although all U.K. universities have developed central student support provision, many have also retained a personal tutor system based in the academic department, or in collegiate universities, the colleges. Such systems are far more common in the pre- than in the post-1992 sector: more than 80% of pre-1992 institutions have a compulsory personal tutor system, in contrast to just more than 40% of the post-1992 sector (Grant, 2006). However, the personal tutor/advisory system is under significant strain even in institutions that are committed to retaining it as a key element in their student support and guidance provision. Even in comparatively well-funded universities, personal tutors now have less time to spend with their students and may not be fully committed to, or skilled in, that role in the face of other teaching, administrative and, in particular, research responsibilities. For financial and pragmatic reasons, the once crucially important separation of academic and personal guidance that underpinned the early development of the personal advisory system has now more or less disappeared.

Despite these difficulties, students value the personal tutor system as it offers opportunities for guidance in the environment with which they are familiar and may be most comfortable. Central student services are of course particularly important when a student's relationship with his or her academic department breaks down, or when a student wishes to discuss issues in a neutral, and perhaps less judgemental and more confidential environment. Student services staff can play a significant role in supporting those academic staff who take on the role of personal tutor, providing them with information materials, training courses and, on a more or less daily basis, offering guidance to individual tutors who are anxious about their students and wish to know how best to advise them. Student services can also play a very important role in clarifying the boundaries between what is and is not appropriate for the tutor to offer, and when students should be referred on to more professional sources of advice. When it works well, the relationship between student services and academic staff can be very effective for students and reduce the workload of faculty.

In terms of the overall models of delivery, there still is much variation in the extent to which there is integration across the range of provision offered. Some services, recognizing that student difficulties are often interrelated, have made considerable efforts to bring together staff working in different functional areas in order to be able respond to individuals holistically. Some provide a "one-stop-shop" where information and guidance across a wide range of areas are provided from a single location. Students are initially seen by trained reception staff, who will attempt to diagnose the key areas of concern. They may themselves be able to help resolve the students' difficulties, but if the issues presented are complex they refer them on to the appropriate specialist or specialists. These might include financial advisers, careers advisors, counsellors, disability officers, study advisers, or other specialists, all working in the same location. In some services, physical integration is prevented by the absence of appropriate accommodation, but attempts are made to ensure that all staff members work to a common set of procedures and policies and that there is appropriate and informed referral between units. Some provision, such as workshops, may be jointly delivered and resources jointly developed.

In other institutions, a head of student services has overall responsibility for a number of semi-autonomous specialized units. Each of the individual functional areas is managed by its own senior specialist who is responsible for the day-to-day activities, while the head of service, in collaboration with his or her senior colleagues, will determine policy and set the overall objectives. The head provides the coordinating role and is the main link to the institution, representing all the services on university committees or other groups. He or she will also be responsible for making sure that all staff are aware of the roles and remits of each of the constituent units, so that there can be informed referral.

There are still some institutions, although these are increasingly rare, where there is no one playing such a co-ordinating role and each of the main areas of provision is separately managed, with minimal or no integration. Mixed models of organization, with integration and coordination of some activities, but more separate management of others is not uncommon. Not infrequently, careers services stand alone and have their own representation in university systems and structures, particularly in the pre-1992 sector. This explains the proportion of AMOSSHE members who have careers services as part of their remit: the figure shown in Table 22.1 is not a reflection of the proportion of institutions that provide a careers service—all institutions offer some form of careers advice and guidance. The early establishment of careers services in many of the pre-1992 institutions has given their heads a strong and well-established position within institutional hierarchies that they fear may be lost if they become subsumed within a broader student service organization.

A rather different and perhaps unique model of student support delivery has been developed at the University of Leeds, which has deliberately moved away from organizational integration to the creation of a community model that explicitly recognizes the role played by student services, faculty, departmental administrative staff, hall wardens, library and computing staff, students' unions and friends and family. Additionally the value for students of engagement in volunteering activities and appropriate part-time employment is explicitly acknowledged in this model. The Leeds Support Services Network includes anyone with a professional role in relation to students and is brought together via a mail-base, formal discussion opportunities, training sessions, and an annual conference. In this model, line management arrangements become almost irrelevant. The internal network is also seeking to develop better communications with relevant outside agencies (Humphreys, 2005; see also Grant, 2003, p. 12).

Different types of arrangement can, to a greater or lesser extent, be aligned with the philosophical models of provision that are found in the literature on student services from the United States. In the "student services" model, service providers are there to offer additional services to support the academic vision of the university, but they are placed alongside and slightly separate from the teaching function of the institution. Such a model might be exemplified by the position of the careers and counseling services at, for example, Oxford and Cambridge. These services, although given much autonomy and a certain prestige, may find it difficult or even impossible to influence teaching or any of the established university traditions that affect student well-being. In these two institutions in particular, the college to which students are attached determines many aspects of their overall experience including their pastoral support; central student services stand outside and somewhat at a distance.

The "student learning" model, which places emphasis on collaboration with academic and administrative staff to create a productive learning environment for students is increasingly the approach taken by U.K. services. This model can facilitate creative approaches to the development of resources and services for students that cross functional boundaries. For example, an approach to helping students with financial difficulties might involve collaboration between financial advisers, a part-time employment bureau, the careers service, and the students' union, with faculty involvement to ensure that course-work deadlines are given well in advance to allow students the flexibility to manage their time effectively (for which further guidance might be offered by study skills advisers or counsellors).

The "student development" model, where provision is organized in line with the developmental phases of a student's progress through his or her university career has not been broadly adopted in the United Kingdom. However, many services will adopt some elements of this approach in aspects of their work. For example, a careers service may develop and promote different elements of its provision to students in their first, second, and third years of study, and a small number of institutions have set up graduate centers, which offer facilities and services exclusively to postgraduate students. Many services are now paying particular attention to the first-year experience and trying to work together and with faculty to improve induction and orientation processes and make these ongoing throughout the first year.

Table 22.2. Reporting lines for heads of student services, by sector (2002–03).

Sector Hierarchical level and line manager	Pre-1992	Post-1992	College of HE/Specialist institution	All
1. Head of Institution/vice chancellor	1		2	3
2. Deputy/Pro Vice Chancelor Registrar/Head of Administration	3 7	10 4	5 1	18 8
3. Academic Registrar or other head of administrative unit	4	4	2	10
Total N	**15**	**14**	10	**39**

Student services in the United Kingdom are becoming more conscious of the need to articulate their missions and their aims and objectives and are developing more reflective and theoretically informed approaches. In the past, the pressures of student demand, institutional expectations, and inadequate funding often drove a reactive and pragmatic approach to development. Nonetheless, there is a more or less universal commitment to a model of service delivery that puts the student at its center and is based on principles of equality of opportunity and of student autonomy and independence. The *in loco parentis* model that characterized some of the early student service developments is now strongly resisted; the aim is to guide students in developing their own problem-solving skills, their self-esteem, and their confidence.

Student Services and their Institutional Relationships

Across the sector, the nature of the day-to day relationships between student services staff and the academic functions of universities varies considerably. In many areas of provision, student services staff can be most effective when they are able to work in close contact with teaching and other administrative staff. For example, if disability officers are able to work with faculty and administrators, they can help (a) ensure that teaching notes are made available to students with disabilities in advance of lectures, (b) train faculty so that they are aware of any specific barriers to learning faced by individual students, and (c) ensure that appropriate adjustments are made to examination and other assessment arrangements.

Opportunities for student service involvement in teaching and the curriculum can be exploited in institutions where students study modular degree courses with a wide choice of options. In some, student services staff members have been able to develop and deliver standalone modules that can be taken as part of a degree course for full academic credit. Such modules commonly address career development and study skills.

Other U.K. courses, particularly those offered in the pre-1992 sector, are highly specialized, and students study one subject or a narrow range of related subjects throughout their entire period of undergraduate study. In these circumstances, the opportunities for input by student services staff may be more limited. There are faculty who are very reluctant to countenance any reduction in the subject-specific components of their courses and may even strongly resist developments that they perceive as undermining the purely academic objectives of their degree programmes. However, other faculty have been more open to curriculum development and have worked collaboratively with student services in the design and delivery of components of academic courses that integrate study skills or career development programs with subject-specific academic learning.

The position of the head of student services within his or her institutional hierarchy is extremely important as it has a crucial effect on the degree of influence they can exert and, of course, their resources. Student services have often felt themselves to be very low in the pecking order of institutional structures, and their role as service providers can separate them from both their academic and purely administrative colleagues. However, this is beginning to change, and heads of student services in some institutions have quite senior roles. Only rarely do they report directly to the head of the institution, the vice chancellor or principal, but many are now only one further step down, reporting either to a pro vice chancellor or to the head of the university's administration. Table 22.2 summarizes the reporting lines of 39 institutions who responded to the relevant question in the AMOSSHE 2002–03 survey (Grant, 2005).

Heads of student services are increasingly gaining membership on key institutional committees and other decision-making bodies, including those responsible for planning and resources and university governance, teaching and learning, academic standards, and quality assurance (Grant, 2005). Where they have this enhanced position, they are more able to stimulate student-centered curriculum and assessment development, administrative systems, and other services, thus assuring that these take full account of the increasing diversity of the student body and the changes in their expectations of higher education.

Funding U.K. Student Services

The primary and often the only substantial income stream for student services comes from government. The four higher education funding councils, for England, Wales, Scotland, and Northern Ireland, act as middle men between government and universities in the allocation of the relevant portion of the national budget. They determine the allocations to the different elements of the grant (broadly, for research, teaching, capital projects, and special projects earmarked to address identified priorities) and thence to each individual institution, in line with government policies and priorities (see, for example, HEFCE, 2005). The HEIs receive grants that have been calculated by a complex formula that takes into account factors as broad and varied as the quality of the academic research output and the number of students. One of the current special funding streams relates to the government's widening participation aims; thus, within the algorithm used for determining institutional funding, the proportions of students from non-traditional backgrounds and of students with disabilities are factored in and identified within the total grant allocation. This funding recognizes the increased costs to institutions of teaching and supporting such students. The overall funding policy, however, is of non-hypothecated allocation.

How institutions use the money allocated to them is very much a matter of individual policy and choice, and individual HEIs decide whether or not all or part of special income streams are handed on to student services. Some institutions have a devolved resource allocation model, with most of the institutional finances allocated to individual academic units and a relatively small proportion retained centrally to fund university wide activities and facilities, including student services. Others operate a more centralized model, although even in these institutions, student services will be in competition with the other central units including estates, personnel, finance, the library, and the IT service.

Student services staff numbers and budget thus vary considerably from university to university. Some operate with many staff and relatively large budgets; others are attempting to provide the same range of services on a fraction of the resource. A recent survey of AMOSSHE members showed that there was no consistency in the level of resource allocated across the sector in relation to size or type of institution (Grant, 2005). Similarly, individual institutions consult their own priorities in allocating resources to the different functional or specialized areas within the overall student service organization. Careers services tend to be relatively well-funded, particularly in pre-1992 institutions, but in institutions with very diverse student bodies, the priorities may be other areas of provision such as financial advice and the development of programs aimed at enhancing student retention.

There is broad consensus among student services personnel that U.K. student services are generally underfunded. Opportunities exist for student services to generate additional income to boost their budgets through a range of means, including sales of services and materials, and sponsorship or grants from local, national, or even European bodies for specific projects. The greatest capacity for sustained income generation is perhaps in the careers area, and quite substantial additional sums can be drawn from employers by offering facilities and opportunities to aid their graduate recruitment. However, it is often the least well-funded services that find it most difficult to invest the initial time and effort required to generate and sustain such income streams.

Additional resources are available to individual U.K. students with disabilities and specific learning difficulties. Following an assessment of individual need by a health practitioner, or, for those with specific learning difficulties, an educational psychologist, grants are allocated by the local authority for the area in which a student lives to cover the cost of any equipment or additional personal or learning support that is necessary for that student to learn effectively. Many students with dyslexia choose to buy their specialized learning support from their own institution, and this has created an income stream that has allowed services to build up their staff with specialist skills in this area.

Student Services Personnel and their Professional Development

The backgrounds and qualifications of staff working in student services in the United Kingdom are very diverse. Some staff have spent all their careers in the field, while others have a range of related and unrelated prior experiences. Heads of student services in the United Kingdom include some who were once academics who developed an interest in student affairs and a commitment to the student experience and moved from a research and teaching post to a service provision role—this is my own background. Others began their careers as specialist advisers, often first with a careers or counseling background and then moving on to a more generic leadership role. Some have a broadly administrative background.

When recruiting staff to take up senior positions within student services, HEIs will usually specify that the applicants should hold an undergraduate degree (although even this may not be seen as absolutely essential), and, preferably further relevant qualifications or training, but they will expect a significant level of relevant experience. This is perhaps something that reflects a long tradition of amateurism that is deeply embedded within the British culture. The lack of a formal qualification is not always a barrier to career success. The judgement is made on output rather than input. There are, in any case, very few U.K. qualifications that are specifically relevant to heads of student services. There is only one master's-level course in the broad area of student service management: an MA in Student Support and Management at the University of Huddersfield. Some student services personnel have embarked on PhD research in areas related to their work. The advantage of the U.K. doctorate is that it can be entirely research based (although training in appropriate research methods is provided). This means that it is possible to undertake a doctorate in the absence of relevant taught elements; specialist supervision is usually offered by staff in Schools of Education. It seems likely that professional qualifications for student services personnel will start to proliferate, and that in the future, they will become desirable, if not essential, for those aspiring to a leadership role.

General management training courses for those working in higher education are offered by internal staff development units and external providers, but these are rarely compulsory. In contrast, training for counsellors and careers advisers is long established though postgraduate and certificated courses. Training opportunities have been developed in specialist areas, such as dyslexia, in response to the development of new areas of provision. In practice, much training is undertaken on the job, together with attendance at short courses and conferences, or, in some areas, more substantial part-time programs.

Professional associations provide a vital element of the continuing professional development of U.K. student services staff. The unique role that they play can leave heads of services rather isolated within their own institutions, and so they have looked outside to the wider sector for support and guidance. The first professional association of heads of student services was founded in 1976 as the Association of Heads of Polytechnic Student Services (AHOPS), with a membership of 12. When polytechnics became universities, AHOPS had to change its name and AMOSSHE, the Association of Managers of Student Services in Higher Education, was born. "Managers" is no longer the most appropriate descriptor for their role,[1] but as is the case with NASPA,[2] the acronym has developed an important identity and there is a reluctance to change it.

AMOSSHE is primarily an organization for the heads of service and full membership is limited to a single Institutional Representative Member (IRM). The association provides training events, an annual three-day conference, a widely used e-mail forum to facilitate exchange of information and views, a Web site for information dissemination, guidance materials and policy documents (for example, AMOSSHE, 2001), and a journal, formerly *CONNECT*, but recently re-launched as the *Journal of Student Services in Higher Education*.

Other professional associations or networks exist for more specialized student services staff including financial advisers, disability advisers, counsellors, mental health support workers, university chaplains, and international student advisers. However, the best and longest (since 1967) established of these is AGCAS, the Association of Careers Advisory Services. AGCAS has more than 1,600 members and an enviable position within the HEI sector. In some respects the established position of AGCAS has limited the development of AMOSSHE, even though AMOSSHE members, with their remit for all elements of service provision, have an overarching role that often encompasses careers services. The AGCAS model of inclusive membership for all those working in careers services is something that AMOSSHE may wish to emulate in the future, not least because it has created for AGCAS a substantial income stream that funds a very wide range of activities and resources.

There has been much debate amongst AMOSSHE members, particularly at Executive Committee level, about whether to keep the restrictive membership or to broaden it to others working in student services. So far the decision has been only to offer an associate-level membership to those with significant managerial responsibility, perhaps as the head of a specialist unit within a larger student services organization; these must be nominated by the head of service.

AMOSSHE has been very successful in recruiting members, with 132 institutions represented, out of a potential 170.[3] Despite this success, the exclusiveness of its membership criteria is a significant limitation to AMOSSHE's income stream and thus the support it can provide for its members. Professional development, lobbying for student affairs at national level, and information dissemination have all been prioritized, and over the last few years, significant strides have been made in increasing capacity in these areas. Where AMOSSHE currently lacks capacity is in undertaking the research that members would like to be able to use to underpin the development of their practice. Those of us in the United Kingdom, including myself, who have joined NASPA look with some envy at the amount of research undertaken by the organization, and indeed by its individual members as exemplified by many of the articles published in the *NASPA Journal*.

---

[1] Those responsible for leading student services now commonly have the title of head or director of student services (or its equivalent); a small handful are called dean of students, a name more commonly used in the United States. This title is generally (although not by all means exclusively) used in institutions that give particular prominence to the development of student affairs, and involve the head of student services in relevant strategic developments at an institutional level.

[2] NASPA, formerly the National Association for Student Personnel Administrators, has changed its name to NASPA–Student Affairs Administrators in Higher Education, but has kept unchanged its longstanding acronym.

[3] A condition of AMOSSHE membership is that the IRM must be a head of service responsible for a significant portfolio of provision; the majority of institutions who are not members are currently ineligible as their student service units are independently managed.

Student Services and the Broader HE Sector: Challenges and Opportunities

Within the broader U.K. environment there is a number of national and governmental organizations and initiatives that are relevant, in different ways, to the development of student services in the United Kingdom. The government's widening participation agenda and its impact on the demographics of higher education have already been discussed; the principles behind that policy are summarized in a recent report from the Department for Education and Skills (DfES, 2004), the U.K. government department whose responsibility includes higher education:

> ...the opportunity to enter higher education should be open to anyone who has the potential to benefit from it, regardless of background. All HEIs need to identify, encourage to apply, admit and support to graduation all those who have the potential to succeed. (DfES 2004, 80)

The government, through the DfES, also determines the levels of fees that can be charged by institutions and the loans and grants provided to support students through their studies. Each university is given an annual sum to be distributed as grants to those students who can demonstrate real financial need; the distribution of these funds is usually the responsibility of student services financial advisors (see Table 22.1). Initially, HEIs were given independence in establishing criteria for allocating these funds. Now criteria and procedures are far more tightly controlled, but AMOSSHE members have played a very important role in advising the DfES, in order to ensure that they understand the difficulties that some students are facing, particularly those from widening participation backgrounds. We have perhaps been less successful than we might have hoped, but there is no doubt that the system is fairer and much more grounded in the realities of student life than it would have been if student services staff had not been consulted.

In a system that is heavily funded from the national purse, it is right and proper that measures should be put in place to ensure public accountability. The funding councils have established performance indicators (PIs) against which each university's outputs and activities are measured. Many of these PIs are not directly relevant to student services, but others, including completion rates and students' employment success are very relevant as they are areas in which student services can have considerable impact (Higher Education Statistics Agency [HESA], 2004).

The expansion of U.K. higher education has created a much more competitive environment for HEIs, who vie with each other to recruit the most able students. A number of league tables have been devised by amalgamating data from the funding council performance indicators, and these are published in the press annually. Statistically, these tables have no validity as they are devised from a number of unrelated or highly inter-related datasets,

some of which are weighted, to produce an overall score. The *Times*, one of the U.K.'s most popular newspapers, uses the following to calculate its Top 100 Universities table: teaching quality, research quality, entry standards, student-staff ratios, spending on library and computing facilities, graduates' final degree classifications, graduate employment success six months after graduation, and completion rates (*The Times*, 2005). Despite their dubious validity, the league tables have become very important in demonstrating and maintaining institutional prestige and thus influencing student recruitment at all levels from undergraduate to postgraduate. The availability of the information online means that these league tables also influence international student choice.

In some institutions league tables have had a beneficial impact on student services by raising their profile. For example, HEIs whose table position is adversely affected by their graduate employment figures have allocated additional resources and attention to careers initiatives. The league tables have also drawn attention to the role of student services in facilitating student progression and achievement and enhancing retention. Although the proportion of the U.K. population entering HE has been relatively low compared to many other countries in the developed world, for a long time the United Kingdom topped the international league tables for its graduation rates as only a very small proportion of those who enrolled failed to complete their degree course. Widening participation, the reduction in the levels of funding both to institutions and to students, and a number of other factors (see, for example, Hall, 2001) have affected U.K. completion rates, although, internationally, they remain very high (Organization for Economic Cooperation and Development [OECD], 2004).

Although the national average for completion is around 85%, the range is very wide: the figures published in the 2005 *Times* league table for the top 100 universities range from 62% to 98.5% (*The Times*, 2005). Even institutions with very good retention rates can no longer be complacent that this position will be maintained by default. The government is also concerned about retention rates and in 2002 established a project to investigate and report on effective approaches to retaining students in higher education. The task, along with funding, was given to two associations: Universities UK (UUK) (formerly the Committee of Vice-Chancellors and Principals), comprising the heads of universities, and the Standing Conference of Principals (SCOP), comprising the heads of higher education colleges. These two bodies are the voices of the HE sector in the United Kingdom. The task group included membership from AMOSSHE, and the resulting report focused specifically on the role of student services in student retention (UUK/SCOP, 2002a).

AMOSSHE has forged a very productive relationship with UUK and SCOP. There are regular meetings between UUK policy officers and AMOSSHE Executive Committee members, and the organizations have collaborated on other joint initiatives. Recent guidance materials developed and published by UUK and SCOP in collaboration with AMOSSHE have addressed mental health policies and practice (Committee of Vice-Chancellors and Principals [CVCP], 2000) and minimizing the risk of student suicide (UUK/SCOP, 2002b). Such joint initiatives are ongoing and the next one, due for completion in 2007, addresses alcohol and drug policies. The collaboration with UUK and SCOP is not only cost-effective for AMOSSHE but also raises the profile of the issues addressed and thus of student services. UUK and SCOP publications are distributed directly to their members and arrive on the desks of vice chancellors and principals. This gives them a far greater chance of being discussed at strategic level than if they were distributed only to practitioners.

A new publication on mental health (Grant, 2006) includes an evaluation of what was found to be the very positive impact of the sectorwide guidance on mental health, including that published by UUK, AMOSSHE and AUCC (the Association of University and College Counselling). Recently, student services, UUK and SCOP have established a committee to promote mental well-being in higher education. This panel reports directly to a newly established UUK Student Experience Committee.

The International Context

We in the United Kingdom envy what from our perspective seem to be much more generous resource levels in the United States, allowing the country to develop high levels of professionalism and resources for its student services personnel and a more powerful role within U.S. institutions.

But compared to most of continental Europe, U.K. services are both very well developed and well funded. The traditional British model of full-time, three-year undergraduate courses, one-year master's programs, and three-year doctorates is not typical of other E.U. countries. In the United Kingdom, the consequences of failure of any element of a degree program are very serious: with only very limited opportunities to retake degree units, failure of one unit can lead to course termination. Therefore, it is of paramount importance for students to be able to access rapidly the support and guidance that will minimise the negative impact of personal difficulties and practical problems on their ability to study effectively. In contrast, in Europe part-time and extended study is more common, as are more flexible degree courses; it is also much more common than in the United Kingdom for European students to live at home during their time as students.

These and other differences between the U.K. and European HE systems perhaps explain why there has not, historically, been the same drive to develop student services in other E.U. countries. Typically, there is more lim-

ited provision in continental Europe than in the United Kingdom, and what does exist has, in many cases, been relatively recently established. The European Union is bringing about a greater convergence in higher education, particularly in respect of the structure of degree courses through the Bologna Declaration (HEFCE, 2003, *The Bologna Declaration*, retrieved August, 2005, from http://www.hefce.ac.uk/partners/world/bol/). European institutions are increasingly interested in exchanging information about student services. A recent conference of student services personnel in Spain invited speakers from both the United Kingdom and France; other intercontinental exchanges are increasing in frequency.

Conclusions and Future Directions

Despite the many difficulties that may face today's students, most thrive in the demanding environment of U.K. higher education. They value their experiences, develop academically and socially, graduate after three, or sometimes more, years of study, and move on to a good first job. Others do not find the experience so straightforward, or they need encouragement to develop their potential; student services can offer such students resources, guidance, and support, or even a crucial lifeline, at any point in their university careers.

The scale and complexity of the jobs of those working in student services is constantly evolving as student numbers grow and students become increasingly diverse. Individual institutions respond to these changes in different ways and while there is much common ground and shared responses, there is no neat definition of "student services" that has relevance across the U.K. HE sector. These organizations are as varied as the sector itself and reflect both the different histories and the current missions and priorities. At any moment in time, government initiatives might be launched and different challenges and concerns emerge, defining new priorities and driving new developments. At present the higher education sector in general is being pressured to be far more accountable for what it does, and this is also affecting student services, which need to demonstrate that they offer high quality provision that is effective and value for money and offer equality of provision for students from a very diverse range of backgrounds.

Students, who are now graduating with very large debts as a result of their university courses, are becoming a great deal more demanding too—they are behaving like customers and consumers, and not, as they perhaps once were, participants in a shared learning experience. Their parents, too, are also expecting more information from HEIs about their children, criticizing institutional facilities and procedures, and challenging confidentiality policies. The introduction of much higher university fees from 2006 onward is also expected to have a significant impact both on student expectations and on the levels of difficulty that the poorest students will experience. Universities are looking to heads of student services to help them respond to these new challenges. The heads of student services, in their turn, look to each other and the mutual support that is provided through AMOSSHE. By fulfilling its mission (a) to provide comprehensive, professional support for the heads of student services in the United Kingdom, and (b) through effective representation, to promote policy change to enhance the student experience, we hope and expect that the association will be able to move from a position of influence to a significant force on behalf of all students in the U.K. HE sector.

For example, the priorities for my own service at the moment include (a) a better integration of the different specialist staff within my services, (b) enhanced relationships with faculty and other staff who interact with students, (c) the development of clearer policy documents and procedures, (d) harnessing the potential of information technology, including developing a much better Web site and other self-help resources, (e) further developing provision for students with mental health difficulties, and (f) attempting to minimize the harm done by excessive alcohol consumption, including developing better social facilities for Muslim students and others who do not drink, and the list goes on.

Most of us who are much over 30 feel, and indeed know, we were extremely privileged to have had a higher education experience that is not available to students today. We were taught in small groups and we had far more personal contact with those who taught us and studied with us, and this allowed us to feel a sense of belonging and importance. Student services can still offer a more individualized contact for those students who need it most, but I would not wish to limit their role to that of the protection of the disadvantaged, the weak, and the vulnerable, important although that role is. There may be a danger here of a return of the paternalism that characterised some of the very early models of central student support in the United Kingdom. There is also an enormous potential for student services to enhance their role in helping all students, including the very able and apparently robust, to find their own ways of meeting the challenges of life and of realizing their full potential. Humphreys (2005, p. 180), in his recent outline of the Leeds community-based model of student service provision, notes the importance paid to the value of creating community in early student affairs development in the United States. Young summarizes this early approach, which although now made much more difficult by the size of most U.K. institutions, must still surely still have some value and be worth reconsidering:

> Students must find a role in relation to others that will make them feel valued, contribute to their feelings of self-worth, and contribute to a feeling of kinship with others. (Young, 1996, 90)

If we can facilitate this process, then we shall have been successful.

References

Association of Managers of Student Services in Higher Education (AMOSSHE). (2001). *'Duty of Care' Responsibilities for Student Services in HE.* Winchester: Author.

Committee of Vice-Chancellors and Principals (CVCP). (2000). *Guidelines on mental health policies and procedures for HE.* London: Author.

Department of Education and Skills (DfES). (2004). *Annual report 2004.* Sheffield: Author.

Goss, S., & Anthony, K. (Eds.). (2003). *Technology in counselling and psychotherapy: A practitioner's guide.* Basingstoke: Palgrave Macmillan Ltd.

Grant, A. (2003, Winter). Where is the evidence? *Association for University and College Counselling Journal,* 11–12.

Grant, A. (2005). The organisation, scale and scope of student service provision in AMOSSHE member institutions. *Journal of Student Services in Higher Education, 1,* 12–20.

Grant, A. (2006). Mental health policies and practices in United Kingdom higher education institutions. London: Universities UK/Standing Committee on Principals (UUK/SCOP).

Hall, J. (2001). *Retention and wastage in FE and HE.* Glasgow: The Scottish Council for Research in Education.

Higher Education Funding Council for England (HEFCE). (2002). *Improving provision for disabled students. HEFCE strategy and invitation to bid for funds for 2003–2005.* Bristol: Author.

Higher Education Funding Council for England (HEFCE). (2003). *The Bologna Declaration.* Retrieved August, 2005, from http://www.hefce.ac.uk/partners/world/bol

Higher Education Funding Council for England (HEFCE). (2005). *How HEFCE allocates its funds.* HEFCE Guide 2005/34. London: Author.

Higher Education Statistics Agency (HESA). (2004). *Performance indicators in higher education in the UK 2002/3.* Cheltenham: Author. (Also available at http://www.hesa.ac.uk/pi)

Humphrys, N. (2005). Values and student support. In S. Robinson, & C. Katulushi (Eds.), *Values in higher education* (pp. 178–188). St. Bride's Major: Aureus Publishing Ltd and the University of Leeds.

Organization for Economic Co-operation and Development (OECD). (2004). *Education at a glance 2004.* Paris: Author.

Swainson, M. (1977). *The spirit of counsel. The story of a pioneer in student counselling.* London: Neville Spearman.

The Times. (2005). *Good university guide.* London: Author. (The league tables also available from Times Online and was retrieved August 22, 2005, from http://www.timesonline.co.uk/section/0.716.00.html)

UNITE. (2005). *Student living report 2005*. Bristol: Author.

Universities UK (UUK). (2004, Summer). *Higher education in facts and figures*. London: Author. (Information is also available at http://www.bookshop.universitiesuk.ac.uk/downloads/facts04.pdf)

Universities UK/Standing Conference of Principals (UUK/SCOP). (2002a). *Student services. Effective approaches to retaining students in higher education.* London: Author.

Universities UK/Standing Conference on Principals (UUK/SCOP).(2002b). *Reducing the risk of student suicide.* London: Author.

Young, R. (1996). Guiding values and philosophy. In S. Komives, D. Woodard, & Associates (Eds.), *Student services: A handbook for the profession*, 3rd edition. San Francisco: Jossey Bass, 83–105.

TWENTY-THREE

UNITED STATES OF AMERICA

JEANNA MASTRODICASA

Student affairs in the United States evolved as the nation's higher education developed, so this chapter will begin with a historical overview. The colleges established during colonial times (e.g., Harvard in 1636, William and Mary in 1693, and Yale in 1701) sought to replicate "the English idea of an undergraduate education as a civilizing experience that ensured a progression of responsible leaders for both church and state" (Thelin, 2003, p. 5). Functions that resemble today's student services were fulfilled by trustees, administrators, and faculty (Fenske, 1989; Thelin, 1996, 2003).

From the beginning of the republic in 1776 through the mid-19th century, colleges were typically small (Thelin, 1996, 2003). The states of Georgia, North Carolina, and South Carolina chartered universities in the early 19th century, but gave them little financial support. However, many colleges were founded in that period, until there were 241 by 1860 (Thelin, 1996, 2003).

In the early 19th century, the classical curriculum was an essential component of higher education (Thelin, 2003). But in 1862, Congress passed the Morrill Land Grant Act, which provided 30,000 acres of public land for the establishment and support of state universities focusing on agricultural and mechanical arts (Fenske, 1989). Those publicly supported colleges did not gain momentum until after 1900, when "legislatures in the Midwest and West started to embrace and financially support the idea of a great university as a symbol of state pride" (Thelin, 2003, p. 12).

Between 1870 and 1910, the modern American university developed along one of two tracks: the German higher education model of research, advanced scholarship, and graduate education or the more traditional model of maintaining the liberal arts undergraduate education (Thelin, 1996, 2003). Institutional size remained generally small; only a few (such as Harvard, Columbia, and the University of Pennsylvania) enrolled more than 5,000 students (Thelin, 1996, 2003).

After World War I, colleges began take on different institutional purposes. Public junior colleges emerged, as did more state normal schools (or teachers' colleges), and technical institutes (Thelin, 2003; 1996). A few of the land grant state universities in the Midwest and West enrolled 15,000 to 20,000, but the majority of universities in the United States still had fewer than 5,000 students (Thelin, 2003; 1996).

World War II is considered a turning point in American higher education, as hordes of veterans returned to the United States and were given federal scholarships for postsecondary education to keep the labor market from being oversaturated (Thelin, 2003; 1996). The Servicemen's Readjustment Act, otherwise known as the G.I. Bill, created portable government student aid, and spurred a tremendous influx of students onto college campuses (Thelin, 2003; 1996).

During the 1960s, the U.S. government passed several initiatives including the 1964 Civil Rights Act, funding for student financial aid, and the Higher Education Facilities Act (Thelin, 2003; 1996). With the explosion of the baby boomers attending college, institutions of higher education evolved to include multicampus university systems and more branch campuses, teachers' colleges, and public community colleges (Thelin, 2003; 1996). By 1972, the federal government focused on increased opportunities for students on college campuses, creating large-scale entitlements for student financial aid (Thelin, 2003; 1996). The issue of access to higher education became more important, with more loan programs, work study opportunities, and institutional funds for scholarships (Thelin, 2003; 1996).

In the 1980s, the states led the movement to focus on student outcomes and accountability (McGuinness, 2001). Since then, the focus on accountability of higher education has sharpened as state and federal funds have been pressed for other purposes. An abrupt downturn in revenues for higher education in the early 1990s marked the start of a steady reduction in the percentage of state revenues at institutions (McGuinness, 2001). McGuinness (2001) suggests that relations between higher education and state government are likely to be especially strained into the next decade, given the trends of escalating demands, severe economic constraints, inherent resistance to change, negative public opinion, and the instability of state political leadership.

Diversity of Institutions in the United States

Higher education institutions differ widely in history, culture, mission, and traditions, as well as size, reputation, resources, geographic region, and academic specialization. Institutions also fit into other categories, such as two-year and four-year colleges, historically Black colleges and universities, Hispanic-serving institutions, tribal colleges and universities, religiously affiliated schools, women's colleges, and for-profit institutions (Dungy, 2003). Student affairs divisions are organized with different missions depending on the type of institution they serve.

Emergence of the Profession of Student Affairs in the United States

Student affairs functions emerged on college campuses after World War I (Nuss, 1996, 2003). Early student affairs professionals sought to provide educational services that focused on the whole student (Creamer, Winston, & Miller, 2001). The original functions included vocational guidance, career placement, and data collection on students' interests (Nuss, 1996). There wasn't a national norm of the roles, organizations, or job titles of student affairs professionals during the early 20th century, but rather the personalities of the individuals and the history and mission of the institutions determined the range of student affairs (Nuss, 1996, 2003; Williamson, 1961). Student affairs professionals and colleges acted in the place of parents—in loco parentis (Creamer, Winston, & Miller, 2001).

The 1937 report *Student Personnel Point of View* is considered to be the most important document in describing the functions of student affairs and demonstrating the appropriate relationship between student affairs and other parts of higher education (Creamer, Winston, & Miller, 2001). This document was the essential source of guidance for student affairs professionals. It focused on more than just the academic performance of the college student: "The concept of education is broadened to include attention to the student's well rounded development—physically, socially, emotionally, and spirituality, as well as intellectually" (American Council on Education, 1994a, p. 109). The 1949 revision (1994b) continued to broaden the means for student growth, as well as the fundamental elements of a student personnel program. The concepts in both reports continue today as a philosophical guide for student affairs professionals (Nuss, 1996).

Most U.S. institutions created two parallel student affairs organizations based on gender, led by a dean of men and a dean of women (Sandeen, 2001). From 1910 until about 1960, these positions were the standard organizational structure in student affairs, assuming that different poli-

cies and procedures were necessary for men and women Several services were duplicated under this arrangement, and it also reinforced a secondary role for women who were often excluded from many opportunities on campus (Sandeen, 2001).

Campus life changed with the huge enrollment boom after World War II as the institutions were forced to accommodate massive influxes of students (Sandeen, 2001; Thelin, 1996, 2003). Higher education—including student affairs—changed dramatically in the two decades after World War II as social, economic, and political forces combined to shift society in the United States (Sandeen, 2001). In the 1960s, issues such as opposition to the Vietnam War combined with new voting rights for 18-year-olds caused widespread disruption as students questioned the role of higher education institutions to serve *in loco parentis* (Sandeen, 2001). Student affairs professionals were given the opportunity to manage the protests and disruptions on campuses and were frequently hired specifically to handle such issues (Sandeen, 2001).

In the late 1960s, the federal courts ruled in *Dixon v. Alabama* that students retain full citizenship rights after they enroll in college (Creamer, Winston, & Miller, 2001). That ended the concept that colleges and student affairs professionals were acting *in loco parentis* (Creamer, Winston, & Miller, 2001).

At the same time at state universities, several traditional student affairs departments had become very large, and a new set of services had evolved from student demands, additional fees, or new legislation (Sandeen, 2001). New services such as financial aid, orientation, academic support services, and recreational sports were added to the traditional student affairs roles of admissions, housing, registration, counseling, and job placement (Sandeen, 2001).

In addition, the traditional roles of deans of men and deans of women were becoming irrelevant to the current culture of the campuses, and in the early 1960s, many institutions consolidated their student affairs divisions with a senior administrative officer who reported to the president (Sandeen, 2001). The various departments were led by directors or deans who reported to that senior student affairs officer and who managed the policies, services, and programs attached to that department (Sandeen, 2001). This structure has remained essentially in place in the United States and has given credence and prominence to the division of student affairs within each institution (Sandeen, 2001).

Student affairs expanded in the 1960s and 1970s because institutions offered solid financial support and because faculty was not interested in student life (Sandeen, 2001). At many institutions, the number of student affairs professionals doubled and tripled in areas seen as necessary to support students (Sandeen, 2001). But in the mid-1970s, financial constraints tightened with inflation and relatively flat enrollments to institutions, so student affairs had to manage essential services with fewer resources (Sandeen, 2001). Student affairs divisions turned to student fees and other fundraising activities to support their efforts, including turning some departments into self-sufficient auxiliary functions (Sandeen, 2001). It was during this time that the institutional priorities began to shape the structure of the student affairs organization, and the senior student affairs officer would face consolidation of departments and the need to lobby the president on student issues (Sandeen, 2001).

As the profession of student affairs matured, practitioners were often turned to for assistance with problem solving on campus and would be asked to manage additional responsibilities, such as intercollegiate athletics, campus bus service, police departments, academic advising, and other areas (Sandeen, 2001). The student affairs organization became a major part of the general administration and educational program of the university (Sandeen, 2001). In the 1990s, growing scrutiny of student affairs resulting in several functions, such as admissions, financial aid, or registration, to shift to other institutional offices, usually reporting to the provost or another vice president (Sandeen, 2001).

Sandeen (2001) states that these changes were caused by the changed expectations and new perceptions of student affairs by those external to the division. Further, he notes that the structure of a student affairs division in a U.S. institution of higher learning is affected by the institutional mission and culture, the professional background of the student affairs staff, student characteristics, presidents and senior academic officers, academic organization, financial resources, technology, and legislation and court decisions (2001).

Functions and Roles of Student Affairs in the United States

Despite wide variations among institutions, college campuses across the country tend to have many of the same student affairs functions (Sandeen, 1996). Student affairs functions have become highly professionalized and specialized in the past 25 years, resulting in improved quality of staff and effectiveness of services (Sandeen, 1996). Dungy (2003) lists several core functions of student services in the United States: academic advising; admissions; assessment, research, and program evaluation; athletics; campus safety; career development; college or student unions; community service and service learning programs; commuter services and off-campus housing; counseling and psychological services; dean of students office; dining and food services; disability support services; enrollment management; financial aid; fundraising and fund development; graduate and professional services; Greek affairs; health services; international student services; judicial affairs; leadership programs; lesbian, gay, bisexual, and transgender (LGBT) services; multicultural student services; orientation and new student programs; recreation and fitness programs; religious programs and services; registration services; residence life and housing; student activities; and women's centers. Sandeen (1996) notes many of those areas have developed their own pro-

fessional associations, creating less communication among those areas.

Creamer, Winston, and Miller (2001) note that student affairs professionals include entry-level staff members who provide direct educational service to students, mid-level supervisors of complex functional areas, and executive-level managers with direct responsibilities for supervising other educators and staff members and managing multimillion dollar budgets. In addition, some student affairs professionals may be functional specialists, and others are more generalists. Even though student affairs professionals have their responsibilities in non-classroom settings, they still have the same commitments to educate students as do faculty (Creamer, Winston, & Miller, 2001). Student affairs professionals are undertaking a growing number of administrative functions due to increased numbers and diversity of students and the addition of more educational functions at institutions (Creamer, Winston, & Miller, 2001).

Organization of Student Affairs Divisions

As campuses change, the organizational model may shift to suit the institution. The institutional mission, culture, traditions, and background of each institution determine the organizational structure of the student affairs division (Sandeen, 1996; 2001). For example, if a college's mission is to educate underprivileged students, their recruitment, financial aid, and retention programs would be likely to have more staff and resources (Sandeen, 1996; 2001). Other factors that affect the organization of a student affairs division on a college campus are the professional background of the student affairs staff, student characteristics, the presidents and senior academic officers, the academic organization, financial resources, technology, and legislation and court decisions (Sandeen, 1996; 2001).

Three examples of student affairs divisions in the United States are discussed below.

A medium-sized public community college, Guilford Technical Community College, located in Jamestown, North Carolina, has 11,657 students enrolled in curriculum programs. (See the college's organizational chart, Figure 23.1.) As of 2005, 73% of the students worked either part time or full time. Guilford Tech has a dean of student support services, who coordinates job placement, testing and assessment, and international student affairs, as well as supervising a director of student life and a director of counseling. The unit is called Educational Support Services, reflecting its focus on services and support for its part-time students. (Guilford Technical Community College, http://www.gtcc.edu/, retrieved June 30, 2005). The senior student affairs officer is at the same level as the senior officers in enrollment services, continuing education and auditing, and institutional research and planning; they all report to the vice president of educational support services.

A small, private college, Rollins College, is located in Winter Park, Florida, and has 3,726 undergraduate students enrolled in arts and sciences. (See Figure 23.2 for organizational chart.) Their student affairs division is "committed to making the academic experience of arts and sciences students rewarding and enriching," as it is complementary to the academic focus of the liberal arts institution (Rollins College, http://www.rollins.edu/, retrieved June 30, 2005). The goals of the division reflect the national trend of focusing on learning outcomes.

A medium-sized public university, the University of Mississippi, is a four-year research institution with its main campus in Oxford, Mississippi. The student population is 16,500 students. (See organizational chart, Figure 23.3.) The services provided through their student affairs division include many of the typical services at these institutions: career services, international programs, student health services, orientation, campus programming, dean of students, and admissions (University of Mississippi, retrieved July 5, 2005, http://www.olemiss.edu). At the University of Mississippi, the vice chancellor for student life reports to the provost; however, many divisions of student affairs at large public research institutions also report directly to the president, depending on that specific institution's mission and culture. Figure 23.3 shows an example of an organizational chart for a medium size public university.

Student Affairs Professional Associations

Because student affairs was originally a field organized by gender, professional associations for student affairs developed separately for men and women (Nuss, 1996). Further, most professional associations were segregated by race, preventing full participation of racial minorities in these organizations (Nuss, 1996). Separate organizations for minorities were founded in 1929 and 1935.

The first association for deans of women was established in 1916, and the vast majority of the early membership came from the northeast and Midwest (Bashaw, 1992; Nuss, 1996). The organization evolved, with several name changes and role changes, until membership dwindled and, as the National Association for Women in Education, it was dissolved in 2000 (Nuss, 1996).

In 1919, the National Association of Deans and Advisers of Men (NADAM) was founded, and in 1951 the organization changed its name to the National Association of Student Personnel Administrators (NASPA). That name change helped to expand the organization, and NASPA began to recruit new members (Nuss, 1996). Although a few women joined the organization, it was not until 1958 that a woman was an institutional representative of NASPA; women did not hold office or participate actively in NASPA until the mid-1960s (Nuss, 1996). Today, more women than men are members of NASPA (E. SolynJohn, personal communication, February 14, 2005).

The American College Personnel Association (ACPA) evolved from organizations related to job placement and guidance. It was founded in 1924 as the National Association of Appointment Secretaries (NAAS) and adopted its current name in 1931 (Nuss, 1996).

As other student affairs roles developed on campuses, professional organizations were created, including the Association of Colleges Unions International (ACUI) in 1910, the American Association of Collegiate Registrars and Admissions Officers (AACRAO) in 1910, the American College Health Association (ACHA) in 1920, and the National Orientation Directors Association (NODA) in 1937 (Nuss, 1996). Today, most functional areas have their own professional association, and ACPA and NASPA are considered the two major professional associations for student affairs.

Both ACPA and NASPA have started using their acronyms, rather than their original names, with taglines that help to better define their organizations (G. Dungy, personal communication, June 21, 2005). ACPA's tagline is College Student Educators International (ACPA), and NASPA's is Student Affairs Administrators in Higher Education (G. Dungy, personal communication, June 21, 2005).

Professional Preparation for Student Affairs

Columbia University's Teachers College began the first formal program of study in vocational guidance for student affairs practitioners, offering the first professional diploma for an "Adviser for Women" in conjunction with an MA degree in 1914 (Nuss, 1996). Currently there are more than 150 graduate preparation programs for student affairs in the United States (ACPA, 2005). To train the profession, individuals typically attend a master's degree preparatory program in student affairs (McEwen & Talbot, 1998). The purpose of those programs is to prepare competently trained professionals to perform the wide spectrum of practice in student affairs on the college campus (McEwen & Talbot, 1998).

According to McEwen and Talbot (1998), the curriculum for the master's degree level for student affairs professionals in higher education should have two objectives: "(a) to provide thorough theoretical background and knowledge related to understanding students, higher education, and the practice of student affairs, and (b) to develop effective student affairs practitioners through guided and supervised experiences in student affairs" (p. 128).

The professional studies component of graduate programs deals with the core knowledge student affairs professionals need, which includes understanding and knowing students, student populations, and the demographics of who attends college and how those students develop and learn in college (McEwen & Talbot, 1998). Appropriate student development theories include psychosocial development, identity development, and campus ecology theories (McEwen & Talbot, 1998).

Figure 23.1. Guilford Technical Community College – Educational Support Services.

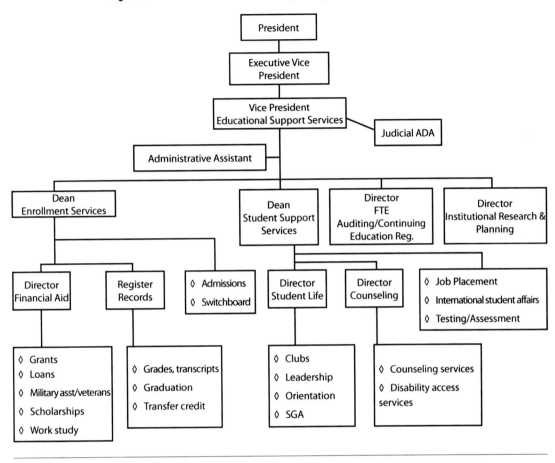

Professional Standards for Student Affairs

In 1979, the Council for the Advancement of Standards in Higher Education (CAS) was organized to establish professional standards for student affairs (Nuss, 1996). In 1986, the council published the first CAS Standards and Guidelines for 19 functional areas of higher education programs in services. As of 2001, CAS has developed 28 sets of functional area standards and guidelines and one set of student affairs master's level preparation standards (CAS, 2005). Today, there are 37 CAS member organizations making up a professional constituency of more than 100,000 professionals in higher education (CAS, 2005).

Relationship between Student Affairs and Academic Affairs

The relationship between student affairs and academic affairs has become a focus of the student affairs literature. A strong relationship is encouraged (Lamadrid, 2003; Schuh & Whitt, 1999). Schroeder (2005) notes that even though the connection was not encouraged in the past, it is necessary in order to achieve student learning. He points out that there are common challenges for both student affairs and academic affairs, such as low retention and graduation rates, campus climate issues for students of color, academic dishonesty, and more.

Those relationships are sometimes built out of necessity, and there has been a dramatic increase in the number of such partnerships over the past 20 years (Upcraft, Gardner, & Barefoot, 2005). The relationship often depends on the personalities and backgrounds of the individuals as well as the size and type of institution (Grund, 2004). Often, it is perceived that academic affairs holds all of the power and there are few incentives for faculty to collaborate with student affairs (Grund, 2004). Further, vice presidents for academic affairs, or provosts, are often left to manage the entire university campus while the president is unavailable. Consequently, provosts are supervising more nonacademic areas including student affairs (Grund, 2004).

Schroeder (2005) and Schuh (2005) call for a redefinition of student affairs to be able to more successfully part-

Figure 23.2. Rollins College – Division of Student Affairs.

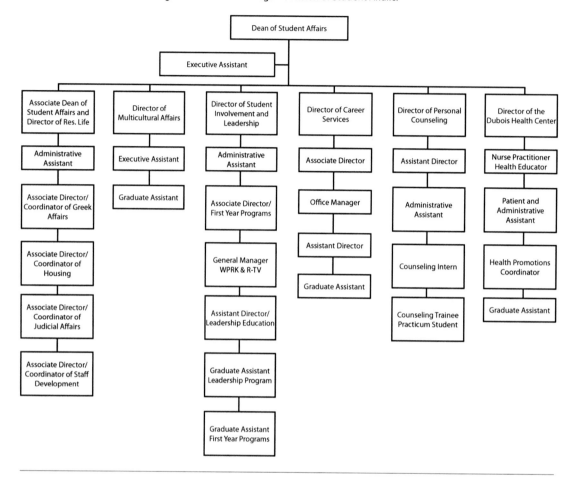

ner with academic affairs to enhance student learning and success.[1]

The Relationship with the Government

Over the past 30 years, mandates from the U.S. government have not only created additional work but have also affected the priorities and budgets of higher education institutions. For example, the G.I. Bill created massive influxes of students to colleges through the 1970s. As a result, housing construction began on campuses with federal support, particularly focusing on building high-rise residence halls (Nuss, 1996).

Section 504 of the Rehabilitation Act (1973) and The Americans with Disabilities Act (ADA) required colleges and universities to spend funds to accommodate physical, emotional, and learning disabilities of its students and employees (Gehring, 2001; Woodard, 2001). Students with a wide range of disabilities attend college in the United States, including those with learning disabilities, hearing or sight impairment, health-related disabilities, and others (Schuh, 2005). As a result of the federal legislation, the participation of students with disabilities has increased dramatically; they now account for approximately 9% of all first-year students entering college in the United States (Schuh, 2005).

The Family Educational Rights and Privacy Act (FERPA, or the Buckley Amendment), passed in 1974, protects educational records from parents or other parties other than students (Gehring, 2001). Originally designed to keep student records from being disclosed without authorization, this federal law prohibits the disclosure of disciplinary records as well as academic records (Gehring, 2001).

---

[1]They cite the Student Learning Imperative (1996) as a source calling for a reexamination of how student affairs operates, so that student affairs would seek specific student learning and personal development outcomes with its programs and services (American College Personnel Association, 1996; Schroeder, 2005; Schuh, 2005). Other publications that encourage the development of stronger relationships between student affairs and academic affairs, specifically focusing on the promotion of learning, include *Principles of Good Practice for Student Affairs* (Blimling, Whitt, et al., 1999) and *Learning Reconsidered: A Campus-Wide Focus on Student Experience* (Keeling, 2004). The latter publication is "an argument for the integrated use of all of higher education's resources in the education and preparation of the whole student" (Keeling, 2004, p. 1).

Other federal laws that affect student affairs include Title IX, which prohibits discrimination based on gender, and the Student Right-to-Know and Campus Security Act, which requires disclosure of crime statistics on campus (Dungy, 2003; Woodard, 2001).

Resources of Student Affairs

Woodard (2001) describes the budget as "the single most important work tool the student affairs administrator uses in developing and implementing activities to meet agreed-upon program activities and outcomes" (p. 245). Financial support of institutions of higher education has moved away from direct funding by governmental sources, such as federal or state dollars. Johnstone (2001) states that many colleges and universities have been "coping with almost perpetual financial challenges, constantly cutting, reallocating, downsizing, outsourcing, and chasing new revenues" (p. 145). Private institutions rely for their income on the tuition paid by the students, but net tuition revenue for many private colleges has not been rising as quickly as the costs (Johnstone, 2001). Increasingly, the costs of higher education are borne by the student and are creating a tighter budget for all of the management of the university. At the same time, there is the perception that the price of college in the United States is too high (Johnstone, 2001).

With less access to funds and less reliance on public financial support, fundraising efforts are becoming a more crucial part of the university's budget Fundraising efforts have become more prominent in student affairs; funds are typically targeted through annual gifts and the support of specific programs by donors (Dungy, 2003).

Research on College Students

The impact of college on students has proven to be a popular source of research for the student affairs profession. For example, Feldman and Newcomb's 1969 work, *The Impact of College on Students*, reviews the research of more than 1,500 studies (Nuss, 1996). The Higher Education Research Institute has been collecting data about incoming freshmen and providing longitudinal studies marking national trends with the Annual Survey of American College Freshmen since 1966 (Upcraft, 2005).

More recently, the level of engagement has become a focus for student affairs, showing that a key factor in student success is student engagement (Kuh, 2005). Kuh (2005) defines student engagement as

> ...the amount of time and effort students put into their studies and other educationally purposeful activities...and how a school deploys its resources and organizes the curriculum, other learning opportunities, and support services to induce students to participate in activities that lead to the experiences and outcomes that constitute student success, persistence, satisfaction, learning, and graduation. (p. 87)

Kuh's (2005) research includes developing the instruments of the College Student Expectations Questionnaire

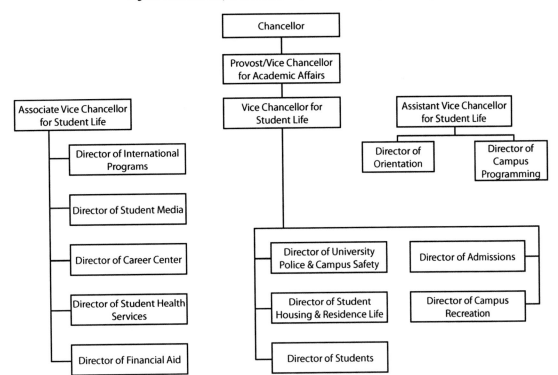

Figure 23.3. University of Mississippi organizational chart (Oxford Campus).

(CSXQ) and the National Survey of Student Engagement (NSSE), both of which measure expectations of college and experiences in college. These instruments are being used at various colleges and universities for institutional research for internal assessment as well as for comparisons to similar institutions.

Contemporary Issues Facing Student Affairs in the United States

Increasing Student Diversity

The demographic profile of the college student is changing dramatically, with a growth or increase in visibility of student subpopulations, including: students who speak English as a second language; students who have psychological or physical disabilities; students who affiliate with a wide range of religions; students of ethnic minorities; international students; lesbian, gay, bisexual, or transgender students; women; and adult learners (Talbot, 2003).

The age of the average college student has risen: 28% of all undergraduate students were 25 or older in the 2002–03 academic year (Ishler, 2005). More women than men now attend college in the United States (56%), and women also tend to graduate at higher rates than men (Ishler, 2005). Gay, lesbian, bisexual, and transgender students are also becoming more visible on college campuses, making up approximately 7% of the student population (Ishler, 2005).

A major shift in college demographics is that non-White students will become the majority on many campuses (Dixon, 2001). It is expected that college enrollment of Hispanic students will increase by 73% and African American students by 23% between 1995 and 2015 (Carnevale, 1999). The type of institution that a student attends often varies by the race/ethnicity of the student. Minority students make up a higher proportion of the student enrollment at public, two-year colleges compared to White students (Ishler, 2005). Further, these increases are felt most strongly at community colleges and public institutions, usually in states adjacent to México or in states that have a large influx of immigrants, such as Florida, California, and New York (Talbot, 2003).

Despite these various demographic shifts, student affairs professionals have continued to be predominately White, and students in the professional training programs tend to be female (Mueller & Pope, 2001; Talbot, 1996).

Campus Climate Issues on Campus

Implications of an increasingly diverse student body include tensions, conflicts, overt racism, alienation, discrimination, and potentially unwelcoming environments on college campuses (Boyer, 1993; Levine, 1993; Levine & Cureton, 1998). Racial incidents and conflicts, racial and sexual harassment, and hate crimes based on race, ethnicity, and sexual orientation all continue to be reported in the national media and the *Chronicle of Higher Education* (Moore & Carter, 2002; Sanlo, Rankin, & Schoenberg, 2002; Talbot, 1992). Since the events of September 11, 2001, there

has been increased scrutiny of international students who study in the United States, and the federal government is placing additional responsibilities on colleges and universities to monitor those students solely because of their ethnic background and country of origin (Arnone, 2002). Student affairs professionals are increasingly asked to address issues of diversity and multiculturalism on campus (Levine, 1993; McEwen & Roper, 1994).

More Active Parents of Traditional-Age Students

In the Unites States, parents are active in their traditional-age student's college experience, as they have been involved advocates in their activities throughout the 12 grades of school (Mullendore & Banahan, 2005). The parents of today's students interact with college staff and faculty much more frequently and for different reasons than previous generations (Keppler, Mullendore, & Carey, 2005). More families attend and are involved in orientation, as they seek a better knowledge of the new college environment (Mullendore & Banahan, 2005). Keppler, Mullendore, & Carey (2005) recommend that student affairs professionals provide opportunities for parents to participate in the college experience, with a result of increased student success, institutional financial support, and enhanced public relations.

Shifts in American Public Policy

Accountability and consumer-focused legislation has marked the past 20 years in the United States, with criticism of American public education and calls for reform to demonstrate effectiveness and efficiency (Dungy, 2003; Thelin, 2003). The 1990 Student Right-to-Know and Campus Security Act created much more information available to students as consumers. Parents, politicians, and the local community have demanded more centralized decision making and more accountability (Dungy, 2003).

The 1990s marked an emphasis on organizational change of institutions of higher education with the goal of accountability (Dungy, 2003). Student affairs has traditionally been a distinct unit with the senior student affairs administrator reporting to the president. However, changes have been occurring nationally to have a department that is a combination of academic affairs and student affairs and that reports directly to the academic vice president (Dungy, 2003; Grund, 2004).

Financial Constraints on Higher Education

Both federal and state resources have shifted away from higher education over the past 20 years (Woodard and Komives, 2003). After World War II, the race to compete with the Russians and the competition in science and technology spurred the federal government to support higher education with tremendous sums. However, since the mid-1970s, when this massive support began to slow, there have been challenges of fiscal constraints (Love and Estanek, 2004). At the end of the recession at the end of the 1980s, even states with traditional records of support, including California,

Massachusetts, and New York, drastically cut financial support for public higher education (Love and Estanek, 2004). At the same time, student avenues for attending college began to focus more on the use of loans rather than grants or scholarships. This decline in financial support has affected student affairs divisions.

Assessment of Student Affairs

The issue of assessing the outcomes of student affairs practice has become part of the current literature, with several publications and meetings focused on assessment. Data are collected about students at each institution, including demographics, grades, test scores, and graduation rates (Dungy, 2003). Upcraft (2003) stated that assessment for student affairs can "improve the quality of student services and programs, guide strategic planning, analyze cost effectiveness, justify student programs and services, assist in accreditation, and more importantly, guide decision making, policies, and practices" (p. 555). Regular professional development opportunities exist with NASPA which encourage the development of assessment skills for student affairs professionals.

Conclusion

The rapid change in student demographics will provide American colleges and universities with a new challenge as a diverse student body enrolls in the future. Student affairs has the opportunity and expertise to guide this change on campus. The continual evolution of higher education in the United States will continue to affect the way student affairs matures as a profession. Also, student affairs today will be affected by trends in public policy and state and f ederal government.

References

American Council on Education. (1994a). The student personnel point of view. In A. L. Rentz, (Ed.), *Student affairs: A profession's heritage* (American College Personnel Association Media Publication No. 40, 2nd ed., pp. 66–77). Lanham, MD: University Press of America. (Original work published 1937).

American Council on Education. (1994b). The student personnel point of view. In A. L. Rentz, (Ed.), *Student affairs: A profession's heritage* (American College Personnel Association Media Publication No. 40, 2nd ed., pp. 108–123). Lanham, MD: University Press of America. (Original work published 1949).

Arnone, M. (2002, September 6). Colleges expect the worst in preparing for new system to track foreign students. *Chronicle of Higher Education*, p.A33.

Bashaw, C. T. (1992). *We who live "off the edges": Deans of women at Southern coeducational institutions and access to the community of higher education, 1907-1960*. Unpublished doctoral dissertation: University of Georgia, Athens.

Blimling, G. S., Whitt, E. J., & Associates. (1999). *Good practice in student affairs*. San Francisco: Jossey-Bass.

Boyer, E. L. (1993). Campus climate in the 1980's and 1990's: Decades of apathy and renewal. In A. Levine (Ed.), *Higher learning in America: 1980–2000* (pp. 322–332). Baltimore: Johns Hopkins University Press.

Council for the Advancement of Standards in Higher Education (CAS). *Twenty Five Years of Professional Services*. Retrieved May 23, 2005, from http://www.cas.edu

Creamer, D. G., Winston, R. B. Jr., & Miller, T. K. (2001). The professional student affairs administrator: Roles and functions. In R. B. Winston, Jr., D. G. Creamer, T. K. Miller, & Associates (Eds.), *The professional student affairs administrator: Educator, leader, and manager* (pp. 3-38). New York: Brunner-Routledge.

Dixon, B. (2001). Student affairs in an increasingly multicultural world. In R. B. Winston, Jr., D. G. Creamer, T. K. Miller, & Associates (Eds.), *The professional student affairs administrator: Educator, leader, and manager* (pp. 65–80). New York: Brunner-Routledge.

Dungy, G. J. (2003). Organization and functions of student affairs. In S. R., Komives, D. B. Woodard Jr., & Associates (Eds.), *Student services: A handbook for the profession* (4th ed.). pp. 339–357. San Francisco: Jossey-Bass.

Fenske, R. H. (1989). Historical foundations of student services. In U. Delworth, G. R. Hanson, & Associates (Eds.), *Student services: A handbook for the profession* (2nd ed.). San Francisco: Jossey-Bass.

Gardner, J. N., Upcraft, M. L., & Barefoot, B. O. (2005). Conclusion: Principles of good practice for the first college year and summary of recommendations. In M. L. Upcraft, J. N. Gardner, & B. O. Barefoot (Eds.), *Challenging and supporting the first-year student: A handbook for improving the first year of college* (pp. 515–524). San Francisco: Jossey-Bass.

Gehring, D. D. (2001). Legal parameters for student affairs practice. In R. B. Winston, Jr., D. G. Creamer, T. K. Miller, & Associates (Eds.), *The professional student affairs administrator: Educator, leader, and manager* (pp. 107–152). New York: Brunner-Routledge.

Grund, N. (2004, Winter). Partnering with academic affairs: Reporting to your provost. *Leadership Exchange*, 10–13.

Ishler, J. L. (2005). Today's first-year students. In M. L. Upcraft, J. N. Gardner, & B. O. Barefoot (Eds.), *Challenging and supporting the first-year student: A handbook for improving the first year of college* (pp. 15–26). San Francisco: Jossey-Bass.

Johnstone, D. B. (2001). Higher education and those "out of control costs." In P. G. Altbach, P. J. Gumport, & D. B. Johnstone (Eds.), *In defense of American higher education* (pp. 144–178). Baltimore, MD: Johns Hopkins University Press.

Keppler, K., Mullendore, R. H., & Carey, A. (2005). *Partnering with the parents of today's college students*. Washington, DC: NASPA.

Kuh, G. D. (2005). Student engagement in the first year of college. In M. L. Upcraft, J. N. Gardner, & B. O. Barefoot (Eds.), *Challenging and supporting the first-year student: A handbook for improving the first year of college* (pp. 86–107). San Francisco: Jossey-Bass.

Lamadrid, L. (2003). *Advancing the student affairs link with academic affairs*. Washington, DC: NASPA.

Levine, A. (1993). Diversity on campus. In A. Levine (Ed.), *Higher learning in America: 1980-2000*. (pp. 333–343). Baltimore: Johns Hopkins University Press.

Levine, A., & Cureton, J. S. (1998). *When hope and fear collide*. San Francisco: Jossey-Bass.

Love, P.G., & Estanek, S.M. (2004). *Rethinking student affairs practice*. San Francisco: Jossey-Bass.

McEwen, M. K., & Roper, L. (1994). Incorporating multiculturalism into student affairs preparation programs: Suggestions from the literature. *Journal of College Student Development, 35*, 46–53.

McEwen, M. K., & Talbot, D. M. (1998). Designing the student affairs curriculum. In N. J. Evans and C. E. Phelps Tobin (Eds.), *The state of the art of preparation and practice in student affairs* (pp. 125–156). Lanham, MD: University Press of America Inc.

Moore, B. L., & Carter, A. W. (2002). Creating community in a complex research university environment. In W. M. McDonald and Associates (Eds.), *Creating campus community: In search of Ernest Boyer's legacy* (pp. 21–68). San Francisco: Jossey-Bass.

Mueller, J. A., & Pope, R. L. (2001). The relationship between multicultural competence and white racial consciousness among student affairs practitioners. *Journal of College Student Development, 42*, 133–144.

Mullendore, R. H., & Banahan, L. A. (2005). Designing orientation programs. In M. L. Upcraft, J. N. Gardner, & B. O. Barefoot (Eds.), *Challenging and supporting the first-year student: A handbook for improving the first year of college* (pp. 391–409). San Francisco: Jossey-Bass.

Keeling, R.P. (Ed.). (2004). *Learning reconsidered: A campus-wide focus on the student experience*. Washington, DC: ACPA & NASPA.

Nuss, E.M. (1996). The development of student affairs. In S. R., Komives, D. B.Woodard Jr., & Associates (Eds.), *Student services: A handbook for the profession* (3rd ed.). pp. 22–42. San Francisco: Jossey-Bass.

Nuss, E. M. (2003). The development of student affairs. In S. R., Komives, D. B.Woodard Jr., & Associates (Eds.), *Student services: A handbook for the profession* (4th ed.). pp. 65–88. San Francisco: Jossey-Bass.

Sandeen, A. (1996). Organization, functions, and standards of practice. In S. R., Komives, D. B.Woodard Jr., & Associates (Eds.), *Student services: A handbook for the profession* (3rd ed.). pp. 435–457. San Francisco: Jossey-Bass.

Sandeen, A. (2001). Organizing student affairs divisions. In R. B. Winston, Jr., D. G. Creamer, T. K. Miller, & Associates (Eds.), *The professional student affairs administrator: Educator, leader, and manager* (pp. 181–209). New York: Brunner-Routledge.

Sanlo, R., Rankin, S., & Schoenberg, R. (2002). *Our place on campus: Lesbian, gay, bisexual, and transgender services and programs in higher education*. Westport, CT: Greenwood Press.

Schroeder, C.C. (2005). Collaborative partnerships between academic and student affairs. In M. L. Upcraft, J. N. Gardner, & B. O. Barefoot (Eds.), *Challenging and supporting the first-year student: A handbook for improving the first year of college* (pp. 204–220). San Francisco: Jossey-Bass.

Schuh, J. H. (2005). Student support services. In M. L. Upcraft, J. N. Gardner, & B. O. Barefoot (Eds.), *Challenging and supporting the first-year student: A handbook for improving the first year of college* (pp. 428–444). San Francisco: Jossey-Bass.

Schuh, J.H., & Whitt, E. J. (1999). *Creating successful partnerships between academic and student affairs*. San Francisco: Jossey-Bass.

Talbot, D. M. (1992). A multimethod study of the diversity emphasis in master's degree programs in college student affairs. *Dissertation Abstracts International, 53*(7), 2198. (UMI No. 9234669).

Talbot, D. M. (1996). Master's students' perspectives on their graduate education regarding issues of diversity. *NASPA Journal, 33*, 163–78.

Thelin, J. R. (1996). The historical overview of American higher education. In S. R., Komives, D. B.Woodard Jr., & Associates (Eds.), *Student services: A handbook for the profession* (3rd ed.). pp. 3–21. San Francisco: Jossey-Bass.

Thelin, J. R. (2003). The historical overview of American higher education. In S. R., Komives, D. B.Woodard Jr., & Associates (Eds.), *Student services: A handbook for the profession* (4th ed.). pp 3–22. San Francisco: Jossey-Bass.

Upcraft, M. L. (2005). Assessing the first year of college. In M. L. Upcraft, J. N. Gardner, & B. O. Barefoot (Eds.), *Challenging and supporting the first-year student: A handbook for improving the first year of college* (pp. 469–485). San Francisco: Jossey-Bass.

Upcraft, M. L. (2003). Assessment and evaluation. In S. R., Komives, D. B.Woodard Jr., & Associates (Eds.), *Student services: A handbook for the profession* (4th ed) (pp. 555–572). San Francisco: Jossey-Bass.

Williamson, E. G. (1961). *Student personnel services in colleges and universities*. New York: McGraw-Hill.

Woodard, D. B. (2001). Finance and budgeting. In R. B. Winston, Jr., D. G. Creamer, T. K. Miller, & Associates (Eds.), *The professional student affairs administrator: Educator, leader, and manager* (pp. 245–267). New York: Brunner-Routledge.

Woodard, D. B., & Komives, S. R. (2003). Shaping the future. In S. R., Komives, D. B.Woodard Jr., & Associates (Eds.), *Student services: A handbook for the profession* (4th ed). (pp. 637–655). San Francisco: Jossey-Bass.

TWENTY-FOUR
SEMESTER AT SEA

The author shares her experience as a student affairs professional during the summer of 2003. She discusses staffing and compares life at sea versus that of a land-based campus. The author also explores how this experience affected not only the students, but her own professional growth and development.

...

Semester at Sea

Semester at Sea (SAS) is a study-abroad program, but with a difference: The journey is as important as the destinations. Faculty and undergraduate students study and learn as they sail around the world each semester. Their home is the *Explorer*, which circumnavigates the globe twice a year (in the fall and spring) and embarks on a regional route in the summer. More than 48,000 alumni of the program have made ports of call in the Middle East (Egypt and Israel), the Far East (China, Vietnam, and Korea), Europe (Spain, Greece, and Russia), Africa (Morocco), and the Americas (Venezuela). They have also visited Cuba, Turkey, Japan, the Philippines, India, Cypress, and Australia, among other countries.

In the spring and fall, voyages last 100 days—50 at sea and 50 in port. The 700 students and 40 faculty and staff (from 250 different universities) spend from three to five days in each of 10 countries. In recent years, students took a 12-credit load (9 credits in summer) from a choice of 80 classes approved by the College of Arts and Sciences at the University of Virginia, and those credits are fully transferable to the student's home institution. The liberal arts curriculum includes classes in architecture, world music, politics, sociology, women's studies, business, geography, and theater arts. (Starting in September 2006, academic sponsorship passed to the University of Virginia.)

For example, the fall 2008 voyage set sail August 29 in Nassau, the Bahamas, and headed south then east to visit Brazil, Namibia, India, Malaysia, Vietnam, Hong Kong, China, Japan, Hawaii, and Costa Rica. The voyage ended on December 14 in Miami, Florida. The summer voyages last 65 days, and regional destinations have included the South and Central America, the Pacific Rim and Europe. Each voyage provides the students, faculty, and staff with an opportunity to reflect, question, and synthesize world experiences through faculty- and staff-led excursions in various ports and the Global Studies course.

Brief History

The first voyage on the *SS Ryndam*, under the name of the University World Cruise, was in 1926. Because of the Great Depression and world war that followed, the next voyage was not until 1963, when a group of California businessmen launched the University of Seven Seas program. Subsequent academic sponsorship devolved to Chapman University, the University of Colorado, the University of Pittsburgh, and, from September 2006, the University of Virginia. Since 1976, a nonprofit corporation, the Institute for Shipboard Education, has had administrative oversight. This corporation named the program Semester at Sea. The current ship, the *Explorer*, is a 24,300-ton motor vessel equipped with classrooms, library, student union, wireless Internet, campus store, fitness center, and two dining rooms. Built by Blohm & Voss shipbuilders in Germany, the *Explorer* is 590 feet long with a beam of 84 feet and a draft of 24 feet. It's said to be the fastest passenger ship today, with a cruising speed of 28 knots (Semester at Sea, n.d. b).

Historically, the operating costs for Semester at Sea have always exceeded its revenue. If not for the vision of the late C.Y. Tung and his family, the program would not have enough money to stay afloat. C.Y. Tung was a cargo ship tycoon from Hong Kong who founded two nonprofit corporations: the Seawise Foundation, Ltd. and the Institute for Shipboard Education. Today the Institute for Shipboard Education remains, and Mr. Tung's dream lives on:

> Mr. Tung expressed his hope that someday a truly international university could be created onboard a ship, where students of different races, lifestyles, and cultures could live, study, and relax together. (Semester at Sea, n.d. a)

Students pay approximately $21,000 for the fall and spring voyage, which includes tuition, meals, and a shared cabin with one other student. For the summer, students pay approximately $10,000. The Institute for Shipboard Education offers more than $2.2 million in need-based student aid. Donations to Semester at Sea make it possible to offer financial grants to 350 students annually (Semester at Sea, n.d., *SAS Facts*, retrieved May 26, 2005, from http://www.semesteratsea.com/media/SAS_Facts.doc). Students also can receive assistance from federal aid and loans.

Academic Life

For the most part, the students and staff aboard the *Explorer* don't even know what day it is, because the voyage calendar only specifies "port days" and "ship days." Academic life is structured differently than on a land-based campus—instead of "MWF" or "TR" classes, there are "A" and "B" days.

The Dean's Memo, which is printed each day and distributed during the lunch hour, serves as the daily calendar of happenings. A typical student day consists of a class period beginning at 0800, followed by Global Studies, which is directed by a faculty member or the global studies director, and is taught in an interdisciplinary manner.

Community College is an opportunity for the staff, faculty or students to share their knowledge or expertise in an informal setting. Topics have included sign language, slide shows of upcoming countries, and a faculty/staff panel on gender roles. Community Colleges are optional except when there are mandatory preport briefings, which are scheduled for the same time slot. The goal of preport is to prepare the students for the country they are about to visit. A key part of that is the interport lecture, delivered by a faculty member or student from a university in one of the countries on the itinerary. They share important information about the culture and social and political situations that students might encounter. Preport is also a time for updates from the field office, medical team, and student life, as well as State Department advisories.

Field Program

The field program is an integral part of the Semester at Sea experience. It offers students a chance to observe and participate in different societies. Faculty members develop and lead field trips called Faculty Developed Practica (FDP), and the field office assists the faculty in designing their programs (as well as offering other activities). Some of the past FDP have included a visit to a South African township, a Dalit overnight stay in India, a tour of the Cu Chi Tunnels in Vietnam, a safari in Kenya, and university receptions in China, Japan, and India. Students can also travel independently in groups, and the field office will help them make arrangements.

Student Life

The student life team comprises the director and assistant director of student life, conduct officer, mental health professionals, and a senior adult coordinator. As director of student life, I was the senior student affairs person and also part of the administrative team. The administrative team comprises the executive dean, academic dean, director of student life, field coordinator, registrar, and assistant dean (who works with the captain and his staff). I was also in charge of hiring resident directors or RDs (6 to 10 for each voyage). In addition to the students, there are 40 adult continuing education passengers to be supervised.

Students are more active in the contained environment of a ship than they would be on a sprawling land-based campus. During the first week of the voyage, the RDs and other members of the student life team organize an "involvement fair." On each voyage, students join one of a number of committees that focus on social service, cultural, recreational, sports, or IT planning and activities. Each RD, besides serving as a resident assistant/advisor, is responsible for overseeing one or more of these student activities. The student life team budget is $3 per student. Students may organize their own committees as well.

In the summer of 2003, the social service group, Students of Service (SOS) Committee, raised $28,000, and the shipboard community voted to distribute the money equally among three organizations: an orphanage and school in Fiji, another orphanage in New Zealand, and the Karri Casner Memorial Scholarship Fund (named after an SAS student alumna who died in a nightclub fire in Indonesia in 1998). The SOS packed up boxes and books left behind from a previous voyage and donated the materials at various ports of call.

The Ambassadors Ball, which also raises money for SOS, is held on the return passage to the United States. The Ambassadors are groups of students on the ship who volunteer to host special guests to the ship such as state ambassadors and local university students.

As you would expect, compared to a land-based campus, space is tight. For example, there is a single, shared recreation space on the outside deck, which alternates as a volleyball/basketball court and aerobics studio. But space doesn't limit the activities. Also, there are religious programs and a number of traditional events, (e.g., Neptune Day to mark crossing the equator). It is not unusual to have the faculty/staff and their families participate in these activities as well. There is, however, a strict rule against students fraternizing with the crew.

Student Conduct

Students are provided online access to the most current edition of the *Voyager's Handbook* about a month before they embark. It outlines the code of conduct, which is similar to other universities, except for some policies specific to Semester at Sea, such as those dealing with public conduct in the societies visited, returning to the ship late, and not following the directives of ship captains, staff, and crew. The assistant director for student life is the primary administrator for student conduct. When necessary, the director assists, and if a student is asked to go home, the executive dean has the final say. There are many challenges that arise on the ship which would probably not happen on our home campus.

Difficulties and Challenges on a Floating Campus

Safety comes first on the ship. To ensure the safety of all passengers, the administrative team and the captain work together. When students do not comply with safety issues, they are held responsible. One of the biggest concerns on the ship and in port is the irresponsible use of alcohol. The legal drinking age for alcohol on the ship is 18 and in most countries visited, students are able to drink alcohol as well.

Another challenge is the unknown: No one knows for sure who will get seasick in bad weather and who will not. Other unknowns include natural disasters or political instability in the ports of destination. Besides monitoring U.S. State Department alerts, Semester at Sea contracts with a risk assessment company to evaluate the different countries visited. The Charlottesville office always has a back-up plan for each port, and the field office has developed relationships around the world with travel agents and other organizations, making it easy for the ship to quickly change its itinerary. The one word that best describes life at sea is flexibility.

Alcohol and Drug Policy

Students cannot bring alcohol onboard. When embarking, students' bags are checked by either ship security and/or the student life staff. The assistant dean, director of student life, and the captain complete random cabin checks a few times on each voyage to check for alcohol and other policy violations. For example, if alcohol is found in a student's cabin and it is the student's first offense, would have some social privileges revoked. Some of the sanctions on the ship are revocation of social events and/or dock time.

Overall, students are given an opportunity to change their behavior, but if after three chances the student's behavior is still not in compliance, the student may be asked to go home from the next port. For students, this sanction can be devastating. On the 2003 summer voyage, three students were sent home, one for inappropriate behavior on a continual basis while under the influence of alcohol, and two for sneaking a Russian girl onto the ship. The Russian authorities caught the students and arrested the girl. This situation caused the ship to be "locked down" for 24 hours. No one who was on the ship could disembark until the lock down was lifted. These students truly learned how their actions affect others.

The drug policy on the ship is strict. In the *Voyager's Handbook*, the drug policy is highlighted and students know they may be randomly chosen to take a drug test. Drug testing is administered by the medical staff. If a drug test is positive, a student must go home from the next port. Students who are taking prescription drugs are required to disclose this information on their medical form (Semester at Sea, 2004).

The student conduct officer, who is part of the student life team, is responsible for enforcing the code of conduct in the evening hours. This person usually works from 2200 or 2300 to 400 or 500, depending how long the students are awake and roaming around the ship. The student conduct officer works closely with the bridge and ship safety officers.

Safety

Before the voyage, the administrative team trains in Virginia (Charlottesville) to review the Institute for Shipboard Education (ISE) Safety and Risk Management Program. The ISE makes decisions on the itinerary based on State Department advisories and other international information. Safety is important on our land-based campuses, but on the ship it is magnified.

A Comparison and Contrast with a Land-Based Campus

The mission each semester is to gain the knowledge and awareness of the different societies that the *Explorer* visits. It is the faculty and staff's responsibility to uphold this mission. Thus, the partnership and respect between the two is not as isolated as it may be on a home campus.

For the most part, because the community is embarking on something new, titles do not matter. The lines between student affairs and faculty, which are so distinct on a land-based campus, are blurred aboard ship, where everyone is an educator—both in formal settings such as the classroom and field programs and in informal settings such as mealtimes and independent travel.

The other difference is the close relationships that develop among the diverse groups on the ship: between faculty and students, students and staff, the families and students, and the senior passengers and students. (On each voyage there are approximately 40 senior adult passengers who are not taking classes for credit but who may choose to audit various courses and participate fully in ship life and Semester at Sea.) Students at times remark how they were involved more on the ship than at their home university or college.

Many times on our college campuses, we do not interact on a daily basis with our university police. On the ship, contact with the captain, crew, and security captain is a daily occurrence. The assistant dean's primary role is to work with the captain and staff. The administrative team learns about maritime law through contact with the captain and staff. The captain is involved with student conduct as well. Safety is a major concern, and students are constantly being reminded that rules are stricter on a ship than on land. There are times in the early part of the voyage that the staff members feel more like parents then student affairs professionals. But toward the end of the voyage, students begin to police themselves and understand the role of the student life staff in keeping everyone safe.

By the end of the voyage, many students understand how their behavior in port reflects on the image others have about America. The effects of their behavior outside of the university or ship are discussed much more than on a land-based campus. On many campuses, the conduct code includes statements about holding students responsible for their behavior off-campus. However, on the ship, the consequences of behavior are understood in a larger context of the world.

Director of Student Life

As the director of student life for summer 2003, it was my responsibility to hire the RDs and assistant director for student life. The process is very different from land-based campus recruiting in that staff is often hired sight unseen. Since the candidates are from all over the country, the luxury of face-to-face interviews is not often possible. Semester at Sea is always looking to hire the best professionals possible, and whenever possible will interview candidates at the NASPA Annual Conference.

A few of the staff members arrived earlier to spend some time together before the required "on ship" time. Discussion groups via the Internet, led by the director of student life, were planned a couple months ahead of time. Topics included setting team expectations and sharing ideas to make the voyage successful.

Benefits and Drawbacks for a Student Affairs Professional

Unlike faculty, student affairs administrators can't easily take sabbatical or administrative leave. I believe in sabbaticals and leave—even if it is unpaid—so student affairs administrators can complete research, write a dissertation, complete a Fulbright or other international exchange, or for an experience such as Semester at Sea.

Many of the administrators on past Semester at Sea voyages have been given a chance to take administrative leave or sabbatical and return to their campuses after Semester at Sea. For me this was not an option, but I felt the program was important enough that in both 1992 and 2003, I sailed and then returned home to look for another job. Semester at Sea was a good transition both times and provided a wonderful personal and professional development opportunity. But all too often, many of the student affairs staff hired are people who have retired because it was not an option for them during their career.

As a direct result of experiences during Semester at Sea, I became better able to appreciate students and scholars from other cultures and to understand the importance of international education and globalization. I am now more involved in learning activities that enable students to experience and appreciate another lifestyle, such as service-learning/community service and study abroad. I even teach a contemporary perspective class in Globalization. Currently, NASPA's International Education Knowledge Community has allowed me to continue my international learning and exchanges.

In retrospect, lessons learned at sea seem to outweigh those learned on land. Interacting closely with students, eating together, and even traveling in port together allowed me to get back in touch with students. At times on our home campuses we lose contact with students as we move up the ladder.

In addition, through my experience with shipboard education, I have a better appreciation of faculty, and I look for opportunities where the experiential learning and the faculty contact with students can be replicated on a land-based campus. Living and learning communities are one way that seems to help provide the connection between the informal and classroom learning. Global Studies was taught in an interdisciplinary approach on the ship, and the global studies director worked with a majority of the faculty to teach this course. The benefits of this type of learning and the experiential component of the field program and independent travel in port cannot be stressed enough. This type of student learning should be replicated on our home campuses. It was not unusual to hear student comments like these about their Semester at Sea:

"I've learned more during the last three months than I have during the past three years at school at home" (Semester at Sea, n.d. a).

"I learned more about myself [here] than I did on my campus. I can talk to anyone now, even if I do not agree with the person...but I can still respect him/her. I am not afraid of anything" (Semester at Sea, n.d a).

References

Semester at Sea. (n.d. a) *SAS program mission and brief history*. Retrieved May 26, 2005, from http://www.semesteratsea.com/media/SAS_Intro_History.doc

Semester at Sea. (n.d. b) *SAS facts*. Retrieved May 26, 2005, from http://www.semesteratsea.com/media/SAS_Facts.doc

Semester at Sea. (2004, August). *Voyager's handbook*. Retrieved June 15, 2005, from http://www.semesteratsea.com/voyages/VoyagersHandbook0804.pdf

PART IV

LOOKING AHEAD

TWENTY-FIVE

STUDENT AFFAIRS WITHOUT BORDERS

Roger B. Ludeman

There is widespread agreement that, for the most part, countries and institutions do not and should not serve higher education students in the same manner. This certainly makes sense when looking at national histories, cultures, economies, social milieus, and, as a result, the approaches to higher education in the various countries (Ludeman, 2002).

Yet there is a growing set of issues and conditions that seem to be pulling the higher education community and, more specifically, the student affairs community toward the time when there will be a global higher education framework. It will be a time when a variety of global issues will need global solutions—there will be global student needs that must be addressed in a global fashion and staff needs that will transcend borders. This appears to be happening in higher education and student affairs as a profession on such topics as cross-border education (International Association of Universities, 2005; Organisation for Economic Co-operation and Development, 2005) and the European Higher Education Area (Bologna Declaration, 1999).

What Challenges Will Higher Education Face in the 21st Century?

What are the more direct challenges that global issues and trends generate for higher education (and student affairs)? How can student affairs staff look at the local situation through global eyes, given the growing set of issues that demand new structures designed to respond globally?

Until recently, student affairs and services providers have not really been included in the learning framework and always seem to be on the outside looking in. Are there roles that student affairs can play on the international scene? What are they, and how can these providers get their foot in the door? What are the issues that are beginning to cross borders and have impacts internationally?

In 1998 UNESCO hosted the first world conference on higher education in Paris. The primary result was the drafting of the World Declaration on Higher Education for the Twenty-first Century: Vision and Action (UNESCO, 1998). The 140 nations present accepted the declaration as representing the challenges and issues for higher education for the 21st century. Note how these are applicable to the student affairs and services profession:

◊ equality and access

◊ education of qualified graduates and responsible citizens (education for work and life)

◊ academic autonomy and freedom

◊ balance between societal needs and higher education activities (relevance of education as balanced with the needs of society)

◊ integration of all levels of education (all one system)

◊ using diverse methods/models to give graduates more choices

◊ seeking quality and accountability through multidimensional and transparent methods

◊ professional development

◊ participation of women in decision making and ensuring they are well represented in all disciplines

◊ respect for cultural context and diversity

◊ the use of technology for renewal and diversification of higher education

Notice how the concept of integrated systems is woven through the challenges.

According to the World Declaration, in order for higher education to be an effective public service it will require support and partnerships from all sectors and with all stakeholders, a strong international dimension to create solidarity and equality, and regional and international credentialing and certification to promote student and staff mobility.

The final priority or challenge laid out in the World Declaration on Higher Education was the most relevant to student affairs and services professionals:

Putting students at the center of all we do in higher education. This has been the main value of the student services profession since its inception (Williamson, 1961). Increasingly, other sectors of higher education and all levels of government recognize the importance of seeing higher education through the developmental and psychological needs of students. It is both reassuring and challenging for the student affairs and services profession to see this student-centered approach emerge a priority for higher education on the international level, just as the profession is trying to establish recognition and value for professional approaches, programs, and services, as well as the training for the people who perform student affairs work.

How will the Student Affairs Profession be Affected by Globalization and Internationalization?

Because the economy and other aspects of life today are becoming global, a number of higher education issues are also becoming global and crossing borders. Among them are student access, financing of students and higher education, health and safety, cross-border education, responding to world crises that affect students and higher education, services for students studying abroad, and new needs in the areas of professional development and networking among student affairs professionals. New organizations on an international level could be formed to deal with these issues.

Traditional methods often fall short. Specialization and national approaches have advantages but ignore the big picture. Integrated and systemic approaches would yield better results.

Successful Models for International Cooperation

What examples does history provide for successfully resolving global issues through cooperation at the international level? Some examples are quite evident. The United Nations turned 60 years old in 2005, as did UNESCO (United Nations Educational, Scientific & Cultural Organization). UNICEF (United Nations Children's Emergency Fund) and WHO (World Health Organization) have been very successful, as has Interpol, in resolving matters across borders yet preserving national integrity at the same time.

The World Bank, G-8, and the World Trade Organization have generated much controversy but also have taken broader views of world fiscal policy. At the 2005 World Economic Forum, for the first time, the idea was introduced of an international tax to help solve the problems of world poverty, HIV/AIDS, Africa, etc.

In February 2005, 55 prominent foreign policy and national security experts from both sides of Atlantic developed what they called *A Compact between the United States and Europe* (2005), a statement in diplomatic agreement format outlining specific policy recommendations on key challenges in foreign policy and security facing the world as a whole today.

Habitat for Humanity (2005) has a very successful history as have many other nongovernmental organizations (NGOs) around the world like E-Law, Environmental Law Alliance Worldwide, a global group of environmental attorneys banded together to give communities and individuals around the world more say in environmental decisions that affect their daily lives (E-Law, 2005).

The Service Corps of Retired Executives (SCORE) and the International Executive Service Corps (IESC) provide a successful model for applying retired talent to problems and situations occurring just about anywhere, and done at the fraction of the cost of normal consultancies because of the volunteer service provided by retired executives from small businesses and larger corporate entities. These are all good models for networking, planning, and action and could potentially be adapted by higher education and student affairs.

Successful Models of International Cooperation in Higher Education

Within higher education there are already several excellent examples of cooperation for working toward resolution of global issues. The Fulbright Scholar and Student Programs have been effective since post-World War II and now include a new annual seminar, the Fulbright New Century Scholars Program whose theme in 2005 was Higher Education in the 21st Century: Global Challenge & National Response.

The UNESCO Higher Education Division continues to coordinate the World Conference on Higher Education, to ensure that the challenges set out in the World Declaration on Higher Education (see above) are followed up with initiatives. One action was the International Barcelona Conference on Higher Education – the Social Commitment of Universities held in October of 2004.

Universities around the world are hosting groups of Chinese government officials who come to study Western style governance (Li; 2005, January 6). Universities are crafting such workshops for governmental and other groups on a regular basis. Higher education is joining forces with government and business entities throughout the world to solve common problems. This is higher education at its best.

In addition to numerous other international initiatives, the International Association of Universities (IAC) has begun to look at the issues involved in making education more borderless. IAC issued a statement entitled, *Sharing quality higher education across borders: A statement on behalf of higher education institutions worldwide* (IAC, 2005). UNESCO and the Organisation for Economic Cooperation and Development (OECD) have jointly issued another statement on cross-border education, *Guidelines for quality provision in cross-border higher education joint-ly elaborated by UNESCO and the OECD* (OECD, 2005).

Several student associations, all of whom have affiliated with UNESCO as NGOs, have gone international in response to many governance and practical issues facing students around the globe. By forming international networks and working within the UNESCO framework, they find better communication with each other and with other NGOs around the globe.

The Internationalization of Higher Education

Internationalization is one area where higher education has not had lasting success. NAFSA: Association of International Educators released a report entitled, *Securing America's Future: Global Education for a Global Age* (2003) that concluded, "Too many Americans lack crucial global skills in the post-September 11 world." This report points out that a prerequisite for international cooperation is an understanding of the importance of and need for such approaches in resolving global issues. The report sets out concrete recommendations to federal and state governments, higher education institutions, and the private sector for addressing the problem, focusing specifically on the need to dramatically increase the participation of college students in study abroad opportunities.

Many of the advances in U.S. international education didn't come until the mid- to late 20th century, including increasing enrollment of international students, adapting the curriculum, and study abroad. Such new areas of study as international relations and internationalization across the entire curriculum have given academic credibility to the study of languages and relationships among nations and cultures. Study abroad became the experiential "platform" from which global learning was launched. Americans finally began to realize that in order to be effective players on the world scene, they had to rethink how to provide international higher education learning for its students, faculty, and staff. The state of the world today demands a fresh outlook on the role of education and its interface with the numerous and inter-related societies around the globe. No nation can afford to be an "island" in the 21st century.

The History of the Internationalization of Student Affairs

What about the student affairs profession and relationships beyond national borders? The history of international involvement by student affairs and services providers varies depending on the part of the world. North American involvement on the global student affairs scene is relatively new, but representatives from Ireland, Germany, and Hong Kong have been coming to NASPA and ACPA conferences since the late 1980s. During the last years of the 20th century, cross-attendance

began at student affairs conferences in many parts of the Western world and along the Pacific Rim.

A number of senior student affairs officers from the United States joined institutional teams that went abroad to study higher education systems or to visit institutional study abroad sites. Several of these same senior officers received Fulbright international education administrator grants to visit Germany, Japan, and Korea to study those higher education systems, with the potential of enhancing study abroad opportunities as well.

As student services providers from abroad formed friendships with their counterparts in other countries, invitations were extended to attend the national and international conferences held by other nations. Some institutions began small staff exchange programs. In 1994 this author was invited to deliver a paper on global cooperation in student affairs at the Franco-German student services colloquium in Bordeaux, France. The conference leaders then invited NASPA to Europe the following year to discuss possible relationships. It was a breakthrough connection between two continents. That same year, this author led a team of 16 U.S. student affairs professionals on the first exchange to France.

During this same time frame, the NASPA International Education Network, now a NASPA Knowledge Community, was being organized in part to create more opportunities for members and student affairs providers in other countries to meet on a regular basis. The idea of the NASPA International Symposium surfaced at the 1995 NASPA Annual Conference in San Diego. Representatives from the United Kingdom suggested that ways be found to provide opportunities for international representatives to attend and present papers at a forum smaller than the NASPA conference.

The first NASPA International Symposium on Student Services took place at the 1996 NASPA Annual Conference in Atlanta. The first worldwide student affairs event, the symposium drew 120 representatives from 21 countries (Ludeman, R. B.; Osfield, K. J.; & Sullivan, M., January, 2005). Focus was on sharing of country-based student affairs delivery systems and the key issues facing students and student affairs providers. That year also saw the first exchange visit to the United States under the NASPA exchange program. A delegation of student services providers from France visited Georgia and South Carolina institutions and the Atlanta NASPA conference and international symposium. Since then, the scope of NASPA exchanges has widened to include France, Germany, United Kingdom, China, Ireland, Australia/New Zealand, México, Spain, United Arab Emirates, and South Africa, with several others in the planning stages.

Today there are a number of international collaborations and national groups with global interests. One of the oldest is the Asia Pacific Student Services Association (APSSA), whose impressive staff attachment training program and ongoing conferences and workshops are meeting the needs of student services staff in the Pacific Rim region. NASPA has continued its entry into the international arena with symposia or courses in Spain, Australia, and South Africa. Katholeek University Leuven in Belgium held a major international conference on the future of social services for students in April 2005.

At the institutional level, there has been much activity in student affairs in the last decade. The University of Florida, Clemson University, Indiana University, and Iowa State University have built international courses or exchanges into their staff development and educational experiences for graduate students and student affairs staff. The University of Wisconsin –Whitewater has held a staff exchange with Instituto Tecnológico de Estudios Superiores de Monterrey in México, and the University of Arkansas has conducted student affairs study tours in Ireland. Graduate preparation programs in student affairs are increasingly becoming "international" in their curriculum and experiential opportunities for students (Lee, 2005). Clearly, the international dimension is becoming much more important for students and, even more interesting, for staff.

Student Affairs Associations and Organizations around the World

How are student services colleagues organized around the world? Are there national groups serving as umbrella organizations under which other groups are connected? Starting with the continent of Africa, here is the situation. South Africa is getting quite organized on all fronts, with two national umbrella groups and several national-level specialty groups. A number of countries bordering South Africa have joined the organizations there (Botswana and Zimbabwe), making these associations regional in nature. Elsewhere in Africa, the national organization of student affairs is quite limited.

National organizations are located in many countries along the Pacific Rim and include Australia, New Zealand, Malaysia, Thailand, the Philippines, Japan, and China. In China, for example, the student affairs officers of the country's 60 normal universities (former teacher training institutions now turned regional comprehensive universities) have formed a national association. Of the Asia Pacific countries, we know the least about Japan, although that is going to change with the development of a new umbrella student affairs association (see Appendix B).

Europe has a fairly long history of national organizations in student affairs dating back to immediately after World War II. France, Germany, Ireland, Spain, and the United Kingdom have thriving national umbrella groups while Portugal has an informal coordinating council. Italy is getting organized with the help of fellow Europeans. The Scandinavian countries have student affairs in their universities but little to no national activity, mainly because social services for students and all citizens are provided by government. Services for students with

disabilities constitute one exception, with a European network well established along with several national groups. Finland has organized a combination virtual/real national health service for university students with counseling available online and health centers located in most urban areas.

As for Latin America and the Caribbean, we know little about national level student affairs organizations, professional or governmental. While these functions are being carried out at the institutional level, organizing on a national level is very limited unless it is tied to the various ministries of education. In North America, Canada and the United States have had national student affairs groups, of both the specialty and umbrella types, for decades. Because student affairs workers are often trained in student affairs preparation programs at the graduate education level, more ongoing professional development is in place, much of that provided by national and regional professional associations. In México, student affairs at the university level is more like the countries to its south, and national activity is quite small except within larger university systems like Instituto Tecnológico de Estudios Superiores de Monterrey with its multi-campus setup.

The development of national student affairs groups in most parts of the world is a relatively new phenomenon; however, as more countries find it necessary to go in this direction, it is a sign that closer coordination and networking are providing benefits. Such activity results in better policy formulation, professional development for student affairs providers, and enhanced communication with government agencies particularly in relation to advocacy on student issues.

Regional Student Affairs Groups

Regional student affairs associations have emerged in areas where countries had a vision that extended beyond their borders. The newest regional organization to emerge is the European Committee for Student Affairs (ECStA) that was formed to carry out the student mobility plan of Erasmus, Socrates, Leonardo da Vinci, TEMPUS, and other European Commission efforts (see Appendix A). The goal is to enable European Union student study in other European countries at no cost except for accommodations and personal expenses, and with complete transferability of study credits. It has been a remarkable effort. The European Association of International Education (EAIE), the European Forum for Student Guidance (FEDORA), and the European Democratic Students (EDS) are also very active as regional consortiums across Europe.

The Asia Pacific Student Services Association is an outstanding example of regional professional development and advocacy for student services. The Caribbean Tertiary Level Personnel Association (CTPLA), founded in 1997, is quite active in this area of the world, where small island countries and territories must come together to share resources in the student personnel services field.

Student Affairs and Services Agencies on an International Level

On the international level the list begins to thin rapidly. The International Exchange of Students for Technical Experience (IAESTE) has been operating for some time. "International" is part of the title of both the Association of College Unions International and the Association of College and University Housing Officers – International; however, the term refers more to some of the memberships coming from countries outside the United States and the existence of a few international internship programs. The same is true of the U.S.-based group, Mobility International, an effective force for promoting and securing study abroad opportunities for students with disabilities, but not an international organization per se.

However, a large number of student groups have organized internationally and are tied to UNESCO as NGOs. Those involved in medicine, agriculture, dentistry, and forestry, as well as the International Union of Students and the International Association of Catholic Students, have been effective vehicles for meeting student needs around the world. These student groups organized globally mainly for political reasons; however they have evolved into excellent service providers and training agencies as well. Student affairs professionals could learn a great deal from these student groups in terms of the group missions and activities and services performed.

The Case for an International Association or Network of Student Affairs and Services Professionals

Finally, what about the idea of organizing student affairs professionals on a global basis? What is the history of the International Association of Student Affairs and Services (IASAS), an effort that has continued informally but has not yet been able to evolve into an ongoing, more established entity?

The idea of organizing student affairs globally was proposed at the 1994 joint conference of the French and German student affairs groups in Bordeaux. In 1996, following the first international symposium in Atlanta, the first meeting was held to discuss formation of such an international organization. From that meeting, a group called ISEVEN was formed, denoting seven initial members from seven different countries: Australia, Canada, France, México, South Africa, the United Kingdom, and the United States. A member from Spain was added immediately thereafter.

Over the next two years, ISEVEN developed a proposal (ISEVEN, 1998) for an international group called the International Association of Student Affairs and Services (IASAS) to promote international education, student mobility, professional development, assistance to develop-

ing countries, and advocacy. The proposed membership structure was similar to that of NASPA, with both organizational and individual memberships. It was to be funded by dues, institutional seed money, grants, and user fees from workshops, conferences, and the like.

This proposal then was sent to the organizations represented by ISEVEN and other national groups in Hong Kong, the Asia Pacific Student Services Association, Germany, and the new European network. These groups were asked to comment on the draft and to endorse the concept in principle. Then, if all parties provided the endorsement, it was to have been studied further by a larger group, with a new draft offered to establish the group in a legal fashion.

Initially there was some resistance from Europe regarding possible duplication of the efforts of existing national bodies. NASPA was opposed at first, but finally endorsed the idea to study the proposal further. This hesitancy raised some concern among the other countries and organizations involved.

Part of the problem was that national groups in Germany, France, and Spain were making excellent efforts in helping developing countries set up their student services programs. This was part of the EU mission and not unlike similar American efforts on many fronts. So this proposal to form an international group could be seen as duplicating the goals and activities of these national organizations.

After a year or so, the idea seemed to lose momentum. Leadership in ISEVEN began to change because the representatives had other personal priorities and some members retired. The idea of an international association or network of student affairs professionals appeared to be an idea before its time. This author decided to put the formal development of IASAS on hold, keeping the idea alive informally by using its name and offering services upon request and whenever possible.

The strategy was to step back for awhile to see if another time or tactic might arise to help IASAS take root more formally. It was time to conceptualize this idea through new lenses, focusing on service and on providing needed skills and ideas at low cost. The new goals would be to assist in professional and organizational development on a global basis through consultations and volunteer assistance on a cost-only basis.

Possible Models for an International Association

Existing models in other sectors included those of the international student groups, the Service Corps of Retired Executives, and the International Executive Service Corps, mentioned earlier in this chapter. Of course, corporate sponsorship and financial support are keys to their success, something that might be a bit more difficult in the public sector, particularly education; however, there are ways to surmount that too through grants, for example. The other model considered was that of Habitat for Humanity, which requires a commitment on the part of individuals and groups to help build housing for those who can't afford it. Certification of need on the part of the clients is an interesting addition to this model.

Accomplishments of IASAS, an Informal Network of Student Affairs and Services Professionals

What this author and several other individuals would like to see eventually is a formal, professional association. But intermediate steps may be necessary to show there is a need for such an entity and to convince people around the world to buy in. One way to show that there is a need for an international network of student affairs professionals is to review what IASAS has already accomplished on an informal basis.

At the International Symposium at the 2000 NASPA Annual Conference in Indianapolis, a UNESCO higher education department official (the keynote speaker) challenged the delegates to develop a publication of good practice in student affairs, a field that she had never heard of as an academic. Over a period of two years, a group developed a manual on student services (Ludeman, 2002) that describes what a good student services or student affairs operation is based upon, believes in, and does; what kind of resources and contacts are available globally; and how to go about developing such an operation. The writing team presented divergent views and used language that was not country-specific, so the manual could be employed anywhere in the world.

UNESCO published this manual in 2002 in three languages: French, German, and English. It was endorsed by more than 25 organizations and numerous individuals around the world. UNESCO has had numerous requests for the publication. An updated second edition is scheduled to be published early 2009. A number of student affairs providers and organizations internationally have used the manual or refer to it in their work. For example, a staff member of the School for Advanced International Studies at Johns Hopkins University used the manual to introduce the concept of student services to higher education institutions in the country of Georgia. The University of Florida has used it in a graduate course, the NASPA International Education Knowledge Community has posted the manual on its Web site, the South African Association of Senior Student Affairs Professionals distributed the manual to all members, and some members of the Confederation of Student Services in Ireland have used it on their campuses.

From graduate students doing research for their theses to practitioners trying to improve efforts on their campuses, the manual has been a helpful tool. It was an inspiration for this author's year-long Fulbright in South Africa where priorities included helping student affairs colleagues all across the country. Assistance has been given to the Financial Aid Practitioners of South Africa (FAPSA), the first student affairs specialty group to organize there since apartheid fell. IASAS is attempting to broker the involvement of the U.S.-based National Association of Student Financial Aid Administrators (NASFAA) group in this process. Finally, for several years, this author and the NASPA International Education Knowledge Community have been encouraging student affairs graduate programs to internationalize their curricula. IASAS and the University of Arizona have collaborated on a survey designed to investigate what changes are being made to recognize the importance of an international dimension in student affairs graduate programs. The initial results were presented at the 2005 NASPA Annual Conference.

Additional Ideas for Activities of the Proposed Network

In addition to the services and activities IASAS has provided or conducted over the last four years, other services and projects could include the following:

◊ Register IASAS with UNESCO as an affiliated NGO to be able to participate in the various UNESCO activities in the area of higher education.

◊ Maintain an international calendar promoting internship sites, professional development activities, conferences, and workshops of national and regional groups.

◊ Collaborate with international student groups on issues of importance.

◊ On a rotating basis, hold IASAS conferences and workshops at the national conferences of other national student affairs organizations in order to make attendance at such conferences more economically feasible.

◊ Serve as a lobby force with such international groups as UNESCO and IAU in order to establish the viability of student affairs professionals on a global basis.

◊ Work with other international groups to enhance cross-border education, particularly in health, counseling, cross-culture experiences, safety, and quality student services.

◊ Develop international professional development and student leadership experiences for student affairs professionals and student leaders, in cooperation with existing national groups and with UNESCO.

The Possibilities for Success Seem Endless. What are the Barriers to Forming Such a Network?

With the array of services and efforts already carried out informally by IASAS, and with those proposed above, there appears to be enough of an agenda for student affairs professionals to organize themselves into an international organization. So, why hasn't IASAS developed more formally? There are several reasons, not the least of which is a strong nationalistic feeling. Also there is the concern about creating another layer of costs and potentially creating needless bureaucracy. More importantly, the vision of student affairs as an international force and coming together in an organized fashion is not quite developed yet in the minds of most practitioners.

The issues are becoming clearer, however. There is a history of success in many areas. Existing national and regional student affairs groups must overcome the limits of traditional borders and think of a world that connects all nations in a chaotic blender, one that maintains individuality, yet confirms membership in one student affairs community that needs to come together to support students and their learning, solve common problems, enjoy great camaraderie and accomplishments, and dream of more integration across borders in the future.

The Way Forward: Key Questions for Student Affairs and Services to Address in Order to Form the Network

Key questions on this subject for the student affairs profession now and in the future are these: Is there a need for an international focus in our work? Can we look beyond our national borders to a world of student affairs? The student affairs profession is at its best when the focus is on students and their needs. How will students fit into this world of student affairs without borders? Why can't a global network of student affairs professionals be established to better serve students? Could this international group enhance student learning outcomes and the chances for student success? The answers to these questions will determine whether a common community of student affairs practitioners can be found and molded, in part, into an international network or association.

References

A compact between the United States and Europe. (February 17, 2005). Retrieved May 20, 2005, from http://www.brookings.edu/dybdocroot/fp/cuse/analysis/USEUCompact.pdf

The American forum for global education. (2003). Many faces of China. Retrieved May 26, 2005, from http://www.globaled.org/announcement041011.php

The European Higher Education Area. (1999). Bologna declaration of 19 June, 1999: Joint declaration of the European ministers of education. Retrieved May 25, 2005, from http://www.bologna-berlin2003.de/pdf/bologna_declaration.pdf

E-LAW: Environmental Law Alliance Worldwide. (2005). About E-LAW. Retrieved on June 1, 2005, from http://www.elaw.org/about/

Habitat for Humanity. (2005). The history of Habitat. Retrieved June 1, 2005, from http://www.habitat.org/how/historytext.aspx

International Executive Service Corps. (2005). IESC activity around the world. Retrieved on May 30, 2005, from http://www.iesc.org/presence.html

International Association of Universities. (2005). Sharing quality higher education across borders: A statement on behalf of higher education institutions worldwide. Retrieved May 26, 2005, from http://www.unesco.org/iau/p_statements/index.html

ISEVEN. (1998, November 16). Proposal to form an international association of student affairs/student services-related organizations or agencies.

Lee, J. (2005). Directory of college student personnel programs with international emphasis. Retrieved June 3, 2005, from http://www.ed.arizona.edu/csppp/index2.asp

Li, Y. (2005, January 6). China's study-abroad program. The Wall Street Journal, A10.

Ludeman, R. B., Osfield, K. J., & Sullivan, M. (2005). The NASPA international symposium: A decade of global dialogue. Leadership Exchange, 3(1), 25.

Ludeman, R. (Ed.). (2002). The role of student affairs and services in higher education: A practical manual for developing, implementing, and assessing student affairs programs and services. Paris: UNESCO, 8.

Marx, G. (2001, March–April). Educating children for tomorrow's world. The Futurist, 43–48.

NAFSA Strategic Task Force on Education Abroad (2003). Securing America's future: Global education for a global age. Washington, DC: NAFSA: Association of International Educators. Retrieved May 26, 2005, from http://www.nafsa.org/content/PublicPolicy/stf/STFEAreport.pdf

O'Brien, T. L. (2005, January–February). Can Angelina Jolie really save the world? The New York Times, Section 3, pp. 1, 3 and 7.

Organisation for Economic Co-operation and Development. (2005). Guidelines for quality provision in cross-border higher education jointly elaborated by UNESCO and the OECD. Retrieved March 17, 2005, from http://www.oecd.org/dataoecd/34/42/34732302.pdf

Service Corps of Retired Executives. (2005). Explore SCORE. Retrieved May 30, 2005, from http://www.score.org/explore_score.html

Shah, A. (2003). Global issues.org. Retrieved May 24, 2005, from http://www.globalissues.org/

UNESCO. (1998). The world declaration on higher education for the twenty-first century: Vision and action. Retrieved May 25, 2005, from http://www.unesco.org/education/educprog/wche/declaration_eng.htm

Williamson, E. G. (1961). Student personnel services in colleges and universities. New York: McGraw-Hill, 13.

TWENTY-SIX

INTERNATIONALIZING THE COMMUNITY COLLEGE

EDWARD T. BONAHUE

At first glance, the priorities of international education and of the community college might appear antithetical. As an assemblage of related curricula and activities within U.S. higher education, international education developed concurrently with the Cold War, from the 1940s through the 1960s. In response to national anxieties regarding socialist expansion, intelligence gathering, and the development of nuclear weapons and space flight, the federal government launched programs in U.S. universities intended to bolster geographic area studies, foreign languages, and study abroad programs. In contrast, the idea of the U.S. community college was founded on providing local access to higher educational opportunities that would serve community needs. Traditionally, most community college curricula consisted of lower-division courses offering an introduction to postsecondary education, adult and continuing education, and vocational education targeted toward local employment. And to be sure, two-year institutions as a whole still take pride in putting service to their local communities first and foremost.

At the same time, it is precisely because community colleges have accepted the challenge of responding to changing community needs that international education is increasingly becoming part of their missions. Especially since the 1980s, the growing political and economic interconnections between nations and cultures have led to a greater demand for multiculturalism and international diversity. Changing demographics within local service areas and changing perceptions of the values and perspectives that ought to infuse higher education have led more and more two-year institutions to create internationally oriented curricula and student activities, and even to include international goals among their institution's strategic objectives. Attempting to clarify the role of international education within two-year institutions in 1996, a report from the American Council on International Intercultural Education (ACIIE) and the Stanley Foundation summarized the new challenge succinctly: "The 'why' of global education is, simply put, the survival of our communities. If community college educators care about the communities they serve, global education is an imperative, not an option" (*Educating for the Global Community*, 1996, p. 2).[1] Since 1996, momentum for international education in the community college has continued to grow and is now making its way into the mainstream of community college education.

In this essay, then, I will first summarize the state of international education in U.S. community and technical colleges and the progress that has been made in this area so far. I also propose that the rationale for internationalizing two-year institutions can be best articulated through the goal of fostering "global competency" among community college students. Next, I will consider internationalization of community college student personnel programming in light of the unique needs and circumstances of community college students, and I propose that there must be an unusually strong link between student activities, student services, and academic curricula in global studies. Finally, for practitioners still at the early stages of internationalizing their institution, I will propose a brief set of action items reflecting best practices in community college internationalization.

To be sure, international programs in community colleges have grown rapidly in recent decades. A report released by the American Association of Community Colleges (AACC) in 2001 found that 82% of the responding colleges featured international components within their curriculum, while 83% sponsored student activities intended to promote global perspectives (Blair, Phinney, & Phillippe, 2001). A similar study conducted by the American Council on Education found that 99% of respondents, or virtually all responding two-year institutions, indicated

---

[1] The increased internationalization of U.S. community colleges has been treated comprehensively by John S. Levin's *Globalizing the Community College* (2001) and by the contributors to *Internationalizing the Community College*, a comprehensive guide to internationalization published in 2002 by the American Association of Community Colleges. For a thorough historical, comparative, and conceptual analysis of the concept of international education in higher education generally, see de Wit (2002).

some activity related to international education (Green & Siaya, 2005). Taken together, the studies suggest that the availability of study abroad opportunities, foreign languages courses, and ESL programs were the most widely offered components of an internationalized curriculum. However, many community colleges are increasingly adding courses focusing on the cultures of other countries and regions, chiefly in the humanities, social sciences, global ecology, and business. A small but growing number of institutions have even offered degree or certificate programs with a global perspective (Green, 2002).

The reasons for initiating an international education program at a community college are manifold, speaking to the multifaceted mission of most two-year institutions. Perhaps first and foremost, colleges keenly feel the need to help students understand something about their interconnectedness within a global community of tremendous diversity. Frequently, the intent is to help students find their own sense of "personal foreign diplomacy," a sense of international awareness that will "reduce provincial thinking, increase acceptance of diversity, and possibly add a little adventure to their lives" (Dellow, 2002, p. 8). Secondly, colleges understand that their mission of training new generations of workers and professionals has an economic impact as well as an intellectual one and that all workers need a global perspective to be effective in their chosen vocations. As industrial and commercial networks of resources, manufacturing, distribution and administration increasingly cross national and continental divisions, students training for employment at almost any level must be prepared to deal with suppliers, partners, and clients and customers located anywhere on the globe. Finally, some schools have even found in international education a kind of quasi-entrepreneurial activity, in that some international education activities—e.g., recruiting new students to the college (and thus to the community) or establishing training programs and partnerships—have the potential to bring new funds both to the college and to the local community.

At the same time, international students have become increasingly aware of the opportunities presented by U.S. community colleges. Between 1994 and 1999, the number of international students enrolled at U.S. community colleges rose 32%. In its annual "Open Doors" report for 2004, the Institute of International Education reported that the number of international students enrolled in community colleges peaked in 2002 at 82,932. In 2002, however, in the wake of September 11, changes in the processing of student visa applications led to a subsequent decline in international student enrollments, which affected community colleges; by 2003–04, the number of enrollments declined more than 7%, to 75,830 international students (Open Doors 2004, 2005). Recently, however, community colleges have joined with institutions nationwide to advocate for a more efficient approval process.

Whether the students hail from abroad or from around the corner, however, the goal with regard to international education is the same: to provide students with an education that will prepare them for an academic and professional future in which nations, peoples, and cultures are increasingly interconnected. In terms of operational educational outcomes, this rationale has been concisely and effectively articulated in the idea of "global competency," the notion that a student with a community college education ought to possess a set of abilities, skills, and knowledge that makes him or her competent to operate in a global society. In the 1996 report *Educating for the Global Community*, the ACIIE and the Stanley Foundation articulate the kind of student-level changes institutions should seek to effect. Their report defines global competency as follows:

> Global competency exists when a learner is able to understand the interconnectedness of peoples and systems, to have a general knowledge of history and world events, to accept and cope with the existence of different cultural values and attitudes and, indeed, to celebrate the richness and benefits of this diversity. (p. 4)

The authors of the report also articulate a knowledge and skill set that students should have by the conclusion of their community college education. This definition of global competency manages to keep the development of student skills and attitudes as a primary focal point, while also recognizing that institutions should have no fear of advocating for "the richness and benefits of diversity."

When community colleges embrace the goal of fostering global competency, however, they take on a considerable task. Anyone who has worked at a community college knows the special challenges facing students in two-year institutions. In contrast to many students in four-year institutions who may have the benefit of living and studying full-time at a residential college or university—benefits including dormitory living, library and computer lab access, on-campus food service, residence life services, and so forth—community college students are almost exclusively commuters. The 2004 Community College Survey of Student Engagement found that the majority of community college students nationwide are responsible for their own finances and are working their way through school. More than 60% work 20 or more hours per week, and even among full-time students, 47% work more than 20 hours per week to make ends meet. One third of all students care for a child or other dependent in their household (*Engagement by Design*, 2005). Many students attending bachelor's-level institutions face these same circumstances, of course, but the level at which these challenges affect community college students as a group cannot be overestimated.

Promoting global competency among community college students, then, is a formidable task, one that is likely to defy anything less than comprehensive, institutionwide efforts at internationalization. Because community college students are so stretched between responsibilities at home, work, and school, attempts to foster global competency through student activities alone might result in a kind of vague international awareness, but will probably fall short of the kind of competency educators would desire. As many as

84% of community college students nationwide report that they "never" participate in college- sponsored extracurricular activities (*Engagement by Design*, 2005). The challenge of promoting global competency through student activities, then, begins with demonstrating for students a compelling reason to remain on campus long enough to do more than go to class. On the other hand, attempts to internationalize academic curricula without support from a complementary program of internationalized student activities is likely to be perceived by students as "academic," that is, as a theoretical exercise or institutional requirement that may not affect them at a personal level.

Those institutions that have most successfully promoted global competency—those recognized by national organizations such as NAFSA: Association of International Educators and the Institute for International Education—have sought to internationalize their student and academic programs in tandem. In this way, international education initiatives within an institution may be united into an integrated, coherent initiative that consistently reminds students of their past, present, and future connection with a global community. [2] As Ping (1999) proposes, the objective is "to extend a global reality of cultural interaction into student organizations and activities; and to make the formal structures of course and degree programs and the pattern of campus life a compatible and reinforcing whole" (p. 15).

A review of the academic literature on internationalization of student services reveals that programs relating to international education tend to go in two different directions: support services for international students and international activities that support the entire college community. From the standpoint of promoting global competency, both are necessary; a college that promotes international activities but has no core of international student involvement will probably end up with a very limited sense of what is real. Conversely, a college that recruits international students and then shows no further interest in international activities is likely to lose a good many of those students over the long term. A community college lucky enough to enroll substantial numbers of international students will probably have an international admissions specialist who works to answer questions and process paperwork related to immigration, academic credentials, initial academic placement, and orientation to the college. On the other hand, larger institutions provide ongoing support to international students through an international student center, which might combine the long-term functions of academic advising or mentoring, organization of international student clubs and activities, and linking with community groups.

At my own institution, Santa Fe Community College, the division of student affairs sponsors a Multicultural Student Center that is charged both with providing long-term support to international students and with serving the entire campus with internationally oriented student activities.[3] Each year, the center accomplishes its mission through a variety of methods: a supplemental orientation for international students each semester helps acquaint new students with college services and key personnel. The coordinator is also involved with connecting international students with activities and clubs that will help them stay engaged and active on campus. The U.S. State Department-sponsored International Education Week, which takes place each November, has been expanded at Santa Fe into an International Education Month, complete with film festival, ethnic music and dancing, demonstrations and sampling of international foods, and other activities. In many of these events, the coordinator for international education activities seeks the support and partnership of academic faculty and administrators, again, for the purpose of bridging the cognitive gap between students' academic and personal lives. Charles Ping (1999) eloquently summarizes the objective behind making this connection:

> Part of the educational task of student affairs is to identify strategies that bring groups and individuals into contact with one another, that encourage interaction, and that modify the deep-seated human tendency to withdraw and cluster together, thus closing out otherness…the strategy is to constantly seek to stir the mix of campus life in order to bring diverse individuals and groups together. (p. 17)

That is, the challenge for integrating international students into the life of the institution is similar to the challenge of working with all multicultural groups: to fight the self-segregation that, though comforting for many, works against the value of diversity that all institutions of higher education commonly embrace.

At the same time, a student's overall development of global competency depends on more academic international education programs, such as the availability of foreign languages, study abroad programming, and, in general, the internationalization of the curriculum. As stated earlier, virtually all community colleges offer students at least one foreign language, and institutions located near a population of either permanent or transient non-English speakers will likely offer ESL classes as well. In addition to these mainstays of community colleges, however, many institutions are internationalizing programs in ways traditionally seen in four-year institutions. For example, geographic area studies programs are growing in various regions of the country

[2] A complete survey of best practices in community college internationalization is clearly beyond the scope of this chapter. In addition to the bibliographic references included with this chapter, up-to-date reports on various best practices in community college internationalization may also be found on the Web sites of the Association of Community Colleges.

[3] Martin J. Tillman (1990) describes a comprehensive program for providing effective support services for international students from their arrival in the United States, through their program of study, and up until their return home (see esp. pp. 89–93). The essays collected in Speck and Carmical (2002) also offer student personnel professionals working with international students a host of suggestions and best practices in the areas of recruitment, visas, academic credentials, orientation, adjustment to U.S. culture, and academic retention and success.

where student and faculty demographics support such curricula, and in large community colleges with sizable cohorts of university-transfer students. In the Southeast and Southwest, and in larger urban centers nationwide, courses and programs in Latin American Studies are becoming increasingly common (e.g., Austin Community College and LaGuardia Community College [NY]); for institutions in California and the Pacific Northwest, the same is true for courses and programs related to Asian Studies and the Pacific Rim. (e.g., Shoreline Community College [Seattle] and the well-known program at Kapi'olani Community College [Honolulu]). More generally, community colleges nationwide are adding courses throughout the academic disciplines—from global issues in agriculture through fine arts, international relations, meteorology, and global business.[4] In many cases, these courses fulfill a general education requirement, so that any student enrolled in the course gains access to the global perspective, not just those students who may have an interest in international topics.

At many community colleges, the internationalization of curriculum is furthered by the development of study abroad opportunities. Traditionally, the option of spending a semester or summer abroad is pursued during a student's junior year, when the choice of a major and professional interests may suggest an appropriate destination that would justify the expense and challenges of traveling and living abroad. In contrast, community college students are almost universally involved either with vocational training or with satisfying lower-division general education and prerequisite courses, and are commonly still developing plans for their academic and professional futures. Given what is known about their financial situations, it almost goes without saying that a great many community college students would not have the financial means to live abroad, or even to take a short-term study tour.

Nevertheless, community college students do go abroad, and they do so in significant numbers. The 2004 Open Doors report indicates that 3,594 community college students traveled abroad in 2002–03, mostly in short-term excursions of several weeks or fewer (*Open Doors 2004*, 2005). At my own institution, Santa Fe Community College, student travel has been successful most often in humanities and social sciences disciplines, where there is considerable flexibility for faculty to create short courses of study oriented around student participation in field work and direct observation of

artifacts and sites abroad. For example, Santa Fe faculty have taken students on anthropology digs in Belize and Peru, on humanities trips to various destinations in Western Europe and China, and on interdisciplinary explorations of language and culture in Central America. In states where it is permitted, some community college study abroad programs have been able to support themselves by tapping into student fees. Funding from student fees may be helpful not only in funding a study abroad office and staff, but also in subsidizing the cost of international travel for students, thereby extending the traditional community college emphasis on open access even to their international study program.

Community colleges also differ from most four-year schools through their emphasis on responding to local community needs, including workforce training, support of local business, and regional economic development. Yet these goals also provide opportunities for internationalization. To the extent that they partner with state and local employers to establish and prioritize training and continuing education programs for workers in a variety of fields, community and technical colleges must be capable of responding to business partners working around the globe. Partnerships with members of the local Chamber of Commerce are likely to lead to the clarification of other business needs for which the college may be able to supply expertise.[5] Significantly, the internationalization of vocational and technical programs may reach a different audience of students than internationalization of university-transfer arts and sciences programs.

Community colleges, then, can promote global competencies in their students through internationalization of the curriculum, student services, and workforce partnerships. If the goal of an institution is to internationalize in such a way as to reach all its students, however, these initiatives should be pursued together. Internationalizing the curriculum will help provide students with knowledge and skills necessary to continue successfully in their chosen academic and professional careers. Internationalizing workforce programs will make community college students more attractive to employers and more competitive in the working world. And internationalizing student services programs will help students understand that the global perspectives they are learning in an academic context apply directly to their personal lives.

In summary, the fostering of student global competency through comprehensive international education programming is wholly consonant with community college education. Whether students are enrolled in university transfer courses, vocational and technical training, or continuing

[4]Federal grant assistance for internationalizing the curriculum is available to community colleges through the Title VI-A Undergraduate International Studies and Foreign Language Program, the purpose of which is to enhance general undergraduate instruction in any field relevant to international education (Cissell and Levin, 2002). See also Prejsnar and Tasch (1998) for a case study on the development of a liberal arts curriculum that came to include coursework in international studies as a general education requirement at the Community College of Philadelphia. Especially fascinating is the account of how humanities offerings continued to include T.S. Eliot and other hallmarks of Western modernism, but at the same time were expanded to include writers such as the Japanese Natsume Soseki and the Senegalese Mariama Ba (pp. 128–32).

[5]Similar to the Title VI-A program (see above), the Title VI-B Business and International Education Program provides assistance to educational institutions seeking to further the competitiveness of U.S. businesses in the global economy. Although the competition for federal grant dollars is always keen, a number of community colleges have to date been successful in winning these annual grants (Cissell and Levin, 2002).

workforce education, they will be well served by institutions preparing them to understand the interconnectedness of peoples and cultures; to accept and work within a world of different cultures, values, and attitudes; and to appreciate global diversity. Clearly, over the past two decades, much progress has been made. However, much remains to be done. While some large community colleges have embraced international education wholeheartedly, and have recognized the development of student global competency either explicitly or implicitly as an institutional goal, many others are just taking their first steps. Moreover, at open-access two year colleges, the financial resources necessary to staff a full-time office of international education may not be available.

Here are some suggestions (adapted from the International Education Initiative of Santa Fe Community College) to those institutions still working to develop an action plan for global education. The model of leadership through a collegewide steering committee is sometimes difficult to achieve due to institutional pressures and diffusion of responsibility. But it can provide a useful structural model for sharing information, clarifying values and goals, and collaborating on various initiatives.

◊ Create a collegewide international education steering committee that will communicate a vision, goals, and benefits for the college community. Involve staff from every part of the college, from the president and board of trustees to clerical and support staff.

◊ Create an action plan that is appropriate for the culture of the school and that incorporates traditional community college values of open access, responsiveness, and accountability.

◊ Conduct an internal scan of the international curriculum, activities, and personnel already available at the college and plan to leverage those resources in appropriate ways.

◊ Join state and national consortia for international education such as NAFSA and CCID. Opportunities for developing grant-funded programs, study abroad programs, professional development and curriculum models, and international workforce partnerships are available from a variety of international education organizations and other community colleges.

◊ Even if impractical at present, initiate planning for eventual establishment of a formal office of international education, in order to institutionalize appropriate goals and activities.

As the trend toward developing international education in community colleges continues, faculty and staff still in the early throes of internationalization have a wealth of resources to consult for reference and upon which to build. In addition to the international consortia already mentioned, colleges should look to the League for Innovation in the Community College an alliance of 20 two-year colleges in the vanguard of student-centered learning innovations. Virtually all League colleges provide international education opportunities through ESL, foreign language, and study abroad programs, either through internal programs or through partnerships with a variety of external partners and consortia. Some colleges, including Seattle, Sinclair, St. Louis, Maricopa, and Johnson County have made tremendous strides in internationalizing their curricula, offering more fully developed selections of courses with international perspectives, as well as various kinds of portable instructional modules on specific topics, allowing for easy dissemination.

References

Blair, D., Phinney, L., and Phillippe, K. A. (2001). *International programs at community colleges*. Washington, D.C.: American Association of Community Colleges.

Cissell, A., & Levin, D. (2002). Federal funding for community college international education programs and activities. In R. M. Romano (Ed.), *Internationalizing the community college*. Washington, D.C.: Community College Press [AACC].

Dalton, J. C. (Ed.). (1999). *Beyond borders: How international developments are changing student affairs practice*. New Directions for Student Services series, Number 86. San Francisco: Jossey-Bass.

Dellow, D. A. (2002). Why do community colleges need to be involved in international activities? In R. M. Romano (Ed.), *Internationalizing the community college*. Washington D.C.: Community College Press [AACC].

Educating for the Global Community: A Framework for Community Colleges. (1996). American Council on International Intercultural Education and The Stanley Foundation.

Engagement By Design: 2004 Findings (2005). CCSSE: The Community College Survey of Student Engagement. Retrieved August 20, 2005, from the CCSSEE Web site http://www.ccsse.org/publications/CCSSE_reportfinal2004.pdf

Fifield, M. L., & Huhra, L. (1993). *Strengthening America's competitiveness: Profiles of leading community college international trade centers*. Washington D.C.: AACC.

Green, M.F. (2002). Joining the world: The challenge of internationalizing undergraduate education. *Change: The Magazine of Higher Learning 34.3*, 13–21.

Green, M. F., and Siaya, L. (2005). *Mapping internationalization at community colleges*. Washington, D.C.: American Council on Education.

Irwin, J. T. (2003). Community Colleges: Changing Individuals, Meeting Global Needs. Retrieved March 1, 2003, from the Institute for International Education website.

Levin, J. S. (2001). *Globalizing the community college: Strategies for change in the twenty-first century*. New York: Palgrave.

Open Doors 2004: International Students at Associate's Institutions, 1999/00 to 2003/04. (2005). Retrieved September 21, 2005, from the Institute for International Education website http://opendoors.iienetwork.org/?p=52925

Ping, C. J. (1999). An expanded international role for student affairs. In J.C. Dalton (Ed.), *Beyond borders: How international developments are changing student affairs practice*. New Directions for Student Services series, Number 86. San Francisco: Jossey-Bass.

Prejsnar, D. C., & Tasch, A. (1998). Mainstreaming international studies in a community college. In J. A. Kushigan (Ed.), *International studies in the next millennium: Meeting the challenge of globalization*. London and Westport, Connecticut: Praeger.

Romano, R. M. (Ed.). (2002). *Internationalizing the community college*. Washington, D.C.: Community College Press [AACC].

Tillman, M. J. (1990). Effective support services for international students. In. R. K. Greenfield (Ed.), *Developing international education programs*. New Directions for Community Colleges series, Number 70, San Francisco and Oxford: Jossey-Bass.

de Wit, H. (2002). *Internationalization of higher education in the United States of America and Europe: A historical, comparative, and conceptual analysis*. Westport, Conn., and London: Greenwood Press.

TWENTY-SEVEN

RECOMMENDATIONS FOR THE NEXT DECADE

Kenneth J. Osfield

The authors featured in this book highlight enormous challenges and opportunities that have
emerged as globalization plays an ever increasing role in world, national, and regional economies
and communities.

Each of the contributing authors was asked to note
emerging issues that will affect higher education and our
institutions' ability to respond to the challenge of globalization over the next decade. The most pressing issues
cited were:

◊ The need for more counseling-related services;

◊ The lack of revenue to run operations and the need
for student services to look toward nontraditional
funding sources (outside the university budget); and

◊ The continuing decline in the number of international student enrolments in the United States but not
necessarily in other areas of the world. There are many
reasons behind this reduction but a few key areas are:
visa policies in the United States, friendlier visa policies
in other countries, and more aggressive recruiting efforts by other countries.

Authors also cited the rising cost of higher education
for students, a problem that will block access for many
students, lengthen the time to complete degrees as students are forced to reduce their course load in order to
work, and spur institutions to look at the length of programs of study. With the lack of funds to run the programs
needed, respondents also suggested that more and more
students will be using student services on campus. So
this is a double-edged sword. Universities and colleges
will need to provide better and more services with less
funding from the institution.

Partnerships were also pointed out as critical to the advancement of internationalization of student affairs and
higher education, partnerships within respective countries, regions, and around the world. These partnerships
will not only afford more opportunities and increased
mobility for students but also provide opportunities for
university and college student affairs administrators. This
increase in student and staff mobility will go a long way
toward improving multiculturalism and a better appreciation of the differences and similarities of people around
the world.

Multiculturalism is another issue the authors cited.
There is a need to educate the world's population about
the differences and similarities of all people, and there is
no better time to achieve that goal than during the college years. Today's college students will be the future
world leaders so it is important to reach out to them and
expose them to the cultures, languages, traditions, religions, life experiences, goals, values, and desires of the
people of the world. Somehow we must begin to see
each other as equal whatever our religion, race, national
origin, language, sex, or political persuasion.

Dalton and Sullivan (chapter 2) talked about the im-
plication of internationalization for future developments
in the student affairs profession. They wrote that "...we
must begin to understand developments in student affairs in other countries if we are to prepare ourselves for
the future. And rather than simply benchmarking our
efforts against peer institutions in the United States we
must also begin to compare our professional efforts with
those of colleagues in other countries". Tejido in chapter
12 put it this way: "Here is our way; show us yours." Mutual
sharing and respect for ones ideas and programs is what
is needed. Tejido asks his readers to "help us help ourselves in the work of improving student services...[but]
be reminded that there can be no universal, all-embracing standard of excellence in student affairs and services,
applicable to all colleges and universities throughout
the world."

What Dalton and Sullivan describe is a position that
many people in student affairs in the United States continue to hold onto and that is the belief that the U.S. way
is the only way. It is true that U.S. colleges and universities forged the way for the development of the practice
of student affairs, and as a result a profession developed.
U.S. colleges and universities have developed both
master's and doctoral degrees in the field of student af-

fairs and student development. At the time this book was written, there were only two other countries known with college-based educational programs in student affairs (England, University of Huddersfield offering a student support and management certificate/diploma/MA; South Africa, University of Kwazulu-Natal, Durban offering a master's in education-higher education). Nevertheless, while other countries may not have devoted degree programs in student affairs, they still manage to run their institutions and provide excellent services to students. We need to look at those services and operations and also share our successes, failures, and best practices.

One of the guiding principles of this book is to present an opportunity for each of us to learn what others are doing around the world and ultimately help each other to develop the best possible services available for our students. One way to accomplish this is to work through the student affairs and services professional associations around the world. In chapter 17 Heyde cites the need for "improved networking or interaction between the relevant student affairs organizations." Propelled by the Bologna Process, the European community is working on improving student services through the European Council for Student Affairs (ECStA), the German Deutsches Studentenwerk (DSW), the French Centre National des Æuvres Universitaires et Scolaires (CNOUS), the Colegios Mayores in Spain, and other organizations.

This effort of working together needs to go beyond our individual continents and become something that is truly global. In 1998 the United Nations Education, Scientific and Cultural Organization (UNESCO) held the first World Conference on Higher Education which resulted in a document called the World Declaration on Higher Education. A result of that conference was the development and publication of *The Role of Student Affairs and Services in Higher Education: A Practical Manual for Developing, Implementing and Assessing Student Affairs Programmes and Services.*

During that conference, some of the delegates saw a need for an association that would work on student issues, and subsequently, Roger Ludeman launched the International Association of Student Affairs and Services (described in chapter 25 with more information available at http://iasas. ehs.ufl.edu). IASAS is waiting in the wings to be the catalyst for bringing together the student affairs and services organizations around the world (see Appendix B for a list of associations around the world). Is it practical and/or possible to have a worldwide association? I believe it is. However, it may take many years to pull together. One way to start would be to hold mini-summits at each of the annual student affairs professional conferences around the world. A meeting of this nature would be more localized, but at least the discussions and dialogue would begin. Given today's technology, the mini-summits could be broadcast via Web cam, video-conferencing, and satellite. ESCtA and NASPA are currently doing something similar during their annual conferences. However, those meetings are held within the context and the name of the association. The International Symposium is NASPA's vehicle to bring together student affairs practitioners from around the world; however, attendance is geared toward NASPA membership. As a NASPA member, I believe that the symposium can be a vehicle for great change in the world of international student affairs and therefore should be open to people from around the world who aren't NASPA members. (Currently, it is open, but nonmembers pay a premium registration fee.)

There was a time when the world came to the United States to study, but the wind is changing. With stricter immigration laws, an increasing number of students are going to other countries for their higher education needs. Countries like Australia, England, and Canada are reaching out and recruiting students from countries where, in the past, the United States had the lion's share of the market. Add to this the improving educational system in some areas of the world (see chapters 14, 17, 19 to 22). Many students are now staying home to study instead of going outside their region.

Another development to watch closely is the expansion of the European Union and accompanying changes. Through the Bologna Process, student and staff mobility will be increased exponentially. As Heyde points out in chapter 17, the principle aim of the process is to "make higher education systems in Europe converge toward a more transparent system." Will this transparent system actually materialize? It is difficult to say at this early stage as there are some major issues that must be worked out. If the Europeans can make the Bologna Process work, the opportunities for students in Europe will be vastly increased.

Finally, I would like to extend a call to the student affairs practitioners around the world to begin to look outside their respective institutions and find ways to continue the internationalization of student affairs and services in higher education. I predict that during the next decade the internationalization of student affairs and services will no longer be an emerging global perspective but a reality.

EPILOGUE

A TIME TO ACT

Doris Ching

The preceding chapters provide a one-of-a-kind glimpse into how student services are delivered in 15 countries around the world. This comprehensive compendium of worldwide information on student services is a *must read* for those who believe that student affairs and services are an integral part of college students' total education. The authors have compiled this book in an effort to provide a source that will serve as a constant reference for those seeking to know how student services are delivered at colleges and universities around the world.

But, the book is anything but just a library reference. The authors stirred my soul and mind with their candid discussions of the intensifying globalization and the inadequacy of U.S. colleges and universities to meet the challenge of preparing students for a complex world of global interdependence. A unique opportunity awaits those who wish to help address the challenge and contribute significantly to an important goal of U.S. higher education.

This book, clearly, is a call to action. At a time when interdependence among countries is high and nations rely on interrelationships for safety and security as well as any hope of international peace, most colleges and universities woefully lag in preparing students for a world deeply-rooted in global economy, politics, and culture. While student affairs professionals can help institutions of higher education achieve their goal of educating students for a global society, many are not equipped to play an international role. Like the general U.S. culture, the student affairs profession has been oriented to the present rather than to the future. The profession may now have a chance to help institutions attain their goals for global understanding by becoming members of a *world* profession and serving as role models for students who otherwise may not be made aware of the profound impact of globalization on their personal lives and on the country as a whole. Student affairs professionals are incited to strengthen their global understanding, and the professional association is urged to expand internationally. In

doing so, both the professionals and the profession can enhance students' campus experiences with perspectives they need to succeed as citizens of a shrinking world.

There is a sense of urgency in initiating the long-overdue direction. U.S. institutions of higher education are not reputed to make timely changes in their curriculum. This has resulted in a lag behind other industrialized nations in economy and culture. A General Motors executive commented, when asked why GM did not enter into more partnerships with colleges and universities, "Their speed is deceptive...they are slower than they look" (*Dateline 2000: The New Higher Education Agenda*, p. 7). As far back as 1982, John Naisbitt wrote in *Megatrends*, "We have not embraced the future...we have extraordinary leverage and influence—individually, professionally, and institutionally—if we can only get a clear...vision of the road ahead" (pp. 249–252).

In 1986, the American Association of Colleges and Universities, in the publication *National Commission on the Role and Future of State Colleges and Universities*, recommended three major areas of focus for an international perspective:

◊ College students must be given a perspective that reflects the world in realistic social, political, economic, and cultural terms.

◊ College students must be able to think, behave, and work effectively in a world of rapid change.

◊ Colleges must assist in resolving international problems with the kind of commitment it gives to similar domestic issues through research, technical assistance, and service.

In 1987, Ernest Boyer, former president of The Carnegie Foundation for the Advancement of Teaching and author of *College: The Undergraduate Experience in America*, wrote:

Our world has undergone immense transformations. It has become a more crowded, more interconnected, more unstable place. A new generation of Americans must be educated for life in this increasingly complex world. If the undergraduate college cannot help students see beyond themselves and better understand the interdependent nature of our world, each new generation will remain ignorant, and its capacity to live confidently and responsibly will be dangerously diminished. (p. 282)

The focus on international education has grown over the past two decades. Most, if not all, universities now include global awareness in their mission statements and strategic plans. But thus far, the overall momentum for assuring that students genuinely understand the impact of global interdependence is not impressive. While the study of foreign languages increased (Welles, 2004, p. 12), and universities added Asian and other languages to the traditional European offerings, and while universities extended their requirements of foreign languages for admission or graduation, many students have not appreciated the value of knowing another language. Universities have not adequately communicated the importance of multicultural understanding, which is summed up in a statement by former Georgetown University President Timothy Healy, "Our ignorance of language keeps us nationally from making the kind of salving contact which ties people together, which enables people to talk person to person, and which in the long run can prevent embroilment, misunderstanding and violence" (Parnell, 1990, p. 90).

Universities are now clearer than they were two decades ago in their pursuit of international students and on the value of international education. Many institutions currently offer effective programs and excellent international experiences for students. However, those opportunities, by and large, benefit a limited number of the total student population. Today, decades after visionary insights and forecasts by respected national educators, the quandary of students' understanding of a multicultural and interrelated world lingers on most campuses.

There are signs that the tide may be turning. In fall 2006, Goucher College became the first college in the United States to require all of its undergraduates to study abroad at least once before graduation. Students may choose a year-long, semester, summer, or brief intensive course experience from among 29 countries. Each student is provided a voucher of $1,200 to defray the cost of the study abroad. Believing "that international awareness is a requirement for anybody who wants to lead a satisfying and successful life in the global community of today," (Goucher College, n.d.), Goucher has chosen *Going Global* as its brand. The college understood the risk of a decreased enrollment of freshmen because of the new requirement, which it responsibly announced widely to its currently enrolled students and prospective freshmen. But the freshman class of fall 2006 was more than 10% larger than the fall 2005 freshman class. The college will conduct standard surveys to determine if the new global focus was a major factor in the new freshmen's decision to attend Goucher (Gail Edmonds, personal communication, August 29, 2006).

Relying on the ability of its student affairs professionals to adapt to new situations and needs of students, Goucher did not provide particular additional in-service preparation for its student affairs staff. However, in previous years, the college found a number of students returning from study abroad with re-entry issues of feeling different, isolated, and challenged as they reflected on their experiences and attempted to process the significance of their new discoveries, especially those who witnessed poverty and other startling conditions for the first time. With the new study abroad mandate for all undergraduates, Goucher anticipates a greater need for counseling on a larger scale, and student affairs and academic affairs faculty and staff are collaborating in preparation of a higher volume of requests to address re-entry and processing concerns (Gail Edmonds, personal communication, August 29, 2006).

Some vice presidents and vice chancellors of student affairs and services of leading colleges and universities already embrace the concept of internationalizing student affairs and services. In August 2006, an informal e-mail survey to 25 distinguished current and emeritus senior student affairs officers at private and public institutions across North America asked, "What is your concept or definition—off the top of your head—of 'internationalizing student affairs and services in higher education'?" The ten responses showed both strong commitment and multifaceted approaches.

The respondents stressed the importance of both infusing on-campus programs and activities with international dimensions and encouraging various paths to study abroad for students and staff. They also suggested that traditional U.S. student affairs practices should be open to influences and best practices from other countries. One idea was to invite student affairs staff on leave from their own universities abroad to be visiting professionals on U.S. campuses. Another suggestion was to include cross-cultural communication in staff development. One respondent suggested that internationalizing student services should involve greater sensitivity to the personal and cultural needs of our international students.

Two respondents gave specific examples of integrating an international dimension into the fabric of the campus:

◊ Emory University plans to integrate its International Students and Scholars Program with all of its other international programs and services (such as study abroad) and to co-locate all the offices, attaching them to a residence hall with an international theme near the center of the main campus (John Ford, Emory University, personal communication, August 8, 2006).

◊ The University of Southern California has created an international residential college to bring domestic students together with foreign students for learning, teaching, cross-cultural exchange, and fun (Michael Jackson, University of Southern California, personal communication, August 14, 2006).

University administrators can incorporate international experiences into the curriculum and work environment, as surely as student affairs professionals can help to increase international education on their campuses. The question is not *if* the curricular and co-curricular transformation will occur. The questions are *when* will it take place, *how* can it be facilitated, and *who* would initiate the process. It is long overdue. The sooner it occurs, the higher our confidence will be raised regarding our graduates' ability to succeed in an increasingly complex world. With Goucher College at the lead, other institutions are apt to add to the momentum. Student affairs professionals must prepare themselves and look forward to an active role in the new direction.

At least 15 U.S. universities' graduate programs that prepare higher education student affairs and services professionals currently include an international dimension. Courses in multicultural and comparative studies educate students in demographic, legal, political, economic, and linguistic differences among nations and encourage students to think globally. Study tours, exchanges, internships and practicum, research, hosting international symposia, and other experiences are preparing graduate students for an important role in the internationalization of student affairs and services (The University of Arizona, n.d.).

As so astutely suggested by the authors of this book, the internationalization of student affairs and services is a concept whose time has come. In order for the internationalization movement to succeed, student affairs professionals must recognize its need and commit to it. Travel, exchanges, service, speaking engagements, and scholarly activities are some of many in-service approaches to internationalize the profession. Staff and student exchanges can have transformational and lasting effects in international awareness and understanding. Student affairs professionals can initiate the internationalization process, and they will need the backing and resource support of their universities to propel the movement.

For student affairs professionals the first step in deepening their global awareness is to expand their knowledge of how colleges and universities in other countries deliver services to students and how their colleagues across the oceans are educated and prepared to serve students. Not surprisingly, there is great diversity in delivery of services and notable differences from country to country in the educational requirements of student affairs professionals, ranging from formal advanced degree programs to informal on-the-job training supplemented with self-sought, in-service education and professional conferences.

It is logical to start the movement at the grassroots, where it can be nurtured and take root. However, the grassroots effort must be accompanied by a national direction, delineated collaboratively with campuses. NASPA–Student Affairs Administrators in Higher Education can provide organizational leadership at the national level. Already conscious of the growing interest in an international direction, NASPA has proactively developed exchanges for student affairs professionals in 11 countries (Australia, China, France, Germany, Ireland, México, New Zealand, South Africa, Spain, United Arab Emirates, and United Kingdom). NASPA also established the International Education Knowledge Community, which has become an active and prominent group in the association and will, undoubtedly, be fully engaged in shaping the national direction.

A combined grassroots-and-association approach to internationalize student affairs and services is rational. The grassroots strategy provides the decentralization that appeals to professionals, and the association involvement provides the national leadership and visibility. In *Megatrends*, Naisbitt reasons that "decentralization is the great facilitator of social change" (p. 129). The combined approach is unifying, and it is predicted to engender enthusiasm and support among NASPA members for a worldwide association or network of student affairs and services professionals, which has presented a challenge for more than a decade.

The time is right for NASPA to organize a think tank to strategize the student affairs and services international education movement. The outcomes of a think tank, potentially, are profound, challenging, and exciting. NASPA can provide instant role model leadership for campuses. For example, if all of NASPA's 21 Knowledge Communities would add an international component to their mission, that single action will spark a flurry of similar actions across American campuses. If all 21 Knowledge Communities would engage in collaborative research on an international question with their counterparts in other countries, the results could advance the entire profession at a world level. If one student affairs professional on each campus would befriend a colleague in another country, hundreds of international relationships would be established. If one student affairs professional in each state of the nation would submit an article to an international journal, significant insights would be shared with hundreds of colleagues around the world. If one student affairs professional in each state would provide an account of his or her campus' efforts to build a sense of community among domestic and international students, other nations will recognize that U.S. universities sincerely welcome the presence of and genuinely value and care about students from other countries. Scores of practical and useful proposals could result from dialogue on advancing the internationalization of student affairs and services from being an emerging trend to becoming a movement.

Student affairs professionals and the profession are called to action. Here is an opportunity for student affairs and services to play an active role in a major goal that will result in better preparation of college students as citizens of the world. The internationalization movement will, simultaneously, contribute to institutions' international goals, support the strength of our nation, and deepen students' and student affairs professionals' understanding of the importance and complexity of global interdependence and interrelationships. A successful movement will be a challenge—and an exciting and rewarding one. It is an opportunity not to be missed. The authors of this book ask that you help us progress from an emerging perspective to a full-fledged movement to internationalize and globalize student services and student affairs. Now is the time to act.

References

American Association of Colleges and Universities. (1986). *To secure the blessings of liberty: report of the National Commission on the Role and Future of State Colleges and Universities*. Washington, DC: American Association of State Colleges and Universities.

Boyer, E. (1987). *College: The undergraduate experience in America*. NY: Harper & Row.

Goucher College. (n.d.). International studies. Retrieved August 29, 2006, from the Goucher College Web site: http://www.goucher.edu/x4737.xml/

Naisbitt, J. (1982). *Megatrends*. NY: Warner Books.

Parnell, D. (1990). *Dateline 2000: The new higher education agenda*. Washington, DC: The Community College Press.

The University of Arizona. (n.d.). Directory of college student personnel preparation programs with international emphasis. Retrieved August 29, 2006, from The University of Arizona, Center for Study of High Education Web site: http://www.ed.arizona.edu/csppp/index2.asp

Welles, E. (2004, Winter–Spring). Foreign language enrollments in United States institutions of higher education, fall 2002. *ADFL Bulletin*. Association of Departments of Foreign Languages, 1–20.

APPENDIX A

TERMINOLOGY FOR THE STUDENT AFFAIRS AND SERVICES PROFESSION

It is important to understand the context in which some of the terminology used in this book is applied. Because the text crosses international borders, it is important that the industry "jargon" be defined in order for all readers to understand the context of the terminology used.

Boletín Oficial del Estado (BOE) – A daily Spanish Government publication in which new laws are published.

The Bologna Process is the most important and wide-ranging reform of higher education in Europe since the immediate aftermath of 1968. The ultimate aim of the Process is to establish a European Higher Education Area by 2010 in which staff and students can move with ease and have fair recognition of their qualifications. This overall goal is reflected in the six main goals defined in the Bologna Declaration:

◊ a system of easily readable and comparable degrees, including the implementation of the Diploma Supplement;

◊ a system essentially based on two main cycles: a first cycle relevant to the labor market, and a second cycle requiring the completion of the first cycle;

◊ a system of accumulation and transfer of credits;

◊ the mobility of students, teachers, researchers, etc;

◊ cooperation in quality assurance;

◊ the European dimension of higher education.

An important goal of the Process is thus to move higher education in Europe toward a more transparent and mutually recognized system that would place the diversified national systems into a common frame based on three outcome levels—bachelor's, master's, and doctoral—and recognize different paths according to which they were achieved.

Campus Climate – Campus climate does not refer to any weather phenomenon but instead refers to a feeling that can be sensed by people on campus, such as the feeling people get when addressing issues of multiculturalism. There may be policies and procedures when it comes to multiculturalism, but what is the actuality of the policies? Do people feel part of the campus or separate?

Campus Structures – The various structures within any campus environment that have been developed to provide the various opportunities for students to learn and prosper. Those structures, whether within student affairs or some other administrative unit, are there to provide the framework by which our professionals develop the programs necessary for students to learn, prosper, and grow.

Colegiales – The members of the Colegio Mayor.

Colegios Mayores – University center for education and accommodation of students.

Collegium – Latin word for college. In Spain, the United Kingdom, and Italy the word later meant university center for education and accommodation (housing).

Consejo de Colegios Mayores (Consejo for short) – Body of directors or rectors of the Colegios Mayores chosen as permanent advisers on matters of Colegios Mayores.

CSAO – See SSAO.

Deutsches Studentenwerk (DSW) – DSW is the national student affairs association overseeing of 61 Studentenwerke (statutory organizations for student affairs) and is funded by contributions from its members and by funds for federal and regional authority projects.

ERASMUS Programme – The higher education action of the SOCRATES II programme. It seeks to enhance the quality and reinforce the European dimension of higher education by encouraging transnational cooperation among universities, boosting European mobility, and improving the transparency and full academic recognition of studies and qualifications throughout the Union (Socrates-Erasmus, n.d.).

European Health Card E111 or E128 – This is a supporting health insurance document that must be prepared in the native European Union country before traveling to Spain. Since June 2004, the European Health Insurance Card is the alternative document for all European citizens.

European Union (EU) – A family of democratic European countries committed to working together for peace and prosperity.

Evolution of Student Affairs and Services – As higher education has changed, so too have the services available to students on campus; and as the services and demands of the students have changed, student affairs as a profession has evolved as well. What works in one country may not be an option in another, and what the needs of students are in one geographical area may not be the needs of students in other areas. Student affairs and services are constantly changing and evolving, and that is as it should be within the context of student development theory. As a campus and its students change, so do the services provided.

Fulbright Scholar Program – The U.S. government's flagship program in international educational exchange. Fulbright grants are made to citizens of the United States and other countries for a variety of educational activities, primarily university lecturing, advanced research, graduate study, and teaching in elementary and secondary schools. The Fulbright Program is sponsored by the United States Department of State, Bureau of Educational and Cultural Affairs (CIES, n.d.).

General Delegate – A person with power to act for or to represent the Consejo de Colegios Mayores in all matters.

Higher Education – One of many accepted terms used when addressing university and college educational systems.

Instituto Nacional de Estadistica (INE) – (English translation: National Institute of Statistics).

International Collaboration – The process by which people from different countries, institutions, and professions work together to achieve a common goal or result.

International Exchange – An opportunity for students, staff, and faculty to take part in some form of formal exchange program with another country. There are many ways for students to take part in international exchange programs, and the best way for them to do that is to contact their international student affairs/services offices. In the context of staff development, there are not as many opportunities. To counter the lack of exchange programs for staff, professional associations such as NASPA–Student Affairs Administrators in Higher Education initiated a formal international exchange program in 1996 with France. Since then, NASPA has signed agreements with 11 other countries. For more information on the NASPA International Exchange Program go to http://www.naspa.org/programs/intl

Internationalization – The process by which a university changes the infrastructure or the campus ecology to keep up with the changing demand for more direct links to higher education outside its own country of origin.

L.O.U. – Ley Orgánica de Universidades (Constitutional Law for the University).

L.R.U. – Ley de Reforma (University Reform Law).

Peak Bodies – A peak body is typically an overarching not-for-profit association or organization recognized as representing the views and interests of relevant associations or organizations within a particular sector or user interest group. The peak body provides services and representation on behalf of its members who generally have similar goals, community service foci, or sector agendas. The peak body provides referent power for purposes such as political lobbying or providing a collective response to government legislation, policy, or initiatives.

People to People International (PTPI) – A voluntary effort of private citizens promoting international understanding through direct people-to-people contacts. The purpose of PTPI is to enhance international understanding and friendship through educational, cultural, and humanitarian activities involving exchange of ideas and experiences directly among people of different countries and diverse cultures. While not a partisan or political institution, PTPI supports the basic values and goals of its founder, President Dwight D. Eisenhower (PTPI, n.d.).

Socrates-Erasmus – For complete details go to http://ec.europa.eu/education/index_en.html. Also refer to ERASMUS program above.

SSAO – The acronym for Senior Student Affairs Officer. This term refers to the most senior person on campus responsible for the administration of student affairs on campus.

Student Affairs – The term adopted by individuals involved with the administration of student services programs. Student affairs is the umbrella term for all student-related functions come under.

Student Demographic – The characteristics of the population under review. Depending upon the university, the actual categories of characteristics will vary. Generally, within the context of the college and university, the demographic characteristics are age, sex, race, disability, veteran status, religion, nationality, sexual orientation, financial status, etc.

Student Development Theory – The study of how students develop and grow within the context of the educational setting. Student affairs practitioners use student development theory to understand the students on their campuses and to plan the student services that are provided on the campus. Student development theory is the cornerstone of student affairs programs.

Student Services – In some instances, this is a subset of the umbrella program of student affairs. However, in many countries the student services component is the primary administrative unit responsible for the coordination of all student-related services. The term is used to describe the actual services available to students on college and university campuses. The actual services provided will vary from campus to campus.

Student Services Delivery Model – The way various institutions provide the organized student services on a campus. There is no set model, and the way services are delivered will vary from campus to campus and country to country.

References

CIES. (n.d.). *About Fulbright*. Retrieved July 8, 2005, from http://www.cies.org/about_fulb.htm/

PTPI. (n.d.). *About Us*. Retrieved from PTPI on July 7, 2005, from http://www.ptpi.org/about_us/

Socrates-Erasmus. (n.d.). *Socrates-Erasmus: the European Community programme in the field of higher education*. Retrieved February 17, 2005, from http://ec.europa.eu/education/index_en.html

STUDENT AFFAIRS ORGANIZATIONS AND ASSOCIATIONS AROUND THE WORLD

COMPILED BY ROGER B. LUDEMAN

The goal of Appendix B is to provide a comprehensive list of national, regional, and international professional associations and organizations of student affairs and services. These groups provide assistance and development opportunities for student affairs and services staff as well as perform advocacy for students, develop positions on key issues, and address policy needs external or internal to the groups themselves.

Included here are student affairs and services groups of which the author was aware at the time of publication. The information was accurate as of the printing of this publication. There are numerous student associations around the world; however, for the purposes of this chapter, those groups are not included.

In the interests of accuracy, much of the material on the following organizations/associations was secured from their respective Web sites, conference papers, and publications or from individuals familiar with the organizations and associations that have been included. Wherever possible, the Web site address has been included for reference purposes. The author hereby acknowledges these sources and appreciates the use of this information and the contribution it makes to better understanding the organizations and associations that support student affairs and services in higher education around the world.

The information on these groups is presented in English, the language of this publication. Most of the websites included herein are already in English or offer the English version. Others can be translated using Google.com by entering the Web site URL in the Google search box and, once the desired site comes up, click on the "Translate This Page" box to the immediate right of that URL.

Africa

Regional

Association of African Universities (AAU). The AAU is an international non-governmental organization set up by the universities in Africa to promote cooperation among the universities and between them and the international academic community. It is the principal forum for consultation, exchange of information, and cooperation among the 185 member universities in 44 African countries. Its primary objectives are to promote cooperation among university institutions in Africa; encourage increased contacts between its members and the international academic world; study and make known the educational needs of African university institutions; and organize seminars and conferences among African university teachers, administrators, and others dealing with problems of higher education in Africa. While student affairs and services is not a fully developed concept in most of Africa, there are university administrators and others who perform those tasks. The AAU addresses issues related to this field of work by identifying and finding solutions for student needs. Web site: http://www.aau.org

Egypt

Supreme Council of Universities (SCU). The SCU was established in 1950 to plan the policymaking of Egyptian university education and scientific research as well as to coordinate matters among Egyptian governmental universities. The SCU issues all policies and decisions related to graduate and postgraduate studies, curricula, and universities' regulations as well as faculty and staff matters. It also determines the annual enrollments and admission rules for different faculties. The SCU sets up a number of committees to assist in carrying out its duties and includes committees on sectors, accreditation of academic degrees, academic work evaluation, and cultural relations, among others. Student affairs is one department of SCU. Web site: http://www.scu.eun.eg/eng/scu-eng.htm

South Africa

Campus Protection Society of Southern Africa (CAMPROSA). CAMPROSA is dedicated to the creation of a free and safe environment on the campuses of South Africa. Through sharing of policies and documentation, workshops, and conferences for institutional and individual members, CAMPROSA informs and educates those who work in this field. The organization also works to improve legislation and funding related to campus security and law enforcement in South Africa. Web site: http://www.camprosa.co.za

Centre for the Transformation of Higher Education (CHET). CHET is a non-governmental organization that strives to develop transformation management capacity and skills throughout the higher education system by integrating skill development training processes with new knowledge production, debates, and information dissemination. CHET mobilizes trans-disciplinary skills for specific projects by tapping available expertise in the national and international higher education sector. CHET provides a forum for interaction between the different structures, stakeholders, and constituencies in higher education and is currently collaborating actively with the Ministry of Education, the Committee of University Principals, the Committee of University of Technology Principals, Committee of College Education Rectors South Africa, and the National Centre for Student Leadership. International collaborators include the American Council on Education, the Association for African Universities, the Commonwealth Higher Education Management Services, and the Centre for Higher Education Policy (Netherlands). Numerous projects have included student affairs practitioners and have included student leadership training and materials and the publication of *A Guide to Student Services in South Africa (2003)* that was a part of The Effective Governance Project. Web site: http://www.chet.org.za

National Association for Student Development (NASDEV). NASDEV initially consisted of the technikon (now universities of technology) cultural program organizers and has become the professional development voice of the advisors of student organizations including the Student Representative Councils (SRCs), the student government groups in South Africa, along with other staff interested in total student development. From their beginning in 1986, their emphasis has been the development of the whole student. Conferences, schools, workshops, and other professional development activities are conducted annually. Web site: http://www.nasdev.org.za

Financial Aid Practitioners of South Africa (FAPSA). FAPSA was formed in 2002, making it the newest student affairs related professional association in South Africa. Its purposes include empowerment of financial aid practitioners, standardization of best practices, and creation of a national forum to discuss relevant financial aid issues. Most universities, technical institutions, the National Student Financial Aid Scheme (NSFAS) staff, and private financial aid providers belong to FAPSA. Work groups have been established in the following areas: merger, National Means Test, measuring academic performance, research on policy, and professional development. Contact: Jameson Ngomane, President. E-mail: ngomanej@nu.ac.za

South African Association of Campus Health Services (SAACHS). SAACHS provides the opportunity for campus health officers to discuss common concerns such as HIV/AIDS and other health issues affecting South African tertiary education students. It also provides professional development experiences including an annual conference and workshops held across the country. Contact: Antoinette Goosen, SAACHS Chair. E-mail: antoinette.goosen@upe.ac.za

South African Association of Senior Student Affairs Professionals (SAASSAP). SAASSAP was formed in 2001 as the umbrella group in support of student affairs staff in South Africa. Projects and priorities include professional development, advocacy of student affairs and students, research, policy development, and quality assurance. A journal (*Thuso*), regional and national conferences, and advocacy at the national level are primary efforts of this group. Contact: Prof. R.C. Bodibe, President. E-mail: cbodibe@tsa.ac.za

South African Student Sports Union (SASSU). SASSU was constituted in 1994 in order to establish a unified, non-racial, national umbrella student sports structure in South Africa. Today SASSU coordinates and promotes all South African tertiary education student sport activities organized at regional, provincial, and national levels. SASSU was founded in order to represent and protect the sporting interests of all students at member institutions based on the principles of unity, accountability, non-racialism, non-sexism, and democracy. SASSU programs are aimed at promoting sporting values and encouraging sporting practice in harmony with, and complementary to, the academic character of tertiary education institutions.

Student Counselling Society of Southern Africa (SCSSA). SCSSA, an association of student counselors within higher education in Southern Africa, was established in 1974 making it the oldest student affairs related group in South Africa, as well as other surrounding countries. The SCSSA mission statement states that, "by combining all our resources into concerted action the SSCSA will become a constructive entity in enhancing our effectiveness to render relevant professional counselling services to students, educational institutions and society in Southern Africa." The central principle that guides the activities of the society is the observation of fundamental human rights. Members also come from other sub-Saharan countries.

Asia and the Pacific Rim

Regional

Asia Pacific Student Services Association (APSSA). APSSA was founded in 1988. Its objectives are to enhance liaison and cooperation among members in the development of student affairs work and student services in the Asia-Pacific region; to assist in the development of student affairs work and to strengthen its role in the development of tertiary education in the region; to promote the welfare of students in tertiary education; and to enhance intercultural understanding and develop intercultural communication skills among members. A biennial conference is held throughout the region and the APSSA Student Affairs Institute for training staff is one of the best projects of the association. Web site: http://home.ust.hk/~sanet/apssa.htm

Australia/New Zealand

Australia and New Zealand Student Services Association (ANZSSA). ANZSSA is the umbrella organization for a wide variety of professional and lay student services providers who share a common concern for the welfare and development of postsecondary education students and their institutions in the two countries. A biennial conference is the major ANZSSA meeting, one that also attracts numerous international participants. Regional and state meetings are the main ANZSSA events between biennial conferences. Special Interest Groups (SIGs) within ANZSSA are free to organize their own specialized activities, often with ANZSSA financial sponsorship. Current SIGs are the Counselors, Heads of Services, Campus Nurses Professional Association, Student Financial Advisers Network (SFAN), TAFE Student Services Network, and Equity. *JANZSSA*, the journal of ANZSSA, is published and distributed to members twice a year. Members are encouraged to contribute a variety of material including scholarly articles, information communications, comments, book reviews, and items of interest to the general membership. Web site: http://www.anzssa.org

International Education Association (ISANA). ISANA is the representative body for professionals in Australia and New Zealand who work in international student services, advocacy, teaching, and policy development in international education. Its members are dedicated to the advancement of international education through leadership, promotion and advocacy of best practice standards for international education, the facilitation of relevant forums, training and information exchange for its membership and the community, and working in partnership with stakeholder organizations including international students, educational, government, business, and community groups. ISANA also recognizes the interests and rights of international students in Australia and New Zealand. Web site: http://www.isana.org.au/AboutIsana.aspx

Student Housing Officers Association of Australia (SHOAA). SHOAA is a privately incorporated association. Its purposes are to: promote and develop the effectiveness of student housing officers, seek the provision of appropriate accommodation for students, encourage a philosophy of service provision, liaise with relevant housing and educational organizations, to work cooperatively with other organizations to further the aims of the association, and affiliate with such organizations as the members in general meeting may from time to time decide. Through its conferences, workshops, publications, and other activities, the members share information and resources, as well as develop policies and undertake campaigns to improve the accommodation options and access for students. Web site: http://www.housing.rmit.edu.au/shoaa/index.html

National Association of Australian University Colleges (NAAUC). NAAUC, founded in 1998, is the peak representative body for Australian tertiary students living on campus. As a not-for-profit association, NAAUC aims to coordinate a network of communications on a national scale, together with fostering goodwill among association members, and liaising with college heads and administration, to provide the best possible advice and referral to Australian colleges and halls of residences. Web site: http://www.naauc.edu.au

China

Association of Normal University Student Affairs in China (ANUSAC). ANUSAC is comprised of the student affairs officers of more than 50 normal universities (for education of teachers) in China. Regular meetings and conferences are held annually that emphasize new trends in student affairs, professional development, international activity, and new policy issues. Contact: Wu Zhigong, President. E-mail: wzhg@bnu.edu.cn

Hong Kong Student Services Association (HKSSA). HKSSA's beginnings go back as early as 1978, and the organization was formally constituted and registered with the government as a charitable society in 1984. A range of activities have been organized both locally and abroad for its members, students, and the community of Hong Kong. It has also become a major channel of communication between its members and their counterparts in the Asia Pacific region and in the English-speaking world. Web site: http://home.ust.hk/~hkssa

Japan

Japan Association of Private Colleges and Universities (JAPCU). JAPCU includes a committee that focuses on issues pertaining to student affairs. Web site: http://www.shidairen.or.jp/english/outline/message.html

Japan Student Services Organization (JASSO). The Japan Scholarship Foundation; Association of International Education, Japan; Center for Domestic and Foreign Students; The International Students Institute; and The Kansai International Students Institute unified to establish the Japan Student Services Organization in 2004. Because of the rapidly changing social and economic climate in Japan, there is an increasing need for universities to provide well-designed education and guidance for diversifying student populations. JASSO provides comprehensive assistance in developing such student support programs and the wide range of support activities that universities implement for their students. Web site: http://www.jasso.go.jp/about_jasso/index_e.html

Japan Association of National Universities (JANU). JANU provides a variety of services and programs for its members including promotion and advocacy, policy research, international exchange, and staff professional development. One of its committees, undergraduate education and student support, conducts research for the improvement of undergraduate education as well as for the improvement of the study environment and career planning assistance for university students. Web site: http://www.kokudaikyo.gr.jp/eng

Malaysia

Malaysian Secretariat of Deputy Vice-Chancellors of Student Affairs Council. The Secretariat, comprised of 17 Malaysian public universities, was founded in 1981 and is the oldest Deputy Vice-Chancellors' Council in Malaysia. The Secretariat was formed to coordinate student activities/programs (student welfare, services, and development) in all 17 public universities in Malaysia. It provides a meaningful and effective platform for interactions and exchange of interests among deputy vice-chancellors of student affairs organizing common interest activities/programs/projects at national and international levels. To carry out its student development agenda, eight councils have been established including the Sports Council (MASUM), Cultural Council (MAKUM), Debating Council (MADUM), Leadership and Training Council (MAKLUM), Student Housing Council (MAPUM), Disciplinary Council (MATDUM), Entrepreneurship Council (MAKMUM), and Counselling Council (MAKUMA). Along with promoting the domestic student development agenda, the Secretariat also develops good relations with universities in other countries, e.g., Hong Kong, Korea, Indonesia, Japan, Australia, New Zealand, and Egypt. The Secretariat also provides avenues for discussions between the Ministry of Higher Education and the deputy vice-chancellors (student affairs) for the purposes of promoting better learning environments and student excellence. Contact: Prof. Madya Dr. Jamaludin Mohaiadin, DVC (Student Affairs), Universiti Sains Malaysia and Chair, Secretariat of Deputy Vice-Chancellors of Student Affairs Council, Malaysia. E-mail: dvc_student@usm.my, jmoh@usm.my.

Philippines

Philippine Association of Administrators of Student Affairs (PAASA). PAASA officially came into being in 1995. Membership includes both public and private institutions of higher education. Annual conventions are held and focus on topics of interest to student affairs providers in the Philippines. Contact: Dr. Evelyn A. Songco. E-mail: osacs@ust.edu.ph

Thailand

Ministry of Education, Commission on Higher Education (CHE). The Thai Ministry of Education and its Commission on Higher Education have shown strong support for student affairs matters. They have established a Bureau of Student Development to stress the importance of the student development and holistic approach to student learning. They also have a Bureau of Higher Education Personnel Administration and Development providing a strong program of professional development and training for higher education personnel. The primary activities initiated by government policy include university games, national arts and culture festivals, learning together and community enhancement programs, international enhancement and global awareness programs, drugs and HIV-AIDS prevention programs, and student exposure for global awareness. Website: http://www.moe.go.th/English/.

Europe

Regional

European Association of Campus Security (EACS). EACS was formed as a nonprofit organization to promote the common interest in the administration of law enforcement programs, including the operation and development of life safety and property safety programs on university campuses, to share and exchange the experiences in security in universities and to promote professional ideas and standards so as to better serve the educational objectives of higher education. EACS holds a congress every two years. Web site: http://www.euro-campus-secur.org/english/bylaws.htm

European Association of International Education (EAIE). EAIE's main aim is to stimulate and facilitate the internationalization of higher education in Europe and around the world, and to meet the professional needs of individuals active in international education. EAIE strives to link international education professionals together in order to help create a global environment where there is mobility and education for all. To this end, the EAIE works to aid in the professional development of internationalizers and to ensure that important information is not only disseminated, but that there is an increased awareness about critical issues so that they can be debated in order to come to mutual understandings. EAIE offers various training courses throughout the year, disseminating important issues via publications, providing a forum with the EAIE-L online, and most importantly, by creating an atmosphere for learning, debate, and networking at the Annual EAIE Conference. The EAIE, with its Professional Sections and Special Interest Groups, ensures that adequate attention is paid to the more specific topics that concern EAIE members as well as the general topics challenging the international higher education arena. Web site: http://www.eaie.nl

European Council for Student Affairs (ECStA). ECStA is an autonomous and independent European umbrella group that promotes the social infrastructure for students at all higher education institutions in Europe. It was formed in 1999, the result of various European conferences on economic and social support for students held in the 1990s, and it serves as a contact and advisory body for the European Commission and European Council of Ministers, as well as international organizations such as UNESCO and the Council of Europe on matters related to higher education student affairs. ECStA promotes the mobility of program students and free movers (students who arrange and finance their own stay abroad). The association serves the objectives stated in article 149 of the EC-Treaty under education, vocational training and youth, namely student mobility, student study, student funding, accommodations, restaurants (food services), guidance and counseling, cultural work, conferences and colloquia, surveys and research, and cultural and exchange projects for students and staff. Web site: http://www.ecsta.org

European Forum for Student Guidance (FEDORA). FEDORA was founded in 1988 to support, guide, and inform students on issues such as study and work opportunities across Europe and student mobility. Large numbers of European students undertake part of their studies at another European university. This has resulted in more students presenting advisers and counselors with new and more numerous challenges. It is in response to these challenges that university guidance staff members have developed a trans-European network for cooperation. FEDORA also is committed to supporting the development of student advisory services in Eastern Europe. Every three years FEDORA organizes a European Congress. FEDORA Summer Universities are devoted to student adviser/counselor training. Web site: http://www.fedora.eu.org.

Higher Education Accessibility Guide (HEAG). HEAG is a guide to accessibility services in higher education institutions across Europe. Web site: http://www.european-agency.org/heag/index.html

Belgium

Conseil Interuniversitaire de la Communauté Française (CIUF). CIUF, founded in 1980 and confirmed in 2003 by law, is a Belgian government initiative. It is a consultative body for the Minister of Higher Education and a discussion body for French-speaking universities on any issue related to university education. Included are providing information on admission requirements, various forms of

financial aid, courses taught in English and French, and information about Belgian universities and Belgium. Web site: http://www.cfwb.be/ciuf/englishpages/indexeng.html

Finland

The Centre for International Mobility (CIMO). CIMO, an organization operating under the Finnish Ministry of Education, offers services and expertise to encourage cross-cultural communication. It administers scholarship and exchange programs and is responsible for implementing nearly all EU education, training, culture, and youth programs at the national level. To support internationalization of educational and training institutions in Finland, CIMO offers training, information, advisory services, and publications. CIMO also promotes and organizes international trainee exchanges and advances teaching of Finnish language and culture in universities abroad and arranges summer courses in Finnish language and culture for international students. CIMO was established in 1991 and it operates under the Finnish Ministry of Education. Beneficiaries of CIMO's services include students, young workers and other young people, and those who work with them. Web site: http://www.cimo.fi/Resource.phx/cimo/mainpage/mainpage.htx.

Finnish Student Health Service (FSHS). FSHS was founded by the National Union of Finnish Students in 1954, having its roots in the 1930s. It covers all university students in 16 cities and the services at 16 health centers that provide students with preventive health care, medical care, mental health care and dental health care. The services are financed by the Social Insurance Institution, the students and student unions, the university cities and the State of Finland. Students are entitled to use the online health counseling service through which FSHS general practitioners and nurses give instructions and advice on health and illnesses. Students receive answers to their questions at the Web site within one to three business days. FSHS is a foundation and students are well represented at all levels within the administration. FSHS has a chief physician, a chief psychiatrist, and a chief dental officer. There are 10 local boards for the administration of health centers. Web site: http://www.yths.fi/netcomm

Finland's Student Housing Ltd (SOA). SOA focuses on cooperation among student housing groups and attempting to satisfy the demand for student housing. SOA activities include promoting the production of student accommodation with the aid of state loans and promoting the management, maintenance, and renovating of the sites. The key roles include communicating with the state administration and political decision makers as well as representing student housing associations in different organizations and planning committees. SOA also promotes research on student housing with the overall aim of ensuring that student housing associations can offer student apartments and services that are of reasonable cost and meet the students' requirements. Web site: http://www.soa.fi/eng/SOA/fsh.html

France

Centre Nationale des Œuvres Universitaires et Scolaires (CNOUS). CNOUS is the national French student affairs organization. It coordinates activities with the 29 regional student services units—the Centres Reginaux des Œuvres Universitaires et Scolaires (CROUS)—and the local units—Centres Lacaux des Œuvres Universitaires et Scolaires (CLOUS)—that are responsible for improving the living conditions of students and working with foreign students and scholarship holders. Each CROUS is responsible for these services in all institutions of higher learning in their region, private and public. Services include accommodation, food, scholarships, social welfare, child care, student employment, research, and cultural and recreational activities. CNOUS and some CROUS units have longstanding relationships with student affairs organizations or higher education institutions in other countries, including those of the European Council for Student Affairs and the United States, among others. Web site: http://www.cnous.fr

Germany

Deutscher Akademischer Austausch Dienst (DAAD). The German Academic Exchange Service is the support organization for all German institutions of higher education. It promotes relations between these institutions and those in other countries through exchanges of students and faculty. Programs are open to all countries and disciplines. Other services include scholarships, information, publications, and counseling and advising. Web site: http://www.daad.org

Deutsches Studentenwerk (DSW). DSW is the national student affairs association overseeing of 61 Studentenwerke (statutory organizations for student affairs) and is funded by contributions from its members and by funds for federal and regional authority projects. DSW is, therefore, both a federal agency and an organization that provides for student affairs staff members across all of Germany. The Studentenwerk organizations in Germany are completely autonomous from the universities or colleges and are fully independent organizations that cooperate closely with the higher education institutions they serve. Many Studentenwerk organizations are simultaneously responsible for several higher education institutions and, in some cases, for institutions at various locations. DSW supports and promotes its member organizations by representing their interests and contributing their expertise to national and federal state legislation; supporting them either collectively or individually by organizing special conferences, compiling working aids, publishing information material, and carrying out initial and continuing education and training; and pursuing an active policy of public relations. Student services offered across Germany include accommodation, food services, financial support, cultural support, health care, services for students with disabilities, and sport. Several publications and research projects are carried out annually. DSW cooperates with the Conference of Rectors, university presidents, the German Academic Exchange (DAAD), and federal and regional authorities. DSW has a long history of relationships with student affairs groups in other countries including Europe (European Council for Student Affairs), the United States, and several countries in Central and Eastern Europe. Web site: http://www.studentenwerke.de/ (German only), English pages geared to incoming international students available at http://www.internationale-studierende.de/en/home/

Ireland

AHEAD – the Association for Higher Education Access and Disability. AHEAD is an independent nonprofit organization working to promote full access to and participation in third level education for students with disabilities in Ireland. AHEAD, founded in 1990, undertakes research in areas relating to disability and third level education and acts in a consultative capacity to the Higher Education Authority, educational institutions, and other bodies in the education sector. The group lobbies to improve access to and increase the participation of students with disabilities in higher and further education in Ireland. It also strives to inform and change national policy in the areas of education and the employment of graduates with disabilities. Web site: http://www.aheadweb.org/home/pages

Association of Graduate Careers Services in Ireland (AGCSI). AGCSI is the professional association for careers services in higher education in Ireland, North and South. It fosters cooperation among the individual careers services, producing a range of careers publications for students and graduates. The AGCSI mission is to lead, support, and develop collaboration among higher education careers services in the development and delivery of high quality careers guidance for students and graduates, and in their work with employers and academics. Web site: http://www.gradireland.com/AboutUs/index.asp

Confederation of Student Services in Ireland (CSSI). CSSI coordinates information on student services throughout the island, producing newsletters and holding biennial conferences and annual events. The CSSI is interested in increasing North–South cooperative ventures in all aspects of third-level education including research and support services. Recent international exchange agreements include one with NASPA–Student Affairs Administrators in Higher Education. Web site: http://www.cssi.edu.ie

Higher Education Authority (HEA). The Higher Education Authority is the statutory planning and development body for higher education and research in Ireland. The HEA has wide advisory powers throughout the whole of the third-level education sector. In addition it is the funding authority for the universities and a number of designated higher education institutions. The principal functions of the HEA include to further the development of higher education;

maintain a continuous review of the demand and need for higher education; assist in the coordination of state investment in higher education and prepare proposals for such investment; allocate among universities and designated institutions the grants voted by the Oireachtas; and promote the attainment of equality of opportunity in higher education and democratization of higher education. In addition, HEA works with higher education institutions to develop university strategic development plans, quality assurance procedures, and equal opportunity policies and their implementation. Web site: http://www.hea.ie

Irish Association of University and College Counsellors (IAUCC). Founded in 1980, IAUCC is a professional association for counselors in all third-level institutions. Since its inception, it has included participants from colleges and universities in both the North and South. Its meetings are usually held in the South, but sometimes in the North. Contact: Marilyn J Terry, head of Student Counselling and Development, University College Cork. E-mail: counselling@ucc.ie

Irish Universities Student Services Network (IUSSN). IUSSN is a network of senior student services officers in Ireland covering five of the seven universities there. Its territory is only the South (the Republic) while CSSI covers both the South and the North (Northern Ireland). Contact: Barry Kehoe, retired Director of Student Affairs, Dublin City University. E-mail: barrykehoe@hotmail.com

National Disabilities Authority (NDA). NDA was established in 2000 under the aegis of the Department of Justice, Equality & Law Reform by the National Disability Authority Act 1999. NDA strives to ensure that the rights and entitlements of people with disabilities are protected. It acts as a national body to assist in the coordination and development of disability policy and undertakes research and develops statistical information for the planning, delivery, and monitoring of programs and services for people with disabilities. NDA members are drawn from all backgrounds and include people with disabilities, parents and caregivers of people with disabilities, and people working in the disability field. Web site: http://www.nda.ie

Italy

Centro di ricerche sull'Orientamento Scolastico-professionale e sullo Sviluppo delle organizzazioni (CROSS). CROSS provides vocational counseling through personal and group interventions. Personal advice (counseling) also is available and includes testing and information services. Contact: Professor Cristina Castelli. E-mail: cross@unicatt.it

Collegi Universitari – The Italian Conference of Colleges (CCU). CCU, recognized by the Ministry of Education, University, and Research (www.miur.it), oversees 14 institutions (with 45 university colleges or residential colleges) in 14 Italian cities. These institutions, some with longstanding traditions, pursue high quality teaching and personal development of students and serve the public interest. They expand on and characterize courses delivered by the various universities, with a wide array of projects that contribute to the student's academic, professional, and personal development. In addition to providing residential accommodation, the colleges offer students interdisciplinary cultural activities, study guidance, and tutoring services. One of the main goals of the university colleges is encouraging international integration; therefore, students also have the opportunity to take part in schemes to study abroad and host undergraduate and graduate students from all over the world. The CCU residential colleges are located in Bari, Bologna, Catania, Genova, Milano, Modena, Napoli, Padova, Palermo, Parma, Pavia, Roma, Torino, and Verona. Contact: Dr Federico Rossi, CCU Secretary's Office. E-mail f.rossi@ceur.it. Web site: www.collegiuniversitari.it

Fondazione Residenze Universitarie Internazionali (RUI). RUI develops and administers international halls of residence. It carries out scholarship and loan services for Italian and foreign students and cooperates with the ministries, regional offices, the EU, and the Council of Europe in carrying out the various aspects of Italian higher education. Web site: http://www.fondazionerui.it/index.jsp. English version: http://www.fondazionerui.it/portal/template/viewTempla te?templateId=ivjv1xsbat_layout_849griisc1.psml

Netherlands

Netherlands Organization for International Cooperation (NUFFIC). NUFFIC is a nonprofit organization that serves as a center of expertise and a provider of services related to internationally oriented education. Its aim is to enhance the opportunities that the Netherlands and its internationally oriented education have to offer to students, researchers, and the providers of higher education and training throughout the world, in both the public and private sectors. Web site: http://www.nuffic.nl/. NUFFIC has another Web site dealing with study in the Netherlands for incoming students: http://www.studyin.nl

Portugal

Conselho Nacional para a Acção Social no Ensino Superior (CNASES). CNASES is a council of 12 people that coordinates student services information nationally, proposing changes in regulations and laws accordingly. CNASES works closely with Servicos de Accao Social (SAS), semi-independent student services structures in each university or polytechnic institute. SAS receives most of its financial support from the government and mainly provides scholarships, student housing, and food service. Contact: CNASES President, c/o DESUP, Ministerio da Educacao. Tel: 351-1-354-72-70.

Spain

Consejo Colegios Mayores Universitarios de España (CCMU). CCMU is comprised of university residential centers or

Colegios Mayores, some dating back to the 17th century. They provide student accommodation, food, cultural, scientific information, credits of free configuration, and sports to residents and serve as faithful allies of their universities. CCMU was formed to serve as a common and effective communication body that solves problems affecting students and the interests of CCMU. Annual conferences are open to nonmembers. Compendia of papers are published and research conducted regularly. Web site: http://www.consejocolegiosmayores.es (Spanish only)

Servieios de Informacion y Orientacion Universitarios (SIOU). SIOU (University Information and Orientation Services) provides quality information and orientation for students in Spanish universities. Contact: Robert Lladro Chapel, director of the Area of Information. Or Polytechnical of Valencia. Web site: http://siou.um.es/english/home.php

Sweden

Talboks-och punktskriftsbibleiteket – The Swedish Library of Talking Books and Braille (TPB). TPB provides students at Swedish universities experiencing difficulties with reading (dyslexia, impaired sight, or mobility) with course literature in alternative formats, such as talking book, e-text, Braille books, or enlarged text. TPB provides course literature in foreign languages and also cooperates with talking book libraries in several countries to borrow both talking books and Braille books. The loans are administered by the university library, and all loans are free of charge. There is a contact person/coordinator, who works with issues relating to educational support for students with disabilities at all universities and institutions of higher educationWeb site: http://www.sb.su.se/studeramedfunktionshinder/english/index.htm. The Swedish Disability Ombudsman (Handikappombudsmannen) can be found at: http://www.ho.se/start.asp?sida=348&lang=en. The TPB Web site: http://www.tpb.se/english/students_service

The Swedish National Board of Student Aid (CSN). CSN is the national authority that handles the financial aid for Swedish students. CSN is the link between the government agencies that offer financial aid and their clients, i.e., students and repayers, as well as refugees and other foreign citizens. The work of CSN includes allocation of student aid and recruitment grants and handling the repayment of student loans. With the use of advanced technology and Web-based services, CSN is able to offer self-service for many clients. Web site: http://www.csn.se/english/default.asp

United Kingdom – England, Northern Ireland, Scotland, and Wales

Association for Student Residential Accommodation (ASRA). ASRA serves workers in UK higher education student housing by providing a network of support and reference. ASRA aims to promote and support its members' professional activities; provides a network for information and professional development; and provides a forum for representa-

tion, consultation, and discussion of professional interests. The organization provides an annual training conference, regional and national meetings, and training events. Web site: http://www.asra.ac.uk

Association of Dyslexia Specialists in Higher Education (AD-SHE). ADSHE was formed in order to share knowledge, inform good practice, and to achieve the following: avoid unnecessary duplication of work, establish commonly accepted codes of good practice, share experiences and overcome feelings of isolation, and work toward establishing parity of provision so that any dyslexic student will be assured of appropriate support throughout the HE sector. Web site: http://www.adshe.org.uk

The Association of Graduate Careers Advisory Services (AGCAS). AGCAS is the professional association of careers professionals in United Kingdom higher education. It numbers among its 132 institutional members the careers services of all the universities and most of the major degree-awarding colleges in the United Kingdom and Ireland, as well as almost 1,600 individuals concerned with the delivery of careers information, advice, and guidance to higher education students and graduates both in the United Kingdom and overseas. Its members collaborate with a small permanent staff toward the ultimate aim of improving the quality of careers information, advice, and guidance they are able to deliver. In addition to a biennial conference, AGCAS conducts workshops and training sessions, holds career fairs, produces media materials including a newsletter, and conducts research on labor markets and graduates and other activities in support of members and their students. Web site: http://www.agcas.org.uk

Association of Managers of Student Services in Higher Education (AMOSSHE). AMOSSHE started in 1976 as the Association of Heads of Polytechnic Student Services. In 1992 the name changed to embrace all institutions of higher education. Currently, 132 institutions in the United Kingdom and Ireland are members, representing the "old" and "new" universities and colleges/institutes of higher education. AMOSSHE provides comprehensive, professional support for the heads of student services in the United Kingdom, and through effective representation, promotes policy change to enhance the student experience. Its aims are to provide high quality support to AMOSSHE members; provide timely and up-to-date information to its members and the sector generally; represent the membership effectively both uniquely and in collaboration with other organizations; seek out, promote, and foster best practice and high quality in student service provision; initiate, promote, and contribute effectively to relevant developments within the higher education and, where appropriate, the further education sector; and secure a solid resource base to underpin AMOSSHE operations and prioritize activities so as to make best use of those resources. Web site: http://www.amosshe.org.uk

Association of University Administrators (AUA). AUA is a professional association for administrators in higher education in the United Kingdom and Ireland that promotes excellence in higher education management, provides information and networking opportunities for its members, forms international links, and enhances the professional profile through its relations with other sectors. AUA is an inclusive membership-led professional body with more than 4,000 members nationally and internationally based in universities and colleges as well as HE-related bodies. The annual conference is the largest in the U.K. higher education sector. A unique credential-based service, the AUA Postgraduate Certificate in Professional Practice (higher education administration and management), is designed by higher education administrators for higher education administrators. Web site: http://www.aua.ac.uk

Association for University and College Counselling (AUCC). AUCC is the umbrella group for counseling in higher education in the United Kingdom. It is a division of the British Association for Counselling and Psychotherapy (BACP—see entry below). Heads of University Counselling Services (HUCS) is a special interest group of AUCC and maintains a Web site on counseling resources for students, staff, and parents (http://www.hucs.org/). The AUCC Web site is http://www.aucc.uk.com

British Association for Counselling and Psychotherapy (BACP). BACP represents all professional counselors and psychotherapists in the United Kingdom and is the largest and broadest body within the sector. BACP ensures that it meets its remit of public protection while also developing and informing its members by a variety of activities including advising schools on how to set up a counseling service, assisting the National Health Service on service provision, working with voluntary agencies, and supporting independent practitioners. BACP participates in the development of counseling and psychotherapy at an international level. It operates special interest divisions and forums that focus on informing members and the public in the following areas and topics: children and young people, healthcare, workplace, higher and further education, spiritual and pastoral, independent and group practice, equality and diversity, and the voluntary sector. Web site: http://www.bacp.co.uk

Graduate Prospects, Ltd. Graduate Prospects is the official graduate careers Web site for the United Kingdom. Its mission is to be the leading U.K. provider of graduate careers and recruitment solutions. Graduate Prospects is the commercial subsidiary of the Higher Education Careers Services Unit *(HECSU).* HECSU is a registered charity that supports the work of higher education careers services in the United Kingdom and Eire and funds major research projects that benefit the higher education careers sector. HECSU is jointly owned by Universities U.K. and the Standing Conference of Principals of Colleges and institutions of higher education in the United Kingdom *(SCOP).* Graduate Prospects works in partnership with the Association of Graduate Careers Advisory Services *(AGCAS)* to maximize the opportunities and support available to all students and graduates throughout their career search. Web site: http://www.prospects.ac.uk/cms/ShowPage/Home_page/p!eLaXi

The Guidance Council. The Guidance Council, a for-profit organization, delivers a range of workshops, training, information, advice, and guidance for learning and work in the United Kingdom. It is the independent campaigning body for career guidance in the United Kingdom. The council helps individuals of all ages to develop, research, and evaluate career guidance provision in all its forms. Some of its projects include working with the national Learning and Skills Council (LSC) to encourage agencies to embed information, advice, and guidance in their activities; developing a national database to promote client success stories; developing staff competence and systems to support frontline guidance workers; and helping organizations that deliver information, advice, and guidance for learning and that work to introduce continuous quality improvement strategies. Web site: http://www.guidancecouncil.com

International Exchange of Students for Technical Experience (IAESTE). IAESTE was founded in 1948 at Imperial College, London. The group operates a practical training exchange program between members in order to enhance technical and professional development and to promote international understanding and goodwill among students, academic institutions, employers, and the wider community. The association has grown to include more than 80 countries worldwide and has exchanged in excess of 300,000 students. Every year, IAESTE exchanges around 6,000 students, playing a key role in the development of technical undergraduates able to make their mark in a global economy. Web site: http://www.iaeste.org

National Association of Disability Officers (NADO). NADO Ltd. is the professional organization for disability and support staff in further and higher education. NADO is for anyone working in the post-16 education sector and involved in the management or delivery of services for students with disabilities. NADO works to improve the professional development and status of disability services staff in the post-16 education sector via education, communication, and leadership, and to promote excellence in the quality and consistency of educational support services provided for students with disabilities. Web site: http://www.nado.org.uk/nado

National Association of Student Money Advisers (NASMA). NASMA acts as a focus for information exchange among practitioners in the field of student funding, bringing together professionals from across the sector and encouraging the free exchange of ideas and consultation with national decision makers on areas concerning student finance and funding. NASMA was formally established in 1996 to create an effective support network and forum for discussion. There are now approximately 450 members across all four countries of the United Kingdom. Members of NASMA are predominantly student money advisers in universities; colleges of higher education; students' unions, guilds, and associations; discretionary fund administrators in higher education institutions; and staff in further education colleges whose remit includes money advice and/or discretionary fund administration. Web site: http://www.nasma.org.uk

National Association for Managers of Student Services (NAMSS). NAMSS aims to provide support and professional development for managers of services that support learners in further education and training institutions. Members of NAMSS are linked to a regional network through which they are able to get information and help, including a national newsletter, a national conference, an e-mail discussion group, local and regional meetings/networks/conferences, research projects, training, and liaison with other national organisations. Web site: http://www.namss.ac.uk

National Disability Team (NDT). NDT is contracted by the Higher Education Funding Council for England (HEFCE) and the Department for Employment and Learning for Northern Ireland (DELNI) to undertake the service of a national team to improve provision for disabled students in higher education. Focus is on bringing those institutions with little or no provision to at least a base-line set of services for higher education students with disabilities. NDT also is involved with developing and disseminating resources relating to the learning and teaching of disabled students. Website: http://www.actiononaccess.org.

The Scottish Higher Education Funding Council (SHEFC). SHEFC was established in June 1992 as a non-departmental public body responsible to the Scottish Executive. It distributes more than £700 million GBP ($1.4 billion USD) each year to higher education institutions in Scotland to provide support for teaching, research, and associated activities. The council also has a statutory function to provide Scottish Ministers with advice and information on matters relating to the higher education sector. SHEFC shares a vision with the Scottish Further Education Funding Council (SFEFC) for tertiary education in Scotland. The council aims to play its role in creating and developing an outstanding and sustainable system of tertiary education, learning, training, and research. Web site: : http://www.shefc.ac.uk

Skill: National Bureau for Students with Disabilities. Skill is an independent charity that promotes opportunities for people with any kind of disability in learning and employment. Since 1974, Skill has been helping young people and adults over 16 years of age with any kind of disability including physical and sensory disabilities and learning and mental health difficulties throughout the United Kingdom. The group provides a free information and advice service for persons with disabilities and the professionals who work with them via a free phone helpline, e-mail, and a Web site. It informs and influences key policy makers to improve legal rights and support for disabled people in post-16 education and training. Skill promotes best practice by keeping professionals up to date and informed about policy changes and by providing the opportunity for exchanging information and ideas through its conferences and seminars, producing informative and practical publications, providing consultancy and staff training for higher education and other organizations, conducting research, and developing projects on education and disability issues to address gaps in provision. Web site: http://www.skill.org.uk

The Student Awards Agency for Scotland (SAAS). SAAS is part of the Scottish Executive and is responsible to Scottish Ministers. Its purpose is to deal with financial support and give advice to eligible Scottish students in higher education throughout the United Kingdom, together with certain related roles in connection with student loans, hardship funds, and educational endowments. Web site: http://www.saas.gov.uk

UKCOSA: The Council for International Education (UKCOSA). UKCOSA is an independent organisation founded in 1968 that provides information, advice, and training about the various aspects of the recruitment and support of international students. It promotes and seeks to protect the interests of students from other countries studying in the United Kingdom; the interests of students from the United Kingdom studying, or wishing to study abroad; and the factors facilitating international student mobility. UKCOSA works with the providers and funders of education to ensure a quality educational experience for international students, monitoring trends and developments, promoting good practice, and lobbying government and other agencies for improvements to policy and legislation. One of UKCOSA's main areas of activity is the specialist advice service giving expert information and guidance on key topics related to international education, particularly to international student mobility. Its members include all U.K. universities, most further and higher education institutions with international students, students' unions, and other bodies. Web site: http://www.ukcosa.org.uk

Universities and Colleges Admissions Service (UCAS). UCAS is the central organization that processes applications for full-time undergraduate courses at U.K. universities and colleges. Web site: http://www.ucas.ac.uk

Latin America and the Caribbean

Regional

Caribbean Tertiary Level Personnel Association (CTPLA). CTPLA was founded in 1997 as the first international division of the ACPA–College Student Educators International. While its affiliation is with a U.S. association, its purpose is to serve the student affairs and services practitioners in the Caribbean region. Contact: Thelora Reynolds, director of Student Services, University of the West Indies, Mona Campus. E-mail: thelora.reynolds@uwimona.edu.jm

México

Asociación Nacional de Universidades e Instituciones de Educación Superior (ANUIES). ANUIES, the National Association of Universities and Institutions of Higher Education, was founded in 1950. Its purpose is to bring together the officers of Mexican higher education of nearly 140 institutions to improve all aspects of undergraduate and graduate academic life. This is done through cooperation, innovation, research, improvement of services, and offering academic programs through extension. Web site: http://www.anuies.mx (Spanish only)

Technologico de Monterrey. Tecnologico de Monterrey is a multi-campus private higher education system located throughout México. It is funded primarily by businesses and corporations and features the latest in technology and instructional techniques. The student affairs division is well developed at each location within the system. Web site: http://cmportal.itesm.mx/wps/portal (Spanish only)

Venezuela

The Ministry of Higher Education (Ministerio de Educación Superior). The Venezuelan Ministry of Higher Education was refounded in 2002. It includes a Vice-ministry of Students Policies (Vice ministerio de Políticas Estudiantiles). This vice-ministry has two offices. The first is the Quality of Student Life (Calidad de Vida Estudiantil) that is in charge of scholarships, transportation, participation, advisory services, etc. The second is the Office of Student Performance (Desempeño Estudiantil) that covers the academic aspects of student life and of universities. Contact: Merly Vanegas, director of Quality of Student Life. E-mail: mvanegas@mes.gov.ve. The Ministry of Higher Education Web site: http://www.mes.gov.ve/ (Spanish only)

Middle East

Iran

Supreme Council for the Youth and the National Youth Organization (NYO). These organizations were formed in 1993 for the purposes of supporting the overall natural growth of the personality of youth in Iran; meeting mental, social, physical and spiritual needs; guiding emotional wants; providing for youth participation in social activities and affairs; defending the homeland of Iran; and preserving and strengthening youth joyfulness toward the development and glory of Islamic Iran. The NYO specifically organizes and carries out programs designed to meet the above purposes. One specific student services organization that was developed as an outgrowth of NYO activity is the Organizing Council of Counselling Centers established in 1996 to provide guidance, counseling, therapy, information, testing, and social work through approved centers across Iran. Web site: www.nyoir.org (Arabic only)

North America

Canada

Canadian Association of College and University Student Services: Student Affairs and Services Professionals in Higher Education (CACUSS). CACUSS is a professional bilingual association representing and serving those individuals who work in Canadian postsecondary institutions in student affairs and services. The group provides advocacy and assistance on issues that affect the quality of student life on Canadian university and college campuses. Since 1973, CACUSS has provided professional development services and programs for members in all the Canadian provinces. Cross-divisional interest groups are formed by members from time to time based on their professional needs and focusing on areas such as peer helping, first year students, new professionals, and leadership education. CACUSS a comprehensive organization consisting of five divisions: the Student Affairs and Services Association (SASA), the Canadian Association of Disability Service Providers in Post Secondary Education (CADSPPE), the Canadian Organization of University and College Health (COUCH), the Canadian University and College Counselling Association (CUCCA), and the National Aboriginal Student Services Association (NASSA). CACUSS holds an annual conference as well as regional workshops focusing on topics of interest to a cross-section of individuals. The Canadian Institute on Student Affairs and Services (CISAS) is a professional development program offered through the CACUSS Centre for Higher Education Research and Development. Its publications include *Communiqué,* a professional magazine for student services professional and Institutional Guidelines for Reviews of Student Affairs. Web site: http://www.cacuss.ca

Canadian Association of Student Financial Aid Administrators (CASFAA). In June 1979, the Canadian Association of Financial Aid Administrators (CASFAA) was formally established as a division of the Canadian Association of College and University Student Services (CAUCUSS). The association was formed to represent financial aid administrators and awards officers in colleges and universities across Canada. In 2001, CASFAA became an independent organization. It provides expertise and a national perspective to the issues of student financial assistance. CASFAA also promotes professional development for its members by offering excellent programs of presentations and workshops during the annual national conferences. CASFAA input has been sought increasingly by numerous agencies, councils, and financial institutions. It also takes an active role in government policy reviews of financial assistance for students. Web site: http://www.casfaa.ca

United States of America

ACPA – College Student Educators International. ACPA is a national student affairs association that advances student affairs and engages students for a lifetime of learning and discovery. Founded in 1924, ACPA has nearly 8,000 members representing nearly 1,500 private and public institutions from across the United States and internationally. Representing the student affairs profession and the higher education community, ACPA provides outreach, advocacy, research, and professional development to foster college student learning. ACPA supports and fosters college student learning through the generation and dissemination of knowledge that informs policies, practices, and programs for student affairs professionals and the higher education community. Among ACPA's major projects are the *Journal of Student Development, About Campus* magazine, and conferences. Web site: http://www.myacpa.org

American Association of Collegiate Registrars and Admissions Officers (AACRAO). AACRAO is a nonprofit, voluntary, professional association of more than 9,000 higher education admissions and registration professionals who represent approximately 2,300 institutions in more than 35 countries. The mission of AACRAO is to provide professional development, guidelines, and voluntary standards to be used by higher education officials regarding the best practices in records management, admissions, enrollment management, administrative information technology, and student services. It also provides a forum for discussion regarding policy initiation and development, interpretation, and, implementation at the institutional level and in the global educational community. In addition to its annual conference, AACRAO provides a variety of services including the International Education Services division that assists with international credential evaluation and international admissions and provides a consultation service and advocacy for international students. AACRAO also follows federal legislation that affects higher education in the admissions, registration, and student records areas. Publications include *College & University,* the AACRAO quarterly journal, and numerous research reports and specialty papers. Web site: http://www.aacrao.org

American College Health Association (ACHA). Since its inception in 1920, ACHA has been dedicated to the health needs of students at colleges and universities. It is the principal leadership organization for the field of college health and provides services, communications, and advocacy that help its members to advance the health of their campus communities. ACHA has 900 institutional and over 2,400 individual college health care members from all sectors of U.S. higher education. To better address individual needs, the membership is divided into 11 regional affiliates and eight discipline-specific sections. In addition to the annual meeting, ACHA projects include the National College Health Assessment, Benchmarking DataShare Survey, con-

sultation services, corporate programs, and cooperative agreements with the Centers for Disease Control and Prevention to address HIV prevention programs. Publications include the *Journal of American College Health* and numerous reports and brochures on specific health issues and strategies. Web site: http://www.acha.org

American Counselling Association (ACA). ACA is a not-for-profit, professional and educational organization that is dedicated to the growth and enhancement of the counseling profession. Founded in 1952, ACA is the world's largest association exclusively representing professional counselors in various practice settings. By providing leadership training, publications, continuing education opportunities, and advocacy services to nearly 52,000 members, ACA helps counseling professionals develop their skills and expand their knowledge base. ACA has been instrumental in setting professional and ethical standards for the counseling profession. The association has made considerable strides in accreditation, licensure, and national certification. It also represents the interests of the profession before congress and federal agencies and strives to promote recognition of professional counselors to the public and the media. Web site: http://www.counselling.org

Association for Student Judicial Affairs (ASJA). ASJA was founded in 1988 as the premiere organization representing higher education student judicial officers. ASJA has a membership of 1,200 members in the United States and Canada, representing over 750 institutions of higher education. ASJA holds an annual conference and a Campus Judicial Institute. Job listings for campus judicial officers and related positions are maintained on the ASJA Web site: http://www.asjaonline.org

Association of College and University Housing Officers-International (ACUHO-I). ACUHO-I is the preeminent professional association dedicated to supporting and promoting the collegiate residential experience by creating value through services, information, and collegial relationships that are indispensable to its members; and continually changing and adapting in ways that assist members in meeting the needs of dynamic campus environments. ACUHO was officially organized in 1951, with the "I" added to the ACUHO name in 1980, indicating the membership's commitment to international expansion. Today, ACUHO-I boasts a membership of more than 5,800 individuals from more than 900 colleges and universities, serving 1.8 million students worldwide, and more than 205 companies. ACUHO-I remains a volunteer-driven association. Career services are provided at its conferences and serves both institutions and members who are seeking employment services. Web site: http://www.acuho.ohio-state.edu

Association of College Unions International (ACUI). ACUI brings together college union and student activities professionals from hundreds of schools worldwide. ACUI is a nonprofit educational organization founded in 1914 and has member institutions in the United States and nine other countries and Puerto Rico. ACUI members work on urban and rural campuses, in two-year and four-year institutions, and at large and small schools. They are union directors and student personnel administrators. They are students, student activities directors, food service administrators, program coordinators, fiscal officers, recreation managers, and deans. ACUI provides professional development for them all through education, conferences, advocacy, and the delivery of services. ACUI is divided into 15 geographical regions, each with its own regional director. This regional structure encourages the participation of students as well as union staff in ACUI programs, activities, and leadership positions. Through regional committees, conferences, and newsletters, students and staff learn about the role of the college union on campus and share in fulfilling that role. Career services for members are available year around. Web site: http://www.acui.org

Association on Higher Education and Disability (AHEAD). AHEAD is committed to full participation of persons with disabilities in U.S. postsecondary education. As an international resource, AHEAD addresses current and emerging issues with respect to disability, education, and accessibility to achieve universal access. AHEAD receives requests for information on topics such as open enrollment, documentation needs for students with psychiatric disabilities, transition issues, job placement, etc. Special Interest Groups are organized around an interest or concern and provide leadership to the AHEAD membership by providing information and referral, organizing professional development opportunities, and networking around a particular topic. AHEAD offers training on the international and local levels through conferences, workshops, and online opportunities. The annual international AHEAD conference brings together professionals in the fields of higher education and disability for a week of information-sharing, networking, and theoretical and practical training. Throughout the year, the organization offers workshops on disability and higher education issues at sites across the country. AHEAD Online is a way for disability service providers and others to gain or augment their formal and practical knowledge. Institutes, courses, and other resources delivered to the practitioner's desktop. Publications include brochures and booklets, books, manuals, videotapes, and *JPED, the Journal of Postsecondary Education and Disability.* Web site: http://www.ahead.org

Council for the Advancement of Standards in Higher Education (CAS). CAS has been the pre-eminent force for promoting standards in student affairs, student services, and student development programs since its inception in 1979. For the ultimate purpose of fostering and enhancing student learning, development, and achievement and in general to promote good citizenship, CAS continues to create and deliver a dynamic and credible *Book of Professional Standards and Guidelines* and *Self-Assessment Guides* that are designed to lead to a host of quality-controlled programs and services. These standards respond to real-time student needs, the requirements of sound pedagogy, and the effective management of currently 30 functional areas, consistent with institutional missions. Individuals and institutions from the 37 CAS member organizations comprise a constituency of more than 100,000 professionals. Web site: http://www.cas.edu

Jesuit Association of Student Personnel Administrators (JASPA). JASPA is a conference of the Association of Jesuit Colleges & Universities (AJCU). JASPA was originally founded in 1954 and continues today to work to promote the mission of Jesuit higher education. Members of JASPA represent the 28 Jesuit colleges and universities in the United States and also include affiliate members from other institutions. JASPA's efforts to educate student affairs practitioners include an annual conference, a five-year summer workshop, summer institutes, newsletters, and various other publications and meetings. Web site: http://jaspa.creighton.edu

International Association of College Law Enforcement Administrators (IACLEA). IACLEA was founded in 1958 for college and university security directors to discuss job challenges and common problems, and specifically to create a clearinghouse for information and issues shared by campus directors across the country. Today IACLEA membership represents over 1,000 colleges and universities and 1,600 individual members located in 20 countries. Included are campus law enforcement staff members, criminal justice faculty members, and municipal chiefs of police. The IACLEA annual conference and the *Campus Law Enforcement Journal* are two of its main services to the law enforcement community. Web site: http://www.iaclea.org

NAFSA: Association of International Educators. NAFSA was founded in 1948 and promotes the exchange of students and scholars to and from the United States and the belief that international educational exchange advances learning and scholarship, builds respect among different peoples, and encourages constructive leadership in a global community. The organization provides numerous services for its members and higher education including public policy research and legislative affairs, professional development and resources, and member services and advocacy. Major projects include the annual conference, specialty workshops and training, immigration advising, special interest groups (SIGs), research and data collection on international education and students, institutional grants, and a job registry. Publications include the *International Educator* magazine, the weekly e-newsletter, *NAFSA. news,* and numerous specialty books and pamphlets. Web site: http://www.nafsa.org

NASPA – Student Affairs Administrators in Higher Education. NASPA, student affairs administrators in higher education, is the leading voice for student affairs administration, policy and practice and affirms the commitment of student affairs to educating the whole student and integrating student life and learning. With over 11,000 members at 1,400 campuses, and representing 29 countries, NASPA is the largest professional association for student affairs administrators, faculty and graduate students. NASPA members are committed to serving college students by embracing the core values of diversity, learning, integrity, collaboration, access, service, fellowship, and the spirit of inquiry. NASPA members serve a variety of functions and roles including the vice president and dean for student life as well as professionals working within housing and residence life, student unions, student activities, counseling, career development, orientation, enrollment management, racial and ethnic minority support services, and retention and assessment. NASPA serves its members through a wide range of services, including outstanding quarterly publications such as the *NASPA Journal* and *Leadership Exchange*, a management magazine, a variety of professional development opportunities for student affairs individuals at all levels within the profession, and a comprehensive, content-rich Web site that is the most widely accessed Web site in the student affairs association community. With over 11,000 individual members and more than 1,200 member campuses, NASPA's leadership is provided by volunteers from member institutions who are elected as regional and national officers. Web site: http://www.naspa.org

National Academic Advising Association (NACADA.) NACADA is an association of professional advisors, counselors, faculty, administrators, and students working to enhance the educational development of students. Its mission is to champion the educational role of academic advisors to enhance student learning and development in a diverse world; affirm the role of academic advising in student success and persistence; anticipate the academic advising needs of 21st century students, advisors and institutions; and advance the body of knowledge on academic advising. Publications include the *NACADA Journal* and several monographs and videos. Events include the annual national conference, the Assessment of Academic Advising Institute, the Academic Advising Summer Institute, and regional and state conferences. Web site: http://www.nacada.ksu.edu

National Association for College Admission Counselling (NACAC). NACAC was founded in 1937 and is an organization of 8,000 professionals from around the world dedicated to serving students as they make choices about pursuing postsecondary education. NACAC is committed to maintaining high standards that foster ethical and social responsibility among those involved in the transition process. The mission of the association is to support and advance the work of college admission counseling professionals as they help students make the transition from secondary schools to higher education. NACAC effectively brings together primary and secondary school counselors, independent counselors, college admission and financial aid officers, enrollment managers, and organizations engaged in guiding students through the secondary to higher education transition process. Activities include an annual national conference, numerous training workshops, college fairs, and government and legislative affairs. NACAC also maintains a career opportunities Web page and service. Web site: http://www.nacacnet.org/MemberPortal

National Association for Equal Opportunity in Higher Education (NAFEO). NAFEO, founded in 1969, champions the interests of historically and predominantly Black colleges and universities (HBCUs) with the executive, legislative, regulatory, and judicial branches of federal and state government and with corporations, foundations, associations, and non-governmental organizations. It serves as an international voice and advocate for the preservation and enhancement of historically and predominantly Black colleges and universities and for Blacks in higher education. It represents approximately 400,000 students and their families and African Americans across the higher education spectrum. NAFEO member institutions are located in 25 states, the District of Columbia, the Virgin Islands, and Brazil. A national legislative mobilization of NAFEO members and supporters is convened annually at its conference held in Washington, D.C., bringing together leaders from academia; government; corporate America; the private, nonprofit and philanthropic sectors; legislators; students; and others for an exchange of information about Blacks in higher education and equal educational opportunities. NAFEO has facilitated internship assignments in government and industry for students enrolled in historically and predominantly Black colleges and universities. Web site: http://www.nafeo.org

National Association of College & University Food Services (NACUFS). NACUFS is the trade association for foodservice professionals at nearly 650 institutions of higher education in the United States, Canada, and abroad. Founded in 1958, NACUFS provides members with a full range of educational programs, publications, management services, and networking opportunities. In addition to colleges and universities, more than 400 industry suppliers are members of the association. These companies exhibit at national and regional showcases, serve on standing committees, and participate in various educational conferences. NACUFS is governed by a board of directors and six regional councils and uses volunteer committees, project teams, and professional staff to deliver service to its members. Web site: http://www.nacufs.org

The National Association of College and University Residence Halls, Inc. (NACURH). NACURH was founded in 1954. It is the leading national organization advocating for the interests and welfare of residence hall students, while also providing opportunities for their personal growth and development.

It is an organization of students committed to developing leadership, honoring diversity, and recognizing achievement, as well as stimulating engagement and involvement among students who reside in college and university residence halls. Through regional and national programs and services, NACURH provides leadership opportunities for students, shares residence hall programming resources and best practices, and coordinates activities with appropriate professional associations and business partners. Web site: http://www.nacurh.org

National Association of Campus Activities (NACA). NACA, founded in 1960, links the higher education and entertainment communities in a business and learning partnership, creating educational and business opportunities for our student and professional members. Cooperative Buying or CO-OP Buying forms the cornerstone of NACA that has evolved into the nation's largest collegiate organization for campus activities, with programs and services designed to reflect the field's increased responsibilities for student leadership development as well as entertainment programming. NACA's activities and services provide a unique forum for business and professional development, information exchange, and networking. NACA offers a wide variety of workshops, publications, educational and business seminars, face-to-face meeting opportunities, and other programs. Web site: http://www.naca.org/NACA

National Association of Campus Card Users (NACCU). NACCU, a nonprofit educational association, was formed in 1993 to provide a responsive, diversified source of campus card-related information and services and works to provide learning and networking opportunities for campus ID card and card industry professionals. NACCU is involved with the collection, dissemination, and interchange of information among the members and others and encourages technological developments and new uses of card systems technology in higher education administration. It also provides opportunities for career development, skill development, and other forms of professional growth by providing conferences, workshops, and seminars. The association offers a monthly newsletter (CardTalk), listserv, Web site, an annual conference, and regional workshops on topics related to campus cards. Web site: http://naccu.org

National Association of College Auxiliary Services (NACAS). NACAS, founded in 1969, is the largest auxiliary services support organization serving higher education and includes colleges and universities throughout the United States, Canada, United Kingdom, Ireland, Australia, and New Zealand. The group provides information and education to professionals in higher education support services. NACAS maintains an extensive catalog of publications, including *College Services*, a bimonthly journal, *NACAS Quarterly*, and a monthly newsletter and maintains a reference library of reprinted articles, papers, RFP templates, monographs, and other resources for members. An online

Career Center connects employers and members with job opportunities. The annual conference is the professional development highlight of the NACAS year. Web site: http://www.nacas.org

National Association of College Stores, Inc. (NACS). NACS, founded in 1963, is the professional trade association representing the higher education retail market reaching 15 million college students annually. NACS has over 3,100 member stores in the United States, Canada, and a dozen other countries, and about 1,200 associate members consisting of suppliers to collegiate retailers. NACS offers its members a wide variety of services including research and information, advocacy, affinity programs, and networking. The NACS annual conference, Campus Market Expo, is the world's largest trade show for the collegiate marketplace. NACS publications include: *The College Store* magazine, *Campus Marketplace*, a semimonthly industry newsletter, and *CM Bulletin*, a weekly e-newsletter. Web site: http://www.nacs.org/.

National Association of Colleges and Employers (NACE). NACE was founded in 1956 and is the leading source of information for career services practitioners on college campuses who advise students and alumni in career development and the employment process, and for human resources professionals who recruit and hire college graduates. NACE represents the interests of more than 1,800 college career services offices at four-year, two-year, technical, and graduate schools and more than 1,900 HR/staffing functions in business, industry, nonprofit organizations, and government. NACE forecasts trends in the job market; tracks legal issues in employer, job search, and hiring practices; and provides college and employer professionals with benchmarks for their work. NACE provides research and information to its professional members through NACEWeb, quarterly surveys of starting salary offers to new college graduates, a quarterly *NACE Journal*, a biweekly newsletter, and surveys of employer and college members. NACE provides members with primary tools for reaching and educating college students through its *Job Choices* publications and JobWeb, the online complement to *Job Choices*. Web site: http://www.naceweb.org

The National Association of Graduate Admissions Professionals (NAGAP). NAGAP is the only professional organization devoted exclusively to the concerns of individuals working in the graduate admissions and recruitment environment. NAGAP is committed to serving the needs and interests of graduate admissions professionals. The Summer Institute for New Graduate Admissions Professionals is a NAGAP program that focuses on the needs of those who have been working in the field, or in their current positions, for less than two years. The quarterly publication, *NAGAP Perspectives*, provides members with information about NAGAP activities, as well as updates on topics of interest to graduate admissions professionals. NAGAP also holds

Graduate and Professional School Fairs throughout the United States. Web site: http://www.nagap.org

National Orientation Directors Association (NODA). NODA was chartered in 1976, and its mission is to provide education, leadership, and professional development in the fields of college student orientation, transition, and retention. NODA offers a number of opportunities for orientation, retention, and transition staff to connect and collaborate with other orientation colleagues and to gain new skills or ideas, including the annual conference, regional conferences, and the Orientation Professionals Institute, a two-day workshop right before the start of the NODA annual conference is designed for professional staff who have spent less than two years with orientation, retention, and transition services on their campus. National and regional networks address special interests such as the adult learner, two-year and small colleges, Canadian colleges, multi-ethnic affairs, GLBT issues, and parent services. Through its awards, scholarships, and internship program, NODA further encourages excellence in orientation, retention and transition programming. Web site: http://www.nodaweb.org

National Association of Student Affairs Professionals (NASAP). NASAP is a professional organization dedicated to promoting excellence in the area of student affairs. With a varied membership spanning across academic, administrative, corporate, and student affairs boundaries, the organization offers a variety of resources, and experiences. The organization was founded in 1954 and its origins can be traced back to two parent organizations: the National Association of Deans of Women and Advisor of Girls in Colored Schools (DOWA) and the National Association of Personnel Dean of Men at Negro Educational Institutions (DOMA). NASAP provides and sponsors several programs and events that address the nature and needs of students and the professional development of student affairs professionals facilitating those programs and services. Web site: http://www.nasap.net

National Association of Student Financial Aid Administrators (NASFAA). NASFAA supports financial aid professionals at colleges, universities, and career schools and is the only national association with a primary focus on student aid legislation, regulatory analysis, and professional development for financial aid administrators. NASFAA is a valued source of accurate, unbiased, and timely information on the federal student aid process for its member institutions. The association also represents the interests of students and financial aid administrators to the Congress, the Department of Education, and other regulatory agencies, working to improve financial aid administration and the delivery of aid to students. NASFAA represents financial aid professionals at nearly 3,000 institutions of postsecondary education, as well as others with an interest in the advancement of student aid. NASFAA is known for its pro-

fessional development activities for its members including the national conference and extensive training programs and materials. Publications include the *Journal of Student Financial Aid,* an *Annotated Bibliography of Literature on Student Financial Aid,* and *Cash for College.* The NASFAA annual conference draws attendees from all across the United States and several foreign countries. Web site: http://www.nasfaa.org

National Career Development Association (NCDA). NCDA is a division of the American Counselling Association. The mission of NCDA is to promote the career development of all people over their life span. To achieve this mission, NCDA provides service to the public and professionals involved with or interested in career development, including professional development activities, publications, research, public information, professional standards, advocacy, and recognition for achievement and service. Web site: http://ncda.org

The National Intramural-Recreational Sports Association (NIRSA). Founded in 1950 at Dillard University in New Orleans by 20 African American men and women intramural directors from 11 historically Black colleges, NIRSA began as the National Intramural Association (NIA). Today, NIRSA is a nonprofit membership organization serving a network of more than 4,000 professionals, students, and associate members in the recreational sports field throughout the United States, Canada, and other countries. It is the leading organization in many areas: training and professional development, intramural sports, sport clubs, recreation facilities, fitness programming, outdoor recreation, wellness programs, informal recreation, and aquatic programs. NIRSA's member institutions represent nearly seven million college students, of whom an estimated five and a half million participate in recreational programs. Web site: http://www.nirsa.org

National Resource Center for the First-Year Experience and Students in Transition. The center's mission is to build and sustain a vibrant campus-based and international educational community committed to the success of first-year college students and all students in transition. It provides opportunities for the exchange of practical, theory-based information and ideas through the convening of conferences, teleconferences, institutes, and workshops; publishing monographs, a peer-reviewed journal, a newsletter, guides, and books; generating and supporting research and scholarship; hosting visiting scholars; and administering a Web site and electronic listservs. Web site: http://www.sc.edu/fye/index.html

National Association of Student Employment Administrators (NSEA). NSEA is an organization of several hundred professionals involved with programs for college students who work. Membership is open to anyone with an interest in administering student employment or hiring students. NSEA supports and promotes student employment through research, publications, professional development opportunities, and the open exchange of information. NSEA is a prime source for current information on federal student employment regulations and expert advice on the Federal Work-Study Program. Through annual conferences and workshops, members are offered training opportunities and the chance to tap into a nationwide network of experienced student employment colleagues. Similarly, employers have access to student employment professionals in the United States and abroad who can help meet their employment needs with well-trained, enthusiastic student employees. Web site: http://nseastudemp.org

Southern Association for College Student Affairs (SACSA). The Southern Association for College Student Affairs is an independent, regional organization whose mission is to be an exemplary organization of practitioners, educators, and students engaged in the student affairs profession. Web site: http://www.sacsa.org

Worldwide Organizations

International Association of Counselling Services (IACS). The basic purposes of IACS are to encourage and aid counseling services throughout the United States and internationally to meet high professional standards, to inform the public about those that are competent and reliable, and to foster communication among counseling services operating in a variety of settings. IACS offers accreditation services and is open to university and college counseling centers and public and private counseling agencies. The group is committed to furthering the visibility of the counseling profession and improving its quality. It has evolved standards that define professional quality, and has established criteria for accreditation which reflect those standards. IACS' roots go back to the 1950s when accreditation was first extended to counseling services. Web site: http://www.iacsinc.org

International Association of Educational and Vocational Guidance (IAEVG). IAEVG is an international association of guidance professionals. Through its members and IAEVG initiatives, it aims to assist students and adults to understand and appreciate themselves, relate effectively to others, develop appropriate educational and vocational training plans, explore career alternatives, and cope with and integrate successfully in society and the labor market. IAEVG advocates for access to guidance for all who seek it and makes recommendations on the quality of guidance services and the training and qualifications of educational and vocational guidance counselors. IAEVG urges governments to develop and maintain policies governing the provision of educational and vocational guidance, including training, research, evaluation methods, and public awareness. Conferences are held every year, with a General Assembly held every four years at which policy matters are addressed and the Board of Directors and Executive Committee are elected. Web site: http://www.iaevg.org

International Association of Student Affairs and Services (IASAS). IASAS serves as an informal network of student affairs and services professionals in higher education around the world (over 30 countries). Its primary goals are to provide high quality and culture-unique consultations, information, publications, and training at low-to-no-cost to student affairs and services professionals and students around the world. As a nonprofit, non-governmental organization, IASAS is comprised of individuals and organizations committed to advancing the cause of whole student development and the student affairs and services profession in higher education. In 2002 IASAS, in cooperation with UNESCO, published *The Role of Student Affairs and Services in Higher Education: A Practical Manual for Developing, Implementing, and Assessing Student Affairs Programmes and Services.* This useful publication presents a picture of student affairs and services as a viable force in higher education, aimed at enhancing student learning outcomes and student success in higher education. It is designed to be applicable to those countries/institutions around the world that are interested in improving current student affairs and services or creating them as a part of the university setting in those countries. Contact: Roger B. Ludeman, executive director. E-mail: iasas@hotmail.com. Web site: http://iasas.ehs.ufl.edu

International Partnership for Service Learning and Leadership (IPSL). IPSL, founded in 1982, is a not-for-profit educational organization incorporated in New York State serving students, colleges, universities, service agencies, and related organizations around the world (14 countries) by fostering programs that link volunteer service to the community and academic study. By studying at a local university and serving 15–20 hours per week in a school, orphanage, health clinic, or other agency addressing human needs, students find that their knowledge of the host culture—and of themselves—takes on greater depth and meaning. IPSL also offers a master's degree in international service. To develop and promote service-learning in institutions of higher education around the world, IPSL sponsors international conferences; conducts research on the effect of service–learning on students, educational institutions, and communities; publishes curricular and other materials related to service–learning; conducts training seminars for faculty members and administrators; and through various activities, helps to develop partnerships between colleges/universities and service agencies, both locally and internationally. Web site: http://www.ipsl.org

Table B1. Quick reference list of associations around the world that provide professional support for people working on college and university campuses.

Acronym	Association Name	Association Contact Information
AACRAO	American Association of Collegiate Registrars and Admissions Officers	www.aacrao.org
AAU	Association of African Universities	www.aau.org
ACA	American Counselling Association	www.counselling.org
ACHA	American College Health Association	www.acha.org
ACPA	College Student Educators International	www.myacpa.org
ACUHO-I	Association of College and University Housing Officers – International	www.acuho.ohio-state.edu
ACUI	Association of College Unions International	www.acui.org/Acui/index.cfm
ADSHE	Association of Dyslexia Specialists in Higher Education	www.adshe.org.uk
AGCAS	The Association of Graduate Careers Advisory Services	www.agcas.org.uk
AGCSI	Association of Graduate Careers Services in Ireland	www.gradireland.com/AboutUs/index.asp
AHEAD	Association for Higher Education Access and Disability (Ireland)	www.aheadweb.org/home/pages
AHEAD	Association on Higher Education and Disability (USA)	www.ahead.org
AMOSSHE	Association of Managers of Student Services in Higher Education (UK)	www.amosshe.org.uk
ANUIES	Asociación Nacional de Universidades e Instituciones de Educación Superior	www.anuies.mx
ANUSAC	Association of Normal University Student Affairs in China	e-mail wzhg@bnu.edu.cn for more information
ANZSSA	Australian and New Zealand Student Services Association	www.anzssa.org or http://www.anzssa.org
APSSA	Asia Pacific Student Services Association	http://home.ust.hk/%7Esanet/apssa.htm
ASJA	Association for Student Judicial Affairs	www.asjaonline.org/
ASRA	Association for Student Residential Accommodation	www.asra.ac.uk
AUA	Association of University Administrators	www.aua.ac.uk
AUCC	Association of University and College Counselling	www.aucc.uk.com
BACP	British Association of Counselling and Psychotherapy	www.bacp.co.uk
CACUSS	Canadian Association of College and University Student Services	www.cacuss.ca/en/index.lasso
CAS	Council for the Advancement of Standards in Higher Education	www.cas.edu
CASFAA	Canadian Association of Student Financial Aid Administrators	www.casfaa.ca

Table B1. Quick reference list of associations around the world that provide professional support for people working on college and university campuses.

Acronym	Association Name	Association Contact Information
CCMU	Consejo de Colegios Mayores Universitarios de España	www.consejocolegiosmayores.es/ (Spanish only)
CCU	Collegi Universitari – The Italian Conference of Colleges	www.collegiuniversitari.it
CHE	Ministry of Education, Commission on Higher Education	www.moe.go.th/english
CHET	Centre for the Transformation of Higher Education	www.chet.org.za
CIMO	Centre for International Mobility	www.cimo.fi/Resource.phx/cimo/mainpage/mainpage.htx
CNOUS	Centre National des Ceuvres Universitaires et Scolaires	www.cnous.frl
CSSI	Confederation of Student Services in Ireland	www.cssi.edu.ie
CTPLA	Caribbean Tertiary Level Personnel Association	e-mail thelora.reynolds@uwimona.edu.jm for more information
DAAD	Deutscher Akademischer Austausch Dienst	www.daad.org
DSW	Deutsches Studentenwerk	www.studentenwerke.de
EACS	European Association of Campus Security	www.euro-campus-secur.org/english/bylaws.htm
EAIE	European Association of International Education	www.eaie.nl
ECStA	European Council of Student Affairs	www.ecsta.org/front/
FAPSA	Financial Aid Practitioners of South Africa	e-mail ngomanej@nu.ac.za for more information
FEDORA	European Forum for Student Guidance	www.fedora.eu.org/
FSHS	Finish Student Health Service	www.yths.fi/netcomm
GC	Guidance Council	www.guidancecouncil.com
HEA	Higher Education Authority	www.hea.ie
HEAG	Higher Education Accessibility Guide	www.european-agency.org/heag/index.html
HKSSA	Hong Kong Student Services Association	http://home.ust.hk/~hkssa/
IACLEA	International Association of College Law Enforcement Administrators	www.iaclea.org
IACS	International Association of Counselling Services	www.iacsinc.org
IAEVG	International Association of Educational and Vocational Guidance	www.iaevg.org
IASAS	International Association of Student Affairs and Services	http://iasas.ehs.ufl.edu/
IAUCC	Irish Association of University and College Counsellors	e-mail counselling@ucc.ie for more information

Table B1. Quick reference list of associations around the world that provide professional support for people working on college and university campuses.

Acronym	Association Name	Association Contact Information
IPSL	International Partnership for Service Learning and Leadership	www.ipsl.org
ISANA	International Education Association	www.isana.org.au
ISESS	Institute for Shipboard Education and Semester at Sea	www.semesteratsea.com/seminar2004/index.html
IUSSN	Irish Universities Student Services Network	e-mail barry.kehoe@dcu.ie for more information
JANU	Japan Association of National Universities	www.kokudaikyo.gr.jp/eng)
JAPCU	Japan Association of Private Colleges and Universities	www.shidairen.or.jp/english/outline/message.html
JASPA	Jesuit Association of Student Personnel Administrators	http://jaspa.creighton.edu
JASSO	Japan Student Services Organization	www.jasso.go.jp/about_jasso/index_e.html
MES	Ministerio de Educación Superior	www.mes.gov.ve
MSAC	Malaysian Secretariat of Deputy Vice-Chancellors of Student Affairs Council	e-mail jamaludin_mohaiadin@yahoo.com for more information
NAAUC	National Association of Australian University Colleges	www.naauc.edu.au
NACA	National Association of Campus Activities	www.naca.org/naca
NACAC	National Association for College Admission Counselling	www.nacacnet.org/MemberPortal/
NACADA	National Academic Advising Association	www.nacada.ksu.edu
NACAS	National Association of College Auxiliary Services	www.nacas.org
NACCU	National Association of Campus Card Users	http://naccu.org
NACE	National Association of Colleges and Employers	www.naceweb.org
NACS	National Association of College Stores, Inc.	www.nacs.org
NACUFS	National Association of College and University Food Services	www.nacufs.org
NACURH	National Association of College and University Residence Hall, Inc	www.nacurh.org
NADO	National Association of Disability Officers	www.nado.org.uk.nado
NAFEO	National Association for Equal Opportunity in Higher Education	www.nafeo.org
NAFSA	Association of International Educators	www.nafsa.org
NAGAP	The National Association of Graduate Professionals	www.nagap.org
NAMSS	National Association for Managers of Student Services	www.namss.ac.uk/

Table B1. Quick reference list of associations around the world that provide professional support for people working on college and university campuses.

Acronym	Association Name	Association Contact Information
NASAP	National Association of Student Affairs Professionals	www.nasap.net
NASDEV	National Association of Student Development Practitioners – SA	www.nasdev.org.za
NASFAA	National Association of Student Financial Aid Administrators	www.nasfaa.org
NASMA	National Association of Student Money Advisors	www.nasma.org.uk
NASPA	Student Affairs Administrators in Higher Education	www.naspa.org
NCDA	National Career Development Association	http://ncda.org
NDA	National Disability Authority	www.nda.ie
NDT	National Disability Team	www.actiononaccess.org
NIRSA	The National Intramural-Recreational Sports Association	www.nirsa.org
NODA	National Association of Orientation Directors	www.nodaweb.org
NRC	National Resource Center of the First-Year Experience and Students in Transition	www.sc.edu/fye/index.html
NSEA	National Association of Student Employment Administrators	http://nseastudemp.org
NYO	Supreme Council for the Youth and the National Youth Organization	www.nyoir.org/eng/default.htm
PAASA	Philippine Association of Administrators of Student Affairs	e-mail osacs@ust.edu.ph for more information
RUI	Fondazione Residenze Universitarie Internazionali	http://www.fondazionerui.it/portal/template/viewTemplate?templateId=ivjv1xsbat_layout_849griisc1.psml
SAACHS	South African Association of Campus Health Services	e-mail Antoinette.goosen@upe.ac.za for more information
SAAS	Student Awards Agency for Scotland	www.saas.gov.uk
SAASSAP	South African Association of Senior Student Affairs Professionals	e-mail cbodibe@tsa.ac.za for more information
SACSA	Southern Association of College Student Affairs	www.sacsa.org
SASSU	South African Student Sport Union	
SCSSA	Student Counselling Society of Southern Africa	
SCU	Supreme Council of Universities	www.scu.eun.eg
SHEFC	Scottish Higher Education Funding Council	www.shefc.ac.uk
SIOU	Servieios de Informacion y Orientacion Universitarious	http://siou.um.es/english/home.php

Table B1. Quick reference list of associations around the world that provide professional support for people working on college and university campuses.

Acronym	Association Name	Association Contact Information
SHOAA	Student Housing Officers Association of Australia	www.housing.rmit.edu.au/shoaa/index.html
SKILL	National Bureau for Students with Disabilities	www.skill.org.uk
TPB	Talboks-och punktskriftsbibleiteket	www.ho.se/start.asp?sida=348&lang=en
UCAS	Universities and Colleges Admissions Service	www.ucas.ac.uk
UKCOSA	The Council for International Education	www.ukcosa.org.uk

CONTRIBUTORS

KENNETH J. OSFIELD has worked for the University of Florida since 1989, when he was hired as an assistant dean of students/director of disability resources. He currently serves as the Americans with Disabilities Act Compliance Officer and an instructor in the student personnel in higher education program at the University of Florida's College of Education. He received his BS (1974) in physical education, health education, and recreation and his MS (1989) in human development, counseling and family studies with a specialization in student personnel services from the University of Rhode Island. He holds an EdD (1996) in higher education administration from the University of Florida.

Active within NASPA – Student Affairs Administrators in Higher Education) since 1989, he is the past chair of the International Education Knowledge Community (2004-06) and is the past Director of NASPA's International Symposium (2002-04). He is the founding network chair of the NASPA Disability Concerns Network (1992-04) (now Disability Concerns Knowledge Community).

MOHD RAZALI AGUS is currently deputy vice chancellor of the students affairs department, University of Malaya. He received his BA (1979) in anthropology and sociology from the University of Malaya, an MSocSc (1981) in sociology from the University of Birmingham, and his Ph D (1991) in city and regional planning from Cornell University.

R. AMBIHABATHY is currently the principal assistant registrar with the Student Affairs Department, University Malaya. He received his BSc (1984) in genetics from the University of Malaya, his MPA (1992) from the University of Liverpool, and an LLB from the University of Wolverhampton.

ANNIE ANDREWS is the director of counselling services at the University of New South Wales, a position she has held since 1998. She received her BA (1976) and Diploma in Psychology (DipPsych) (1979) from the University of Queensland. She is an active member of the Australian and New Zealand Student Services Association (ANZSSA). She was the executive committee of ANZSSA from 1997 to 2005 and served two terms as co-president.

LISA BARDILL MOSCARITOLA is dean for students affairs at Pace University. She received her B.S. (1987) in marketing from the University of Akron, her MS (1989) in higher education and college student personnel from Florida State University and both an EdS (1998) in mental health counseling and a PhD (1998) in leadership from Barry University. She is a past president of the Southern Association for College Student Affairs (SACSA-2003-04). She is a past director of student life on the Institute for Shipboard Education and Semester at Sea (2003) and has been active within NASPA's international affairs, where she has assisted the International Symposium as the sponsor coordinator and also as the national chair for the International Education Knowledge Community (2006-08).

FRANÇOISE BIR is the director of student life for CNOUS (Centre Nationale des Œuvres Universitaires et Scolaires) in France. She received her BA (1977) in public law from ENA (National School of Administration) in France. For her dedication and service to higher education in France, she was awarded the "Academic Medal" in 1995.

EDWARD T. BONAHUE serves as chair of the Department of Humanities and Foreign Languages at Santa Fe Community College (Gainesville, Florida) where he is also co-chair of the college's International Education Initiative. He holds a BA in English from Wake Forest University (1987), an MA in modern drama from the University of North Carolina (1991), and a PhD in English Renaissance literature from the University of North Carolina (1996).

TONY W. CAWTHON is an associate professor and interim department chair for the Department of Leadership, Counselor Education, Human and Organizational Development at Clemson University. He holds a BA (1981) in psychology and sociology and an MA (1983) in sociology from the University of Tennessee – Knoxville. He earned his PhD (1995) in counselor education and student development from Mississippi State University.

DORIS CHING was vice president for student affairs at the University of Hawaii from 1987 until her retirement in 2005. She received a BEd and MEd in secondary education from the University of Hawaii, and an EdD degree in educational administration from Arizona State University. She chaired the Education and International Division of the Pacific International Center for High Technology Research from 1983–86. In 1998, she represented the United States at the Asia Pacific Student Affairs Association in Hong Kong. In 1999, she became the first woman of color to serve as president of NASPA–Student Affairs Administrators in Higher Education, and from 2002 to 2004, she served as president of the NASPA Foundation Board of Directors.

JON C. DALTON is an associate professor in higher education and director of the Hardee Center for Leadership and Ethics at Florida State University. He is a former vice president for student affairs at Florida State University and Northern Illinois University. He holds an EdD in higher education from the University of Kentucky (1974), an MDiv from Yale University (1966), an MS in higher education from the University of Kentucky, and a BA in philosophy from Franklin College. A long-time leader in the field of student affairs and advocate of international experiences, he helped shape NASPA's International goals and commitment when he was president in 1994-95.

SUAN ENG is the deputy director (Student Services) at the Office of Student Affairs, National University of Singapore (NUS). She received her BA (1969) in Chinese studies and Asian history from the University of Singapore.

DALA TAJI FAROUKI was the student activities coordinator at The American University in Dubai at the time this chapter was written. She is now management consultant with PricewaterhouseCoopers. She received her BA in English from Tufts University and a master's degree in higher education administration with a concentration in international education from George Washington University (2005).

ANNIE GRANT is the dean of students and director of student services at the University of East Anglia (UEA) in Norwich, Norfolk, United Kingdom. She holds a BA (1968) an MA (1973) in archaeology and anthropology and a PhD (1997) in archaeology, all from the University of Cambridge. She has been an active member of AMOSSHE, the UK Association of Managers of Student Services in Higher Education since 1993 and a member of its Executive Committee since 2001.

JENNIFER HANSON is the dean of student services at the American University in Dubai. She holds a PhD from Purdue University in curriculum and instruction, with a concentration in cross-cultural education, multicultural education, curriculum design, and English as a second language. She also holds a master's degree in reading and language arts from the University of Pennsylvania and a bachelor's degree in elementary and special education from Penn State University. She is certified to teach reading, language arts, elementary education, and ESL.

PAMELA A. HAVICE is currently an assistant professor in counselor education at Clemson University, where she has been an integral part of developing a distributed learning environment for the delivery of the study abroad course for the student affairs academic program. She received her BSN (1980) and an MS (1984) in counseling from Fort Hays State University. She completed her PhD (1999) in educational leadership and higher education at Clemson University.

ACHIM MEYER AUF DE HEYDE is the secretary general of the Deutsches Studentenwerk (DSW), a position he has held since 2003. He holds a BS in economics (1977) and a BS in business administration (1978) from Freie Universität Berlin. He is very involved with European student affairs and is the current president of the European Council for Student Affairs (ECStA).

ENRIQUE IGLESIAS HIDALGO is director of the Colegio Mayor Universitario "Cardenal Cisneros," Granada University, Spain. After finishing his studies in theology at the Franciscan Center of Studies in Chipiona (Cádiz) in 1966, he went on to complete an MA in sociology from the Instituto Social Leon XIII in Madrid (1967) and a PhLic from Granada University (1973). Very involved in Spanish higher education, he has been elected as General Delegate of the National Council of Colegios Mayores since 1978 (27 consecutive years) and is a member of the steering committee of the Council, a position responsible for guiding national discussions with the Ministers of the Spanish Government. He was elected by the European Commission as the Spanish representative for the design and implementation of the Erasmus Programme.

SANDY HUBLER is vice president for university life at George Mason University. She received her BA (1980) in physical education from Wooster College, an MEd in college student personnel administration from The Ohio State University, and her EdD (1998) in international and multicultural education from the University of San Francisco. She is the former director of NASPA's International Symposium (2000-02) and was the national chair of the NASPA International Education Knowledge community from 2002 to 2004.

HEIDI HUANG YU is a part-time counselor and graduate student of English Literature in the School of Foreign Languages (SFL) at Sun Yat-sen University (SYU).

KWOK HUNG LAI is currently the senior student affairs officer at the Hong Kong Institute of Education. He holds a BSocSc (1981) in social work from the Chinese University of Hong Kong and an MSocSc. (1994) and a PhD (2003) in sociology from the University of Hong Kong. He has been the treasurer of Asia Pacific Student Services Association (APSSA) Executive Committee since 2002. He also serves on the Executive Committee of the Hong Kong Student Services Association.

OUYANG KE-QUAN is a lecturer and the associate vice-secretary of Communist Party Committee. He is currently the executive director for the student affairs office of Ling Nan (University) College, Sun Yat-sen University. He holds a BSc (1979) in physics and a BPhil (1987) in ideological and political education from Sun Yat-sen University.

SHARON M. KARKEHABADI is a PhD candidate in education policy, planning, and leadership in higher education in the School of Education at The College of William and Mary. She received her master's in social foundations of education with a cognate in women's studies from the department of curriculum and instruction at Virginia Tech in 1991. She received BA degrees in English and philosophy from George Mason University in 1988.

BARRY KEHOE recently retired from Dublin City University after 25 years as the director of student affairs at Dublin City University (DCU). He received his BA and MA in philosophy and theology from Angelicum University and also an M Ed in education (counselling and management) from Trinity College (Dublin).

ROGER B. LUDEMAN is executive director of the International Association of Student Affairs and Services (IASAS). He received his BS in education from the University of South Dakota (Springfield), an MEd in secondary education/psychology from the University of South Dakota (Vermillion), and he his MEd in counselor education/educational psychology and PhD in counselor education/educational psychology from the University of Pittsburgh. Ludeman served as the director of the NASPA International Symposium and Exchange Program, efforts he initiated in the mid-1990s. He also served as chair of the NASPA International Education Knowledge Community during that period.

DANIEL MACKEBEN is the director of external relations for the School of Management at George Mason University, where he leads development and marketing communications initiatives for the business school. He received his BS (1982) in marketing from Illinois State University, an MEd (1984) in college student personnel administration from Colorado State University, and his EdD (1998) in international and multicultural education from the University of San Francisco.

JEANNA MASTRODICASA is the associate director of the honors program at the University of Florida. She received her ABJ (1992) in public relations and JD (1995) from the University of Georgia, an MS (1997) in college student personnel from the University of Tennessee, and her PhD (2004) in higher education administration from the University of Florida.

JULIE ADKINS NHEM is currently working as a paralegal in San Francisco.. She received her BA (2001) in anthropology and Spanish and her ME degree in higher education administration from the University of Arkansas, Fayetteville.

LESLIE A. OWEN is a program assistant at the University of Florida International Center. One of her main responsibilties lies in coordinating the Coca-Cola World Citizenship Program (WCP). Leslie earned a BS (1998) in biology from the University of Georgia and her MS (2004) in student personnel in higher education from the University of Florida.

OLGA RYBALKINA is currently the director of multicultural services at Palm Beach Atlantic University and teaches multicultural courses in the Department of Graduate Counselling and Psychology. She received her PhD in higher education administration and her MEd in higher education from the University of Toledo. She also holds an MA and BA in Russian and English languages and literature from the Eastern Ukrainian University. She is currently (2006-08) the NASPA IEKC chair and past director of the NASPA International Symposium.

ROBERT SHEA is the founding director of the Department of Career Development & Experiential Learning at Memorial University of Newfoundland. He holds undergraduate degrees in political science (1985) and social work (1989) and a master's in educational leadership (1995) from Memorial University of Newfoundland. He is a past (2005-2006) president Canadian Association of College and University Student Services (CACUSS).

CATHRYN STEVENS is currently working at Furman University as the associate project director at the Richard W. Riley Institute of Government, Politics and Public Leadership. She holds an MEd in counsellor education with emphasis in student affairs.

MARTHA SULLIVAN retired from Tulane University as the vice president and dean of student affairs (1989-2003). She holds a BA in history from Newcomb College (1960), an MA in French from Laval University (1961), and a PhD in French from Tulane University (1970). She is a long-time supporter of international student affairs and is a past Director of the NASPA International Symposium (2004-06).

CAROL TANG has been the head of student affairs at the Hong Kong Institute of Education since the establishment of the Institute in 1994. She holds a BSocSc (1971) in social work from Chinese University of Hong Kong, an MEd (1984) in early childhood education from the University of Hong Kong, and an EMBA (2001) from the University of Western Ontario. She was the chairperson of the Hong Kong Student Services Association from 2003 to 2005, contributing to the promotion of interaction and cooperation among student affairs practitioners for the advancement of student affairs and services in Hong Kong.

MANUEL M. TEJIDO received his AB (1968) in philosophy from San Beda College (Manila, Philippines), an MA (1972) in Science of Sacred Theology from Ateneo de Manila University, and a PhD (1987) in religious education from Ateneo de Manila University. He was assistant dean for student affairs at the Ateneo de Manila University from 1995 to 1999. Since 1996, he has been involved with the Asia Pacific Student Services Association (APSSA). He became its president in 2000. He has also been an active member of two local professional student affairs organizations, the Philippine Association of Administrators of Student Affairs (PAASA) and the Catholic Educational Association of the Philippines, serving on the National

Capital Region Student Affairs Committee (CEAP/NCR-SAC) for many years.

HOWARD S. WANG has been the associate vice president for student affairs and executive director for the Student Health and Counseling Center at California State University, Fullerton, since 2003. He received his BA (1971) in biology from the University of Oregon, an MS (1974) in clinical microbiology from the University of Wisconsin, an MA (1981) in higher education administration, and a PhD (1992) in higher education administration from the University of California, Los Angeles.

JEANINE WARD-ROOF is currently the dean of students, at Florida State Univeristy. She received her BA (1988) in communication from Ohio University, an MA (1990) in college student personnel from Bowling Green University, and her PhD (2003) in educational leadership and higher education from Clemson University. She has served as president of the National Orientation Directors Association and South Carolina College Personnel Association.

Degree information for the authors listed.	
EdD	Doctor of Education
PhD	Doctor of Philosophy
JD	Juris Doctorate
PhLic	Until recently most Spanish degree courses lasted five years. Students would be awarded a diplomatura (general degree) if they completed three years of study, and they would receive their licenciatura (lic) (honours degree) after another two years. For the Doctorate they need two more years and to write and defend a "doctoral thesis."
BA	Bachelor of Arts
AB	Bachelor of Arts
BS	Bachelor of Science
BSc	Bachelor of Science
BPhil	Bachelor of Philosophy
MS	Master of Science
MA	Master of Arts
MBA	Master of Business Administration
EMBA	Executive Master of Business Administration
MSocSc	Master of Social Science
BSocSc	Bachelor of Social Science
ABJ	Bachelor of Arts in Journalism
DipPsych	Diploma in Psychology
MPA	Master of Public Administration
LLB	Bachelor of Laws
BSN	Bachelor of Science in Nursing
MEd	Master of Education
ME	Master of Education